The Essex Genealogist

Volume 5

1985

Essex Society of Genealogists, Inc.
Essex County, Massachusetts

HERITAGE BOOKS
2015

HERITAGE BOOKS
AN IMPRINT OF HERITAGE BOOKS, INC.

Books, CDs, and more—Worldwide

For our listing of thousands of titles see our website
at
www.HeritageBooks.com

Published 2015 by
HERITAGE BOOKS, INC.
Publishing Division
5810 Ruatan Street
Berwyn Heights, Md. 20740

International Standard Book Numbers
Paperbound: 978-0-7884-0508-2
Clothbound: 978-0-7884-6087-6

The Essex Genealogist

VOLUME 5, NUMBER 1 FEBRUARY 1985

CONTENTS

THE ESSEX GENEALOGIST is published quarterly: February, May, August
& November for $7 per year, by the Essex Society of Genealogists,
Lynnfield Public Library, 18 Summer Street, Lynnfield, MA 01940.
Second Class Postage paid at Lynnfield, MA 01940. ISSN: 0279-067X
USPS; 591-350. POSTMASTER: Send address changes to ESOG, Lynnfield
Public Library, 18 Summer Street, Lynnfield, MA 01940

Letter from the Editor

February 1985 - our fifth year of publication begins! We are pleased to report that TEG is healthy on all fronts; financially solvent and teeming with contributions from our growing readership. Our query editors are still willing to handle the myriad minutiae of that department; our stalwart collators are still arriving on the 10th of the month to make their numerous peregrinations around the tables where 17,400 sheets of printed matter lie waiting; and your Editor still finds enjoyment in the month-long task of keying onto disk the articles submitted for TEG.

We are especially pleased with this issue which contains more than the usual number of original manuscripts, helpful advice and information for genealogists. Two articles will be serialized this year. The Saville Family, submitted by Gail Goodwin Nekorowski, will run through all four issues of 1985, and the Gerry (Geary) Family will run through two issues.

The Nichols Family, submitted by Ann Williams, is a typical example of early genealogical work that appears in manuscripts throughout New England libraries. The format is confusing to read and filled with ambiguities. Nevertheless, the information is invaluable and we must appreciate the work our ancestors did. We hope our readers will compare the various forms of genealogical work that appear in TEG (i.e.; the Proctor material in the Nov 83 issue, as well as the Saville and Gerry articles in this issue). We hope you will agree that "The Register Format" used by that prestigious journal as well as by TAG, is the clearest to follow. Also, it is the only accepted method by most national journals today, so genealogists should try to follow it when writing the history of one family. The Gerry family is an example of the Register Format.

Once again we have a "witch" article - this time submitted by Eleanor Spiller. For some unknown reason, there seems to be a strong rekindling of interest in that dark and enigmatic episode in our Essex County history. Essex Institute in Salem has initiated a "Friends of Salem Witchcraft" for descendants of persons involved in the "infamous episode," with a one-time membership fee of $20.

Here in Essex County we are all agog with the daily reports issuing from the Rebecca Nurse Homestead in Danvers, where the television crews for PBS (Channel 2) are filming "Three Sovereigns for Sarah." It will be a 3-part mini-series scheduled for broadcast in May and it features Vanessa Redgrave as Sarah Cloyce. Danvers Archivist, Richard Trask, is working as a consultant, and when the staging people actually constructed (on the Rebecca Nurse property) a replica of the old Salem Meeting House, Richard made several trips to "our" Old Meeting House in Lynnfield for details. Lynnfield's Old Meeting House is the third oldest Meeting House still standing on its original green, and it is the only one that typifies the simple Puritan architecture.

On a more personal note, I wish to thank all of you for your kind good wishes on my recent marriage. My husband and I have a combined family of seven children, seven grandchildren and three living parents, who are scattered over seven states from California, New Mexico, Florida, Georgia, North Carolina, New York and New Hampshire! That should keep us out of mischief!

Until May . . . Keep up the good work.

Marcia Wiswall/Lindberg

Teg Feature Article

THE DISTAFF SIDE DID MAKE A DIFFERENCE

(A Story about the Contributions some Colonial Women Made to their Homes and Communities)

by Mrs. Laurence W. L. Barrington

Women have been vital factors in all the great movements of mankind. In America, the Pilgrim women, enduring that first winter in New England, provided proof of their courage. During the Revolution women played an important part in the fight against tyranny. Our West could not have been settled without the skill and bravery of the pioneer women.

The domestic experience separated their world from that of men. Most women spent their years in farm households. A wife was expected to obey her husband's orders. He controlled family finances; she had little knowledge of legal terms or property transactions. No household task was more time consuming or symbolic of woman's inferior role than spinning and weaving. Marriage was almost universal, divorces difficult to obtain, while most widows re-married. Women bore five to seven live children and averaged twenty-eight months between births. The role of spinster was unenviable as she was a perpetual dependent on relations.

The Revolutionary war years disrupted the normal pattern of society, resulting in a more independent outlook on life for women. Although traditional denigrating attitudes would continue until the 1790s, the re-evaluation of domesticity eventually culminated in the nineteenth century's glorification of woman's household role.

Nothing prevented women from working; nor did the kind of work affect social standing. Women could be seamstresses, nurses, or perhaps, teachers. Women often ran roadside inns or served as midwives. A drygoods or grocery shop were options for a widow who had resources to stock merchandis.

Occupations included mounting and repairing fans, laundering laces and dyeing fabrics. In Philadelphia, Jonathan Crathorne's widow, Mary, continued his business of manufacturing mustard and chocolate. Foodstuffs and clothing were within woman's accepted sphere, but some went farther afield, caning chairs, making soap and candles. Elizabeth Russell was a coachmaker, Sarah Jewell made rope, and Mary Salmon shod horses. Some eleven women ran printing presses, ten of whom published newspapers before 1776.

Women were active in religion. Mother Ann Lee, daughter of an English blacksmith and totally illiterate, introduced the Shaker religion to America. Mary Fisher and Ann Austin were the first Quakers to come to this country, while Mrs. Barbara Heck, in 1766, with four members, established a Methodist Society.

Anne Hutchinson and a group of women held vague, mystical theological discussions at her house. Ann criticized the spiritual heads of the Massachusetts Colony at a time when the church was the center of all authority. Records indicate she was banished because of her revelations and excommunicated for lie. Actually, she was too brilliant and progressive for the ministers and magistrates. Welcomed to Rhode Island by Roger Williams, after her husband's death, she went to Pelham Manor, New York, where, in 1643, she and her children, except one taken captive, were slain by Indians. A notable and picturesque figure, Anne Hutchinson's life represented a forecast of the liberty for which America stands.

In 1705, Madame Sarah Knight, a widow, rode on horseback from Boston, through the wilderness, to New York and back, at a time when no man ventured more than twenty miles from town until the church offered prayers for his safety. She had protection by hired guides, the western post, or such travellers as she met. Her journal includes explicit descriptions of inns and taverns. Her vivid pictures of customs and places she visited, plus the uniqueness of her journey, make her a woman of note. Back in Boston, she opened a school in her home on Moon Street, among her students being Benjamin Franklin and Samuel Mather. Later in life she operated a successful tavern near New London, purchased mills and speculated in Indian lands. Quite a Colonial dame!

Elizabeth Murray was perhaps the first woman philanthropist. A Scottish immigrant, she opened a dry goods store in Boston, prospering because she learned the benefits of judiciously timed sales, regular bookkeeping methods and a careful watch of finances. Elizabeth Murray married three times, first to a merchant, Thomas Campbell, with whom she had no antenuptial agreement. At age thirty-four she married seventy year old James Smith, a distiller and one of Boston's wealthiest men, with whom she demanded a marriage settlement and guarantee her property would be preserved intact. With her third marriage to Mr. Ralph Inman, a Cambridge farmer and merchant, she had a stringent marital settlement. By then a wealthy woman, she helped five nieces establish busines- ses, aided an unwed mother, Janet Day, to open a sewing school and financed a shop for orphaned sisters, Anne and Betsy Cuming. Elizabeth Murray exemplifies how widowhood and financial independence affected the eighteenth century woman's perception of self and her role.

On December 4, 1766, an "ad" appeared in the PENNSYLVANIA GAZETTE indicating a Mrs. Lydia Darragh "intends to make grave clothes and lay out the dead." When the British occupied Philadelphia, officers frequently met at the home of this Quaker family. One evening the family was ordered to retire so early Lydia became suspicious and kept her bedroom door ajar and overheard plans to attack at nearby White Marsh. The next morning, obtaining a permit to pass through the British lines on the pretext of needing flour, she walked to the mill, left her bag, then pressed on toward the American camp. Meeting an officer whom she recognized, she told him of the proposed attact, thus intercep- ting the British plan.

In 1634, Leonard Calvert, brother of Lord Baltimore, brought some three hundred colonists to Maryland, including Thomas Green, his successor as Colony Governor. Four years later, Margaret Brent arrived with family, servants and nine others. This woman was one of the most remarkable figures of early Colonial life. Whether a friend, cousin, or an intimate of Calvert's was never determined, but nevertheless, she was at his bedside when he died. Pointing at her so all could see, he said, "I make you my sole executrix; take all and pay all." Thus, Margaret Brent became, literally, Maryland's ruler. Moving into Calvert's house, she managed all his property. As executrix, she served as Lord Baltimore's attorney, thereby controlling his property as well. On January 21, 1648, she demanded the right to vote and have a seat in the General Assembly. In fact, she concluded she deserved two votes, one for Baltimore and one for a dead man. Governor Green, usually weak and vacillating, refused Margaret's demand, the only request ever denied her. Although Margaret Brent failed in her effort for representation and voting rights, nevertheless, she became the first American woman to advocate that right.

Eliza Lucas was born in Antigua in 1723, daughter of British officer, Lt. Colonel George Lucas. Brought up and educated in England, the family eventually moved to South Carolina, where her father, now Governor, started extensive

4

plantations near Charleston. War with Spain demanded Eliza's father leave her, at age sixteen, to care for a sickly mother, a little sister, the management of a large house and three plantations. Frequently she visited Colonel Pinkney and his wife. Recognizing Eliza's intelligence, the Colonel lent her books, discussed literature with her and encouraged her interest in music and botany. After his wife's death, now Chief Justice, he persuaded young Eliza to marry him. They lived in England five years, where they were widely entertained, even by Royalty. Judge Pinkney died soon after returning home, but Eliza carried on the responsibilities of her family and plantations. Experimenting with crops, she mastered the secret of the preparation of indigo, so that its export to England, just before the Revolution, was a source of wealth to the Colony, its annual value being more than one million pounds. This cultivated and artistic Colonial daughter's contribution to society was pre-eminent among women landowners.

The fall of Charleston May 12th, 1780, erased hopes for an early end to hostilities. Women proposed a nationwide relief movement, beginning in Philadelphia June 10th, 1780, with the publication of a broadside entitled THE SENTIMENTS OF AN AMERICAN WOMAN, composed by Esther Reed. By July, she and thirty-six women raised more than three hundred thousand Continental dollars from sixteen hundred persons.

It is difficult to conclude a treatise on the contributions of Colonial women without naming briefly such persons as Anne Bradstreet, the first American poet, or Phillis Wheatley, an African slave, brought to this country about 1755, who sent her verses to George Washington, who acknowledged her genius. Mrs. John Davenport, wife of the New Haven minister, looked out for the extensive property interests of John Winthrop, the younger, when political business kept him in England. Few narratives are more exciting than that of Mary Rowlandson and her two children, captured by Indians in Lancaster, Massachusetts, and forced to live with them until ransomed by friends for twenty-seven pounds. Her journal is one of the most descriptive and valuable of Indian life and customs. Mercy Otis Warren, friend of Abigail Adams, was a pamphleteer, dramatist and historian. Hannah Dustin, Molly Pitcher and Deborah Sampson, are noted as the most famous and fierce of all women fighters. Nancy Hart, a Georgian, single-handedly, captured a group of Tories, while Emily Geiger and Deborah Champion served as teen-aged messengers during the war.

Many more women could be named who enriched Colonial life. In the arts and sciences, in literature, the field of education and social advancement, their gifts were outstanding. As we reflect on the accomplishments of these forebears, we realize their struggle for recognition did not end with the Colonial period. Few more fundamental questions still confront the modern world than a solution as to what should be woman's status in society.

###

SOME NOTABLE COLONIAL WOMEN

1. Abigail Smith Adams   1744-1818
2. Hannah Adams   1755-1831
3. Ann Austin   -1665
4. Anne Bradstreet   1612-1672
5. Margaret Brent   1600-c1661
6. Esther Edwards Burr
7. Deborah Champion   1753-
8. Mary Cooper
9. Mary Fisher Crosse   1624-1690

10. Lydia Barrington Darragh 1729-1789
11. Elizabeth Wooley Davenport   1650s
12. Elizabeth Digges
13. Hannah Dustin   1657-
14. Sarah Pierpont Edwards   1710-1758
15. Deborah Read Franklin   c1707-1774
16. Emily Geiger   Fl. 1760s-1770s
17. Elizabeth Schuyler Hamilton
                               1757-1854

18.	Nancy Hart	1735?-1830	29.	Elizabeth Poole	1599-1654
19.	Barbara Ruckle Heck	1734-1804	30.	Sarah Prince	
20.	Anne Marbury Hutchinson	1590?-1643	31.	Esther Deberta Reed	1746-1780
21.	Sarah Kemble Knight	1666-1727	32.	Mary White Rowlandson	1635-1678
22.	Mother Ann Lee	1735-1784	33.	Deborah Sampson	1760-1827
23.	Susan Livingston		34.	Cornelia Van Cortlan Scuyler	
24.	Sybil Ludington	1761-1839			Fl. 1700s
25.	Dolly Payne Madison	1768-1849	35.	Mary Coffin Starbuck	1645-1717
26.	Elizabeth Murray	1726-	36.	Mercy Otis Warren	1728-1814
27.	Eliza Lucas Pinckney	1723-1793	37.	Martha Washington	1731-1802
28.	Molly Pitcher	1754?-1832	38.	Phillis Wheatley	c1753-1784
	(Mary Ludwig Hayes McCauley)		39.	Jemima Wilkinson	1752-1819
	40. Margaret Tyndal Winthrop	1591-1647			

##

QUOTATIONS   (What Men have said about women)

"She looks well to the ways of her household, and does not eat the bread of idleness."   (Proverbs 37, verse 27)

"Let a woman learn in silence with all submissiveness. I permit no woman to teach or to have authority over men; she is to keep silent." (1 Timothy, Chapter 2, verses 11 & 12)

"Women are expected to tend the hearth and find happiness in their chimney corners." (Governor Livingston of New Jersey)

##

BIBLIOGRAPHY

1. Benson, Mary Sumner. Women in Eighteenth Century America. Port Washington, New York: Kennikat Press.
2. Brooks, Geraldine. Women in America. New York: Arno Press, 1974.
3. Dexter, Elizabeth Anthony. Colonial Women of Affairs. Cambridge, MA: Houghton Mifflin, 1924.
4. Earle, Alice Morse. Colonial Dames and Good Wives. New York: Frederick Unger, (Republished) 1962.
5. Earle, Alice Morse. Home Life in Colonial Days. New York: Macmillan, 1898. (Alice Earle, 1926)
6. Encyclopedia of American History. New York: Harper, 1953.
7. The Heritage of America. Boston: D. C. Heath.
8. Hollingsworth, Anne. Colonial Days and Dames. Philadelphia: Lippincott, 1895.
9. Index to Women of the World. Westwood, MA: F. W. Faxon Co., 1970.
10. Kelley, Joseph J., Jr. Courage and Candlelight. Harrisburg, PA: Stackpole, 1974.
11. Minnegerode, Meade. Some American Ladies. New York and London: G. P. Putnam & Sons, 1926.
12. Norton, Mary Beth. Liberty's Daughters. Boston: Little Brown, 1980.
13. Notable American Women. 1607-1950. Cambridge, MA: Belknap Press, 1971.
14. World Book Encyclopedia. Chicago, IL. (Vol. 18)

##

Crest and Shield

By Lyman O. Tucker

WARD

SUB CRUCE SALUS

OR	AZURE
GOLD	BLUE

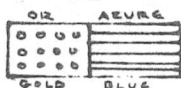

ARMS: Azure, a cross flory Or.

CREST: A wolf's head erased proper,
        langued gules.

MOTTO: Sub cruce salus

#############################

Andrew, Watertown 1634; d. CT
George, New Haven, Branford, CT
Benjamin, Boston 1639
John, physician; Boston, Ipswich
John, Conn. & N.J.
Lawrence, Bro. of George, Ct & N.J.
Marmaduke, Newport, RI, 1640
Miles, Salem, 1639
Nathaniel, Hartford, Ct; Hadley, MA
Samuel, Hingham, Charlestown.
Samuel, Marblehead, 1665
Thomas, Milford, MA 1657
William, Sudbury, Marlboro, MA

WARREN

PRO PATRIA MORI

ARG	OR	GULES	AZURE
WHITE	GOLD	RED	BLUE

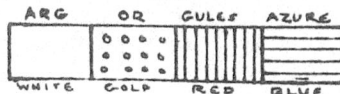

ARMS: Gules, a lion rampant, a chief
        chequy Or and Azure

CREST: Out of a coronet a demi-eagle
        displayed

MOTTO: "To die for one's country"

#############################

Abraham, Salem, Ipswich, MA
Arthur, Weymouth, MA
Ephraim, Boston, MA
James, Kittery, ME
John, Watertown, MA
John, Exeter, NH; Boston, MA
John, Ipswich, MA
Peter, Dorchester, Milton, MA
Ralph, Salem, MA 1638
Richard, "Mayflower" passenger
Thomas, Salem, MA
William, Hartford, CT
William, Boston, MA

7

It Happened in Essex County

By Corinne Wilmoth Witham

CAPE ANN CHAPTER, DAUGHTERS OF THE AMERICAN REVOLUTION RECEIVE A LEGACY

The Cape Ann Chapter of the Daughters of the American Revolution have received a legacy of a home and meeting place from the late Shirley Elizabeth Klein, a member of the local Chapter, who died December 6, 1983, leaving her home at 95A Granite Street, Pigeon Cove on Cape Ann, to the Cape Ann Chapter. Under the terms of Miss Klein's will, one member, and possibly two, may reside there. Miss Phillis E. Harvey, a member of the Cape Ann Chapter (and a member of ESOG), has the honor of being the first resident.

Shirley Elizabeth Klein was born in Blue Island, Illinois, on May 13, 1924, daughter of Hazel Elizabeth Airey and Alden J. Klein. A graduate of DePauw University with a masters from the University of Illinois, she made her career in the newspaper field, owning the Press Rubber Company of Blue Island, and travelling extensively for her company on legal matters. Although she grew up in Illinois, Miss Klein's roots were in this area of New England, going back to the first Peter Lurvey, who settled in Ipswich in 1675. It was his great-grandson, Moses Lurvey, who was Miss Klein's Revolutionary ancestor; and through him, she became a member first of the William French Chapter, Bellows Falls, Vermont, on 1 July, 1962, and later transferred to the Cape Ann Chapter, Gloucester-Rockport, Massachusetts, 18 October 1968.

Moses Lurvey, great grandson of Peter[1] Lurvey, was born in Gloucester, Massachusetts, 30 October 1753, and died in Barnard, Vermont, 23 November 1836. His wife was Elizabeth Potter, born 28 August, 1753, and died in Barnard, Vermont, before 16 December 1831. They were married on January 11, 1776 in the Church of the Linebrook Parish, Ipswich, Massachusetts. Moses enlisted on Cape Ann, April, 1775 for eight months under Captain Barnabus Dodge, Colonel Gerrish. He re-enlisted as Sergeant on 1 January, 1776, for one year under Captain Josiah Fay and Colonel Jonathan Ward.

How Shirley Elizabeth Klein came to Cape Ann from Blue Island, Illinois, and purchased a home at 95A Granite Street, Pigeon Cove, Rockport, is interesting to genealogists. It was a long trail of research, many times discouraging. Born in a small town, called Blue Island, Illinois, which joins Chicago on the Southwest, she had never heard of Cape Ann, with its rock-bound coast. At one time, Blue Island was an island in Lake Michigan, but as the waters of the lake receded, the island became part of the mainland. Its elevation was the highest point in Cook County. At one time, it was French territory and explored by Marquette, La Salle, and Joliet. There are many stories as to how the city got its name, the most reliable being that it was named by the Illini Indians because from Lake Michigan the high ridge appeared blue, as the forest land was surrounded by a blue mist.

In 1834, the first settler, in the true respect, because he was not a trader, trapper or hunter, came to this section of the country. Thomas Courtney of English origin, was his name, and ten years later, other settlers of English origin came, followed by a German migration. Shirley's great-great grandfather

Frederic Klein came from Nonnenrole, Hesse, Dormstadt, Germany in 1849. On Shirley's maternal side, her great-great grandfather was Norman Townsend, who, with his wife, Fanny Lurvey Townsend, came from Barnard, Vermont in 1879. Both families supported themselves by farming. The land in Illinois was flat, fertile and free from stones. The early settlers of English and German origin either intermarried or married their own countrymen or countrywomen. In Shirley Klein's case, English married German. As a child, she recalled going with her German grandfather into a German smoke shop where he purchased cigars and met other German-speaking friends. One asked her grandfather, "Heinrich, is this the granddaughter with the Yankee mother?" Her grandfather answered, "Yes, and I am proud of her." When Shirley returned home, she asked her mother "What is a Yankee?" and was told that a Yankee was a person of English origin who came from New England.

After graduating from college, she moved to the East and was employed at White Plains, New York, as executive assistant to the general manager of Macy-Westchester Newspapers, publishers of eight dailies and three weeklies. Coming from a small, friendly farming town, she found it difficult to adjust to the New York City area. As a gift to her mother, she decided to take her back over the migratory path her family had travelled, and the research started.

No birth or death records were kept in Blue Island, Illinois, before 1900, but in the "Genealogical and Biographical Record of Cook County, Illinois," containing biographical sketches of permanent citizens of Cook County, she found her great uncle Alonzo Townsend listed, and this information gave her the first exposure she ever had to Cape Ann. She thought Cape Ann was a city, and on September 17, 1960, wrote to the Town Clerk, Cape Ann, Massachusetts. The reply from there informed her that Cape Ann was a Cape, not a city, and composed of Gloucester and Rockport.

In the meantime, she wrote the Town Clerk of Barnard, Vermont, and learned that Moses Lurvey (her Revolutionary ancestor) had been born in Gloucester, Massachusetts. Her next step was to make contact with the Vermont State Registrar of the Daughters of the American Revolution. Prior to that she had made contact with William Parry of the New England Publishers Assoication, who referred her to Mr. Alexander Stoddart, publishers of the Essex County Newspapers, who in turn, put her in touch with the late Mrs. Isabel Hill of the Sawyer Free Library in Gloucester, who proved to be a great help.

Miss Klein's search took her to the Old Colony Historical Society in Taunton, Massachusetts, where she found their Vital Records had been burned in 1838. This was another dead end. But many of Taunton's records were duplicated in Providence, Rhode Island. From here, she travelled to Barnard, Vermont, and there she saw the old burial ground and took pictures of Moses Lurvey's gravestone. There was no stone for his wife, Elizabeth Potter Lurvey, and as Shirley journeyed through New England cemeteries, she found that women were not too important, and often had unmarked graves.

Her next travel was to Cape Ann, where she arrived the 5th of October, 1961. Here she found that the Lurveys had lived on Dog Town Common, once inhabited by over one hundred people but now a deserted village, with only ancient cellar holes where once stood the homes of the early settlers. Many stories have been written about Gloucester's deserted village, stories of witchcraft, of a changing population, where Gloucestermen left their families to go to the Revolutionary war from which many never returned. Geologists have studied Dogtown Common, for here is the end of the terminal moraine where great boulders stand today as mute testimony of the time the great glacier approached this spot and then started to recede. It is a natural Salisbury Plain of which icebergs and ocean currents were the Druidic builders where the sea-birds fly across the Cape, and the sweet-bay and green ferns are imbedded in a softer, deeper setting as the years go by. It is the only place in America where the cellars of the first settlers remain.

Most of Shirley Klein's clues came from her family bibles which the family had carried to the mid-west. Her ancestor's service papers are listed in Pension Papers at the DAR Library, Washington, D.C., volume 43, page 129. He applied for pension 4 May 1819 and his place of residence at that time was Barnard, Vermont, but his residence at the date of enlishment was Cape Ann (afterwards called Gloucester).

Undoubtedly her roots drew her back to Cape Ann, and she purchased the property at 95A Granite Street where she resided until her death on December 6, 1983. A $500 contribution was also bequeathed to the DAR Library, Washington, D.C.

I wonder what the first Peter Lurvey who settled in Ipswich in 1657, would say if he knew that one of his descendants, Shirley Elizabeth Klein, had willed her home to the Cape Ann Chapter of the Daughters of the American Revolution, where another descendant, Miss Phyllis Harvey resides under the provisions of Miss Klein's will, and that this article was researched and written by another descendant, and no doubt will be read by many other descendants scattered over our country.

****

"The Tall Ships of Annisquam" by Barbara Brown Marden in the November 1984 TEG was most interesting to me as many of the men mentioned were my ancestor grandfathers.

Edward Harraden was born in Devonshire, England, and came to Ipswich in 1654, and from there to Cape Ann. His wife: Sarah ---- b. 1630; d. 14 May 1699

Benjamin Harraden was b. 11 Sept 1670; m. Deborah Norwood, daughter of Sir Francis Norwood and Elizabeth Coldom.

Philip Stainwood (Stanwood) came from England with his wife Mary. She d. 3 Jan 1678 and he d. 7 August 1672.

Abraham Robinson was the first child born of English parents on Cape Ann in 1644. He d. 1746 at 102 years of age. He m. 7 July 1668 Mary Harraden, b. 1649 in Ipswich, 28 September 1725. She was daughter of Edward Harraden and Sarah Haskell. Tradition states that Abraham was the son of Reverend John Robinson, the pastor to the Pilgrims.

Samuel York from North Yarmouth, Maine, moved to Gloucester. He m. Hannah Hoyt. He was b. 1645; d. 18 Mar 1718.

My husband, Karl, descended from the Henry Witham who built his house in Lobster Cove. Also his grandfather were Thomas and Nathaniel Sanders, also well-known for their ship building.

Corinne B. Witham

GILES COREY

By Eleanor V. Spiller

Except for the times when he is referred to as having been pressed to death, little is known about Giles Corey by most people. In truth he was a most colorful character in the community. Since he was an ancestor, I wished to know all that I could about him. By searching dozens of histories, deeds, and other papers; by putting together a comment made in one place and a sentence from another source, a story of a man began to come together. The following account was compiled by chronologically arranging the "dribs and dabs."

GILES COREY (Cory, Corry, Kory, Coree) was born circa 1619 in England, married (1) Margaret ---- by whom he had the children we definitely know of by records of the Essex County Quarterly Court. (see below) He married second Mary Brite on 11 April 1673. Her gravestone in the Charter St. Cemetery, reads: "Mary Corry Ye wife of Giles Corry aged 63 years dyed August Ye 27 1684." Caleb Moore stated that when he was in Virginia with his father, the latter bought Mary, Cory's 2nd wife, out of a London ship. Giles third wife was Martha, about whom we'll talk more. Martha was a white woman from England. She spoke English well and was supposed to be English. She had a son, a mulatto, named Benjamin or Benoni, who was living in 1699, at the age of 22. She married Giles Corey in 1685, after the boy was born.

Corey lived in what is now Peabody - about 10 rods westerly of the West Peabody jct. R.R. station adjoining the southerly side of the location of the Salem and Lowell RR. He was apparently an agitator most of his life according to the record in references. In the Salem Court 28 June 1649 Giles was fined for stealing wheat, powder, soap, flax, tobacco, bacon, port, butter and knives from Mr. Curwin and Thomas Anthrom. In October 1668 petitions against imposts were called forth by the Massachusetts General Court. Giles Corey was one of many to sign.

About the last of November, 1675, as Mrs. Mary Corey testified, Elizabeth, wife of Zachariah Goodale, told her that the latter's brother Jacob Goodale had been to Zachariah's house and got into the cellar and took some apples. Zachariah was then coming in with a log of wood, and laying it down, he took a stick and "pade (paid) hem to som porpos." About 10 days later, in December, Giles Corey unreasonably beat Jacob with a stick of about an inch in diameter nearly a hundred blows in the presence of Elisha Kebee, who told Corey that he would knock him down if he did not forbear. About 10 days later, Corey went to the house of Zach Goodale and told him that his brother Jacob had had a fall. He was afraid he had broken his arm, and desired him to take Jacob to Mrs. Mole's in town. Jacob was then 34 years, and up to that time had been lusty. Now, Jacob went "very ravel" and stooping, and he was very pale and his eyes sunken. Thereupon, Zach went to Corey's house and saw Jacob who was there. The roads were slippery, and Corey said that his horse was not caulked, so could not go with him. Jacob went so badly, Zach asked him if he had any other hurt than his arm, but he would not tell. Zach then requested that some one go with them since he was afraid to take him alone; whereupon Goody (Mrs.) Corey went with them. Jacob died a few days later, and an inquest was held. The jury was of Nathaniel Felton, Francis Nurse, Anthony Buxton, Michael Shaflin, Jeremiah Meacham, John Traske, Thomas Small, Samuel Very, Thomas Preston, John Cooke, Joshua Rea, Eleazer Giles. They made the following report "we find several wrongs he hath had in his body as upon his left arm and upon his right thigh a great bruise which is very much swold and upon the reins of his back in color differing from the other parts of his body we caused an incision to be much bruised and run with a jelly and the skin broke upon the outside of each buttocks." For his abuse Corey was fined.

A small house belonging to John Proctor, which stood on the northerly side of Lowell St. (Peabody) about 150 rods easterly of the Georgetown branch of the Boston and Maine RR, was partially burned in July 1678. The roof and that part of the walls above two feet upward from the upper floor was burned away. This occurred about two hours before day, and but for the timely appearance and strenuous efforts of John Phelps and Thomas Fuller, who were passing, it would have been wholly destroyed. Proctor suspected that Giles Corey set the fire. A warrant was issued on the 24th for his appearance at court, as he had done so many ill things to his neighbors, --- threatened and suggested fires, etc. He proved that he was at home and abed all the night of the fire, and was discharged.

Giles Corey moved for consideration for land that "is made use of for a highway." The selectmen answered that he "shall have a small stripe of land near that which was Roger Moreys meadow" about 2 acres. Another time a man named Morrow granted to Giles a spot or hole of meadow near Henery Phelps house and near his own meadow. It seems he was constantly engaged in gathering and transferring land.

Giles could throw all the younger men and often proved it. Records of the First Church, Salem (pages 170-171, dated 26 April 1691) read "Giles Corey a man of 80 years of age having been a scandalous person in his former time and God having in his later time awakened him into Repentance he stood propounded a moneth, and making confession of such evils as had been observed in him before." He was received into the Church with consent of the brethren.

The Salem Witch trials were to a great extent the result of the fanatical views expressed from the pulpit by the clergyman Cotton Mather who systematized, organized the thought and defended demonology in America. Ten bored children, 9 years to 20 years old, at an impressionable age, influenced by tales, fortune telling and incantations of a family black servant from the Barbadoes were the actors and instigators of this heinous crime against their fellow colonists. The childrens well-timed fits, convulsions, strange sightings and pressure from parents, cleric and medico began seven horrifying months. The months March through September 1692 were pitiless and pitiful for 125 persons accused of witchcraft. Warrants were issued and ´offenders´ - "those in compact with the Devil" were tried, by magistrates John Hathorne and Jonathan Corwin (Curwin).

Martha Corey was arrested 19 March; excommunicated 27 March; jailed in Boston in April; tried 9 September; executed 22 September. Giles Corey - over 80 years old - was carried away by the delusion for a time, and unwittingly with his testimony contributed to the conviction of Martha. Soon afterward, however, he denounced the proceedings and was himself thrown into jail. Copies of some of the accusations have been included in this family history.

He was arrested 18 April. (Essex County Archives and Danvers Archives are filled with depositions against him for inane reasons.) In better times, Giles had conveyed properties to some of his daughters and their husbands - for love. Wisely, while in jail, Giles, on 25 July 1692, made his will and conveyed all his remaining property - house, lands, moveables, etc. to his sons-in-laws William Cleaves and John Moulton. This also prevented confiscation of the property by the Crown or Provincial government at his death.

He was both tried and excommunicated 18 September 1692. He refused to plead for he had observed the futility of it. Not guilty to the court meant nil. Hence, the court resorted to the old English usage of applying pressure (peine forte at duce). There is in the Danvers Archives a document including the X (his mark) or signature of Giles Corey. The old man was taken to a public place, stripped of his clothing and laid on his back on the ground where boulders were heaped upon his chest, crushing the air from his body. "When in the agony of finally expiring his tongue obtruded from his mouth, some observer crowded it back down his throat with the thrust of a cane." Giles Corey was the only one to suffer thus. This pressing had nothing to do with witchcraft for if he had refused to plead on the charge of burglary, etc, the charge would have been the same. Certainly Giles Corey had courage, for he must have known this would be his fate when he did not plead his case.

In 1703, the heirs petitioned and the General Court repaid the heirs of persons executed; and the condemned and not executed the pecuniary damages they severally sustained. Some 600 pounds were paid out to the estates of these people. Heirs of Giles Corey and his wife received 21 pounds.

On 6 March 1712 the excommunication was erased and blotted out. An infamous era over, families, state and nation began to build an illustrious history.

GILES COREY. b. circa 1619 England, d. 19 Sept 1692 Salem. He married (1) Magaret -----; m. (2) 11 April 1673 Mary Brite, b. 1621, d. 27 Aug 1684; m. (3) 1685, Martha, b. ----, d. 22 Sept 1692.

    Children of Giles Corey and Margaret -----:
i   Martha, b. ----, d. 1683; m. 1675 William Cleaves, b. 1654, d. 1714.
          Children: i   John Cleaves, b. 1676 at Beverly.
                  ii   Eleanor Cleaves, b. 1678 at Beverly.
                  iii Martha Cleaves, b. 1680 at Beverly.
ii   Margaret, b. ---, m. (1) at Beverly, William Cleaves; m. (2) 3 May
        1716 Jonathan Biles.
          Children: i   William Cleaves, b. 23 July 1686 at Beverly.
                  ii   Hannah Cleaves, b. 31 Mar 1688 at Beverly.
                  iii Robert Cleaves, b. 21 July 1689 at Beverly.
                  iv Ebenezer Cleaves, b. 13 Oct 1691 at Beverly.
                  v   Benjamin Cleaves, b. 23 Oct 1693 at Beverly;
                       d. 23 Oct 1693; m. 25 Jun 1719 Rebeckar Conant
iii   Deliverance, b. 5 Aug 1658 at Salem; m. 5 June 1683 Henry Crosby.
iv   Elizabeth, b. ---; m. 16 Sept 1684 at Marblehead, John Moulton.
v   Mary, b. ---; d. before 11 Feb 1697/8; m. 29 May 1673 John Parker.
          Children: i   Giles Parker, b. 16 Apr 1675 at Salem.
                  ii   Martha Parker
                  iii Mercy Parker, b. 12 Apr 1676 at Salem, d. bef
                     2 Feb 1677.
                  iv Joseph Parker, b. 17 Sept 1680 at Salem.
                  v   Margaret Parker, b. 11 Feb 1682 at Salem.

vi John Parker, b. 30 Mar 1674 at Salem.
vii Mary Parker, b. 2 Feb 1677 at Salem.

(ANN PUTNAM V. GILES COREY)

The Deposition of Ann Putnam who testifieth and saith that on 13th of April 1602, "I saw the Apperition of Giles Cory com and afflect me urging me to writ in his book and so he continewed hurting me by times till the 19th April being the day of his examination; and dureing the time of his examination Giles Cory did tortor me a great many times and also several times since Giles Cory or his Apperance has most greviously afflected me by beating pinching and almost Choaking me to death urging me to writ in his book also on the day of his examination I saw Giles Cory or his Apperance most greviously afflect and torment Mary Walcott, Mercy Lewes and Sarah Vibber and I veryly beleeve that Giles Cory is a dreadful wizzard for sence he has ben in prison he or his Apperance has come to me a great many times and afflected me."

(Essex County Archives, Salem - Witchcraft Vol. 2, Page 41)

REFERENCES FOR GILES COREY

1. First Church of Salem Records 1629-1736, pgs 170, 171, 193, 219.
2. Danvers Archives.
3. History of Salem, Vol II 1638-1670, by Perley.
4. Salem in 17th Century, by James D. Phillips, pgs 290-308.
5. Essex County Quarterly Court Records.
6. NEHGR Vol 9, pg 85.
7. Deeds Essex County Courthouse, Salem, Mass.
8. Notebook of - "Some Inscriptions from Charter St. Cemetery, Salem, copied August 1901-1902 by William D. Dennis.
9. History of Danvers - Fel
10. Chronicles of Old Salem - Robotti.
11. Rebecca Nurse - Tapley.
12. Giles Corey will.
13. Depositions agains the Coreys.
14. A Book of New England - Z. Humphrey.

****

MORE ON THE SALEM WITCHES

(Reprinted from The American Genealogist (TAG), 59:245, "1983)

By Ruth Ann Wilder Sherman, Associate Editor of TAG

Dr. David L. Greene's series of splendid articles on Salem "Witches," which has been appearing recently in TAG, has attracted a considerable number of inquiries, particularly among new subscribers. To answer these questions, we solicited from our above-named friend and contributor the names of those about whom he proposed to write, and his plans for the series. Here are the facts:

All 20 persons who were executed for witchcraft in Salem, MA in 1692 are listed below. Each will eventually be featured in an article. Those with asterisks have already appeared in print. (See ordering information below.)

Bridget Bishop*
Rev. George Burroughs
Martha Carrier
Giles Cor(e)y
Martha Cor(e)y
Mary E(a)sty
Sarah Good(e)

Elizabeth How(e)
George Jacobs**
Susanna Martin***
Rebecca N(o)urse
Alice Parker
Mary Parker
John Proctor

Ann Pudeator
Wilmot Reed/Redd
Margaret Scott
Samuel Wardwell
Sarah Wild(es)
John Willard

If there is enough interest among readers, and sufficient materials are available, the series may also cover the four accused witches who died in prison: Lydia Dustin, Ann Foster, Sarah Osborne and Roger Toothaker.

Each article will provide a full analysis of contemporary material related to an executed witch. To this will be added a documented account of the individual's descendants for three generations. The author and the editors feel that these articles will show that significant historical problems can be solved, or at least clarified, by use of the techniques of scientific genealogy.

Dr. Greene originally planned to write on all 20 of the witches himself, then to gather revised versions of the articles into a book, but such in-depth research has proved to be extremely time consuming. At Dr. McCracken's suggestion, others were invited to contribute to the series, articles modelled on those already published. At the moment Glade Ian Nelson is working on the Rev. George Burroughs. Although Dr. Greene still expects to write most of the balance of the articles, he would be happy to hear from competent genealogists who have, already underway, research on specific witches, and who would be interested in participating in the series. Please write directly to David L. Greene, Ph.D., F.A.S.G., Route Three, Clarkesville, GA 30523.

* Bridget Bishop: TAG, July 1981, vol. 57 #3, p. 129.
** George Jacobs: TAG, April 1982, vol. 58 #2, p. 65.
***Susanna Martin, a two-part study: Part 1, TAG, Oct 1982, vol. 58 #4, p193

(Back issues of TAG may be obtained for $3.50 each from Dr. George E. McCracken, 1232 39th St., Des Moines IA 50311).

***Susanna Martin: Part 2, TAG, Jan. 1983 vol. 59 #1, p. 11. $3.50 from the publisher. (RuthAnn Sherman, 128 Massasoit Dr., Warwick, RI 02888)

A TRIP TO OLD ENGLAND

By Paul A. Hillman

In July Louise and I spent a most enjoyable 25 days touring England, Scotland and Wales with an English couple we met on a Romanian trip several years ago. It was wonderful riding through the beautiful countryside and seeing cathedrals and castles and not having to drive between narrow hedgerows on the left side of the road.

My genealogy work consisted of following the life of William Brewster of the Mayflower and some of his friends. We went to Scrooby, a small town northeast of London and saw the home he lived in and where he attended church. Next we went to Cambridge University and saw where he and John Harvard had attended college. After William Brewster finished his studies at Cambridge, he returned to Scrooby to become a religious leader, and with William Bradford and others, attempted to escape to Holland through the port of Boston. I sat in the cell he was locked up in and the court upstairs from which he was released.

While we were in Boston, we visited the cathedral (Boston Stump). A plaque there is dedicated to our 2nd Governor, Thomas Dudley, and a stained-glass window is dedicated to his daughter Ann Bradstreet of our Essex County. We visited the quay from which the Mayflower sailed in 1620 and the adjoining church where all the passengers prayed, and the cemetery where Captain Jones was later buried.

At Plymouth, we stood on the dock steps from which the Mayflower sailed. On a plaque next to the Mayflower is another plague commemorating the sailing of the ship Sea Venture to Virginia in 1609. Our Mayflower ancestor, Stephen Hopkins was a passenger on this voyage, and they were shipwrecked at Bermuda. Some managed to get to Virginia and our Stephen returned to England and was a Mayflower passenger in 1620. Our Mayflower was scrapped on the Thames River a few miles west of London several years after her voyage to America, and her timbers and beams were converted to a barn which we visited at old Jordans near Beaconsfield, Bucks, England.

A "bed and breakfast" trip like this through England is highly recommended because you can really see the countryside and meet local people.

###

NEW ENGLAND HISTORIC GENEALOGICAL SOCIETY RECEIVES GRANT

Congratulations are in order to the New England Historic Genealogical Society which was just awarded a $500,000 Challange Grant from the National Endowment for the Humanities. The 3-year grant, to be matched $3 to $1 was awarded for the purpose of strengthening the Society's services to members and building collections. As it is the first such grant received by the Society, it represents a valuable vote of confidence in their resources and services. Details of this challenge and of the Society's Twenty-First Century Fund program will be given at a later date. ESOG encourages all of its members to become involved with the New England Historic Genealogical Society, which must be recognized as the greatest genealogical treasure-trove in New England.

Research in Progress

RECORDS OF THE SAVILLE FAMILY

By Richard D. Saville; submitted by Gail Goodwin Nekorowski

<u>Thomas Savell</u> was the founder of the family in Gloucester bearing his name. Of his birth and parentage and personal history previous to his appearance in Gloucester, about 1720, nothing is definitely known. In answer to inquiries as to these points, one of his grandsons (William Saville) writes: "Thomas Savill was born in Malden, Massachusetts, tradition says in 1701." Another grandson (Thomas) records in his family bible: "Thomas Savell was born April 17, 1699." This latter record being definite as to dates is probably founded upon facts derived from an authentic source and may, therefore, be regarded as correct. The place of our ancestor's birth is not easily determined. It is not known upon what authority the statement of William Saville, that he was born in Malden, is based. The records of that town from 1693 to 1736 have been carefully examined by the town clerk with reference to this matter and he reports that he "cannot find the name of Saville or any name similar therein." The records of the town of Boston, where Thomas is said to have lived for some time previous to his removal to Gloucester, have also been consulted and although the family name frequently appears in them, no trace of him can be found there.

It is known that persons bearing our name (variously spelled Savil, Savill, Savel, Savell) were among the early emigrants from Yorkshire, England, to this country and they established themselves chiefly at Braintree and vicinity. The name still exists (1881) in that region and it is possible, if not probable, that Thomas Savill was a branch of that stock, although the records of the towns of Braintree and Weymouth which have been examined furnished no confirmation of this theory. The births of many children named Savill are recorded, but among these no "Thomas" is found.

John J. Babson in his history of Gloucester says: "Thomas Savill is said by his descendants to have come to this town from Malden and families of this name were early in Massachusetts but it is not known to which our settler belonged. He was a cooper and took up his abode in Annisquam." To supply the lack of evidence as to our remote ancestry, various traditions have arisen in the family. William Saville (grandson of Thomas) writes: "About the year 1755, it was ascertained that he (Thomas) was related to a great family in England of which Sir George Savill was a member and in all probability his uncle. My father (Jesse) clung to his belief that he was a descendant of a noble and wealthy family and that at some future time our propinquity will be established and perhaps our inheritance to a great estate."

Another tradition, or another version of the same, is to the effect that a wealthy English gentleman, George Savill by name, was an early emigrant to America and, having established himself at or near Boston, soon returned to England for the purpose of arranging his business and property in view of his determination to make America his future home. Having accomplished this object, he again took passage for this country but was never heard from, the vessel on which he embarked having, as we supposed, foundered at sea. His wife, who had remained in this country during her husband's absence, had meanwhile given birth to a son and this son was our ancestor, Thomas Savill. Had proper measures been taken in season he would, it is said, have inherited a large property of his father, but this was not done and the whole estate, having been advertised according to law in England and no claimant appearing, went eventually into the King's treasury.

It is claimed that at a later period papers were discovered which, had they been in good preservation, would have proved the son's heirship and recovered to him the property that rightfully belonged to him, but unfortunately these papers had been so mutilated by rats as to destroy their value as legal evidence. The tradition further avers that had the son been named "George," as the father had intended, his claim to the property would, not withstanding faulty evidence in other respects, have been established; but for some reason, not apparent, his mother gave him the name of "Thomas" and thus unwittingly deprived him of the inheritance to which he was entitled. Rhoda (great grand-daughter of Thomas) Savill, who related to the writer this story, says she has often heard her grandfather (Jesse) regard the statements he made always with great earnestness and with a firm belief, apparently, in their truth.

These traditions must pass for what they are worth. They do not afford a very satisfactory basis for genealogical research, the chief thing in their favor being that Jesse Saville seems to have believed them, or something like them. It is evident that he considered himself a descendant of a "nobel and wealthy family of England." He was not a weak-minded man likely to be captivated by silly fables, but was regarded on the contrary as a man of steady common sense, clear headed and practical. His aid and advice were often sought by his townsmen in matters of importance and he filled offices of trust and responsibility under the colonial government.

From what sources were his convictions as to his ancestry derived? Must not his father (Thomas) have furnished the facts, and if so is it credible that he should have misled his son in this way? On the other hand if these traditions have any substantial foundation, how does it happen that they were unconfirmed by any recorded facts? But, whether substantial or visionary, they are all that is now within our reach. Those who might at an early period have thrown some light upon the subject from personal knowledge, have passed away. Possibly at a future day some curious or persevering member of the Saville family may, by a thorough examination of all sources of information, both at home and abroad, be enabled to substitute for this shadowy traditon well authenticated facts. Until then we must remain content with such facts of history or fiction as our defunct friends have handed down to us.

Having learned the cooper's trade either in Malden or Boston, Thomas Savell moved about the year 1720 to the village of Annisquam, a part of the town of Gloucester. Here he engaged in business as a cooper and married, January 24, 1721, Mary Harraden. He early built or purchased a house in which he ever after lived, where all his children were born and where he died March 19, 1783. His wife, the mother of all his children, died June 10, 1775.

The house which sheltered this family for so many years was situated upon a high eminence far apart from other dwellings and was a conspicuous object, both from the land and the sea. The cellar alone remains (1881) to tell the passing traveler of a former human habitation. Of those who were born under this humble roof none remain among the living and their descendants are widely scattered.

Thomas Savell is represented to have been an upright, conscientious man, a devout Christian and a rigid conformist to the Levitical law. A grandson, William Saville, who was born in the old house (his father occupying the easterly half) says: "With them the Sabbath began on Saturday at sunset and ended at the same period on Sunday. Every article of food for the Lord's day was prepared beforehand and a strict observance of the sacred hours was required of all his household. Often have I looked with strained vision to see the last ray above the horizon at the setting of the glorious luminary, that I might exercise my limbs from the spellbound situation in which I was compelled to study over and over the Assembly of Divine Catechism."

Our respected ancestor must have experienced, during his long pilgrimage, a good share of earthly cares and perplexities. His income which was derived chiefly from his occupation as a cooper was small and precarious. The shop in which he carried on his trade was a rude structure built of stone gathered from the surrounding pastures and laid by his own hands against the side of a large boulder situated a short distance easterly from his dwelling. Although a humble establishment, it afforded, no doubt, all the facilities that his limited business required.

In addition to his employment as a cooper, he cultivated, with the aid of his children, a few acres of land adjoining his dwelling and which were a portion of his estate and thus supplied some of the more pressing wants of his famiy. The sea too was near at hand and it is to be presumed that from this source his table was sometimes supplied.

If our ancestor was poor in this world's goods, his was not an exceptional case in those early days, but was the common lot of all his friends and neighbors. It is pleasant to reflect that however small may have been his early possessions, his life gave evidence that he was rich in faith and a conscience void of offense. The limitations and perplexities of his earthly career may have been but needed preparation for the freedom and joys of the better kingdom.

The boulder above referred to has always been an object of interest to those of Thomas Savell's descendants who have been accustomed to visit the "old place." It was a large cleft rock and could easily be seen from far different points on the Cape. It was with much regret that the writer on a recent visit found that the present owners of the place had caused it to be blasted and cut into paving stones.

Another boulder on the northerly side of the house had shared the same fate, giving evidence that the old land marks of the place, around which cluster so many interesting associations, will all, ere long, be obliterated. Let us be thankful that the past, at least, is secure and that memory is stored with so much that shall recall the trials and lives of our ancestors.

COPY OF THE LAST WILL AND TESTAMENT OF THOMAS SAVELL

"In the name of God, Amen, I, Thomas Savell, of the town of Gloucester, in the County of Essex, cooper, being sick and weak in body but of perfect mind and memory, thanks be to God, calling unto mind the mortality of body and knowing that it is appointed for all men once to die, do make and ordain this my last will and testament, that is to say:

Principally and first of all, I give and recommend my soul into the hands of Almighty God that gave it, and my body to the earth to be buried in decent Christian burial at the discretion of my executors, nothing doubting but at the general resurrection I shall receive the same again by the mighty power of God. And as to touching my worldly estate, wherewith it has pleased God to bless me in this life, I give, demise and dispose of the same in the following manner and form, viz:

First, I give and bequeath to my grandson, Thomas Savell, Jr., one half dozen earthen plates, for my name.

I also give and bequeath unto my daughter, Mary Whitredge, her heirs and assigns, two pieces of land on Harraden's Point which came by her mother, also two acres of woodland coming by her mother, and also an equal share with my sons, John and Jesse Savell, in the household furniture I shall die possessed of.

I give and bequeath also unto my sons, John and Jesse Savell, the remainder of all my real and personal estate, to be equally divided between them, they paying twenty pounds each to my daughter, Mary Whitredge, before mentioned, the same to be possessed by them and their heirs forever.

I hereby constitute my sons, John and Jesse Savell, jointly and severally to be the executors of this my last will and testament.

Signed, sealed, pronounced and declared to be the last will and testament of Thomas Savell aforeseaid in the presence of us, this fourth day of March 1783. (signed) Thomas Savell.

(Signed) Prest. Barnet Harkin, Edward D. Burke, Paul Morgan.

###############################

The present spelling of the name "Saville" was adopted about the year 1783 by the descendants of Thomas and has since been maintained by all the family. Thomas, himself, however still adhered to the spelling to which he had been accustomed and signed his name "Savell" to the will executed in 1783, a few days before his death.

The various modes of spelling the family name indicate only the freedom of former days in this particular. Every man spelled his name as he pleased. The Saville name is very ancient and of Norman origin, but in early English records, as well as in those of a later period in this country, there is a great diversity in the manner of spelling it.

The following record of the family of THOMAS SAVELL is copied from the family bible of his grandson, Thomas, and is presumed to be substantially correct, although it differs in some particulars from another account furnished by William Saville:

THOMAS SAVELL, born April 17, 1699, died March 19, 1783.
Mary Harraden, born February 5, 1704, died June 10, 1775.

The above were married January 24, 1721.

CHILDREN

1. Thomas, born April 17, 1722, died March 19, 1724.
2. Hannah, born September 26, 1724, died May 6, 1727
3. James, born July 12, 1726, died July 14, 1726.
4. John, born July 12, 1727, died November 1790; married Susanna Harraden, May 30, 1751. The birth of two daughters is reported as follows:
   Mary, born August 23, 1753.
   Elizabeth, born May 13, 1755.
5. Mary, born 23 May 1729; died March 23, 1808; married William Whittredge 8 December 1755.
6. Thomas, born August 4, 1731, died of smallpox in 1769.
7. Hannah, born December 14, 1733.
8. Oliver, born February 28, 1736, died young.
9. Oliver, born July 31, 1738, died at sea.
10. Jesse, born December 16, 1740, died March 11, 1823.

Of all the children of Thomas and Mary Savell, Jesse seems to have been the only one who perpetuated the name and from this honored root has sprung all the various branches of the Saville family of Gloucester.

JESSE SAVILLE, born December 16, 1740, died March 11, 1823.
Martha Babson, born October 8, 1745, died April 19, 1785.

They were married October 6, 1763.

CHILDREN

Thomas, born October 18, 1764, died May 7, 1845.
Abiah, born June 12, 1766, died February 18, 1843.
John, born April 16, 1768, left home April 1779 and never more heard from.
William, born Mary 17, 1770, died January 12, 1853.
James, born October 16, 1772, died June 6, 1805.
Martha, born December 1774, died December 13, 1801.
Oliver, born January 20, 1777, died on passage from India, March 14, 1801.
Epes, born March 6, 1779, died July 1820.
David, born March 13, 1781, lost at sea on passage from India with the whole
    company of the ship "Winthrop and Mary" about 1800.

JESSE SAVILLE married for his second wife, Hannah Dane of Hamilton, Mass. The intention was recorded January 21, 1786.

CHILDREN

Mary Dane, born March 7, 1787.
Hannah, born December 24, 1790.

Upon his marriage with Martha Babson, JESSE SAVILLE became an occupant of the easterly half of his father's house before described. During the war of the Revolution he removed with his family to New Boston, N.H. How long he remained there is not now definitely known, but after the close of the war we find him again at his old home in Gloucester. Probably some of his children were born in New Boston. With the exception of this absence and a brief period at Ipswich, his long life was spent on the spot of his birth. To his occupation of cooper he added the business of tanning in a small way, having learned the trade at

Ipswich. He was at one time an officer of the customs under the colonial government. Babson in his History of Gloucester says: "The strict performance of what he considered his duty made him odious to his townsmen and for it he suffered severly in his person and property."

It is surely not to his descredit that he suffered persecution and outrage for opinion's sake. May the mantle of his courage rest upon his descendants through all generations!

(To be continued)

BETHIA, THE WIFE OF SAMUEL GASKILL

By Janet I. Delorey, 496 Main Street, Shrewsbury, MA 01545

There has been some confusion regarding the identity of Bethia, the wife of Samuel Gaskill, an early resident of Salem, Massachusetts. This confusion has found its way into print, stating as fact that Bethia was the daughter of Thomas Gardner, Jr. and his wife, Hannah.

Through the efforts of Dr. Grayson Mitchell of Kingston, NY, records were obtained that prove beyond doubt that Bethia was an unrecorded daughter of John and Mary (?) Woodin. Although her birth record is missing, due perhaps to the fact that John Woodin, in his occupation of Mason or Bricklayer, resided in various towns including Haverhill, MA, Hampton, NH, Salisbury, MA, Newbury, MA and Rowley, MA, we submit that two records from the Essex County Probate Court and the Essex County Registry of Deeds prove the relationship.

On January 30, 1721 at Essex County Probate Court, "Letters of Administration on ye Goods & Estate of Jn Woodin Sen who dyed att Carolina, formerly of Haverhill in ye County aforesd Deceased Intestate was granted to Samll Gaskill of Salem who marryed Bethia Daughter of ye Dec...". And, on September 29, 1730, a deed was recorded at Essex County Registry of Deeds from Bethia Gaskill to Robert Peaslee. "...I Bethiah Gaskill of Salem in ye County of Essex in His Majesties Province of the Massachusetts Bay in New England, widow and Daughter of John Woodin formerly of Haverhill in & in ye County & Province above Mason or Bricklayer Deceased...".

Samuel Gaskill, born 23:11m:1663 at Salem MA (Salem VR), a son of Samuel and Provided (Southwick) Gaskill, was dead by 1725 when his will was probated (Essex County Probate Court Records). Thus, his wife, Bethia, was a widow in 1730 when she deeded land to Robert Peaslee.

22

GERRY (GAREY, GEERE, GEARY) FAMILIES
OF ESSEX AND MIDDLESEX COUNTIES

By Marcia Wiswall/Lindberg

There were seven Geary (Gerry) "Heads of households" that came to Essex and
Middlesex Counties in the Massachusetts Bay Colony in the 17th and early 18th
centuries. The name was spelled variously Garey, Gary, Geare, Geary, Geere,
Gere and Gerry, and, in one form or another, appears in the records of Charlestown, Lynn, Marblehead, Reading, Roxbury, Salem, Stoneham, Wakefield and Wenham.

A typescript entitled "Genealogical Record of the Gerry Family," by Wilton F.
Bucknam (Hereafter "Bucknam") at the New England Historic Genealogical Society
in Boston, claims that there were three brothers; Arthur, Dennis and William,
who came on the "Abigail" in 1635 to Salem. But there is no documentation to
substantiate this claim. The Passenger List of the "Abigail's" voyage in 1635
has been published (Edward Banks, Planters of the Commonwealth, p. 161-167) and
only Dennis Geere and family appear on that list. Mr. Bucknam is undoubtedly
the W.F.B. who submitted a lengthy article (No. 1113) in Notes and Queries from
the Boston Evening Transcript, published July 8, 13, 20, 22, 27 and August 12
and 19, 1908. Throughout Mr. Bucknam's work, no sources are cited, and the
phrase "family tradition" appears frequently. Nevertheless, there is much in
Bucknam's work that is useful and we have included parts of it here. References
to Bucknam's manuscript at NEHGS will be given as "Bucknam." References to
Buckman's article in the Transcript will be given as "TR 1113." Further confusion concerning the various Geary/Gerry families is due to the "adoption" of the
name of "Elbridge" by several Gerry groups - after Governor Elbridge Gerry
became well known. Actually, that distinguished gentleman's ancestors did not
arrive until the early 18th century.

The seven Geary, Gerry (etc.) "Heads of households" that appear in the early
records are as follows:

1) Arthur Gary of Roxbury - 1638.
2) Benjamin Garey of Lynn - married in 1693.
3) Dennis Geere of Saugus - 1635.
4) Stephen Gearie of Charlestown - 1679.
5) Thomas Gery (Geary) of Charlestown, Reading and Stoneham - about 1668.
6) Thomas Gerry of Marblehead - 1730.
7) William Geare of Salem and Wenham - 1639.

There appears to be no connection between the various names listed above, with
the possible exception that William Geare of Wenham may be the father of Thomas
Geary of Stoneham, and Benjamin Garey of Lynn may be the son of that Thomas
Geary. The published data on the seven immigrants is given below, listed in
chronological order of "first record in America."

1. DENNIS GEERE - SAUGUS - 1635

Dennis Geere, age 30, with wife Elizabeth ----- , age 22, and two daughters,
Elizabeth, age 3, and Sarah, age 2, came in the "Abigail" in 1635 and settled
at Saugus. He died two years later, as his will, dated 10 Dec 1635, probated 6
August 1637, recorded in Boston and London, bequeathed to wife and daughters; to

cousin Ann Pankhurst; to Elizabeth Tuesley; Roger Carver of Bridhemson and John Russell of Lewes in Sussex, to be overseers of his estate in England. He bequeathed also in New England, to Thomas Topper, Thomas Braines, Thomas Launder, Benjamin Nye and Thomas Grenuill; and made provision for the return of his family to England. The residue to be bestowed on the plantations within the province of Massachusetts Bay. The colony of Massachusetts received 300 pounds. (Henry F. Waters, Genealogical Gleanings in England, Baltimore: Genealogical Publishing Co., Inc., 1969; I:7)

Waters gives further information concerning what is probably the same family. "Thomas Geere, of the parish of Falmer, near Lewes, co. Sussex, 6 March 1649, proved 25 April 1650, by Dennis Geere, son and executor. To wife Mary. To eldest son Thomas Geere and his wife Mercy, and their children, Mercy and Mary. To grand-children Dennis and Richard Geere and grand child Thomas Geere. To the poor of Falmer and the poor of Stamer. Youngest son, Dionice Geere, executor. Friend John Russell, of Southover, near Lewes, and Stephen Towner, of Kingston, to be overseers. Witnesses, Richard Banckes and Thomas Russell.

---

2.   ARTHUR GARY (GAREY) - ROXBURY - 1638

Arthur Gary was baptised in Bishop's Stortford, Hertfordshire, England 20 May 1599, son of Nathaniel and Joane (-----) Gary. He married there Frances Warman, b. 1601. He was an early settler of Roxbury, was admitted Freeman 14 March 1638; was one of the earliest members of the Roxbury Church (Rev. John Eliot pastor). He died in Roxbury 17 Dec 1666, aged 67. Frances Warner Gary died in Roxbury 10 Oct 1672.

Children of Arthur Gary and Frances Warner:
i   (Deacon) William Gary, bpt 22 Aug 1628 in Little Haddam, Hertfordshire, Eng. Settled in Roxbury. Married (1) Hannah Curtis; married (2) Elizabeth Parker of Woburn. No issue
ii   Nathaniel Gary, b. Eng. ca 1631, married at Roxbury Ann Douglas. He died early of small pox and his widow married (2) Thomas Bishop. Children: Hannah, d.y.; Elizabeth (twin), m. William Abbott of Andover; Mary, d.y.; Nathaniel, m. (1) Ann Rice, m. (2) Mary (Fairbanks) Allen; Sarah, m. (1) John Holt of Andover, m. (2) John Preston of Andover; William, m. Susanna (-----), moved to Pomfret, CT; Rebecca, d.y.; Hannah, m. Caleb Phillips, moved to Bellingham; Samuel, m. (1) in Dedham, Sarah Lovell, m. (2) Martha Thurston; Debora, d.y.; Dorcas, d.y.
iii   Samuel Gary, b. 22 Sep 1638 in Roxbury, Mass.; m. (1) Elizabeth Parker; m. (2) Martha Clark. Samuel died 12 Oct 1730. No issue.

(Laurence Brainerd, Gary Genealogy . . ., p. 27-33)

---

3.   WILLIAM GEARE - SALEM, WENHAM - 1639   (See account on page 27)

4.   THOMAS GEREY - STONEHAM - ABOUT 1668   (See account on page 28)

5.   BENJAMIN GAREY - LYNN - BY 1693   (See account on page 29)

---

6.   STEPHEN GEARIE - CHARLESTOWN - BY 1679

"Stephen Gearie. Servant to R. Russell; bellman; age 28 in 1679; testified in case Ballatt vs. Bussell; age 38 in 1690; m. Mary Manuel 14 Aug 1673. Issue. - Ann. b 17 Jan 1679. . . Will, Jan 2 (probated 16), 1691-2 devised to wife Patience, now with child. His master, S. Ballatt, overseer. House and land valued at 76 pounds." (Wyman, 402)

> Child of Stephen and Mary Manuell; (born in Charlestown)
>
> i   Ann Gary, born 17 Jan 1679.

> Child of Stephen and Patience (-----) Gary: (born in Charlestown)
>
> ii   Stephen Gary (posthumous), born 1691/2. When about twenty years old he removed to Taunton, Mass. where on Nov. 9, 1711, he married Mary Gilbert. Seven children all born in Taunton. The name of this family remained "Gary."

---

7   THOMAS GERRY - MARBLEHEAD - 1730

Captain Thomas Gerry (ancestor of Governor and Vice President Elbridge Gerry) was born 15 March 1702 at Newton Abbot, Devonshire, England, son of Daniel and Lydia Gerry. He came to America in 1730 as Captain of a trading vessel from London and later became a merchant at Marblehead. He married (1) at Marblehead, Elizabeth Greenleaf, who was born at Marblehead 1 June 1716. He married (2) 6 May 1773 Mrs. Elizabeth Lemmon, presumably widow of Dr. Joseph Lemmon of Marblehead.

> Children of Thomas Gerry and Elizabeth Greenleaf:
>
> i   Thomas, b. 1735, m. Tabitha Skinner
> ii   Samuel, b. 1737, d. 1738.
> iii   Elizabeth, b. 1740, d. 1740.
> iv   John, b. 1741, m. Sarah Wendell.
> # v   Elbridge, b. 17 July, 1744, m. Ann Thompson. (See page 32)
> vi   Samuel, b. 1746, d. 1750.
> vii   Elizabeth, b. 1748, m. Burrell Devereux.
> viii   Samuel Russell, b. 1750, m (1) Hannah Glover; m (2) Sarah Thompson
> ix   Rebecca, b. 1752, d. 1752
> x   Daniel, b. 1754, d. 1754.
> xi   Daniel, b. 1758, d. 1759.

(The name "Elbridge" came down from Governor Elbridge Gerry's great-grandmother, Elizabeth Elbridge who married Samuel Russell. Rebecca Russell married Enoch Greenleaf, and their daughter Elizabeth Greenleaf married Captain Thomas Gerry. (William Richard Cutter, Genealogical and Personal Memoirs relating to the Families of Boston and Eastern Massachusetts, p. 49-50)

(See biography of Governor Elbridge Gerry, p. 34)

##

BIBLIOGRAPHY

Banks, Charles Edward, Planters of the Commonwealth

Brainerd, Lawrence, Gary Genealogy; The Descendants of Arthur Gary of Roxbury,
   Massachusetts; with an account of the posterity of Stephen Gary of Charlestown, Massachusetts; and also of a South Carolina Family of this Name. Boston, Mass.: T.R. Marvin & Sons, 1918.

Bucknam, Wilmot F. Genealogy of the Gerry Family (Typescript at the New England
   Historic Genealogical Society, 101 Newbury Street, Boston, Mass.)

Cutter, William Richard, Historic Homes and Places and Genealogical and
   Personal Memoirs Relating to the Families of Middlesex County, Mass. 4 Vols.
   New York: Lewes Pub., 1908.

Cutter, William Richard, Genealogical and Personal Memoirs Relating to the
   Families of Boston and Eastern Massachusetts. New York: Lewis Pub., 1908.

Deane, Silas. A Brief History of the Town of Stoneham, Mass., from its
   First Settlement to the year 1843; with an account of the Murder of Jacob
   Gould, on the Evening of Nov 25, 1819. Stoneham, Mass. : Sentinel Press, 1870

Fairfield, Wynn Cowan, Descendants of John Fairfield of Wenham. Volume 1,
   First Five Generations. Bound typescript at NEHGS, Boston, Mass., 1953.

Notes and Queries from the Boston Evening Transcript, 1908, Vol. XLVIII.

Perley, Sidney. History of Salem, Massachusetts. 3 vols. Salem, Mass.:
   Sidney Perley, 1924.

Pope, Charles Henry. Pioneers of Massachusetts. Boston: C.H. Pope, 1900.

Probate Records of Essex County Probate Records. Salem, Mass.

Records and Files of the Quarterly Court of Essex County, Mass. (1636 - 1686).
   Salem, Mass.: Essex Institute, 1911 - 1975.

Stevens, William B. History of Stoneham, Massachusetts. Whittier, 1891.

Sweetser, Dana. Notebooks at Lynnfield Public Library.

Vital Records of Massachusetts to the end of the year 1849. (Lynn, Marblehead,
   Reading, Salem, Stoneham, Wakefield, Wenham.)

Waters, Henry F. Genealogical Gleanings in England. Baltimore: Genealogical
   Publishing Co., Inc., 1969.

Wyman, Thomas Bellows. Genealogies and Estates of Charlestown, 1629 - 1818
   Boston: David Clapp and Son, 1879.

****

GENEALOGY OF THE GERRY (GEARY, GEREY) FAMILY OF STONEHAM, WAKEFIELD & LYNN

The Geary (Gerry) family of Stoneham presents a genealogical problem that appears to be insolvable. A Thomas Geary is the first to appear in the early Stoneham records, and early genealogists had various theories as to his origins. Wyman does not associate him with any other Geary family. Savage and Pope do not mention him at all. Silas Dean, in his brief History of Stoneham, written in 1870, claims that:

"Thomas Gerry, the immigrant ancestor, is said to have been of Irish ancestry. He was a boatswain on an English man-of-war. When in Boston he fell in company with Patrick Hay, a Scotchman, and they decided to settle in this country. He was allowed to leave his ship on condition that he return to service if war with France broke out."

The most comprehensive study of the Stoneham Geary family was undertaken at the turn of the century by Wilmot F. Bucknam, who published his research in a manuscript at the New England Historic Genealogical Society and also in a series of "notes" in the Boston Evening Transcript. (Note No. 1113, which ran in the July and August, 1908) Mr. Bucknam, unfortunately, does not cite sources and makes frequent use of the phrases "family tradition" and "family papers."

First of all, Mr. Bucknam claims that William, Arthur and Dennis Geary were brothers who came together on the Abigail in 1635. This assumption appears to be without foundation, except for the use of some similar names in all three families. William Geare settled in Wenham; Arthur Gary settled in Roxbury; Dennis Geere, of Saugus, died young and his two daughters returned to England. (See account of Arthur Gary on p. 23 and Dennis Geere, p. 22)

Secondly, Mr. Bucknam claims that Thomas Geary of Stoneham was a son of William Geare of Wenham, although William Geare's children are given in Salem & Wenham VRs and no Thomas is listed. However, there was a Thomas Geare in Wenham, according to the Wenham VRs, which give: "Shuball Geare, son of Thomas, b. at Wenham 19 Mar 1676." No further record is found in Wenham or Salem. A year previous to this, on 4 May 1675, a Thomas Geare applied for land at Reading (Bucknam: Transcript, 1113)

Further confusion comes from two court records; one at Essex County Court (VII:293) when Thomas Geare deposed in 1679 that he was "about 33 years of age" which would make his birth date 1646. In another deposition in 1662 (quoted in Wyman) Thomas Geary was "24 years of age," which would make his birth date 1638, eight years younger than the Wenham Thomas. Perhaps some day further information will come to light, but for this paper, we shall use Bucknam's supposition that Thomas Geary of Stoneham was a son of William Geare of Wenham.

FIRST GENERATION

1. <u>WILLIAM GEARE</u> was of Salem in 1639, where he was made a freeman and granted two hundred acres of land in 1649. He removed to Wenham, where he afterward lived and was recorded "deacon." His wife was Tryphena (Triphenia), last name not known. William died 13 November 1672 (Records and Files of the Quarterly Court of Essex County, Massachusetts, VII:158. hereafter "Essex C.R.") (Bucknam gives William's death as 15 Oct 1658, but that is an obvious error.) The

inventory of William's estate, "amounting to 86 pounds, taken 10:1:1673. by Tho. Fiske and Richard (his mark) Hutton, and allowed Mar. 25, 1673, upon oath of Triphany Geare, the widow. There being two daughters left, the estate was ordered to remain in the widow's hands and if she married, she was to give her daughters 20 pounds each. . ." Tryphena died 15 October 1671. "William became a member of the church in Wenham in 1644, and selectman in 1658 or 9, also a commissioner to end small cases. It would seem that as selectman he died in office, was a poor man and left no estate, probably meeting with some misfortune. His widow, Triphena Geary was helped by the town." (TR 1113)

Children of William Geare and Tryphena:

(Given by Bucknam (TR 1113)

i   Samuel, b. Salem, 14 Mar 1641
ii Mary, b. Salem, 14 May 1643
iii John, b. Salem, 23 June 1644
iv Ephraim, bpt at Wenham 1647
     died at Wenham 15 Oct 1658
v   Sarah, b (?) m. 26 Mar 1666
     John Fairfield.
vi Triphena, b (?) m. Daniel Killam.
2 vii Thomas, b. about 1647

(Given by Perley, History of Salem)

i   Ephraim, d. 15 Oct 1658 (?)
ii Samuel, bpt. 14 Mar 1641
iii Mary, bpt. 14 May 1643
iv John, bpt. 23 June 1644
v   Deborah (?)
vi Triphena (?)

(Church Records, 1st Church, Salem)
    Samuel, bpt 14: 1m: 1641
    Mary, bp 14: 3m: 1643
    John, bp 23: 4m: 1644

SECOND GENERATION

2. THOMAS GEARY (William), perhaps the son of William Geare of Wenham, was born in 1638, according to his deposition in 1662 in which he states that he was 24 years of age. (Thomas Bellows Wyman, The Genealogies and Estates of Charlestown (Boston, 1879), 402. Hereafter "Wyman")

Bucknam gives the following account of Thomas[2].

"Thomas Geary (William), born in Wenham about 1646, early of Reading and Stoneham, was previously of Wenham, where he had a wife Sarah and a son Shuball, born in 1676. Soon after this he is of Reading, having applied to the town of Charlestown May 4, 1675, for land in Charlestown End. It seems it is left to the selectmen and after the usual red tape of time he gets it laid out but appears to have occupied it on the plan of a dollar down and another some time, all to be paid in six years. The rate was twenty shillings per acre. Tradition tells us he was quite athletic in nature and while clearing it encountered a pack of wolves, backed up against a tree and swung his axe right and left till the many dead caused the living to run away. It being dark, he left them till morning when he returned, clipped off their ears and went to Charlestown and claimed the bounty, which was sufficient to raise the mortgage on his land. He was by deposition aged twenty four in 1662; he was appointed to minor offices by the town of Charlestown and a tythe collector at one time. He was a soldier in the expedition to Canada and died on his return in November, 1690, tradition says at Goff's Falls, N.H. There were several children of this family, but only three are accounted for. His widow is not accounted for in the record."

Thomas Geary's estate was taxed in 1688, and in the inventory of his estate, valued at 159 pounds, his house was valued at 70 pounds. He left a widow, Sarah -----. (Wyman) Torrey (New England Marriages) gives her surname as "Lepingwell" or "Lepingwell."

Children of Thomas Geary and Sarah (Leffingwell?):
  ? 3   i   Benjamin, b. ca 1672; m. Abigail Goold (Gould).
  ? 4   ii   Thomas, b. ca 1674; m. Hannah Streeter.
  ? 5   iii   Shuball, b. at Wenham, "son of Thomas" 19 Mar 1676 (Wenham VR)

THIRD GENERATION

3. **BENJAMIN GEARY**[3] (Thomas, William) perhaps the son of Thomas and Sarah Geary, was at Lynn for a time (Wyman). He married 15 May 1693 Abigail Goold (Gould) who was born 30 (10) 1672, daughter of John Goold and Abigail Belcher of Charlestown (Wyman, 426). (The "Record Book of First Church of Charlestown," as given in NEHGR 29:72) gives the marriage of Benjamin and Abigail as 1693 3/15). He resided in the homestead of his father, near the Reading line, and later built a new house near by a little south of the old homestead on Farm Hill, in Charlestown End, now Stoneham. He acquired land in both Reading and Stoneham and was an influential man in his day. The administration of his estate was by Thomas Gould and recorded in the Essex Probate Court. (TR 1113)

Children of Benjamin Geary and Abigail Goold (Gould)
  6   i   Benjamin, b. 8 Mar 1694/5; m. Elizabeth Damon.
  7   ii   John, (Bucknam calls him twin to Benjamin: source not known);
             m. Elizabeth Wyman.
       iii   Abigail, b. 2 Mar 1696/7; m. 12 Jan 1713 (Wakefield VR) Thomas
             Hodgman, son of Josiah and Elizabeth Hodgman. Ch: Elizabeth,
             1715; Josiah, 1721; Benjamin, 1722; Jonathan, 1725; Thomas,
             1727; David, 1729; Timothy, 1731; John, 1733. (Lilley Eaton.
             Genealogical History of the Town of Reading; 93)
  8   iii   Thomas, b. 20 Oct 1700 (TR 1113); m. Abigail Vinton.
  9   v   James, b. -----; m. Sarah -----. (?)

_____

4. **THOMAS GEARY**[3], (Thomas, William) perhaps the son of Thomas and Sarah Geary, married 10 April 1701 Hannah Streeter. (Wyman, 402) He bought land in Charlestown end as early as 1703; also sold later to his "son-in-law," Thomas Gould. He bought the Deacon Nathaniel Lawrence homestead of the heirs in 1725 and settled on it and lived and died there. (TR 1113)

Children of Thomas and Hannah Streeter:
       i   Sarah, b. 29 May 1702; m. at Medford, 23 Oct 1724, John May, son
             of John, Jr. and Ann Parker, of Charlestown. Children,
             all born at Stoneham: Sarah, 5 Oct 1725; Mary, 17 Feb 1728;
             John, 25 June 1729; Thomas, 19 Mar 1731; Rebecca, 21 Mar
             1733; James, 16 Feb 1735; Benjamin, 12 July 1738; Hannah,
             29 Apr 1740; Hannah, 23 Nov 1744.
  10   ii   Thomas, Jr., b. 2 June 1704; m. Phebe Wyman.
       iii   ?Reuben, b. c1706; m. 16 Feb 1731 Katharine Brown (Wakefield VR)
       iv   Mary, b. 5 Aug 1708; m. Henry Jefts, Jr. of Billerica.
       v   A daughter, b. -----; m. Thomas Gould. (Thomas Geary sold land
             to son-in-law Thomas Gould. Wyman, 402)

5. SHUBALL GEARY[3] (Thomas, William), perhaps the son of Thomas and Sarah Geary, was born in Wenham 19 March 1676 (Wenham VR).

> "Tradition says he went to the vicinity of Lancaster and took up
> unoccupied territory. This appears to have some foundation as the
> early families had relatives there whose identity does not now appear,
> but family names in common with each other are used, also others from
> here of later generations removed to that part of Worcester County
> "among their relatives." He is also said to have been a soldier in the
> Colonial Wars and taken up granted land. A David and a Robert Geary
> (Bucknam must mean David and "Joseph" as they are the two sons he lists
> for Shuball.) appear in Sterling, the latter baptized in 1718, both
> marrying sisters. There seems to be a possibility of their being
> children of Shuball, according to the data from which much of this
> article is drawn as to family records." (TR 1113)

Children of Shuball Geary:
| | i | David, m. Louisa Goodale. |
| 11 | ii | Joseph, bpt 1718; m. Ruth Goodale. |

FOURTH GENERATION

6. BENJAMIN GEARY[4] (Benjamin, Thomas, William), was born 8 March 1694/5 (Wyman, 402). He married (1) 5 April 1716 Elizabeth Damon (Wakefield VR) who was born in 1693, daughter of Thomas Damon and Lucy Ann Emerson (Eaton, History of Reading, 61). "He appears to have lived both sides of the Stoneham-Reading line, and evidently occupied the homestead that was over the line in Reading." (TR 1113)

Children of Benjamin Geary and Elizabeth Damon:

	i	Benjamin, b. 4 Mar 1719 (TR 1113); bpt 22 Mar (Wakefield VR); m. m. 21 Feb 1760 Elizabeth Farwell of Townsend, Mass., b. Lunenberg; 17 Sep 1740, dau. of Thomas & Elizabeth Farwell. No further records on this family. (TR 1113)
	ii	Elizabeth, b. 25 July (TR 1113); bpt 30 July 1721 (Wakefield VR) Died in infancy. (TR 1113)
	iii	Abigail (TR 1113 says "twin"), b. 5 Apr 1724 (TR 1113); bpt 16 May 1725 (Wakefield VR); m., as Abigail Garey (int.) 11 Aug 1745, Obadiah Walker of Lunenburg (Lynn VR)
	iv	Elizabeth (TR 1113) says "twin"), m., as Elizabeth Garey (int.) 12 Mar 1738/9 Timothy Bancroft. (Lynn VR)
12	iv	Edward, b. 10 July 1730 (TR 1113); bpt 18 July 1731 (Stoneham VR); m. Phebe Holden.

---

7. JOHN GEARY[4] (Benjamin, Thomas, William), twin of Benjamin, Jr. (TR 1113), married 12 Mar 1723, Elizabeth Wyman, born 11 Nov 1700, daughter of Nathaniel and Mary (Winn) Wyman of Woburn. (TR 1113) (Eaton gives Mary (Richardson) Wyman. He resided on a ten-acre lot given him by his father and confirmed to him by his father's will and located south of his father's homestead.

Children of John Geary and Elizabeth Wyman:
     13   i   John, b. 22 Sep 1727 (Stoneham VR); m (1) Susannah Williams;
                   m. (2) Ruth Richardson.
           ii   Elizabeth, bpt. 29 Mar 1730 (Stoneham VR).
     14   iii Nathaniel, Jr. b. 26 Feb 1730/1 (Stoneham VR); m. Mrs.
                   Susannah (Hay) Hill.
           iv   Elizabeth, b. 22 Feb 1734. (Stoneham VR); m. 28 June 1751, Capt.
                   Thomas Eaton, 3d, born Reading, son of Thomas and Lydia
                   (Pierce) Eaton. Ch: Thomas, James, Betsey.

---

8. THOMAS GEARY3 (Benjamin, Thomas, William), was born 20 October 1700 (TR
1113). He married Abigail Vinton, born 28 Dec 1704, daughter of John Vinton and
Abigail Richardson of Stoneham.
Woburn (Wyman, 1059).

Children of Thomas Geary and Abigail Vinton:
     15   i   David, b. 27 Nov 1728 (Stoneham VR); m. Keziah Holden.
           ii   Abigail (twin), b. 30 Aug 1734 (Stoneham VR);
           iii Thomas (twin), b. 30 Aug 1734 (Stoneham VR)

---

9. JAMES GEARY4 (Benjamin, Thomas, William), was b. -----. He married, probably
at Lynn, Sarah -----.

Child of James Geary and Sarah:
           i   Thomas, b. 30 Apr 1740 (Lynn VR) (No further record)

---

10. THOMAS GEARY4 (Thomas, Thomas, William), son of Thomas Geary and Hannah
Streeter, was born at Charlestown End, 2 June 1702. (TR 1113). He married 23
October 1724 Phebe Wyman, born at Woburn, November 1702, daughter of Nathaniel
and Abigail (Winn) Wyman. "By the papers from which some of this article is
drawn, she was sister of Elizabeth, brother John's wife, and Ruth, the wife of
Thomas Gould, who settled in Sutton. They appear to have removed from Stoneham
in later life, and the homestead passed to another branch of the Geary family."
(TR 1113)

Children of Thomas Geary and Phebe Wyman, all born at Stoneham:
           i   Jonathan, b. 24 May 1729.
           ii   Phebe, b. 4 May, 1730.
           iii Thomas, b. 15 Mar 1732.
           iv   Susanna, b. 3 Mar 1734.
           v   Nathan, b. 1 May 1735.
           vi   Keziah, b. 23 Apr 1737.
           vii Keturah, b. 10 May 1739.
           viii Catherine, b. 4 May 1740. (Stoneham VR has Catturn, bpt 11 May)

---

11. JOSEPH GEARY4 (Shuball, Thomas, William), son of Shuball Geary, was
baptized in 1718. "He was born, per gravestone, at Sterling, Mass. and died
there 13 April 1781, in his sixty-first year. He married, 1741, Ruth Goodale of
Marlboro. His will, dated April 1779, remembered son, Reuben; daughters Hannah
Darby, Phebe Ross, Sarah Sawyer and Lois Willard." (TR 1113)

Children of Joseph Geary and Ruth Goodale:
    i   Hannah, b. 6 July 1743; m. ----- Darby.
    ii   Phebe, b. 7 Aug 1745; m. ----- Ross.
    iii   Sarah, b. 31 July 1747; m. ----- Sawyer.
    iv   Reuben, b. 7 Dec 1749.
    v   Ruth, b. 14 Jan 1742; m. 27 Nov 1800 Joseph Roper & died in PA.
    vi   Lois, b. 11 June 1754; m. ---- Willard.
    vii   Joseph, b. 2 Aug 1756.
    viii   Joseph, b. 19 July 1760.

FIFTH GENERATION

12. EDWARD GEARY[5] (Benjamin, Benjamin, Thomas, William), son of Benjamin Geary and Elizabeth Damon, was born 10 July 1730 (TR 1113); bpt 18 July 1731 (Stoneham VR). He married 7 December 1750 Phebe Holden, born at Woburn, 9 October 1727, daughter of John and Mary (Damon) Holden, who were married at Reading 17 Dec 1724. He resided for a time at Woburn, later was at Lunenburg, Mass. (TR 1113)

Children of Edward Geary and Phebe Holden, the first born at Woburn, the rest at Lunenburg:
    i   Edward, Jr. b. 1 Sep 1752.
    ii   Phebe, b. 30 Sept 1755.
    iii   Mary, b. 7 Feb 1759.
    iv   John, b. 25 Aug 1761.
    v   Elizabeth, b. 26 Feb 1764; m. 30 Nov 1781, Jonathan Adams.
    vi   David, b. ----; m. Lucy Thompson.

---

13. LT. JOHN GEARY[5] (John, Benjamin, Thomas, William), son of John Geary and Elizabeth Wyman, was born 22 September 1727 (Stoneham VR); and was baptized 1 October 1727 (Wakefield VR). He married (int.) 23 September 1749, Susanah Williams (Lynn VR). (Stoneham VR gives "John, Jr. and Mrs. Susannah Williams of Lynn") John, as Ens. John, married (2) January 1767 Ruth Richardson, who was born 28 March 1733 and died 9 March 1806 (Bucknam) (Stoneham VR gives 9 Mar 1807 C.R. 1808, age 73 y). Lt. John Geary died 22 February 1825, age 97 y. 5 m. (Stoneham VR) "He was a pioneer settler of Hillsboro, New Hampshire, and was buried on the spot where he cut the first tree for his homestead, making a temporary shelter till he could erect a log house. He was a Lieutenant in the militia." (TR 1113)

Children of John Geary and Susannah Williams:
    i   Susanah, b. 14 Dec 1750 (Stoneham VR).
    ii   Joseph, b. 27 June 1754; perhaps m. 3 Oct 1775 Ruth Nichols (Wakefield VR).
    iii   Mary, b. 28 June 1759; perhaps m. 25 Mar 1783 Nathaniel Bacheller (Wakefield VR. C.R.)

Children of "Lt." John Geary and Ruth Richardson:
  16   iv   Benjamin, b. 1 Sept 1767 (Stoneham VR); m. Persis Danforth.
  17   v   John, b. 25 Sept 1771 (Stoneham VR); m. (1) Elizabeth Morgan; m. (2) Hannah Monroe.

---

14. NATHANIEL GEARY, JR[5] (John, Benjamin, Thomas, William), son of John Geary and Elizabeth Wyman, was born 26 February 1730/1 (Stoneham VR). He married, 29 June 1767, Susannah (Hay) Hill, baptized 19 April 1742, daughter of Peter and Dorcas (Gould) Hay of Stoneham. She was widow of John Hill, born in Stoneham 9 Feb 1736. By her first marriage she had: John, Jr. who married Ruth Boutwell. After the birth of John Hill, Jr., they removed to Harvard, Mass. where he was drowned in the Nashua River at Lancaster 30 May 1764. (TR 1113)

Children of Nathanial Geary and Susannah Hill (Stoneham VR):

i	Nathanael, b. 26 July 1767. (At Harvard, Mass. - TR 1113)	
ii	Susanah, b. 10 Apr 1769; m. Israel Whiting of Harvard (TR 1113).	
iii	John, b. 23 Sep 17--. (TR 1113)	
iv	Abigail, b. ----.	" "
v	Peter, b. ---, 1776.	

---

15. DAVID GEARY[5] (Thomas, Benjamin, Thomas, William), son of Thomas Geary and Abigail Vinton, was born 27 November 1728 (Stoneham VR) and was baptized 18 May 1729 (Wakeifled VR). He married 30 March 1748 Mrs. Keziah Holden (Stoneham VR). He died 16 September 1798 "in his 70th year." (Stoneham VR. C.R.)

Children of David Geary and Keziah Holden:

	i	Abigail, b. 2 Apr 1749 (St. VR); m. 1771 John Green, b. 1747, son of Col. David Green and Ruth ---- (Eaton, 84)
18	ii	David, b. 3 Sept 1751 (St. VR); m. (1) Elizabeth Damon; m. (2) Anna Bucknam; m. (3) Sarah Richardson.
	iii	Keziah, b. 16 Apr 1754 (St.VR) m. Jonas Green (NEHGR 11:346).
	iv	Thomas, b. 25 June 1756 (St.VR); "sailed from Boston, lost at sea or made a slave by the Turks" (NEHGR 11:346)
	v	Rebekah (Rebecca), b. 8 Oct 1758 (St.VR); m. 21 Nov 1782 at Reading, Elisha Newhall (Wakefield & Lynn VR). They lived in Malden. (NEHGR 11:346).
19	vi	Reuben, b. 17 Nov 1760 (St.VR); m. Johannah Okes (Oakes).
	vii	Joshua, b. 2 Dec 1762 (St.VR).
	viii	Jesse, b. 8 May 1765 (St. VR).
20	ix	William, b. 31 Mar 1767 (St. VR); m. Margaret Picket.
21	x	Daniel, b. 3 Nov 1769; m. Joanna Geary.

(To be continued)

##

ELBRIDGE GERRY

By Walter McIntosh

Elbridge Gerry, signer of the Declaration of Independence and Vice President of the United States, was one of Essex County's most famous sons. He was born 17 July 1744 in Marblehead, the son of Thomas and Elizabeth (Greenleaf) Gerry. He graduated from Harvard in 1762, and although he had prepared to go into medicine, his merchant father prevailed upon him to go into his business where he became a partner and was eminently successful.

In 1772 he heard the call to public service, and was elected to the General Court of the Province of Massachusetts and was a member of the House 1772-75. In 1773 Samuel Adams introduced his celebrated motion for the appointment of a "Standing Committee of Correspondence and Inquiry," and Gerry, although one of the youngest members of the House, was chosen for the committee and served as one of its most active and influential members.

ELBRIDGE GERRY.

In December of 1775 he was appointed to the Continental Congress where he served 1776-81 and again 1782-85. He was a delegate to the Constitutional Convention of the United States in Philadelphia in 1787. He did not like the proposed constitution, and spoke no less than 119 times during its consideration. When it was approved by a majority vote of the convention, he quickly became a supporter of it as the law of the land. He was elected to the first two U.S. Congresses as an anti-Federalist, serving during the period 4 March 1789 - 3 March 1793. In 1797 he was dispatched to France with Marshall and Pinckney on a diplomatic mission to negotiate a settlement between the two countries over serious differences which had sprung up.

He campaigned for the Governorship of his state in 1801, but failed. A second try in 1805 was successful, and again in 1809 he was elected for a two year term. In 1812 he was elected Vice President of the U. S. with his fellow Democrat, James Madison as his Presidential running mate. He served from 4 March 1813 until his death in Washington, D.C. a year and a half later on 23 November 1814.

Elbridge Gerry married in New York City, 12 Jan 1786, Ann Thompson, dau. of Charles and Hannah (Harrison) Thompson. His wife died at New Haven, CT 17 Mar 1849. They had 10 children: Catherine, Thomas, Elbridge, Thomas, James, Anne, Eliza, Helen, Eleanor, and Emily. (For ancestors of Elbridge Gerry, see p. 2)

As a final note, Elbridge had a grandson, Elbridge[5] active in politics in Maine, who was a U.S. Congressman, and a great grandson, Peter[6], who served as both a Representative and a Senator from Rhode Island.

GENEALOGY OF THE NICHOLS FAMILY OF MALDEN AND LYNN

Written in 1868 by John Nichols[7]. Submitted by Ann Williams of Lynn

(Editor's note: This article is reproduced verbatim with no attempt
to correct obvious errors)

I JAMES NICHOLS, the first, lived in Malden, Mass. in 1660, married in April
the same year, Mary Felt, was made freeman in 1668, and died in 1694. (30 March
- Malden VR) Their children were Mary (2), James (2), Abigail (2), Nathaniel
(2), Sarah (2), Elizabeth (2), Anna (2), Samuel (2) and Caleb (2).

II JAMES NICHOLS, (2) was b. at Malden in December 1662, married (1) Hannah
Whittemore, b. 15 Nov 1686 of Woburn. Their children were Hannah (3), James (3)
died 1689, Ester (3), Abigail (3), James (3). His second wife was Mary Biles;
their children were Joshua (3), Caleb (3), and Jemima (3).

II NATHANIEL NICHOLS, (2) had children (his wife not recorded) viz. Nathaniel
(3), Samuel (3), Sarah (3), Josiah (3), Elizabeth (3), John (3), Mary (3), Anna
(3).

II SAMUEL NICHOLS (2) had one child, Elizabeth (3).

III JAMES NICHOLS (3) married Tabitha Floyd, she died 1723; had James (4),
born 1720, died 1740, John (4), b. 1723, married Elizabeth Burditt 1748. Their
children were John (5), born Sept 16, 1749, died Jan 23, 1821, married Phebe
Oaks, daughter of Jonathan Oaks, Feb 27, 1772. (these two, John (5) and wife,
were my grandfather and grandmother) Elizabeth (5), Ebenezer (5) died 1761,
Tabathy (5), Ebenezer (5), Nathan (5) and William (5).

V JOHN (5) and Phebe Oaks had children: John (6) born March 15, 1773, married
June 26, 1796 Lydia Chadwell of Lynn, daughter of Harris and Ruth Chadwell; she
was born June 29, 1775 and died August 31, 1802. The other children of John (5)
and Phebe his wife, were David (6) who married Polly Watts and left one child
viz. Richard (7) who lives in Chelsea. Phebe (6) who married Ezra Holden of
Malden and died October 8, 1868, aged 89 years and 8 month, Thomas Oaks, (6)
Their children were Phebe (7), Ezra (7), Eli (7), Dana (7), Hannah (7) and
Marian (7) who live in Malden at this date 1868.

VI ELIZABETH NICHOLS (6) who married Luther Johnson, who removed to Petersburg,
Va. and died March, 1823. One of their children lives there and one in Malden,
who married David Faulkner.

VI JAMES NICHOLS (6) born May, 1784, married Rebecca Barton. Some of their
children are living. Mary (7), in Roxbury, Sarah (7) in Cambridge, and John (7)
in Fitchburg. He died April 6, 1846.

VI WILLIAM NICHOLS (6) born July, 1785, married Sarah Bates for first wife, she
died. His second wife was Isabel Bates. He died Dec, 1858. Their children
were Sarah (7) who married Mr. Marsh who lives in Wartown (?) William (7) who
lives in Boston, Fanny etc.

VI EDWARD NICHOLS (6) born Jan 28, 1789, married Susan Truman. He died May,
1842. She died Jan. 1854. Their children were Maria (7), who married Mr.

Frothingham of Charlestown; Elizabeth (7) and Susan (7) married and removed to the West. Gilbert (7) lives in Charlestown. Charles (7) lives in Chelsea. Edward (7) lives in a town west of Boston.

VI **ESTER R. NICHOLS** (6) born Nov., 1791, married William Whittemore, Feb. 1811; he died Nov. 29, 1859; Their children were Esther (7), Henry (7), Joseph (7), William (7), George (7), Eliza (7), Charles (7), Nathan (7), John N. all living in Everett. Maria, who died a number of years since, and a daughter who died Dec. 1867.

VI **THOMAS OAKS** (6), son of John (5) and Phebe, was born Sept. 1, 1794; married April 9, 1820; Susan Frost, who was born Oct. 1801. He died July 2, 1871. They had two children; a son who died a number of years since, and a daughter who died Dec. 1867.

VI **ANDREW NICHOLS** (6) was born April, 1797; married 1820, Hannah, daughter of Ebenezer Nichols. She died Nov. 1871. their children: Andrew (7), Franklin (7), Thomas (7), and Ebenezer (7), they all living in Everett except Andrew (7), who died a number of years ago.

The other children of John (4) and Elizabeth Burditt were Elizabeth (5) born Jan 11, 1752, married May 2, 1771, Joseph Dyer and died 1818. Sarah (5) born Oct 24, 1754, married Nov 6, 1774, Jonathan Oaks, and died June 16, 1830. James (5) born March 17, 1757, died 1780. Ebenezer (5) born April 21, 1759, died Sept. 10, 1761. Tabitha (5) born April 7, 1761, married May 6, 1787, Benjamin Bill, her second husband March 11, Winslow Sargent, and died May 5, 1805. Ebenezer (5) born April 21, 1763, married April 5, 1792, Esther Sargent, who was born August 8, 1766, and died April 6, 1854. He died Aug. 1, 1836. Nathan (5) born April 18, 1765, married Feb. 20, 1792, Dorcas Smith; he died Aug. 19, 1841; she died 1867. William (5) born Nov. 24, 1767, married in 1791 Nancy Wait, and died Sept. 1849; their children were William Stephen Wait (6) and Lemuel (6), Nancy (6), Sarah (6) and one other whose name I have not remembered.

Thus it is ascertained that James Nichols, our first ancestor, was among the first settlers of our country for he was here as early as 1635; we have some evidence that this branch of our family was related to the Nichols family that settled in Brooksby (now Danvers).

From the foregoing, we learn that my father John Nichols (6) was a son of John Nichols (5) and Phebe Oaks, who was born in Malden March 15, 1773. When at a proper age, he came to Lynn and served his time as an apprentice at the shoe business with Hanson Newhall who was grandfather to my wife. When he became the age of twenty-three, he married Lydia Chadwell, daughter of Harris Chadwell and Ruth of Lynn; they were married June 26, 1796. their children, John Nichols (7) who is the writer of this record was born June 11, 1797 and was married to Mary Newhall, daughter of Allen Newhall and Micha Newhall, of Lynn, July 1, 1818 in Epping, N.H. Her parents removed there from Lynn, 1816. She was born in Lynn Oct. 9, 1798 and died July 7, 1863. their children were John Edwin Nichols (8), born Feb. 28, 1820 and married Harriet C. Atkinson, 1848. Nathan Augustus (8) born July 25, 1824, married June 1, 1843, and died Oct. 12, 1870 aged 45 years, without children; married Sarah A. Williams. Mary Frances (8) was born Dec. 29, 1826 and married Charles Lakeman from Ipswich, Oct. 1847. She died Feb. 22, 1853, aged 26 years and 3 months. They had one child, Ida Frances Lakeman, born March 2, 1852, married December 18, 1870 to Alex Gilmore. Lydia Caroline (8), the fourth child of John (7) and Mary Nichols was born Oct. 12, 1830, married Francis Flagg from Lincoln, Dec. 1847; their children were Edward Lesley (9), Mary Emma, Jennie Louise, Harriet Maria (8), fifth child of the above, was born Sept. 4, 1833, married James Marble from Haverhill, Mass. ----; their children were Carrie, Maria (9), Frank Herbert (9) Eva Stanton (9), and Lena Marcelia.

NATHAN NICHOLS (7), the second child of John Nichols (6) and Lydia Chadwell, was born Dec. 20, 1798, married Harriet Herbert of Newburyport, April 22, 1824. their children were Harriet Elizabeth (8), born May 12, 1825, died May 12, 1827. Nathan Herbert (8) born Dec. 17, 1826, Charles Augustus (8) born August 2, 1828, died Jan 24, 1864, Thomas Parker (8) born August 28, 1830. John Harris (8) born Oct. 15, 1833, Melville Shepard (8) born July 28, 1836, Richard Johnson (8) born June 15, 1839, Timothy Johnson (8) born Dec. 31, 1841, died -----, George Herbert (8) born April 20, 1845. Nathan (7) died Sept 5, 1858; his wife Harriet was deprived of her reason and was carried to the Insane Hospital at Worcester, but died previous to her husband, Feb. 15, 1857, a worthy and affectionate woman.

HARRIS NICHOLS (7) the third child of our parents was born Feb. 6, 1801 and married Hannah Allen, who died in 1838. they had two children born in Lynn, Joseph (8) and William Henry (8). He married for his second wife, Emily Hawkins; they had four children; Frederick (8) who was killed in the Rebellion in South Carolina, 1864, George (8) who lives in Illinois, James, and Emily who was deaf and dumb and died in 1868.

JOHN NICHOLS (6) and Lydia Nichols, our parents, after marriage lived together in a house that formerly set on a part of the land where the City Hall now sets, six years, and she died August 31, 1803 suddenly with lung fever, with a strong faith in Christ, and in hopes of a blissful immortaility (such has been my information). Her remains has laid over in the Old Burying Ground 70 years with her parents, brothers and sisters who have died since.

THOMAS PARKER NICHOLS (8) born Aug. 28, 1830, married Caroline Smith, May 5, 1853. Their children were Carrie Helen (9) born March 24, 1854 at Malden, Mass. Frank Herbert (9) born April 14, 1856, Fred Hammond (9) born November 25, 1861, Sarah Lizzie (9) born July 5, 1865. these last three children were born in Lynn.

CARRIE HELEN NICHOLS (9) married John Cushman Aborn of Lynn, March 19, 1885. (No children)

FRANK HERBERT NICHOLS (9) married Emily Clark (daughter of Joseph and Sarah Ann Clarke) of West Upton, Mass. at her home, Oct. 24, 1883. Their children were Louise Mudge (10) born March 25, 1887, and Mildred Aimee (10) born Sept. 11, 1889, both born in Lynn (at No. 60 Vine Street) (Mildred unmarried)

FRED HAMMOND (9) married May 25, 1886, Annie Louise Attwill, a second daughter of Isaac Meade and Harriet Elizabeth Attwill of Lynn at the family residence 121 Ocean Street. Their children were born at No. 10 Prospect Street, Lynn. The first Miriam Cecelia (10) born May 15, 1888 (unmarried) and the second Thomas Attwill (10) was born April 22, 1891.

SARAH LIZZIE NICHOLS (9) married June 3, 1886 at 11 Prospect St. to Samuel Swasey Shepard of Marblehead. (No children)

The Ahnentafel

The Ahnentafel is an Ancestor Table, or list. It follows the numbering system of standard Ancestor Charts; i.e.: yourself is 1, your father and mother 2 and 3. A father's number is always double that of the child; 13 is a child of 26 (father) and 27 (mother). This is a good way to preserve in print what is known of your ancestors. It also serves as an exchange column for those working on like surnames. Subscribers are encouraged to submit their ahnentafels only through six generations (#63). It does not matter if some are unknown.

Ahnentafel of Lillian A. Pierce (Graffam). P.O.Box 587, Houlton, ME 04730

I	1	Lillian Ardelle Pierce	1915-	Saugus, Lynn, MA: Oceanside, CA; Houlton, ME
II	2	Bertram Henry Pierce	1892-1978	Hingham, Saugus, MA; Kittery, ME Oceanside, CA
	3	Pearl Frances Belcher	1895-1964	Saugus, MA; Kittery, York, ME
III	4	John Warren Pierce, Jr.	1870-1928	Melrose, Weymouth, MA
	5	Lucietta Gertrude Lord	1874-1957	Hingham, MA
	6	William Francis Belcher	1864-1935	Dedham, Saugus, MA
	7	Emma Whitford Putnam	1865-1933	Chelsea, Saugus, MA
IV	8	John Warren Pierce	1840-1923	Woburn, Brocton, MA
	9	Adelaide Augusta Wheelwright	1847-1921	Cohasset, Hingham, MA
	10	William Henry Lord	1845-1928	Quincy, Hingham, MA
	11	Hannah Whiton Gardner	1842-1932	Hingham, MA
	12	William Belcher	1838-1913	Quincy, Cambrdige, MA
	13	Lydia Lord	1845-1915	Roxbury, Boston, MA
	14	William Putnam	1829?-1868	Chelsea, MA
	15	Georgiana Nason	-1909	Saugus, MA
V	16	John R. Peirce	1804?1870	Malden, MA
	17	Sarah Waite	1815-1843	Malden, Woburn, MA
	18	Lewis L. Wheelwright	1825-1889	Cohasset, MA
	19	Mary Nile Sherman	1829-1869	Marshfield, Cohasset, MA
	20	Peter Ross Lord	1816-1863	Lebanon, ME, ?
	21	Sarah Ann Philbrick	1817-1866	Rye, NH
	22	Charles Gardner	1807-1873	Hingham, MA
	23	Hannah Whiting	1803-1884	Hingham, MA
	24	William Belcher	1791-1857	Quincy, MA
	25	Celia Beal	1796-1875	Hingham, Boston, MA
	26	William Hugg Lord	-1864	Dedham, MA
	27	Sarah Mussinger Frizzell	1828-	Walpole, MA; ?
	28	Ephraim Putnam?		
	29	Rachel Cram?		
VI	34	Nathaniel Waite	1787-1856	Malden, MA
	35	Sarah Neagles	1796-1884	Malden, MA
	36	Gershom Wheelwright	1790-	Cohasset, MA
	37	Hannah L. Ellmes	1797-	Scituate, MA
	38	Mark J. Sherman	1789-	Marshfield, MA
	39	Betsy Bailey	1794-	Marshfield, MA

40	John Lord	1782-	Lebanon, ME
41	Polly Ross	1783-1856	Lebanon, ME
42	James Philbrick	1780-	Hampton, NH
43	Abigail Peviere	1782-1862	Rye, NH
44	Charles Gardner	1778-1838	Hingham, MA
45	Silence Sprague	1774-	Hingham, MA
46	Sylvanus Whiting	1775-	Hingham, MA
47	Hannah Stodder	1778-1865	Hingham, MA
48	Elijah Belcher, Jr.	1762-1819	Braintree, MA
49	Lucy Newcomb	1759-1833	Quincy, MA
50	Elisha Beal	1761-1830	Hingham, MA
51	Lydia Tower	1761-1833	Hingham, MA
52	Jeremiah Lord?	1782-1858	Kennebunk, ME
53	Lydia Rideout?		
54	John Frizzell	1802-	Walpole, MA
55	Annie Thompson	-1838	Walpole, MA

##

Ahnentafel of Merle G. Graffam, P.O.Box 587, Houlton, ME 04730

I 1	Merle Grant Graffam	1918-	Bridgeport, CT; Lynn, MA; Houlton, ME
			Oceanside, CA; Houlton, ME
II 2	Harry Bion Graffam	1886-1957	Bangor, ME; Worcester, Lynn, MA
3	Lottie Judson Sawyer	1886-	Lynn, Worcester, MA; Desert Hot Springs, CA
III 4	Jesse Lewis Graffam	1854-1919	Bangor, ME
5	Ida Belle Grant	1859-1914	Bangor, Lincoln, ME
6	Charles William Sawyer	1848-1933	Brewer, ME; Lynn, MA
7	Flora Deering	1851-1944	Brewer, ME; Lynn, MA
IV 8	Leander Lewis Graffam	1830-1908	Westbrook, Togus, Bangor, ME
9	Jeanette Dora Lombard	1829-1906	Gorham, Bangor, ME
10	Joseph W. Grant	1837-1904	Frankfort, Bangor, ME
11	Rachel Ann Glidden	1837-1906	Sebec, Bangor, ME
12	Charles Nathaniel Sawyer	1816-1891	Cherryfield, ME; Lynn, MA
13	Abigail Leach	1826-1919	Brewer, ME; Lynn, MA
14	Samuel Deering	1816-1896	Scarborough, Brewer, ME
15	Mary Ann Downes?		
V 16	Caleb Graffam	1780-1851	Westbrook, ME?
17	Mary B. Swett	1799-1849	Gorham, ME?
18	Richard Lombard	1795-1880	Gorham, ME
19	Temperance Lewis Hamlin	1796-1864	Gorham, ME
20	Moses Grant, II	1810-	Frankfort, ME
21	Mary Boden		Lowell, ME
24	Josiah Sawyer	1787-	Harrington, ME
25	Rebecca Grindle	1790-	Sedgwick, ME
26	George Leach	1805-1874	Penobscot, Brewer, ME
27	Betsy Door	1803-1875	Penobscot, Brewer, ME
28	Joshua Deering	1794-1844	Gorham?, Brewer, ME
29	Susah Berry	1789-1851?	Scarborough, Brewer, ME
VI 32	Enoch Graffam	1753-1827	Windham, Raymond, ME
33	Charity Mayberry	1755-	Windham, ME
34	Joshua Swett	1761-1851	Westbrook?, Gorham, ME?
35	Mary Bailey	-1849	

```
       36   James Lombard          1768-1808  Gorham, ME
       37   Bethiah Smith          1776?      Eastham, MA?
       38   Samuel Hamlin          1753-1834  Gorham, ME
       39   Molly Clay             1756-1833  Biddeford, Gorham, ME
       40   James Grant            1781-1865  Berwick, ME
      _41   Betsy Green
       48   Josiah Sawyer          1763-1842  Cape Elizabeth, Harrington, ME
       49   Elizabeth Brown
       50   John Grindle
       51   Joanna Hutchins
       52   John Leach             1760-1845  York, Penobscot, ME
      _53   Polly Simpson          1771-1845  York, Penobscot, ME
       56   Samuel Deering         1768-1839  Gorham, ME
       57   Nancy Larrabee         1775-      Scarborough, ME
```

##

Ahnentafel of Marion Ryker (Chiarello), 1444 Kenmore Ave., Buffalo, NY 14216

```
I    1   Marion Ryker           1916-      Oneida Castle, Buffalo, NY
II   2   E(dward) Leon Ryker    1892-1975  Garrattsville, Buffalo, NY
     3   Harriet Jane Martin    1891-      Camroden, Rome, Buffalo, NY
III  4   Edward Ryker           1849-1921  Jeff. Co., Ind.; Oneida Castle, NY
     5   Lucy L. Joslin         1861-1952  Burlington, Oneida Castle,
                                           Vernon Center, NY
     6   John Peter Martin      1864-1943  Western, Rome, NY
    _7   Carrie Curtis Smith    1868-1943  Floyd, Rome, NY
IV   9   Jane Ryker             1820-      Jeff. Co., IN
    10   Nathan F. Joslin       1829-1902  Burlington, NY
    11   Sarah Jane Gifford     1841-1919  Whitestown, Burlington, NY
    12   Theodore Mills Martin  1834-1920  Western, NY
    13   Catherine Lusher       1837-1910  Remsen, Western, NY
    14   Matthew W. Smith       1829-1902  England or at sea, Camroden, NY
   _15   Jane Little            c1847-1932 Middleton, Ire.; NYC, Rome, NY
V   18   John Ryker             c1794-1822/5 Shelby Co., KY; Jeff. Co., IN
    19   Nancy Ledgerwood       1797-1833  Kentucky; Scott & Jeff. Co., IN
    20   John F. Joslin         1791-1869  RI; Burlington, NY
    21   Ludy Fisk              1797-1883  Otsego, Burlington, NY
    22   Samuel Gifford         1800-1887  Schuylerville, Whitestown, NY
    23   Phoebe Reynolds        1803-1876  Whitestown, NY
    24   David Martin           1798-1848  Western, NY
    25   Teressa Denison        1800-1874  Stephentown, Western, NY
    26   Peter Lusher           1796-1870  France; Remsen, NY
    27   Catherine Lesher       1803-1891  France; Remsen, NY
    28   John F. Smith          1782-1873  Yorkshire, ENG; Westernville, NY
   _29   Mary Robotham          1787-1849  Yorkshire, ENG; Westernville, NY
VI  36   Samuel Ryker           1769-1832/3 Closter, NY; Jeff. Co., KY;
                                           Canaan, IN
    37   Barbara Fullenwider    1771-1829  Jeff. (now Shelby Co.), KY;
                                           Canaan, IN
    38   Samuel Ledgerwood      c1772-1842 VA; Bourbon Co., KY; Clark Co.,
                                           KY; Jeff. Co., IN
   _39   Jane Hillis            c1780-1850 VA; PA; Clark Co., KY; Jeff Co.,IN
    42   Nathan Fisk            1772-1857  Hampton, CT; Burlington, NY
    43   Eunice Ford            1771-1831  Hampton, CT; Burlington, NY
```

44	Thomas Gifford	c1770-	Schuylerville, Northumberland, NY
45	Rhody Tully		Schuylerville, NY
46	Jacob Reynolds	1761-1831	Chatham, NY
47	Sarah Hart		Chatham, NY
48	Ebenezer Martin, Jr.	c1771-1850	Rhode Island, Floyd, NY
49	Sarah Capron	c1775-	RI; Floyd, NY
50	Latham Denison	1771-1847	New London, CT; Stephentown, Floyd, NY
_51	Elenor Tefft	1780-1846	Stephenton, Floyd, NY
54	Nicholsen Lesher		Germany; France
_55	Catherine -----		Germany; France
58	Robert Robotham	1760-1840/2	Yorkshire, ENG; Western, Floyd, NY
59	Jane Mooring		died in England

###

Ahnentafel of Alan H. Hawkins, 14 Adelbert St., So. Portland, ME 04106

I	1	Alan H. Hawkins	1947-	Lincoln, Millinocket, South Portland, Cape Elizabeth, Falmouth, ME
II	2	Herschel James Hawkins	1906-1977	Masardis, Lincoln, ME
	3	Madaline Dorothy Gipson	1910-	Burlington, Lincoln, Falmouth, ME
III	4	Hayward Ludlow Hawkins	1878-1946	Kingsclear, Douglas, Millville, NB; Masardis, Lincoln, ME
	5	Eunice Estelle Goding	1881-1955	Masardis, Lincoln, ME
	6	Ralph Emerson Gipson	1887-1964	Burlington, Lincoln, Mattawamkeag, ME
	7	Gertrude Gerry	1890-1970	Lincoln, Mattawamkeag, ME
IV	8	James Ludlow Hawkins	1841-1899	Douglas, Kingsclear, Millville, NB; Ashland, Masardis, ME
	9	Emma J. Grant	1854-1882	Douglas, Kingsclear, Millville, NB
	10	Llewellyn Goding	1842-1916	Corinna, Maardis, ME
	11	Hannah Howes	1839-1905	Ashland, Masardis, ME
	12	Wellington Jipson	1849-1915	Burlington, E
	13	Edith Ellen Davis	1857-1928	Burlington, ME; Lowell, MA
	14	Granville W. Gerry	1845-1923	Old Town, Moro Plantation, Lincoln, ME
	15	Anna Mae Ludden	1858-1943	Lee, Lincoln, ME
V	16	James Hawkins	1812-1889	Douglas, NB
	17	Rebecca Burt	1813-1895	Douglas, Burt's Corner, NB
	18	Thomas Grant	c1805	Douglas, NB
	19	Mary Devlin	c1815	Douglas, NB
	20	Amasa Goding	1797-1884	Livermore, Corinna, Masardis, ME
	21	Dorcas W. Goss (Rowe)	1798	Danville, Levant, Corinna, Masardis, ME
	22	George W. Howes (House)	c1807-	Ashaldn, ME
	23	Adeline Speed	c1817-	Ashland, ME
	24	James Jipson	1824-1903	Monroe, Burlington, ME
	25	Jane Neal	1825-1899	Belmont, Burlington, ME
	26	Benjamin Warren Davis	1814-1902	Fairfield, Burlington, ME
	27	Thankful W. Costigan	1836-1877	Burlington, ME
	28	Eli Gerry	c1820-	Old Town, Patten, Lincoln, ME
	29	Nancy Keezer	c1825-	Old Town, ME
	30	John Emerson Ludden	1823-1882	Canton, Lee, ME
	31	Susan Averill	1828-1907	Pittston, Lee, ME

VI 32	John Michael Hawkins	1786-1877	Douglas, NB
_33	Nancy Todd	1790-1874	Douglas, NB
40	Jonas Goding	1766-1849	Watertown, MA; Jay, Livermore, ME
41	Elizabeth Parker	1769-1851	Roxbury, MA; Jay, Livermore, ME
42	Thomas Goss	1780-1872	Gloucester, MA; Danville, Levant Masardis, ME
_43	Elizabeth Witham	1778-	Gloucester, MA; Danville, Levant, ME
48	William Jipson	1789-1870	Wells, Monroe, Lincoln, Burlington, ME
49	Abashaba Booden	1794-	Swanville, Lincoln, Burlington, ME
50	Johnson Neal	1778-	Belmont, Burlington, ME
51	Betsey Patterson	1788-1865	Belmont, Burlington, ME
52	William Davis	c1750-1836	Huntington, LI, MY; Dartmouth, MA; Starks, Fairfield, ME
53	Jane Allen	c1770-	Dartmouth, MA; Starks, Fairfield, Sydney, ME
54	William Costigan	1803-1871	Sunkhaze (Milford), Burlington, ME
_55	Olive Hurd	1813-1864	Harmony, Burlington, ME
60	John Brown Ludden	1793-1876	Turner, Canton, Dixfield, Lee, ME
61	Hannah Woodbury	1796-1881	Danville, Turner, Canton, Dixfield, Lee, ME
62	David Averill, Jr.	1800-1866	Greenfield, NH; Temple, Pittston, Lincoln, ME
63	Mary M. Lee	1804-1864	Dresden, Pittston, Lincoln, ME

TRIVIA QUIZ

After John Jones died, his widow Sarah Farwell married John Wheeler, whose first wife had been Sarah Stearns, daughter of Isaac Stearns and Sarah Beers, the second wife of Sergeant Thomas Wheeler, the father of John Wheeler by his first wife Sarah Merriam, the daughter of Joseph Merriam and his wife Sarah Goldstone, who married second Joseph Wheeler and were the parents of Rebecca Wheeler, who married Peter Bulkeley grandson of Reverend Peter Bulkeley, whose sister Frances by her husband Richard Welby had a daughter Olive who married Henry Farwell and had a son John who married Sarah Wheeler, the daughter of Timothy Wheeler, brother of Joseph Wheeler and Thomas Wheeler, the latter having by his wife Ann Halsey, Sergeant Thomas Wheeler, the father by his second wife Sarah Beers, of Ephraim Wheeler, who married Elizabeth Spalding, daughter of Benjamin Spalding and his wife Olive Farwell, sister of John Farwell, father of Sarah Farwell, John Jone's widow. What was the relationship of John Jone's widow to her second husband before their marriage?

By Raymond D. Wheeler, RD 1 Box 25, Dolgeville, NY 13329 (Published in NEHGS Nexus, I:3)

Tools of the Trade

GENEALOGICAL RESEARCH AT BOSTON PUBLIC LIBRARY MICROTEXT DEPARTMENT

By William H. Schoeffler

A wealth of valuable genealogical information is available to researchers in the Boston Public Library and this extensive collection is once again open seven days a week, as well as evenings, Monday through Thursday. More than a city-dweller's preserve, the BPL issues library cards to any Massachusetts resident and even allows out-of-state visitors to obtain courtesy cards valid for a full month.

Genealogical researchers will find the most useful collections of the BPL concentrated in two separate departments in the Research wing (the old half of the building fronting on Darmouth Street). These are the Microtext Department, located in the southeast corner of the old building on the first floor, and the Social Science Reference Room, located at the north end of Bates Hall, the main reading room on the second floor.

This article will discuss items to be found in the BPL Microtext Department, including the federal censuses for New England, ship passenger lists, Massachusetts court records, town records, newspapers, and city directories.

The Microtext Department has a wide variety of primary and secondary source materials that will delight the genuine researcher. Principal among the primary sources are the National Archives microfilm of the federal census records for the New England states from 1790 to 1910. Needless to say, this does not include the 1890 census, which was almost completely destroyed in a fire before the days of microfilm. However, the BPL does have the microfilm of the 1890 Union veterans and widows schedule for Massachusetts, which some users may find a modest substitute. The National Archives Soundex for the 1880 and 1900 census records are also available, but users should check the Guide to Genealogical Research in the National Archives to fully understand the limitations of these indexing aids. Information describing the Soundex code is posted in the microtext department.

A second group of National Archives microfilms which researchers will find at the BPL Microtext Department is ship passenger arrival lists and indexes. Of greatest local interest is the 115 reel series of Boston passenger arrival lists held at the National Archives, which cover the period 1820-1891. The library also has the 282 reel film of an alphabetical card index of passenger names from 1848 to 1891, but this must be used with caution. Curiously, although this index is a National Archives film, the cards were prepared from passenger lists held by the Massachusetts State Archives, rather than its own collection, so obvious problems arise. Names appearing in one copy of the list may not appear in the other, and entire lists found in one collection may be missing from the other. Even more curiously, the State Archives has a microfilm of its own Boston lists, but not of the index. If users do not find the name in the Boston index, they should always check the approximate date of arrival in the film of National Archives passenger lists just in case. Microfilm indexes for Boston passenger arrivals are also available in the library for 1899 and 1902-1906, although the lists themselves are not. A few additional Boston arrival lists are in the separate 16 reel series called "Atlantic and Gulf Ports and Ports of the Great Lakes," covering 1820-1873. The 188 reel "Supplemental Index" is a companion to this entire series. The microtext department also has the six reels of New Bedford passenger arrival lists covering 1902-1921.

While these federal records are quite useful, many researchers will find the Library's collection of county and local records even more valuable, particularly for research in the colonial period. Some of the most significant genealogical information is found in probate records, and the Microtext Department has an extensive collection of filmed probate records from Middlesex, Suffolk and Hampshire counties. Given the Library's evening and weekend hours, these microfilms allow many people tied down to regular jobs during courthouse hours an opportunity to consult these primary records. The Middlesex and Suffolk microfilms were prepared by the Mormons for the Genealogical Society of Utah, while the Hampshire County probate records were filmed by the New England Archives Center for Springfield's Connecticut Valley Historical Museum.

Of these three, the Middlesex County probate microfilms are by far the most complete and easy to use. Covering the period 1648-1871, they include the files of original documents, the original records volumes (beginning in 1654) and 19th century transcripts of the first 14 volumes. The document files themselves are arranged by docket number, which roughly follow alphabetical order in this "Middlesex First Series." Alphabetical indexes to these Middlesex docket numbers are available both on film and in book form at the microtext department. One particularly noteworthy feature of the Middlesex County probate microfilms is the inclusion of a special handwritten volume of 17th century probate matters culled from the records of the Middlesex County Quarterly Courts but not found in the probate files. This single volume was prepared in 1917 by a probate court clerk and is described as "Miscellaneous index and records, 1659-1692."

The microfilm of the Suffolk and Hampshire County probate records at the BPL are not nearly as extensive as the Middlesex records, nor are they as easy to use. In both cases, only the record volumes have been filmed, while the original papers and the docket indexes were overlooked. This oversight makes use of the Suffolk probate records particularly difficult, because the docket numbers were assigned roughly in chronological order rather than alphabetically. Each individual record volume has an index of its holdings, but researchers familiar with the Suffolk probate records know its docket index is an invaluable guide to the locations of all surviving records. If filmed, for some reason the BPL does not have it. Moreover, only the first 150 volumes of the Suffolk Probate record volumes, covering the years 1636-1852, were filmed. Apparently the filmers did not realize the significance of the useful 42-volume "New Series," which contains record copies of many colonial-period probate documents that were not copied into the original record volume series. The Microtext Department does have the three-volume alphabetical index to the Suffolk County docket numbers, which gives the year of probate and the type of proceedings, but without the numerical docket index books, the researcher has only a hint to an estate's first chronological appearance in the record volumes. Record copies of subsequent papers for an estate may appear in the same volume or in later volumes.

The usefulness of the Hampshire County probate records on microfilm also suffers from a lack of adequate indexing, but it still provides researchers in eastern Massachusetts with local access to valuable Connecticut Valley information. Hampshire County record volumes 1-150 have been filmed, covering years 1660-1820. These records contain all estates probated in Hampshire County, which included what is now Berkshire County until 1761, Hampden and Franklin Counties up to 1811, and even Suffield, CT, while it was part of Massachusetts. Although the lack of an index may be disappointing, these 32 reels are particularly well catalogued. The contents of each reel, listing the inclusive dates of each filmed volume, appear on the catalog card found under "Hampshire County." This cataloging treat is sorely missed for the Middlesex and Suffolk County probate records.

Another set of court records found in the Microtext Department is the 138 reels of Suffolk County Court of Common Pleas minute books, covering the years 1701-1855. These minute books provide a brief description of each case to come before the court, together with a notation about its disposition that day. Frequently, this indicates which party won and whether an appeal was taken. As is often true with court records, these minute books have virtually minimal indexing (by plaintiff only) but occasional gems of information found in them can make the tedious search worthwhile. (A plaintiff-defendant index to these court records will be serialized in the new Mayflower Descendant.)

In addition to court records, the Boston Public Library Microtext Department holds a variety of town records dating from the colonial period. The two most significant collections are a 225-reel set of Boston secular records, which includes records of all of the annex towns, and a 145-reel set of similar town records for 44 Middlesex County towns. These Middlesex town records run through 1830 and include virtually all of the county's prominent colonial centers. A 38-page descriptive guide to the entire Middlesex series aids the user, and the film of each volume includes a descriptive inventory of its contents. The Microtext Department also has films of the records from selected other towns, as a glance through the card catalog revealed the presence of Gloucester town records, too. Less substantial in size, but possibly more useful to the genealogist is the Microtext Department's collection of local tax lists covering the colonial period for 21 communities, including Dedham, Salem, Danvers and Marblehead. These lists for the most part date from the mid-18th century, but some are as early as the 1663 tax list for Reading.

These are just a sampling of the official records found in the Microtext Department's own card catalog. Researchers should be aware that an ever-increasing amount of government documents are being published in microtext form. While these are stored and used in the microtext department, they are catalogued only in the Government Documents Department, at the northeast corner of the Research Wing's first floor.

A description of these official records discussed so far by no means exhausts the resources available in the Microtext Department. In fact, it is probably best known as the repository of newspapers on microfilm. The department holds an extensive collection of newspapers from most Massachusetts cities and towns, as well as selected principal cities throughout the country. Full details on these newspaper holdings are found in black guidebooks at the request desk, in which the listing for Massachusetts alone runs some 53 pages, although some more obscure newspapers remain available only in bound form. (Consult the Main Card Catalog.)

Other collections derived from newspapers are of even more direct interest to the genealogist, particularly the obituary indexes and the renowned genealogical columns for the old Boston Transcript and the Hartford Times. Several useful printed indexes and compiled obituary listings are available in the Micotext rooms, too. Eighteenth century obituaries from Boston newspapers are well covered in the three red Boston Athanaeum volumes, while the multi-volume Columbian Centinel series is extremely useful for obituaries from the 1784-1840 period. references to more recent obituaries can be found in a five-volume index to the Boston Transcript, 1875-1930, while the library staff has been maintaining a special card catalog index to obituaries from several Boston papers from 1932 to the present, although this has some gaps. For the period 1840-1875, researchers must resort to a slip index at the Boston Athanaeum, which may soon appear in print. When it does, it will be a welcome addition covering a period that is now quite lacking in such sources. Other obituary indexes of note in the microtext department include the two-volume index to the New York Times, 1859-1979, which is most helpful about people of national prominence. Another New York Times aid now available on the shelves in the Microtext Department is far more extensive than this obituary index: a comprehensive 22-volume Name Index to the annual New York Times index volumes.

Few readers are unaware of the remarkable genealogical columns that ran in the Boston Transcript for almost fifty years and almost that long in the Hartford Times. Even so, they may not realize that the Microtext Department has a special set of films or fiche devoted exclusively to these columns. Moreover, the department houses a thorough name index to the Transcript columns from 1901 through 1935. These cards are arranged in strict alphabetical order within five-year groups. The microfiche collection of the Hartford Times genealogical columns includes annual indexes to its contents.

No researcher should ignore the extensive collection of city directories now available in the microtext department, either. A private company has been publishing microtext versions of almost everything in print prior to 1860, including about 240 cities and counties, as well as regional parts of some states. A more limited group of directories for 78 major cities is available for the 1861-1901 period. The Microtext Department has obtained virtually this entire series through 1881 and has most of the available cities through 1901. Meanwhile, it is completing this collection as funds allow, and plans to order the next series when it becomes available. While most of these directories are on microfiche, some are on microfilm. Complete details about the current holdings can be learned by consulting the staff member at the request desk.

Finally, a wide variety of other useful sources can also be discovered by simply browsing through the card catalog of the Microtext Department. This serendipitous method revealed the astonishing Harbottle Dorr collection of the Massachusetts Historical Society. Here, on four reels is a collection of Massachusetts newspapers during the years immediately prior to the American Revolution, including the Boston Gazette, the Boston Evening Post and the New England Chronicle, all with contemporary handwritten annotations and a manuscript index. Also available are the George Bancroft papers, several series of Presidential papers, a listing of "uncatalogued materials" in the reference section of the Social Science Department of the BPL, a description of "Early records of the 17th Century Churches in Massachusetts which became Unitarian," and a guide to 288 primary sources in the U.S. for vital records.

Despite these interesting discoveries, serendipity should not be a necessary part of thorough research. Unfortunately, it is almost required due to the haphazard consistency of the Microtext Department's card catalog to its own holdings, and this remains a major complaint hindering the usefulness of the department. Few of the collections discussed in these pages are adequately described or cross-referenced, so even if a card is found it is all too often difficult to determine what the film contains. Users must consider all possible headings when looking for any particular collection. In fact, sometimes it is worthwhile to begin the search in the Reference Library's main card catalog on the second floor, but even this approach is not always foolproof. Still, current efforts to improve the microtext card catalog have made some noticeable progress over its almost useless state of just a few years ago.

(Courtesy of the Newsletter of the Massachusetts Genealogical Council: III:3)

46

WHITE GRAVESTONE PHOTOGRAPHY

By Harold Everitt and Sid Russell

Our shaving cream and squeegee method of photographing dark gravestones was enthusiastically received. With the popular acceptance there also came many requests for a way to improve the white cemetery marker photographic possibility. Happily we have found a method for dealing with that problem. With a true Yankee eye to economy and practicability, we discarded the shaving cream in favor of wallpaper wheat paste colored by RIT dye.

First, with a scrub brush and Spic and Span we washed down the stone and rinsed it thoroughly. Next we covered the entire stoneface with a white wallpaper paste undercoat (leaving the engraved letters empty), then squeegeed the surface leaving a thin paste mask all over the stone. We mixed some of the paste with black RIT dye and painted it over the engraved area making sure that the letters were filled. Again we squeegeed, and the stone was camera ready. We snapped the picture and washed the stone. Even the black paste washed off easily. It can be noted in our picture that the area adjacent to the engraved portion is darkened through use of the squeegee. One might shade the whole stone in like manner for a better picture or use only a dark gray paste mixture for letter contrast. The latter would produce a lighter surface shading. Either way can leave the lettering highly legible.

Best mixed at home are the white wallpaper wheat paste (about 3 cupsful for a medium stone), and the RIT dye (1 1/8 oz pkg with about a pint of water). It takes very little of the dye mixture to color the paste. Needed equipment: bucket, jug of water, paint brush, stirrer, putty knife, scrub brush, squeegee, rags. A small stiff artist's brush is useful for imperfections. We used a dish-washing liquid bottle as a squirt bottle and found it very handy for the final wash and rinse operation.

We have made comparison studies of shaving cream versus white paste on dark stones. The cream is lighter, the paste adequate. Colored film makes prettier pictures but for the more enduring genealogical gravestone record, we suggest the use of black and white. One final thought - our methods will not restore a crumbling stone, only help to bring out the engraved part which is still there.

Miscellaneous Notes

STALLARD FILE ESOG's first major project; the transcription of the 1850 census for Essex County has been completed. Although ten persons originally worked on the project, more than 72% of the records were transcribed by Burrell Stallard of North Andover, Mass., who did the work on a home-made microfilm reader. In honor of Mr. Stallard's noted accomplishment, the Board of ESOG has voted to name the file The Stallard File. The file is housed in the Lynnfield Genealogy Room in blue boxes that contain alphabetically-arranged cards for 131,189 names of Essex County persons! Our sincere thanks are extended to Burrell Stallard.

NOTES AND QUERIES FROM THE BOSTON TRANSCRIPT Lynn Public Library has a unique resource in its "Boston Transcript." It is the only library to begin with 1894 when the Transcript published "Notes and Queries," a forerunner of its well-known genealogy column. The columns themselves are preserved at Lynn in 237 hardbound scrapbooks covering 1894-1941. A unique catalog card file of the "Notes and Queries" covers: Dec 28, 1895 - Dec 8 1930; Apr 29, 1935 - Aug 28, 1935; May 6, 1939 - Apr 26, 1941. Through 1919, the indexing included the given name, but from 1920 on, it was by surname only. Boston Public Library has an index to the Transcript Genealogical Column but lacks the years 1894-1901. The American Genealogical Biographical Index (AGBI) includes the "Boston Transcript" Genealogy Column, but since BPL's index was used, AGBI also lacks the information for 1894-1901. (Submitted by Ludovine Hamilton)

FAMILY SOCIETIES LIBBY For information on the John Libby Family Association and the John Libby Homestead Corporation, contact Prescott Libbey Brown, Secretary, 67 Old Kent Road North, Tolland, CT 06084. Its 80th Annual Reunion was held in September 1984 at Scarborough, Maine where the original Libby settled in America. GOODWIN The GOODWIN Family Organization held its seventh Annual Reunion in August 1984 in South Berwick, Maine. For information on this organization, contact Alice B. (Goodwin) Sharp, 13430 Mirella Street, Pensacola, FL 32507. SHELDON The SHELDON Family Association held its Annual Meeting in August 1984 in Warwick, RI. For information, contact Mrs. R. T. Phelon, 2032 Oak St., West Suffield, CT 06093.

BOSTON VITAL RECORDS Boston's own collection of vital records are now open in Room 201, City Hall. Researchers may use the collection, including original records from the colonial period for Boston and the several annex towns, for a fee of $4/hour, 9 - 5, Mon - Fri. In a separate move, the city's Church Record transcripts will also find a new home in Room 201. Researchers will no longer have to pay separate fees to consult both sets of records. Both changes were recommended by the Society Engaged in the Restoration of Vital Records (SERVA) Committee. Researchers will find Room 201 a significant improvement over the basement storage room in the School Committee Building. (From MGC Newsletter; Winter, 1984, reported by Bill Schoeffler)

ESSEX INSTITUTE Essex Institute in Salem is now closed on Mondays. Library hours are Tuesday through Saturday, 9 - 5.

Our Readers Write

ENGLISH/GERMAN DESCENT I noticed in the Feb '84 TEG, p. 44 a statement that "more Americans trace their ancestry to Germany than to any other country." The Boston Globe of 21 Oct 1984 states:

> "According to the 1980 federal census, there are 49.6 million Americans of mainly English descent. Of German descent there are 49.2 million; Irish, 40.2 million . . . "

I believe people may have misinterpreted the report when it was first issued, i.e. that, not counting those of English descent, most of the others were of German descent.

Constance Hanscom, 200 Orchard St., Belmont, MA

BAKER/WOODBURY I am sending you the page that Doug Wenny and I have been working on for so long to insert in the "Woodbury Genealogy" typescript in your library. I am especially anxious to get this page inserted, as it is my ancestor, John BAKER who has been "killed off" before he was born. Doug and I are also working on an article about the first four generations of the Baker family of Beverly (and Salem) but want to take more time on it. Every time I attempt to write an article, I appreciate more than ever the effort and time taken by the author-contributors to TEG, The Register, TAG, etc.

Woodbury, Hannah[2] (John[1]), bapt. 25 Dec 1636 at 1st Chrurch, Salem; m. 26 Apr 1658 at Salem, Cornelius Baker, (Robert[1]) of Salem (later Beverly); He died 29 Dec. 1716 at Beverly. (Beverly VR)

Children of Hannah Woodbury and Cornelius Baker:
- i Hannah, b. 14 Oct 1660 at Salem; d. 6 Nov 1662.
- ii Hannah, b. 28 Nov 1662 at Salem.
- iii John, bpt. 29 Mar 1665 at Salem; d. 10 June 1673 at Beverly (BVR)
- iv Samuel (twin) bpt 21 July 1667 at Salem; d. bef. 1668.
- v Cornelius (twin) bpt 21 July 1667 " ; d. 1 Sept 1714; m. Abigail Sallows (Essex Antiquarian, 5:164)
- vi Jonathan, bpt 19 Sep 1669 at Beverly (BVR) d. soon bef. 27 Jan 1706/7 (admin.); m. Mary Trask?, who m. 2nd Samuel Balch, Jr.
- vii Abigail, bpt 6 Sep 1672 at Beverly; d. 1 July 1714 (BVR); m. John Hill 12 Oct 1657.
- viii Priscilla, bpt 11 Oct 1674 at Beverly.
- ix Bethiah, bpt 27 May 1677 at Beverly.
- x John, bpt 1 Dec 1678; m. Deborah Morgan; d. 1719 (Bev. Ct. Rec. found in a Baker folder at Bev. Hist. Soc. by Caroline M. Sparks).
- xi Jabez, b. 6 Mar 1682 at Beverly; d. 24 Aug 1758 at Gloucester; m. 15 June 1703 at Salem, Rachel Allen (Salem VR)

. . . Caroline M. Sparks, 24 Peirce Rd., Deerhurst, Wilmington, DEL 19803

"My family's ancestry is very old," said one club member. "We can be traced back to the early kings of Europe." Turning to another member, she asked, "And how old is your family, my dear?" "I really don't know," the lady replied with a sweet smile. "Our records were lost in the great flood."

The Mail Bag

MORTIMER/MCPHERSON/MCLEAN I would like to contact descendants of Mary Isabelle (McPherson) and Henry (Harry) Mortimer of Lynn, MA. Mary was daughter of Alexander McPherson and Isabella Cameron and was b. P.E.I. ("at sea") 16 June 1853, d. 6 July 1931 at Swampscott, MA. Harry was son of William Mortimer and Isabelle McLean and was born P.E.I. 2 August 1854, d. 2 March 1911 at Lynn, MA. Children of Mary and Harry included: John A., b. Sep 1880; Harry H., b. Jan 1882; Minnie M., b. July, 1888; George G., b. Jan 1892. Was Mrs. A. L. Ellis a daughter?   Mrs. Jack Dieterle, 6 Carmen Court, Novato, CA 94947

WILSON I am looking for the ancestry of James Wilson, b. 1756, place unknown; d. 1822, Etna, ME. Lived in Lisbon, ME in 1800 where son Gowen was born. Another son, David was b. 1791; a third son may have been Putnam. Gowen married Sarah Cameron in 1833 in Ludlow, NB, returned to Newport, and moved to Presque Isle in 1838, where he died in 1871. David married Deborah Bradford of Turner, and died in Newport in 1828. Because of the name Gowen, I am assuming that James was of the Gowen Wilson of Kittery family. If anyone is working on this family I would appreciate any help you can give me in locating the parents of James Wilson. I have an extensive card file on this family and would be glad to answer questions.
    Dorothy Wilson, RFD Box 658, Ellingwood Corners, Winterport, Maine 04496

DURKEE/LORD (FORD) I am having a real problem with an Ipswich family. Thomas Durkee (son of William the emigrant) married an Elizabeth Lord or Ford. The vital records give it as Ford, while Hammet gives Lord. I went over all of the early wills and as many land records as I could in Salem and found almost no Fords in Ipswich, so have concluded that Lord is probably right, but no Lord family had an Elizabeth of the right age. The Elizabeth with the right birthday in Hammett appears to be a typographical or recording error. Does anyone have information on this?   Bernice B. Gunderson,
    Society of Genealogy of Durkee, 11150 Pine Street, Lynwood, California 90262

FBI RECORDS I quote an interesting letter appearing in a recent Illinois State Genealogical Society Qarterly... "Dear Editor: Most genealogists seem to forget that there is one record that they, and only they, can send for, that being their FBI record. Most patriotic Americans will have an FBI record if they were in the military, or worked in a place that required a secret clearance. Under the Freedom of Information Act, you may request copies of these records. Address your letter to: Freedom of Information-Privacy Acts Branch, Records Management Division, U.S. Department of Justice, Federal Bureau of Investigation, Washington, D.C. 20535. (signed) S/Sgt Paul Hennefeld, USAF Ret, 54 Overlood Rd., Upper Montclair, NJ 07043."   Walter McIntosh, Danvers, MA

GOOD WIVES Essex County (MA) and York County (ME) researchers will find pleasurable as well as profitable a book by Laurel Thatcher Ulrich, entitled Good Wives, Image and Reality in the Lives of Women in Northern New England, 1650-1750, pub. by Knopf, 1982.   Winnifred Pierce, Ann Arbor, MI

Society News

FORTHCOMING MEETINGS

February 23.   Saturday, Old Meeting House at Common in Lynnfield.
                   Social Hour 12:00. Lecture promptly at 1:00
NOTE   **Speaker: Roger W. Joslyn**, F.A.S.G.
DATE   Topic: "Getting the Most out of Census Records."
               (Note: Fee for this lecture: $1 members; $1.50 non-members)

March 16.   Saturday, Old Meeting House at Common in Lynnfield.
                   Social Hour 12:00. Lecture promptly at 1:00
                   Speaker: Ruth Ann Harris of Northeastern University; History
                      Department.
                   Topic: The Irish in New England, and the "Pilot" Project.

April 20.   Saturday, **Haverhill Public Library**
                   All-day open work meeting. Genealogy Room will be reserved
                   for ESOG members only. Bring your lunch or eat nearby. Coffee
                   and cookies will be served.

REPORTS OF PREVIOUS MEETINGS

<u>December 15</u>. The Annual Christmas Party at the Centre Congregational Church.
Mother Nature didn't hinder 124 who came from Maine, New Hampshire, Gloucester,
Scituate, Acton and all points between. What a warm, friendly group! And the
food!! All sorts of attractive dishes so m-m-yumily good!!! With appetites
appeased, the stage was set for what is now a party tradition - numbers were
drawn for the 12 table centerpieces; raffle tickets for the 3 poinsettias (proceeds for the book fund) and as everyone joined in singing the old familiar
carols, the hall echoed our Chirstmas spirit. Each year more members bring
Show and Tell. Two outstanding contributors were Barbara Staples, who showed
slides depicting her "little" ancestor - an authentic midget; and Dr. Tom
Devaney who brought laughs as he told the history of his ancestors - displaying
a fig leaf from the family tree and other "objets d'art" interspersed with
authentic family memorabilia. Around 4 P.M. our 10th Christmas party came to a
close, and as we left for home, Merry Christmas and Happy New Year filled the
air.

<u>January 19</u>. Our workday and Book Auction at the Lynnfield Library. Again the
Ole Gal fouled us up with a nasty snowy day, but 51 stalwart ESOGers defied her.
Most came early to spend the day - north from New Hampshire and up from Plymouth
County. It's nice to see our "family" working together - helping each other -
and when a common ancestor shows up, heads sure get close! At 1 P.M. Donald
Doliber, our auctioneer, conducted a spirited and fun-filled auction with his
mini-reviews and comments that brought forth chuckles as folks did their bid-
ding. All but one book found a happy home. Marcia Wiswall/Lindberg told about
new acquisitions and called attention to the book truck laden with new books and
journals for members to peruse. Marcia also asked for volunteers to help keep
the genealogy room in order and five members came forward to form a much-needed
task force.

Queries

GUIDELINES FOR SUBMITTING QUERIES
Readers may submit free queries. No
query to exceed 50 words. No limit
on number of queries. Ask specific
questions re parentage, birthplace,
marriage, children, etc. Use identifying detail such as name, date,
or place. Type or print on 3 X 5
card. Use abreviations listed at
end of February Query section.
Deadlines for queries: Jan 1, Apr
1, July 1, Oct 1. Send queries to:
Ludovine Hamilton/Katherine Little,
77 Edgehill Road, Lynn, MA 01904.

BACHILER/BATES/WEARE/MASON/BEEDLE
Seeking anc & info on (Rev.) Stephen
BACHILER, BATCHELOR, etc. B ca 1560/1
Wherwell, Hampshire, Eng., d 1660/1 "in
his 100th year" in Eng., after spending
many years in the American Colonies; m/1
Ann BATES, m/2 Christian WEARE 1623/4,
m/3 (Mrs.) Helen MASON 26 Mar 1627, m/4
(Mrs.) Mary Magdelane BEEDLE.

BELL/GUNTERMAN/DESPAIN
Seeking info & anc of Isaac BELL b ca
1715 (of) Hardwick, Sussex, NJ; d after
1778; w name unk; s Zephenian b ca 1743
(of) Newton, Sussex, NJ; d ca 1813 Green
Co., KY; m Sophia GUNTERMAN. They were
par of Nancy BELL who m (Capt.) Solomon
DESPAIN.

CREEL/MOTT
Seeking info & anc Elizabeth CREEL b ca
1600 (of) Cambridge, Cambridge, Eng.; m
Adam MOTT.

JORDAN/WILSON/KIMBALL
Seeking anc & info on Francis JORDAN b
ca 1610 (of) Ipswich, MA; d Apr 1672,
Ipswich, MA & his w Jane WILSON b ca
1614 of Ipswich, MA. They m 6 Sept
1635. Their dau Mary b 16 May 1641
Ipswich, m (Sgt) John KIMBALL 8 Oct 1666
Ipswich, MA.

MOTT/CREEL/LOTT
Seeking info & anc John MOTT & w. Par
of Adam b 1596 Cambridge, Cambridge, Eng

d 12 Aug 1661 Portsmouth, Newport, RI;
m/1 Elizabeth CREEL; m/2 (Mrs.) Sarah
LOTT.

POTTER/ANTHONY
Seeking info & anc of Susanna POTTER b
1620 (of) South Kingston, Washington,
RI; d 1675; m John ANTHONY. Michael K.
REYNOLDS. Box 776, Bountiful, UT 84010.

################################

ABBOT
Samuell ABBOT b 20 Sept 1727 Newbury,
MA. Looking for par & ch. Corr
welcome.

COKER/MOODY
Wish par Robert COKER b 1606 overseas, d
19 Nov 1678 Newbury, MA & w Mary MOODY &
2/w Catherine. Corr welcome.

HATHORNE/BARTLETT
Looking for par of Sara HATHORNE &
Tirzah BARTLETT of Newbury, MA. Corr.
welcome. Roland AMUNDSON, Box 1505,
Valleyview, Alberta, Canada.

################################

BROWN/GARLAND
Who were par of Mariam BROWN who m
Thomas GARLAND of Benton, ME 14 Feb
1833?

DECKER/MESERVE
Sarah DECKER w of Clement MESERVE of
Portsmouth, NH was b 10 May 1709 dau of
John DECKER of Exeter, NH 1672. Who
were his par?

MOORE/GARLAND
Wish par of Mariam MOORE m Josiah
GARLAND at Biddeford, ME in 1767? Need
bp for Josiah.

WOODBURY
Wish par, bp, bdt & w of Samuel
WOODBURY, fa of Experience b Beverly, MA
11 Apr 1722.

WORMWOOD/GARLAND
Who were par of Ellen WORMWOOD who m
Thomas GARLAND b at Ellsworth, ME ca
1770?

Are there any known genealogies of the above named families of NH or ME that I might read or borrow? Paul A. HILLMAN, 283 Lowell St., Lynnfield, MA 01940.

#################################

WESTON/WESSON

Seeking par of Jonathan WESTON (WESSON) b 1753 in MA d 1828 in Marcellus (now Skaneateles) Onondaga, NY. Liv for a while in Fitzwilliam, Cheshire, NH.

Seek par of Mary (Molly) w of Jonathan WESTON (WESSON) b Aug 1759. D in Marcellus, Onondaga, NY bef 1828. Wish bp, mpl & ddt.

Desire mdt, mpl, & w for Jonathan WESTON (WESSON), Jr., b Jan 1784 in Fitzwilliam, NH s of Jonathan, Sr. Liv in Marcellus, Onondaga, NY. Where did he res after m?

Desire bp, mdt, mpl & name of w for Aaron WESTON (WESSON) s of Jonathan, b Mar 1790/1. Liv in Marcellus, Onondaga, NY until m. Where did he res after m? Patricia C. OLSEN, 1229 So. Barkley, Mesa, AZ 85204.

#################################

CARR

George CARR d 1682 Salisbury, MA, of CARR's Island. Where did he come from when he appeared in Ipswich, MA 1633? Statements in The Carr Family, E. I Carr, 1894 re his arr & depart. from Plymouth, MA are in error accord to research librarian at Plimouth Plantation.

CURRIER/BARTLETT

Wish par of Mary CURRIER b 8 Mar 1770 (g.s.record), prob Newbury? M Joseph BARTLETT of Newbury 1 Jan 1797.

CURRIER/POOR/PRESSEY

Did John s of Capt. John CURRIER m Mary POOR (accor to J.J.CURRIER) or Judith PRESSEY (accord to J.L. CURRIER), prob before 1770. Ch prob b Newbury(port), MA.

CURRIER/TODD/TOPPAN

Wish par of William CURRIER m Elizabeth TODD 4 Mar 1760 Newbury, MA. Did their s Joseph m Abigail TOPPAN?

TOPPAN/CURRER

What is the proof that Abigail TOPPAN, dau of John TOPPAN m Joseph CURRIER 9 Apr 1785 in Newbury, MA. NVR does not give name of her fa.

MILTON/PARSONS

Wish par b of John MILTON m Hannah PARSONS of Newburyport, MA 9 Nov 1802. He was native of Eng. & d at sea. Mrs. Arthur J. WASHBURN, 496 Highland Ave., South Portland, ME 04106.

#################################

DARLING

Seeking info on DARLING families of Salem, Essex Co 1640-1693. Cynthia SCHOTT, P.O. Box 3989, Lawrence, KS 66046.

#################################

BRAGG/SHORES

Seek bdt, ddt par & anc of Sally SHORES poss of Eng who m William BRAGG of North Vassalboro, ME 14 Apr 1816 in Winslow, ME>

BROWN/EMERSON

Seek par & anc of Betsey BROWN of Campton, NH who m William EMERSON 2 Dec 1819 in Plymouth, NH. She d 27 Sept 1880 in Newbury, MA/

FELLOWS/HODGDON

Seek par & anc of Salome FELLOWS poss of Wakefield, NH who m Joel D. HODGDON of Ossipee, NH 17 Nov 1844 in Newburyport, MA. Need ddt of Salome & Joel.

BUSHEY/RICH

Seek par & anc of Angelette BUSHEY who m Robert C. RICH of Tremont, ME 22 Apr 1838 in Salem, MA. She d visiting in Newburyport 24 Sept 1887 but liv in Dover, NH.

CARTER/GOTT

Seek par & anc of Charity CARTER d bef

1801 m/2 Peter GOTT 1776 in Gloucester,
MA. Peter d Swan Island, ME 31 Mar
1839.

COOK/LUNT
Seek bdt ddt par & anc of Hannah COOK
who m Johnson LUNT 28 Apr 1771 of
Newbury, MA.

DOWNES/LUNT
Seek bdt ddt par & anc of Massey DOWNES
poss fr York, ME who m Samuel LUNT 6 May
1802 in Newbury, MA.

EMMONS/GOTT/ANDROSS
Seek par bdt ddt & anc of Eunice EMMONS
who m 13 Nov 1729 Stephen GOTT in
Gloucester, MA. Stephen was s of Samuel
& Margaret ANDROSS GOTT.

ROBERTS/HODGDON
Seek bdt ddt mdt par & anc of Sarah
ROBERTS who m Caleb HODGDON of Ossipee,
NH b 30 Apr 1796.

WYATT/NOYES
Seek par & anc of Mary WYATT b 15 Dec
1745 in Newbury, MA. M (int.) Capt.
John NOYES of Newbury 24 Oct 1767.
Evelyn Noyes DORFLER, 6410 Sherwood
Road, Baltimore, MD 21239.

#################################

BOVEE/CARGILL/ARNOLD
Elizabeth BOVEE m Cumberland, RI 1801
Daniel CARGILL b 17 Sept 1773 s of James
& Dorcas (ARNOLD) of Smithfield &
Cumberland. Desire par any info BOVEE
family.

HENDERSON/ENCHES (INCHES)/ALLEN
Melinda HENDERSON b ca 1796 d Sherburne,
NY 7 Apr 1822 ae 26 m Dr. Thomas INCHES.
Was Melinda dau of William & Sarah
(ALLEN) HENDERSON "of Ringe, NH?"

INCHES/LAMBERT/FOWLER/SHIPPEE
Thomas INCHES m Boston, MA 30 Dec 1703
Rachel LAMBERT dau of Jesse & Deborah
(FOWLER) s Thomas b Boston 26 Aug 1718 m
Smithfield, RI 1745 Margaret SHIPPEE.
Desire par VR of 1st Thomas. VR of
Rachel.

NICHOLS/WILEY
Wish par of Alexander NICHOLS b ca 1716
d 18 Aug 1799 ae 83, Ward, MA. Was "of
Dudley" m Oxford 26 Feb 1739 Margaret
WILLEY b Oxford 14 Mar 1721 d Ward, MA.
Dau of Joseph & Jane (Jennett)

SPAULDING/NOTT/ROCKWELL
Wish VR of Rhoda SPAULDING dau of
Sampson & Temperance (NOTT) of
Canterbury, CT & Orwell, VT m Moses
ROCKWELL b Cornwall, VT 27 Oct 1790.

VAN VALKENBURG/BREWER (BRUER)/BURROUGHS
Hannah VAN VALKENBURG b Granville, NY d
Sparta, WI 1907 dau of Francis & Nellie
(BREWER/BRUER) m John BURROUGHS. Desire
par of Francis & John.

WARREN/HILDRETH
Jacob WARREN bpt 8:12m:1673 Chelmsford,
MA d Plainfield, CT 3 Sept 1727 s of
Jacob & Mary (HILDRETH) m ca 1690 Sarah
---- who d 1759. Desire par of Sarah.
Mrs. Margaret S. ROSE, 2011-20th Street,
Portsmouth, OH 45662.

#################################

FOSTER/SOUTHWICK
Need par, dts, anc Betsy FOSTER b 10 Dec
1791 S. Danvers, MA, m William SOUTHWICK
3 Sept 1809 d 1825.

KILBURN/SOUTHWICK
Need par, dts Lucy KILBURN b 10 June
1755, Rowley, MA m William SOUTHWICK 4
Feb 1778, d 24 Aug 1825 S. Danvers, MA.

KING/SOUTHWICK
Need dts, par, anc Sarah Elizabeth KING
m William SOUTHWICK 6 Aug 1748, Salem,
MA, now Peabody.

MANSFIELD/WALTON
Need dts, par, anc Lydia MANSFIELD
(Lynnfield) m Joshiah WALTON, Reading 19
Nov 1795.

MANSFIELD/WALTON
Need dts, par, anc Rebecca MANSFIELD b
Reading, m Timothy WALTON 17 Oct 1766.

MASON/TARBELL
John L. MASON b 10 Dec 1898 Chichester,

NH m Sally TARBELL 15 May 1828, NH; d 2?
Nov 1857 near Winnetka, IL. Liv
Charlestown, Danvers, Lynn, MA. W d
Lynn 1895. Had 7 s, 1 dau. Need par,
anc, dts. Mrs. C. A. Southwick, Jr.,
P.O. Box 282, Hope, NJ 07844.

#############################

CHASE/HARVEY
Seek par & anc Judith CHASE b Oct 1727
prob at Amesbury, MA. m David HARVEY Feb
1746.

HAYDEN/THAYER/HOLBROOK
Need all data on Phebe HAYDEN who m
Uriah THAYER in 1781. Also, on Alice
HOLBROOK who m Jeremiah THAYER in 1747.

PHILLIPS/RUSSELL
Wish info on Kezia PHILLIPS of New
Ipswich, NH, m Silas RUSSELL 22 Aug 1764
Rindge, NH. They mov to Sutton, NH in
1773.

TRIPP/MILLER
Need anc & desc of Ada B. TRIPP b New
Bedford, MA 1832, m Frederick MILLER, d
1888 at Westport, MA. Need data on
Frederick, also. Sid L. RUSSELL, 90
Ford St., Lynn, MA 01904.

#############################

COLE/GOULD/ANDREWS
Need anc & dts Rebecca COLE m/1 19
Feb/Apr 1712 Henry GOULD, Jr. of
Ipswich, MA; m/2 8 Dec 1731 Thomas
ANDREWS.

HILLIER/SARGENT
Deborah HILLIER b 30 Oct 1643 Yarmouth,
MA, m 19 Mar 1662 John SARGENT, s of
Rev. William SARGENT. Need any info on
Deborah's par. Hugh HILLIER d ca 1647 &
w Rose ----.

HYDE
Need anc & info on Samuel HYDE b 24 Apr
1747 & his fa the Rev Samuel HYDE b ca
1720. Rev Samuel a Baptist minister
often preached in Methuen, MA & was bur
there 22 Oct 1775.

MERRIAM/JONES/BREED
William MERRIAM, Jr. of Concord, Boston
& Lynn, MA m/1 Elizabeth ----; m/2 11
Oct 1676 Anne JONES. Was Elizabeth dau
of Allen BREED of Lynn?

PICKERING/FLINT
Need info & anc John PICKERING b ca
1615, m ca 1636 Elizabeth ----. They
were par of John PICKERING of Salem, MA
m 1657 Alice FLINT.

ROGERS/MERRILL/PILLSBURY
Wish anc & dts of William ROGERS & w
---- par of Hannah ROGERS b 1776
Newbury, MA m 4 Sept 1797 Joseph MERRILL
b 10 Sept 1770 Newbury s of Richard
MERRILL & Mary PILLSBURY.

SHERIDAN/MACMAHON/MCDERMOTT
Henry SHERIDAN & w Elizabeth MACMAHON
had 7 ch all b in St. John, N.B.
Elizabeth & ch mov to Salem, MA after
Henry's d in 1847. Need all info on anc
of Henry's par & Elizabeth's par Michael
MACMAHON & Mary MCDERMOTT of Ireland.

VEIZEI (VEAZIE)/CUMMINGS/DIXON
Need dts, info, & anc of Joseph VEIZEI b
France & w Mary CUMMINGS b P.E.I., Can.
par of Ann VEAZIE m William DIXON in
P.E.I., Can & d 10 Sept 1898 ae 86 yrs,
7 mos in Boston, MA.

VIALL/SARGENT
Mary VIALL b 23 Aug 1711 m 29 May 1729
Nathan SARGETN & liv in Chelsea, MA.
Mary said to be dau of Nathaniel VIALL.
Need info on Nathaniel & Mary's mo.

WHEELER/CHAMBERLIN
Thomas WHEELER of Charlestown, MA m 5
May 1673 Elizabeth CHAMBERLIN. Need anc
of Elizabeth & info on Thomas' par Isaac
WHEELER & Frances ----. Anne Merrill
GOULETTE, R.R. 3, Box 120, Dexter, ME
04930.

#############################

RHODES
Henry RHODES b 1 June 1674, need dts, w,
pl.

RHOADS

Hannah RHOADS m John RHODES 21 May 1752, need dts, pl, par & anc.

SHILLABER/RHODES

Hannah SHILLABER m Samuel RHODES 12 Sept 1781 Congregational Church, Saugus, MA. Need bdt, bp, par, & anc. Mrs. C.A. Southwick, Jr., P.O. Box 282, Hope, NJ 07844

###

ABBREVIATIONS FOR QUERIES

about (circa)	ca	father	fa	parents	par
age	ae	family (-lies)	fam	place	pl
after	aft	female	f	possible	poss
ancestors	anc	first	1st	probated	pro
arrived	arr	first husband	1/h	record(s)	rec
and	&	first wife	1/w	regarding	re
answer	ans	following	fol	relative	rel
baptised	bpt	from	fr	removed	rem
before	bef	genealogy	gen	requested	req
between	bet	grand	g	reside	res
birth date	bdt	grandchild	gch	Reverend	Rev
birthplace	bp	granddaughter	gdau	Revolutionary War	RevW
born	b	grandmother	gmo	Self-addressed,	
brother(s)	bro	grandparents	gpar	stamped envelope	SASE
buried	bur	grandson	gson	second	2nd
cemetery	cem	great	gr	siblings	sib
census	cen	great grand-	gg-	sister	sis
certificate	cer	husband	h	soldier	sol
child(ren)	ch	identity	iden	son(s)	s
Civil War	CivW	information	info	territory	terr
correspondence	corr	in-law	/law	tradition	trad
County	Co	i.e.	mo/law	township	twp
cousin	csn	intention of mar.	int	unknown	unk
date(s)	dt	known	kn	unmarried	unm
daughter	dau	lived (living)	liv	verify	ver
Deacon	Dea	location	loc	vicinity	vic
death date	ddt	male	M	volume	vol
descendant(s)	desc	manuscript	Ms	wife	w
died	d	marriage (-ried)	m	widow(er)	wid
died young	d.y.	marriage date	mdt	Vital Records	VR
divorced	div	married first	m/1	year(s)	yr(s)
emigrant (-grated)	em	mother	mo	World War I	WWI
enlisted	enl	moved	mov	World War II	WWII
estate	est	no date	ndt		
exchange	xch	obituary	obit		

The Essex Genealogist

VOLUME 5, NUMBER 2   MAY 1985

CONTENTS

THE ESSEX GENEALOGIST is published quarterly: February, May, August,
& November for $7 per year, by the Essex Society of Genealogists,
Lynnfield Public Library, 18 Summer street, Lynnfield, MA 01940.
Second Class Postage paid at Lynnfield, MA 01940. ISSN: 0279-067X
USPS: 591-350. POSTMASTER: Send address changes to ESOG, Lynnfield
Public Library, 18 Summer Street, Lynnfield, MA 01940.

Letter from the Editor

In keeping with our policy of publishing typescripts of our Society's lectures, we offer in this issue <u>Genealogical Research in New York City</u> by Timothy Field Beard, F.A.S.G. Although the topic does not conform with our priorities of Essex County - Massachusetts - New England, nevertheless, the New York area is of interest to many of our members. We have also found that as our members/researchers increase their knowledge and abilities, they find they are reaching out to help others who are just starting. In this regard, we must all try to absorb all that we can about genealogical research in other areas.

The Saville Family concludes in this issue, but the article on the Gerry family has been postponed. The complications of trying to sort out the family groups that removed to the Lancastrian Towns in Worcester County, and the scarcity of complete records in those areas, has deemed it imperative that more work be done before publishing. I hope to research the Worcester and Middlesex Probate and Land Records before committing the Gerry (Geary, Gary) family to print. The results should be ready by the August or November issue. Meanwhile, if anyone has any unpublished data on the Gerry (Geary, Gary) families prior to 1800 in the areas of Lancaster, Leominster, Sterling, Stow, Harvard or Bolton, I would appreciate hearing about it.

To those who have sent material to TEG and have not yet seen it in print, please be patient! TEG is still a one-person operation, and I simply have not had time to send acknowledgements of material received. Often, I intend to use an article but it does not fit into a particular issue, or it is put aside for a more timely article or a more pertinent one. But I do go through the box of material for each issue and pull out what will fit in. Please do not submit originals of your material. Send a <u>copy</u> and keep the <u>original</u> yourself. We do appreciate the material that is sent. Someday soon, we must form a publishing committee that will help to sift and screen material. As time goes on and the success of TEG becomes more firmly established, the base should be broadened to include an organization of people involved in its preparation. We are also looking for someone who will assist in transcribing lectures for publication. Let me know if you are interested.

Again a reminder to those who are sending queries. <u>Please</u> send your queries on <u>3 X 5 cards</u>, and put only one query on each card! Also, it would help our query editors a great deal if you would put your name and address on the <u>lower</u> <u>right-hand</u> <u>corner</u>. Thank you for complying with this request.

I trust you are all looking forward, as I am, to summer research. With longer days and warmer climate, it is so much easier to get out to where the records are! We hope you will all pull together your research and submit the same to TEG.

Marcia Wiswall/Lindberg

##

RULES FOR SUBMITTING ARTICLES TO TEG
1. Articles should be typed and properly documented according to the <u>MLA Handbook</u>, <u>Cite Your Sources</u>, or a similar written manual.
2. Articles should have some relation to Essex County or to general genealogical research. Families or groups who migrated to or from Essex County would be suitable subjects.
3. TEG reserves the right to accept or reject any article.
5. TEG does not assume responsibility for the content of articles printed.

##

TEG Feature Article

GENEALOGICAL RESEARCH IN NEW YORK CITY

(A lecture given to the Essex Society of Genealogists at Lynnfield
17 November 1984)

By Timothy Field Beard, F.A.S.G.

About a month ago I spoke at the New England Historic Genealogical Society and they had a small, sedate group, so I was not expecting this large voluble crowd. I hope I have enough handouts.

It was very appropriate this morning - as I was awakened by my clock-radio, I heard the word "Mayflower" and I immediately jumped up - as being a native of Massachusetts. They were talking about the now famous "Mayflower Madam" in New York. They said that she and her family had been taken out of the Social Register. I hope this doesn't mean all 3000 descendants of William Brewster and Thomas Rogers were taken out (those were her ancestors) - let's hope they don't go that far! It was appropriate, though, that it should be the "Mayflower Madam" that was mentioned today, because I'm going to speak to you about an institution that had as one of its benefactors a lady very much like Sidney Biddle Barrows, the "Mayflower Madam."

THE NEW YORK PUBLIC LIBRARY

The New York Public Library, on 42nd Street in New York, is a private library. The building belongs to the city, but the library is a combination of the libraries belonging to John Jacob Astor and James Lenox. John Jacob Astor was that famous fur trader who came over from Germany in the late 1800s, made a great fortune. He was very interested in books and learning, so he created the Astor Library which was open to all. It was in downtown New York and is now a public theater. James Lenox was a Scot who came from a famous Scottish mercantile family and made a great fortune. He was more interested in books than in business, so he began to collect books. John Jacob Astor died in 1848 but his library was supported by his family after his death. James Lennox died in 1870 and his library continued on. Then Samual J. Tilden, who was Governor of New York State, died in the 1880s and left a vast fortune to New York State instead of to his family. The reason for this was that his family would not recognize his mistress who lived next door. His nieces and nephews ostracized her - would not speak to her at all. So his money was left for "some sort of institution" - the trustees would have the say over this. And so, in the 1890s, it was decided that the old reservoir in New York, no longer used, would be moved uptown, and on the site of this resevoir, they would put a library. They would combine the Astor Library and the Lennox Library with the money of Samuel J. Tilden. So in 1911, what we now know as the New York Public Library - Astor Lennox Tilden Foundation, was opened. This has become one of the greatest libraries in the world, and they were very fortunate in having these two basic libraries. James Lennox was a great bibliophile, and his collection had a great deal of local history and genealogy. And John Jacob Astor hired a man named James Cogswell, who also was interested in local history - British history and American history and genealogy. Cogswell bought in England (at a sale when one of the great mansions in England was sold) most of the British local histories that had been published before the 1840s - many went back into the 1600s. Now Great Britain was the first place where people began to study local history with all the individuals in the county in mind. In continental Europe, they were only interested in the nobility and the titled families. There was not as much interest in the average people, or "peasants" as they called them in Europe. We called them "yeomen" in England. A few years ago someone mentioned something about English "peasants" and I was really quite upset, because they didn't have "peasants" in England. They were "yeoman farmers."

Well, you had all these books gathered together - all the town and county histories of the U.S. that had been published at that time. And the wonderful thing was, that they had hired a librarian who continued to collect all the local histories and genealogies that they could find. In a very short time, the Library at 42nd Street became noted for its genealogical collection. And it was so accessible! It wasn't like the Library of Congress where sometimes you couldn't find the books - and that has continued up to this day because if some congressman asks for the books, he takes them away and they are not there. The NYPL is a Reference Library. Books do not leave. Now there is a problem with this. The building has not been updated the way many buildings have been, and the stacks of the library open onto 42nd Street - carbon monoxide flows in and all these wonderful books are crumbling. That's why the librarians don't last too long there. (I don't think I'd still be alive if I stayed much longer!) But the books are disintegrating and even that wonderful rag paper has a hard time standing up to monoxide. It's too bad that they haven't seen fit to air-condition/humidity control the stacks. It's so nice when you go the New England Historic Genealogical Society and see how pleasant a place it is in which to work, and how well cared for the books are. It's not as large a collection as the NYPL but it's a wonderful place to work.

U. S. HISTORY - AMERICAN HISTORY AND GENEALOGY DIVISION - ROOM 315N

Room 315N at the NYPL is not a spot to visit in the summer. There are no windows - no air-conditioning - no working vents. But it certainly is worthwhile to visit, so go in the Spring and Fall. This room is now called the U.S. History - American History and Genealogy Division. This long name was a sop when they closed the American History Division a few years ago, which was a very tragic event. All the state histories and the histories of the other countries in this hemisphere were there. They are still available to the public, but they have no one overseeing them and no one to help you. The collection was probably one of the more important collections in this country. Many scholars at the time wrote about it to the "New York Times" but it didn't do any good. The wonderful catalog, still called the Local History and Genealogy Catalog of the NYPL, is available at Newbury Street (NEHGS) and other libraries in the New England area. If you use that catalog first (The 18-volume Green set done by G.K. Hall) you will be able to discover what was in the NYPL up to 1971. After that, there are blue and red volumes and then green volumes, then a tan catalog - and now they've put a computer in! Now it is much more difficult to get into the more modern material they've collected since 1971. And the microfilm section has no separate catalog, so it is difficult. Sometimes, if the film is a genealogical film, you may want to go to the desk in Room 315N to ask about census film or passenger lists, etc. The wonderful collection of English local history was moved from Room 315N at the time the American History Division was closed, so these volumes have to be ordered from the central stacks, and that is another difficulty because sometimes they can't be found. There is no one really over-

60

seeing these volumes. You must sign in when you go into Room 315 N. Usually the service is pretty good.

MAP COLLECTION

There are other Divisions besides the Genealogy Room that are very important for the genealogy collection, and they are in my book: How To Find Your Family Roots. I think probably one of the most valuable collections is the Map Collection. As anyone knows, you can't do genealogy without consulting maps. It is hard enough in this country with all the changes in boundary lines, but if you're doing work, say in Poland or Austria, it is so important. A fellow came in the other day and he just bought the London Times Atlas of World History (in this country, Hammond is handling it and it's a wonderful book - about $75) He was using it because his mother was from Poland before the 1st World War. Of course Poland disappeared from the map of Europe from 1790 to 1917 and it was Austria. To have to then get maps of Austria, you have to go to 18th century maps. Even in England today, the counties have changed. Some counties have disappeared from the map of England. If you just went out and bought a map of England today, you'd find there's no Huntingdon anymore. It has vanished; that Somerset is now one-half Avon and one-half Somerset. Avon doesn't appear on the map 10 years ago. So maps are so important. And the Map Collection at the NYPL is one of the best in the world. You can get photocopies of these maps. If you want want photocopies, they will send you up to the photographic department.

ART DIVISION

The Art Division is very important, because there's so much information buried there. I note in my book, books about craftsmen, for instance. If you have an ancestor who's a clockmaker or a cabinetmaker or perhaps a silversmith, you might be able to find information about them in the Art Division.

SLAVONIC AND ORIENTAL DIVISIONS

Anyone who is doing research in the Salvonic area would go to the Slavonic Division. They have wonderful volumes in Polish and Russian. You would have to get someone who knows the language. Most people who come to the library to do genealogy do not know the language, but they may have an older relative who does. The Oriental Division is another Division. No one here looks like they might have an Oriental ansestor, but you never know. A lady in New York came in one day - she was a "Signer" - a descendant of Benjamin Franklin, in fact. She also had seven great grandparents who were Japanese. There are a great many descendants of William Brewster living in Japan, because in the mid-18th century, a lot of Sea Captains went over there. Some of them settled in the Pacific Islands, had children, and at the time of the second World War, many of those people went to Japan because they already were partially Japanese. Their descendants are now living in Japan. It would be sort of fun (I know the five-generation project won't catch them) to find some of these Japanese descendants of William Brewster!

GENEALOGICAL PERIODICALS

Most of the periodicals of a genealogical nature are in the Genealogy Division (now called the U.S. History - American History & Genealogy Division) They have something like 2000 genealogical periodicals from all over the world).

61

I brought a few just to show you: <u>Irish</u> <u>Ancestor</u>, <u>Families</u> (which is from the Ontario Genealogical Society in Canada), <u>New Jersey</u> <u>Genealogical</u> <u>Magazine</u>, of course the famous <u>TAG</u> (<u>The</u> <u>American</u> <u>Genealogist</u>), <u>The</u> <u>Scottish</u> <u>Genealogist</u>, <u>The</u> <u>Norfolk</u> <u>Ancester</u>, (Journal of the Norfolk and Norwich Genealogical Society), <u>Maryland</u> <u>&</u> <u>Delaware</u> <u>Genealogist</u>, <u>Journal</u> <u>of</u> <u>the</u> <u>Afro-American</u> <u>Historical</u> <u>and</u> <u>Genealogical</u> <u>Society</u>, <u>New</u> <u>Orleans</u> <u>Genesis</u>, <u>Genealogical</u> <u>Journal</u>, <u>New York</u> <u>Genea-</u> <u>logical</u> <u>and</u> <u>Biographical</u> <u>Record</u>, <u>North</u> <u>Carolina</u> <u>Genealogical</u> <u>Society</u> <u>Journal</u>. This goes on and on, and when you get these titles that are in Finnish and Swedish, it really is something. Of course you get into the problem of the foreign language and no one is there to translate for you. So either you make photocopies of things or try to get someone to come in with you who knows the language.

PERIODICALS DIVISION

In the Periodicals Division itself, there are some wonderful historical periodicals where there is genealogical material. After those are bound, they are put in the stacks of the library, so they can be extremely helpful. I know one time I was looking at <u>Country</u> <u>Life</u>, which has a lot of local history and genealogy, and I found a house where my 4-greats grandmother's house was on the cover and inside a whole article. I didn't even know it was still standing.

MICROFILM READING ROOM

In the microfilm reading room most of the people are doing genealogy. The Library does have a wonderful collection of the "New York Times," and the "New York Herald Tribune" that go back to the beginning, but the major portion of the microfilms deal with the <u>Census</u>, <u>Passenger</u> <u>Lists</u> and <u>Pension</u> <u>Records</u>, and they have bought most of the things from the National Archives. They have the Passenger Lists from the port of New York from 1820-1903 and these are now available that cover from 1945 and you can see those at the National Archives in Washington. I doubt that the Boston Branch of the National Archives in Waltham has the New York Port Lists. (They have all the Boston lists.) In the library in Bayonne, New Jersey, which is New York's branch of the National Archives, they have just the New York area. And they don't have the Passenger Lists. That's why we bought them at the NYPL. Unfortunately there's not a full index to them. The first index goes from 1820-1846, which is great. However, not everything is there. Not everything that survived in that period. And often you will look at the scraps on film and it looks as if its been eaten away or something happened to it. Someone did tell me that the rats got into the manuscript, so that you can see that not everything is there. And I've found some ancestors that came in that period but for others, I know the exact date that they arrived in New York and they're not there. So the lists were probably destroyed before the W.P.A. got them. But that second bulk of lists from 1847 to 1896 is not indexed. We now have so many people who are interested in genea- logy that it would be a wonderful project if someone would index those lists from 1847 to 1903, which is just a small period of time, but the index is larger than the index from 1820 to 1846. So you see the problem you get into in indexing records of that period.

NATURALIZATION RECORDS - BAYONNE, NEW JERSEY

There are some indexes of the Naturalization Records from 1797 to 1906 over in Bayonne. You don't find a lot in the Naturalization Record for the people in the middle of the 19th Century. Once in a while it may say that they were sujects of the King or Wurtenburg or something, but too often they just say that they were German.

NEWSPAPER ANNEX

However, there is another source at the NYPL that is not at 42nd Street. The Newspaper Annex is at 43rd Street between 10th and 11th Avenues. At the Newspaper Annex there are some wonderful newspapers from all over the world - many of them in their original condition. It's nice to use the "New York Evening Post," say 1836, and it's almost as white as the snow because of its rag content. Of course the minute you get into the 1860s, you get into pulp paper, which is crumbling, and that's why they've had to microfilm things of that period. But the "Staats Zeitung," the famous German newspaper, is available. I know one fellow, all of whose ancestors were German and arrived in the early 1840s - and he was stuck because all their obituaries that he found in English and all the death certificates and censuses - all said just "born in Germany." He had no way of knowing from where they had come because it had now been four or five generations since these people died. He went to the "Staats Zeitung" and found obituaries for all of them with the parents' names and the places where they were born. Newspapers are often forgotten and I'm always encouraging people to try to abstract their local newspapers if they can. You get so much wonderful material there that is not available in the Vital Records or Church Records or in any of the public records, or hasn't survived. Not long ago, I found that one volume at the library had a great great grandmother of my wife's who died in Alabama in the 1860s - where they kept no Vital Records. The newspaper not only gave her exact birth, and the place where she was born in North Carolina, but it gave the names of her parents. It was a volume of abstracts of obituaries from a religious newspaper. So never underestimate what you may find in a newspaper. Are there apt to be indexes to those? No, not usually. The only newspaper in this country that was indexed for many years was the New York Times. It's awful how few newspapers in the country have indexes. There are a lot of bibliographies. Gregory's Union List of Newspapers which unfortunately was done as long ago as 1937, does list all the newspapers at that point and retrospectively back to 1820, and would say if the NYPL had those - or in Boston on microfilm. It lists who are the holders of various issues of the paper and so fourth.

CITY DIRECTORIES AND SOCIAL REGISTERS

The Annex also has a wonderful collection of City Directories from all over the world. But the best Directories were done in this country. Dorothea Spear did a Bibliogrpahy of these that goes up to 1861, and all of those Directories have been put on microfiche and some of the ones after 1861 have been put on microfilm. They are available at NYP but also at other libraries - certainly at Boston. But the NYPL has originals of those volumes and the films are at 42nd Street. Also they have all the old Social Registers and various School Directories that were published in this country. There were Dow's Blue Book for New York and The Philadelphia Blue Book. All these things are very helpful in locating people if they were in a city. I wish someone would reprint City Directories for 1860, 1870 and 1880 because they're very useful if you are doing any census work. Even though you have some Soundex Indexes for the 1880 and 1900 and only some for 1910, the City Directories are helpful in locating the indivuduals. The New York City Directories did not list all the members of a household. They would usually list the working members of the household. There are other City Directories possibly, such as Chicago or Albany that might list

all the members and some of the City Directories even list the death date for
a person.

SCHOMBURG CENTER FOR BLACK CULTURE

There's one other section of the library that you may not think applies to
you but it does. It's the "Schomburg Center for Black Culture." And almost all
the census records are there. This part of the library had the money and were
able to buy the census records - all the census records for the United States
from 1790 through 1910. If you are at the NYPL at 42nd Street, you can have
sent down 4 reels at a time, or you can go up to the Schomburg Center, which is
up at 135th Street (It's in Harlem and you would probably want to go during the
daytime). It's heavily guarded and they do request IDs. At 42nd Street they do
have all of New York, Connecticut and New Jersey Federal Census Records and some
of the New York state census records. These State Records were very good and
sometimes better than the federal because they give the county of birth if the
person was born in New York State, and with all the movement in New York in the
1850s and 60s, it's very important, for instance, to find that someone who was
living up in Ontario County was born in Duchess County.

NEW YORK GENEALOGICAL AND BIOGRAPHICAL SOCIETY

Skipping on to another library which is a very pleasant place to work is
the New York Genealogical and Biographical Society. It has a very good collection of American genealogies and local histories for New England and New York.
It also has a large southern collection because New York is filled with souther-
ners and has been since the early days. There are, for instance, North Carolina
Marriage Bonds - the Barbour Collection of Connecticut Vital Records (that's
also at NYPL). There are lots of miscellaneous Census Records and Directories
and there's that wonderful set of microfilm dealing with the Signers of the
Declaration of Independence - genealogies of the "Signers," the originals of
which are at the Fellson Club in Louisville. Unfortunatly, nothing has ever
really been done on the descendants of the "Signers." But the manuscript is
wonderful and if you have a question about a "Signer," you can go and check the
films, you may see if indeed you have a connection. They have wonderful Vital
Records and abstracts of Vital Records from New York State. Now New York has
not been very good about getting their records published. We have not had a
good State Archives and a good State Library. They're trying to improve upon
them, but it's still in more or less of a primitive state. The New York Genealogical and Biographical Society takes a great many periodicals - probably a
couple hundred - and they have an excellent "New York State" room. You have to
be a member if you're going to use the manuscripts and microfilm. Sometimes
it's worth joining for a year if you're going to go down to New York. You also
get the "New York Genealogical and Biographical Records" issued quarterly. It's
somewhere around $35 or $40 a year for membership.

PATRIOTIC SOCIETIES

There are, in that building, a great many patriotic societies, and some of
those libraries are open occasionally. The Holland Society, which is open to
membership to men who can prove they descend in the male line from a Dutch
settler who settled before 1672 in Manhattan. You can find that library open
once a week on Friday. It has a wonderful collection of New York Dutch Church
Records from all over the state. Of course, there's the Mayflower Society - it
has a small library. The St. Nicholas Society (men) - New Yorkers before 1785;

The Daughters of Holland Dames - that's a lady who's descended from an immigrant that was born in the Netherlands; the Daughters of Cincinnati (jokingly referred to as the "Daughters of Sin"); The Society of the Cincinnati for the state of New York; the Veterans of Foreign Wars; the Society of Colonial Wars, etc. They're all gathered together in that building, so they're easy to find, and if you have a question, the secretaries can usually answer them.

OTHER BUILDINGS IN NEW YORK

"The Abigail Adams House" has Massachusetts connections - she was the daughter of John Adams. This was her home and it's called "Smith's Folly" because only the stalls were built before her husband went bankrupt in about 1799. Even if it was just the stable, it's quite a lovely little building, and it is the home of the Colonial Dames of America. The National Society of Colonial Dames has a very beautiful house on 71st Street that they built probably in the 20s or 30s, and their library is open and has a very good collection of genealogies. The Sons of the Revolution have Fraunces Tavern, the building where George Washington bade farewell to his officers. It has a library, but unfortunatly (I was the librarian at one time & was always embarrased by this) the library is not open to the public. In fact, the library now is so hidden by desks and things that you can't even get to it. It's very unfortunate because they have a wonderful collection of volumes dealing with the Revolution. The more public buildings are the Municipal Archives, at 52 Chamber Street. At this very moment they may be moving across the street. They always say they're going to move across to 31 Chamber Street - the Hall of Records. 52 Chamber Street is the famous "Boss Tweed" building. It's the Tweed Court House which cost New York about 50 times more than the building actually cost as Boss Tweed walked off with all the funds. So they are now in the basement of the Tweed Court House. It's very easy for them to move because all they've got is a bit of microfilm and some microfilm readers. The records themselves are evidently stored out on Long Island. This great mass of bundled collections of the public records of New York - we don't even know what they are or almost how to find them. I think when someone was talking about going through them, so many of them had been mutilated, and famous signatures that might be there such as Alexander Hamilton, had all been clipped off and sold to dealers - and as a matter of fact, they tried to throw them all away at one point, and some one of the city officials stepped forward and wouldn't allow it, because there are tax lists - the records of the city (and some go back into the 17th century). They did, for instance, at one point, throw out all the apprentice records. Fortunatly, a second-hand paper dealer recognized what they were and sold the records to the New York Historical Society - so they are there. But New York has been casual with their records, and they're casual now with their microfilm If you write in for a certificate, some times you may have to write two or three times. The Hall of Records is at 31 Chamber Street. And that is where the Deeds and Wills are - the Surrogate Court and the Deeds for New York City. Again, don't expect a great deal of the people who work there. Unfortunatly, they are the volumes in the Historical Room, and if they let you in there, you can get the volumes yourself off the shelf. There are indexes going from 1664 up to the present. If you start asking for records, you'll get sort of harassed and harangued. But pay no attention. They are there to answer your questions.

Two other places right near there are The Department of Health at 125 Worth Street, which has the Vital Records for the City - the birth records from 1897 and the death records from 1920 on. The records before that time are all on microfilm at the Municipal Archives. The Death Records at the Municipal Archives go back to 1798, but they don't give parentage until 1880. One other place down town right near there is the Marriage License Bureau. They have been keeping records since 1866 for Manhattan, New York County. New York County is just Manhattan. Before 1898, New York City was just Manhattan and parts of the Bronx. Parts of the Bronx gradually began to be added to New York City in 1874 and it wasn't until 1914 that Bronx County was formed. So if you want a marriage for someone who was married in the Bronx in 1900, you would go to the Marriage License Bureau on Chamber Street in the New York City Hall and you would get their marriage there. If they were married in 1915 in the Bronx, you would go uptown to the City Clerk in Bronx County. If you're getting a marriage in Queens, you go over to Jamaica and get the marriage records. If you have a marriage on Staten Island, you go over there. If you're getting a marriage in Brooklyn, you go to Brooklyn, King's County, and get the marriage there. The confusing one is Staten Island, which is Richmond County! Unfortunately, the marriages of the city have never been all collected together.

ANSWERS TO QUESTIONS FROM THE FLOOR

Unfortunately in New York State, there was no law about Vital Records until 1880, so before that, you have to find cemetery records. The D.A.R. has done wonderful work in copying the tombstone inscriptions in the various towns. You should use the Master Index to the D.A.R. Church, Town and Cemetery Records in New York State - the Master Index is a printed volume. They have these volumes in Washington, D.C. at 1717 B Street and they have them at the NYPL and in Albany for New York. Each state has these collections. They have done an Index to the New York Collections. Of course, there are Bible Records. There may be some in the State Library. Also there are Census Records. If you could find Church Records, it might help. Sometimes, people living in rural areas didn't even go to the churches they might have gone to if they had a choice, because there were so few churches around. Even though they might have been Presbyterians or Episcopaleans, they might have gone to the Dutch Reform Church because it was the only church there. So, in rural areas, you should look at all the churches.

In Albany, they now have on microfiche, the Records at the State Department of Health from 1880. Deaths and Marriages have a 50-year limit, so it will be up to 1934 you can look at them; and 75 years for births. There are annual indexes. In New York City, there are published volumes from 1888. The records before that time, you can use yourself at the Municipal Archives. There are Manuscript Indexes that you can use. The printed records have crumbled so that most of them you have to use on film at the NYPL. You can not use them, unfortunatly at the Department of Health. For some reason, you can't use the indexes there. But all of them should be at the NYPL on film or in the original printed form. That's Births and Deaths from 1888, and Marriages go from 1888 to 1937. Then the arrangement of the Indexes is crazy. Some of the early ones before (before '98) include only Manhattan and part of the Bronx. After that time, they're arranged by Burroughs. There are five sections and finally in 1937, they came to their senses and put it all in one alphabet. So you get used to it.

##

Timothy Field Beard, F.A.S.G. is a native of Great Barrington, Mass. He is now Director of the Hodge Memorial Library at Roxbury, Conn., where he resides. He is author of How to Find Your Family Roots, and genealogist for the Roosevelt Family Association.

Crest and Shield

By Lyman O. Tucker

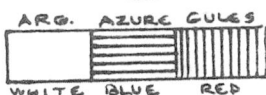

ARMS: Argent, two chevronels azure,
a canton gules.
CREST: A tree (oak) a pendant
therefrom two weights

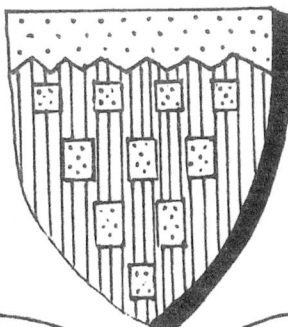

****

Rev. Gregory, born Olney, Northhamp-
tonshire, England, 1610, came to
New England in 1644, locating at
Providence and Warwick, R.I.
Richard, born England about 1606,
from the County Meath, Ireland,
admitted freeman at Boston, Mass.
1642, two years later removed to
Charlestown, Mass.
Thomas came to Lynn, Mass. 1630, and
in 1637 removed to Sandwich, Mass.
and in 1646 to Barnstable, Mass.
(Holmes: "Directory")

ARMS: Gules, ten billets Or, a chief
indented of the second.
CREST: A goats head erased argent
ducally crowned and gorged Or.

****

John was at Roxbury, Mass. before 1636.
Samuel, born at Groton, parish of Manchester, County of Lancaster, Eng.
1592. Came to Boston, Mass. 1636,
soon after went to Plymouth, Mass.
thence in 1638 to R.I. and settled
at Warwick. He was Assistant Deputy.
Clothier. Author of "Simplicities
Defence..." 1646. Life and times of
Samuel Gorton, 1907. Coat of arms
enrolled. (Colket: "Founders..")
Thomas, freeman, at Portsmouth, RI 1655
(Holmes: "Directory")

THE SOUTH LYNNFIELD STORY

By E. Gerry Mansfield

The first record that relates to the area now called South Lynnfield, or at one time, the South Village, was in 1635. The Colonial Records state:

> "There are 500 acres of land and a fresh pond with an island containing about two acres, granted to Sir John Humphrey Esq; lying between north and west of Saugus, providing he takes no part of the 500 acres within five miles of any town now planted. Also it is agreed that the inhabitants of Saugus and Salem shall have liberty to build four houses upon the said island, to lay in such provisions as they shall deem necessary in time of need."

The acreage stated in this grant comprises much of the area of South Lynnfield. Sir John Humphrey was a native of Dorchester in England – a man of considerable wealth and good reputation. He was one of the most influential in promoting the settlement of the colony, was chosen Deputy Governor in 1630 and Assistant in 1632, both of these appointments before his arrival. He arrived at Lynn in 1634. Previous to his arrival he had received several liberal grants in the Lynn and Swampscott area, mainly along the waterfront. This is where he resided. He was a Justice in The Quarterly Court and was prominent in Town and Colony affairs. He returned to England in 1641 and died in London in 1661. In the same year his Administrators, Joseph Humpfrey and Edward Batter claimed title to this 500 acre Grant. However no attempt was ever made to recover it.

On December 6, 1642, this tract of land was delivered to Robert Saltonstall of Boston, as an execution issued upon the judgement in an action brought by Mr. Saltonstall against Mr. Humphrey. In 1645, Mr. Saltonstall conveyed the same to Stephen Winthrop of Boston. After a few years this tract of land came into possession of Mr. Winthrop's daughters; Judith, wife of Richard Hancock of London; and Margaret, wife of Captain Edmond Wiley also of London. Mrs. Hancock received the southwest half and Mrs. Wiley the northeast half, which she conveyed to James Menzie of Boston in 1698. In 1695 Mrs. Hancock conveyed to Bartholomew Gedney of Salem, 420 acres, being two-thirds of one half. Mr. Gedney died in 1697 and the property was divided between his two daughters, Mrs. John Richards and Mrs. Benjamin Alford, both of Salem.

In 1723 another division was made; one half was purchased by Joseph Newhall and the other by Andrew Mansfield in 1724. According to the deeds, the land was divided equally, and the purchase price paid by Andrew Mansfield for his 120 acres was 565 pounds. To the best of my knowledge, the Humpfrey Grant included about all the land east of Summer Street, excluding the land granted in 1638 distributed by the Town of Lynn. It is quite evident that the Humpfrey Grant contained much more than the stated 500 acres, as there is more than that figure in each half. This information I have copied from the original deeds. There remains to this day one of the bounds of the original Humpfrey Grant of 1635. It is located near the corner of Salem and Locust Streets. There is a large rock, painted white, and to the best of my knowledge this is the southeatern boundary. Incidentally, Salem Street was laid out in 1660 as a road from Salem to Reading. Locust Street originally was a right of way, laid out in 1697 to the Gedney Farm purchased by Andrew Mansfield in 1724.

Joseph Newhall was the son of the first white child born in Lynn. The Newhall and Mansfield family names were predominant for many generations and at one time there were some sixteen houses in the village of South Lynnfield that was the home of either a Newhall or a Mansfield. Other family names familiar in the early history of the village were Aborn, Abbott, Brown, Copeland, Gerry, Hawkes, Hobson, Hayward, Jackson, Lawrence, Monroe, Palmer, Richardson, Russell and Spinney, to name but a few. How strange it is that so few of these family names remain today.

By occupation the majority were tillers of the soil, although the making of shoes soon became an important part in the life of the community. One of the early manufactures were the Spinneys and their shop located on the second floor of the old store which was on the corner of Salem Street and the old Newburyport turnpike; in other words at Lynnfield Square. Other members of the Spinney Family operated the store for many years. Incidentally, about the turn of the present century, this old building was moved about a half mile on Salem Street, remodeled into a dwelling house and still remains. There were other shoe manufacturing establishments in the village, two of them of considerable size; namely Henry Law's factory on Locust Street and Clarence Moulton's on the turnpike. These have long since passed into oblivion.

The Lynnfield quarries, operated by some of the Newhall Family, were well recognized for the high quality of granite. Consequently it was in great demand for several years. Remains of this once flourishing industry can be seen at the abandoned quarry off Ledge Road.

The most famous building in the village was the Lynnfield Hotel, built about 1804 by the Newburyport Turnpike Company and located on the turnpike near what was Lynnfield Square. So popular was this resort that the village was often called Lynnfield Hotel. In fact when the first railroad through the town was opened on August 21, 1850, the station was given that name. In its ninety years of existance it had several proprietors; the first was Noah Newhall, and the last was Samuel Bruce. However, on the evening of May 7, 1894, it was destroyed by fire. During the same year, the first telephone in Lynnfield was installed in the old store, which was near the Hotel and proved to be of great service in calling for aid from the Peabody Fire Department. Another Hotel was soon built, located a short distance from the old one, near the present site of Donovan's store. This was called "The New Lynnfield Hotel." However, after a few years it also was destroyed by fire.

During the year of 1836, the first Post Office in Lynnfield was established in the old store, so called, in South Lynnfield. The first Post Master was Theren Palmer. Some thirteen Post Masters have served this office which was located in various places prior to the time when one Post Office served the entire town.

Suntaug Lake, or Humpfreys Pond (the original name) and the surrounding area has an interesting past, some of which should be mentioned here. In 1850, a great tragedy happened when several members of a Sunday School picnic were out on the lake in a flat bottom boat, with a paddle-wheel propelled by a man in the same manner you would peddle a bicycle. Suddenly a gust of wind sent a spray of water onto the boat, causing everyone to move to the other side of the boat. Thirteen young people were drowned. The story is told that the boat was never used again. This tragedy happened near the Town Lyne House.

On the shores of the lake in 1861 was the Civil War Encampment in the area between the Town Lyne House and Moulton Drive. This was called Camp Stanton. Incidentally, some seventy years later, during the first World War, another encampment was located in the immediate area, precisely where the Holiday Inn now stands, as well as the area included in the present Rte 1/128 interchange.

In 1857, the South Church (now the Lynnfield Community Church) was built. The generosity of Josiah Newhall, who gave the land as a gift, was much appreciated and no doubt was some-what responsible for the Church being built at that time. The original location was near the present Eastern Savings Bank building.

The coming of the railroad to this part of town in 1850 was the reason for the Boston Ice Company building a large block of ice-houses on the shore of the lake. They were in use for only a short time, for in 1865 they were destroyed by fire. About the same time an open-air theater was promoted by the railroad and others. This was also on the shores of the lake, somewhere between Locksley Road and the lake. This venture never proved to be successful.

The first school in this part of town was built about 1810 on the present site of the fire station, and was called the Newhall ward or District School. Previous to this time, most of the children in this part of the town went to a school lcoated on Route One, at the corner of Lake Street. This was called District nine, of Danvers (now Peabody). I have in my possession a list of scholars dated 1806; and many of the names represented families residing in Lynnfield, particularly Newhalls and Mansfields. My Great, Great Grandfather was School Committeeman for this district at this time, and I have several interesting documents. For instance, there is a receipt from a Betsey Putnum, dated 1806, for $16 for teaching school "sixteen weeks." Times have changed, haven't they?

Street cars were once a familiar sight in this part of Lynnfield; for a period of some twenty years. Beginning on May 5, 1898, they operated continuously until 1981. These cars ran from Salem through Peabody and Lynn-field to North Saugus, where one could change for either Lynn or Wakefield. The story is told about one of the conductors when arriving at North Saugus, which at that time was rather sparsely settled, would announce "North Saugus change here for all points of the world!"

Although the old Lynnfield Hotel became famous in its time, it does not compare with that of the more recent "Suntaug Inn." This was known far and near as one of the most famous eating places. The first Inn was built around the turn of the century, and was totally destroyed by fire on January 3, 1918. it was immediately rebuilt and remained famous for many years until it was once again destroyed by fire in 1966. Among the various proprietors was Cora Egalston who was also recognized for her generosity when she presented the Town of Lynnfield with its first motorized fire apparatus (which is still cared for by the Lynnfield Fire Department and wins regular awards at the antique fire apparatus shows). The Suntaug Inn was again rebuilt and is now operated under the name of "Bali-Hai" and continues to be a very popular eating place.

70

There was another famous eating place located near the shores of the lake. In fact, it was on the site of the Civil-War Encampment, which, incidentally, was later the private estate of David P. Ives of Salem. About 1920, "Hap Ward" and his wife, known as "Lucy Daley" (both were Theatrical people), purchased the property and built the once famous "Wardhurst Club." Of the old houses, few remain that were built before 1800. The oldest house now standing was built in 1740 by Deacon Daniel Mansfield, on Salem Street, and is now the residence of Mr. and Mrs. Richard Thorngren.

I probably should mention that the majority of Newhalls came from the Joseph Newhall house, still standing on Lynnfield Street just beyond the town line in Lynn. This house was built about 1700. And the Mansfields came from the old homestead which was located on Locust Street just over the Peabody town line. This house was built about 1680 and was in the Mansfield family from 1724 to 1959, when it was demolished for State Highway purposes.

\#

MONUMENT TO MEMBERS OF THE BOSTON TEA PARTY

Submitted by Lyman O. Tucker

In the Hope Cemetery in Worcester, Mass. is a monument dedicated to the members of the famous "Boston Tea Party." A beautiful obelisk of Italian marble, made by Tateum & Horgan, marble workers in Worcester at that time, the shaft is four feet square at the base and thirteen feet high, standing on a foundation of granite. It is located on the corner of Chestnut and Aspen Avenues, a short distance from the main entrance to the cemetery. On three sides of the monument are the names of the family of Captain Peter Slater, including his mother and his fifteen children, giving the time of their decease and their ages. On the fourth side are the names of the "Patriots" above which is inscribed:

"NAMES OF THE PATRIOTS WHO THREW THE BRITISH TEA INTO BOSTON HARBOR 16 DEC 1773

Peter Slater	Ebenezer Stevens	Thomas Porter	Joseph Lee
Benjamin Tucker	William Russell	Seth Ingersoll Brown	Thomas Moore
Paul Revere	Joseph Bassett	Adam Colson	Daniel Ingollson
John Spurr	Amos Lincoln	Samuel Doliber	Matthew Loring
John Dickman	Samuel Peck	John Crane	Joseph Eayres
Jonathan Parker	Lendall Pitts	Joseph Shedd	T. Gammall
John Brown	Henry Purkett	Thomas Chase	William Mollineux
George R.T.Hewes	Rich'd Hunnewell,Jr	S. Coolidge	Nathaniel Green
Joshua Wyeth	Nath'l Frothingham	Thomas Urann	S. Howard
David Kennerson	Sammuel Gore	James Brewre	Wm. Pierce
Joseph Palmer	Moses Grant	Thomas Bolton	Samuel Sprague
James Swan	Nicholas Campbell	Edward Proctor	Benjamin Clark
Joseph Mountford	Jose(ph) Payson	Thomas Gerrish	John Hooten
Peter McIntosh	Benjamin Rice	Samuel Sloper	John Prince
James Starr	Robert Sessions	Wm Hurdley	Thomas Gerrish
Josiah Wheeler	D. Thomas Young	Thomas Spear	Edward C. Howe
Thomas Melville	Abraham Tower	Isaac Simpson	----- Martin

(Copied from Caleb A. Wall's The Historic Boston Tea-Party of December 16, 1773 available at the Lynn and Boston Public Libraries)

A MAN - A LEGEND - A HERITAGE

By Helen P. Bosworth

What better time than May - fresh and colorful with all the beauty of spring - to tell about a man better known by his legendary name and who some folks believe to be only a myth. This story begins in Essex County when Edward Chapman, with his wife Mary, came from Yorkshire, England, to Ipswich in 1639 to plant the family tree. One of the spreading branches was his son John who married Martha Perley and moved to Tewksbury where on 13 September 1746 a son, Nathaniel, was born. After the birth of their last child, John and Martha removed to Leominster. Nathaniel was now of age and married Elizabeth Simons whose parents had come from Woburn.

Nate was a carpenter and he and Elizabeth lived on a farm "a stone's throw from the Nashua River." On 10 November 1770, Elizabeth, their first child was born, followed by a son on 26 September 1774. Nate said there had always been a John in the family until he came along, so named the boy John. Like many of our ancestors, Nate was a militia-man and served in the Revolution. While with Washington in New York - Capt. Pollard's Company of Carperters - his second son, Nathaniel, was born on 26 June 1776, and Nate returned home. He and Elizabeth were taken into full communion into the Congregational Meeting and their children baptized. Elizabeth's health had been declining and she died on 18 July 1776 - the infant soon after.

It wasn't long before Nate, with his two children, set off along the Connecticut River Valley and settled in Long Meadow (now Longmeadow) in the southern part of the state. In July 1780, he married as his second wife, Lucy Cooley, by whom he had a number of children. Here John learned his three R's but what impressed him most and filled his young mind with wonder was an apple the schoolmaster impaled on a sharpened stick and lighting a candle stub, held them up for the children to see saying, "Behold, the apple, it is like the planet Earth on which we dwell. See how it spins on its axle and revolves around the candle's light which represents the sun - thus does the Earth spin in infinite space." John carried this image, and the Bible he later acquired, throughout his lifetime.

After the Revolution, land grants were given to families who agreed to band together and settle 4-5 years in a place and establish a community. The trek west began. As the story unfolds, founded on fact and family tradition, John, now age 18, "aglow with western fever," and his half-brother Nathaniel, age 11, set out from Longmeadow in 1792 to go west. By shanks mare they reached the cabin of an uncle in western New York where Nathaniel fades away.

John worked as an orchardist for awhile but he had a mission burning in his mind and believed that if you followed the rivers they would take you anywhere. He hadn't gone far before he joined the Swedenborgians - a faith based upon the doctrines of Edmund Swedenborg (1688-1772), scientist, theologian, who, in his search for an explanation of the universe, came upon God and believed himself divinely appointed to "unfold the spiritual sense of the Holy Scriptures." Although John was an intelligent young man, he may not have wholly understood this new creed, but in his own way made use of the "heart of it" - the love for all creation, and with the only skill he knew, that of an orchardist, would serve mankind. Thus the work and legend of John Chapman began to take shape.

John washed and collected only the best apples seeds, and with a full knapsack, traveled into the wilderness, almost always on foot, to cultivate and plant his nurseries that would produce the fine saplings for his orchards, he nurtured with tender loving care, from Ohio to Virginia, Indiana, Illinois,

72

Michigan, Iowa - following the rivers he knew would take him anywhere. John didn't believe in grafting trees, only that they should grow as God intended. There were Baldwins, Northern Spy, Pippin, Red Astrachan, Winesap, Russet...

Chapman was a gentle and humble soul - his home the great outdoors and Nature his provider. As the years rolled by he became shoeless, his clothes worn and tattered, his hair and beard long and matted. People thought him queer, but as they grew to know him, welcomed him and loved him. Like St. Francis of Assisi, the animals and the birds followed him. At first the people called him "Apple John", then, with love, "Johnny Appleseed".

As Johnny traveled about harvesting his seed, he collected stories and had a way of telling them that held his audience as if by magic, but he didn't like to talk about himself. During his lifetime, he kept his vow and faithfully served mankind. When they were sick he helped them with his knowledge learned from the Indians; read from his Bible and gave them solace; taught them to plant and care for their orchards; brought news and messages as he traveled from one community to another and could exchange talk with the best of them around the tavern hearth. As new territories opened, he would come upon relatives and enjoyed visits and listening to family gossip.

Johnny had been wandering a long time now and was getting old and his body tired. In 1844, he paid his last visit to Ohio where "he walked the land of his youth, saw the fruit of his labor and the harvest of his years." He offered his gnarled hand to kin and friends, exchanged cordial talk, said his final fare-wells and returned to Indiana. His brother-in-law, William Broom, who married his favorite step-sister, Persis, had built a new cabin on Johnny's 74 acres near the Broom home. They thought it time to stop wandering and settle down there but Johnny sought the home of a friend by the St. Joseph River where there was an old abandoned cabin in which he had sometimes slept. He built a fire and in his wet, tattered clothes, sank down upon the ancient hearth sick unto death. He had no warm bed for his weary and aching body; no fresh sheets or bed gown; no cool pillow to lay his burning cheek; only a cup held to his fevered lips and a look-in now and then to see how the old man was. The years had made tough fibre of Johnny and he lingered. On 18 March 1845, Johnny Appleseed died of the winter plague (pneumonia) and was buried in Fort Wayne, Indiana, in the quiet Archer Cemetery overlooking the St. Joseph River where a little fence guards his grave and crab apple blossoms scent the spring air.

The cemetery is now part of the 300 acre Johnny Appleseed Memorial Park and in the distance the Johnny Appleseed Memorial Bridge. When the park was dedicated, people from all walks of life came from near and far to pay tribute to a man so well loved. A Swedenborian minister read from Johnny's own Bible - "He leadeth me beside the still waters." A Chapman descendent came from Leominster to represent the town of his birth, told of the annual apple festival and the monument erected on the site of the Chapman home.

Though Johnny denied himself the common necessities of life, he is supposed to have owned considerable property. What if he had known it would take the court ten years to settle his estate of hundreds of acres and thousands of trees? Johnny Appleseed has been immortalized through the decades by poets, authors, playwrites. When I see the apple trees laden with blossoms and whiff the delicate perfume, I say "Thank you, Johnny, for sowing the seeds of a heritage you gave us - radiant spring beauty - luscious fall fruit."

##

Note: Do any ESOG members relate to "cousin" or "uncle" Johnny through his Chapman or allied lines?

Research in Progress

MARTIN - DURKEE CONNECTIONS

(From "The DURKEE FAMILY NEWLETTER" - reprinted with permission from Editor
Bernice B. Gunderson)

The emigrant ancestor of the Martin family was George Martin of Salisbury,
who arrived from England in 1639 in the employ of a Mr. Winsley. This probably
refers to the custom of settlers coming from Europe 'indented,' that is bound to
someone financially for a sum of money, as thirty pounds, or a time as four
months, services for their passage and espenses. George was a blacksmith and
apparently practiced that profession for his entire lifetime. In 1643 he bought
Job Cole's land rights in East Salisbury and he took the oath of fidelity in
1646. The name of his first wife was Hannah (possibly Green) and by her he had
a daughter Hannah who married Ezekiell Wathen or Worthen. His wife Hannah, died
in 1646 and on 11 Aug 1646 George married Susanna North in Salisbury. She was
the daughter of Richard and Ursula North of Salisbury (and the Susanna Martin
who was hung as a witch in 1692 - see below). George and Susanna had nine
children, two dying in infancy. The second son of George and Susanna was also
called George and later became known as George, Sr. He moved to Amesbury and
later to Chebacco Parish in Ipswich. His name appears among the residents
having pasturage for horses on the common in 1697 and he was a commoner or
proprietor in 1707. We do not know if he pursued his father's occupation of
blacksmith or not but he may have combined this with farming. The name of his
first wife has never been discovered. The birth-records of his children, who
were all born in Chebacco Parish, give only the father's name. Sometime in the
early 1700s the Durkees and the Martins became friends and on 4 June 1709 the
intentions were published for the first marriage between the families for George
Martin, Jr. and Mercy Durkee. The following year on 29 April 1710, the
intentions of John S. Martin and Jane Durkee were published. During this
interval the first wife of George Martin, Sr. died and on 21 February 1712/13
George Sr. published his intentions to marry Elizabeth Durkee, elder sister of
Mercy and Jane. This resulted in Elizabeth becoming the step-mother of her
sisters and the sister-in-law of her step-sons!

In 1704, William Durkee, Jr., brother of Elizabeth, Mercy and Jane, had
married Rebecca Gould and they became the parents of a large family consisting
mostly of daughters. On 1 April 1729 Ebenezer Martin, another son of George
Martin, Sr. married as his second wife, Jerusha Durkee, second daughter of
William, Jr. and Rebecca. This was followed on 12 May 1737 by Sarah, a sister
of Jerusha marrying her cousin George Martin, 3rd, the son of George Jr. and
Mercy (Durkee). Relationships now became hopelessly entangled.

On 14 April 1734, George Martin, Sr. died leaving as his widow Elizabeth
(Durkee). By this time his sons George Jr. and Ebenezer had removed to Windham,
Connecticut, with the Durkee family and his son John S. Martin (whose wife was
Jane Durkee) and his son-in-law John Howard were appointed administrators of his
estate. For some reason they were slow in providing their step-mother Elizabeth
(Durkee) with her rightful share of George Sr.'s estate and on May 3rd she
petitioned the court for her portion. George and Ebenezer in Windham received
their shares on May 25th. The estate was valued at 881 pounds.

The marriages between the Durkees and the Martins continued when Elizabeth Martin married Eliphalet Durkee on 29 Nov 1787. Their relationship is interesting. Eliphalet was the son of Henry Durkee and his wife Relief Adams. Henry was a son of William Durkee, Jr. and a brother of Jerusha and Sarah Durkee who had already married Martins. Elizabeth was the daughter of David Martin and his 1st wife Elizabeth Hende. David was the son of George Martin, 3rd and his first wife Grace Howard. Grace was most likely the daughter of John Howard and Mary Martin, daughter of George, Sr. John Howard was one of the Administrators of George Martin's estate. George 3rd of course had married as his 2nd wife Sarah Durkee, daughter of William Jr.

In the next generation Lora Martin married Benjamin Durkee. Again, a complicated relationship. Benjamin was the son of Capt. Benjamin Durkee and his wife Abigail (Durkee). Abigail was a sister of the Eliphalet mentioned above. Lora was the daughter of Nathaniel Ford Martin and Jerush (Linkon). Nathaniel in turn was the son of Joseph Martin and Elizabeth Ford and the grandson of Ebenezer Martin and Jerusha Durkee!

There were two other Durkee-Martin marriages but these relationships are not so clear. In 1768, Mary (Baker), widow of Nathaniel Durkee married Samuel Martin, Sr. The relationship between Samuel and the George Martin family is not known, but they were likely related. There was a Samuel Martin early in Francestown, New Hampshire. This Nathaniel Durkee was a son of Thomas Durkee who was a brother to the Elizabeth, Mercy and Jane Durkee already mentioned as having married various Martins. Nathaniel and Mary (Baker) had a son Nathaniel who married a Keziah Martin of Lyme, but her relationship to either of these Martin families has not been proved. There are likely other hidden relationships and intermarriages between these families that we have not yet discovered but the association of the families remains to this day. (Bernice Gunderson is descended from the marriage between George Martin 3rd and Sarah Durkee.)

* *

GEORGE MARTIN, Sr. & his second wife **ELIZABETH DURKEE** had no children.

GEORGE MARTIN, JR. and his second wife, **MERCY DURKEE** married in 1709 and
    had 4 children:
  Mercy, b. 25 Jun 1710; m. Amos Leach.
  George, 3rd, b. 19 Apr 1712; m. (1) Grace Howard; m. (2) Sarah Durkee.
  Sarah, b. 31 Mar 1721; m. (1) John Marsh; m (2) Manassah Martin.
  Anna, b. 15 Jul 1725; m. Ebenezer Stowel.

(Mercy Durkee Martin died 1 Aug 1730 and George Martin, Jr. married (3) Mercy Linkon. He d. 15 Aug 1755 in Windham, CT. Mercy's gravestone is one of the earliest Martin graves and represents primitive gravestone art.)

JOHN S. MARTIN and **JANE DURKEE** were married in 1710 and had 6 children:
  Martha, b. 6 Jun 1711; m. Thomas Brown.
  John, Jr., b. 17 Oct 1712; m. Elizabeth Thomson.
  Elizabeth, b. 18 Oct 1715; m. David Goodridge.
  Joshua, b. 18 Dec 1717; m. (1) Sarah Storey; m. (2) Elizabeth Knowlton; m.
    (3) Charlotte -----.
  Mary, b. 24 Sep 1720; probably died young.
  George, b. 23 Sep 1722; m. Eunice Burnham.

(John S. Martin remained in Ipswich when the rest of the family moved to
Windham, CT, and with his brother-in-law John Howard, administered the
estate of his father, George Martin, Sr. This family later lived in Lunenburg, MA. The date of Jane (Durkee's) death has not been found. John died
in Ipswich in 1760.)

EBENEZER MARTIN married first Mary Millard and by her had 2 children. He mar-
  ried second, on 1 April 1729 **JERUSHA DURKEE** and they had 9 children:
Joseph, b. 29 Mar 1730; m. (1) Elizabeth Ford; m. (2) Elizabeth Coy; m. (3)
  Zerviah Dayley.
Ebenezer, b. 31 Mar 1732; m. Susan Plumb. (He was a minister in Windham)
Jerusha, b. 8 Jun 1734; m. Joseph Utley.
William, b. 11 Mar 1736; m. Naomi Upton.
Elizabeth, b. 1 Aug 1738; m. Ebenezer Griffen.
Amasa, b. 7 Oct 1740; probably died young.
George, b. 14 Mar 1742/3; m. Dorothy Brown.
Benjamin, bl 28 Feb 1744/5; m. Lucee Clark.
Lucee, b. 9 May 1747; m. Nathaniel Flint.

(Ebenezer died in Windham 13 Jul 1775 leaving his widow Jerusha. It is
possible she re-married but no records have been found.)

GEORGE MARTIN married (1) Grace Howard (probably his cousin) and had 2 sons;
  Jonathan, died age 1-, and David who m. (1) Elizabeth Hende; (2) Dinah
  Utley; and (3) Sabra Sharp. George married (2) 12 May 1737 **SARAH DURKEE**
  and had 11 children:
Grace, b. 6 Mar 1737/8; m. Amos Utley.
Sarah, b. 1 May 1739; m. Henry Brown.
Gidwon, b. 24 Sep 1740; m. Rachel Heath.
Aaron, b. 30 Jul 1742; m. Eunice Flint.
Marcy, b. 18 Apr 1744; died unmarried in 1817.
Jonathan, b. 24 May 1746; died as an infant.
Rebecca, b. 3 Jul 1747; m. Asa Geer.
Lucy, b. 6 May 1749; m. Samuel Flint.
George, twin, b. 7 Apr 1751; died young.
William, twin, b. 7 Apr 1751; m. Anna Slate.
George II, b. 16 Nov 1753; m. Sarah Simmons.

(George Martin, 3rd. died 30 July 1794 GS and is buried in South Cemetery,
Hampton. Sarah (Durkee) died 5 Dec 1807 recorded in Windham but not buried
beside her husband. Some report her as being buried in West Randolph, VT
where her son Gidwon and daughter Lucy Fling lived.)

ELIPHALET DURKEE and **ELIZABETH MARTIN** were m. 29 Nov 1787 and had 4 children:
  Eliphalet Jr., b. 18 Jul 1789; died unmarried.
  David Martin, b. 24 Apr 1792; m. Miranda Spencer; lived in Chautauqua County,
    New York.
  Elizabeth, b. 18 Feb 1797; m. Darius Knight.
  Chloe, b. 18 Mar 1803; died unmarried in 1813.

(Eliphalet, Sr. d. 17 June 1813 & Elizabeth 5 Jun 1815. Both are buried in
South Cemetery, Hampton, Connecticut.)

BENJAMIN DURKEE and **LORA MARTIN** were married 26 August 1804 in Windham, Connecticut. They had 6 children:

Lora, b. 26 Jun 1805; d. 1834, probably unmarried.
Arba, b. 19 Sep 1807; m. Hannah Chaffe.
Alba, b. 2 Oct 1809; d. unmarried 1827.
Annah, b. 3 Nov 1815; m. Edward C. Grant.
Alonzo (or Lorenzo) Martin, b. 15 Nov 1821; probably died young.
Mary Almira, b. 12 Oct 1824; d. a child in 1827.

(Benjamin and Lora removed to Vermont in about 1808, living in Tunbridge, Brookfield and Randolph. Benjamin died 9 Aug 1862 and Lora 23 Feb 1828. Both are buried in Brookfield.)

NATHANIEL DURKEE and **KEZIAH MARTIN** were married about 1750 and had 5 children:
Erastus, b. about 1750/1; married, but wife not known.
Nathaniel, b. 23 Sep 1757; m. (1) Lucy Warner; m. (2) Catherine McRae; m. (3) Mrs. Melinda Bartlett.
Samuel, b. ca 1759; m. Rhoda Mott.
Keziah, b. 24 May 1761; m. (1) Dr. Elisha Camp; m. (2) Capt. Enoch Ely.
Mary, bpt. 10 Mar 1766; m. David Merwin.

(Nathaniel and Keziah apparently moved to New York, but the location and dates of their deaths is unknown.)

###

SUSANNA (NORTH) MARTIN - ANOTHER SALEM WITCH

Susanna (North) Martin was the second wife of George Martin (1st) and the mother of George Martin, Sr. She was one of the innocent victims of the witchcraft mania and was executed as a witch in 1692. Susanna was above the average in intelligence and moral courage, an outspoken, fearless woman, very far from being a hypocrite. At the time of her trial she had been a widow for six or seven years. Her children were all of age, so the management of the farm fell upon her, and she came in contact with rough, uncivil persons who would not venture to treat men so ill. Captain Jonathan Walcot and Sgt. Thomas Putnam charged her with acts of witchcraft upon Mary Walcot, Abigail Williams, Ann Putnam and Mercy Lewis of Salem village.

TESTIMONY OF JARVIS RING Jarvis Ring testified on 13 May 1692 that 7 or 8 years previous he had been several times afflicted at night by somebody or something coming upon him when he was in bed. Something would lay upon him and he could neither move nor speak. Sometimes it made a noise which was heard by others, but when they came near him it would be gone. He never saw anything except one time when he saw Susanna Martin. She bit his finger and then laid upon him as before. The print of the bite is yet to be seen on the little finger of his right hand for it was hard to heal.

TESTIMONY OF THOMAS PUTNAM Thomas Putnam, aged 40, testified on June 30th that he had been conversant with most of the afflicted persons, namely Mary Walcot, Mercy Lewis, Elizabeth Hubbard, Abigail Williams, Sarah Vibber, and Ann Putnam, Jr. and had often heard them complain of Susanna Martin torturing them. He has seen marks of several bites and pinches that they said she hurt them with. Also, on 2 May 1692, the day of the examination of Susanna Martin those persons were most greviously tortured during the time of her examination for upon the glance of her eyes they were struck down and almost choked. And upon the motion of her finger they were afflicted and if people had not clenched her hands or held her head aside, the afflicted persons would have suffered more.

TESTIMONY OF SARAH ATKINSON Sarah Atkinson, aged 48, testified on 30 June 1692 that sometime in the Spring about 18 years since, Susanna Martin came into her house at Newbury from Amesbury. It was in an extraordinary dirty season when it was unfit for anyone to travel. When she walked into the house Sarah asked if she came from Amesbury on foot. She said she did. She asked her how she could come at this time on foot and she bid her children to make way for her to come to the fire and dry herself. She replied that she was as dry as Sarah and Sarah was startled that she was so dry and told her she would have been wet up to her knees if she had come so far on foot. She (Susanna) replied that she scorned to have a "Drabled tayle."

TESTIMONY OF BARNARD PEACH Barnard Peach, age 43, testified on May 11th that 6 or 7 years previously he was living in Jacob Morall's house in Salisbury. He was in bed on a Sunday night and he heard a squabbling at the window. Then Susanna Martin of Amesbury jumped thru the window dressed in the same hood, scarf, and dress she wore at a meeting the same day. She drew his body into a hoop and laid upon him for 1-2 hours during which time he could not speak. Finally he grabbed her hand and bit three fingers hard enough to break them. She then went down the stairs and out the door. He called the other people in the house. There was a bucket at the door with a drop of blood on the handle, two more on the snow and a print of her two feet about a foot from the door, but there were no other footprints.

SUSANNA'S TRIAL, 2 MAY 1692 As soon as Susanna entered the courtroom many people had fits. Abigail Williams identified her as Goody Martin who had hurt her. Others by fits were hindered from speaking. Elizabeth Hubbard and John Indian said she had not hurt them. Mercy Lewis pointed to her and fell into a fit. Ann Putnam threw her glove at her. Susanna laughed.

Accuser: Why do you laugh?
Susanna: Well I may at such folly.
Accuser: Is this folly? The hurt of these people?
Susanna: I never hurt man, woman or child.
Mercy Lewis: She hath hurt me a great many times and pulls me down.
Susanna laughed again. Mary Walcot and Sue Sheldon also accused her of afflicting them.
Susanna: I have no hand in witchcraft.
Accuser: What ails these people?
Susanna: I do not know
Accuser: But what do you think?
Susanna: I do not desire to spend my judgement upon it. I desire to lead myself according to the word of God.
Mercy Lewis: You have been a long time coming to the court today but you came fast enough at night.
Her accusers said they could not come near her.
Accuser: What is the reason they cannot come near you?
Susanna: I cannot tell. It may be the Devil bears me more malice than another.
Accuser: What is the reason they cannot come near you?
Susanna: I do not know but they can come if they will or else I will come to them.

SECOND TRIAL On 27 June 1692 Susanna was again brought to trial and accused of a number of acts.
   1. She made a threat concerning John Allen's oxen.
   2. She "afflicted" Abigail Williams.

78

3. She frightened and choked Elizabeth Brown and caused her to become insane.
4. She caused John Pressey of Amesbury to become lost and to see strange lights.

THE DEATH WARRANT Susanna was convicted along with Sara Good, Rebecca Nurse, Elizabeth How and Sarah Wildes on Tuesday 19 July 1692. The warrant was signed and they were hung that same day.

BOYNTON - AN ESSEX COUNTY/OHIO CONNECTION

By Margaret S. Rose, 2011 20th Street, Portsmouth, Ohio 45662

JOHN BOYNTON, the three times great-grandfather of **ASA BOYNTON, SENIOR**, was born at Knapton, Wistingham, East Riding of Yorkshire, England in 1614, and came to Massachusetts and settled at Rowley in 1630. He was a tailor and married Helen Pell of Boston. He died February 18, 1670 and was the father of eight children, one of whom was **CAPTAIN JOSEPH BOYNTON**. He was born in 1644 and married Sarah Swan by whom he had eleven children. He died December 16, 1730. One of his sons, **SERGEANT RICHARD BOYNTON**, was born November 11, 1675, and married Sarah Dressler and had seven children. He died December 25, 1732. One of his sons, **NATHANIEL BOYNTON**, the father of Asa, was born August 18, 1712. He married Mary Stewart, 1736, by whom he had twelve children, and Asa was the eleventh in order of their births.

ASA BOYNTON was born 4 March 1760, and married Mary Edmunds, daughter of Joseph and Mary Edmunds, of Lynn, Massachusetts April 10, 1781. She was born in Lynn August 9, 1762. They resided first at Lynn and then moved to Grafton County, New Hampshire at Piermont. In 1806 he came to the French Grant (Ohio) for the purpose of looking out a location. He went back to New Hampshire and negotiated the purchase of 3,800 acres of the Gervais Tract, and 650 acres outside, from Rosewell P. Hunt, brother of Samuel Hunt and executor of his last will and testament, for the sum of $9,000. Samuel Hunt died 27 July 1807. The mortgage was foreclosed and the 3,800 acres were sold to Earl Sproat at

Sheriff's Sale for $5,700, April 18, 1810. Boynton got a warranty deed from Rosewell P. Hunt, dated January 15, 1810.

ASA BOYNTON and his family made the trip overland from New Hampshire to their new home in 1810.

Children of Asa Boynton and Mary Edmunds:
i   Mary, b. 17 Dec 1781; d. 4 May 1797
ii   Asa, b. 4 Aug 1784; d. 30 Aug 1802
iii   Lucy, b. 6 July 1787; d. 29 Nov 1787
iv   Lydia, b. 21 Feb 1789; m. James B. Prescott 12 Nov 1815; d. 23 Feb 1825.
v   Joseph E., b. 21 Feb 1791; m. Betsey Wheeler 18 Jan 1813; d. 17 Aug 1817.
vi   Charles C., b. 29 Dec 1792; m. Rhoda Sumner, dau. of Capt. Edward C.
            Sumner of Peacham, VT, 13 Mar 1814; d. Aug 1837.
vii   Cynthia, b. 13 Jun 1795; m. Benjamin Locke 22 Dec 1814.
viii   Lucy, b. 22 Nov 1797; m. George William 30 Nov 1818; d. 3 Nov 1883.
ix   William L.
x   Mary, b. 9 July 1802; m. Thomas Rogers 1 June 1822.
xi   Jane Ann, b. 7 Mar 1805; m. Thomas Whittier 19 Dec 1821; d. 19 Nov 1891.
xii   Asa, b. 21 July 1807; m. Julyia Bertrand, 25 Dec 1828; d. about 1880.
xiii   John L., b. 17 July 1811; m. Felicite Bertrand 13 Feb 1836; d. 12 Aug
            1858.

ASA BOYNTON built several mills for grinding wheat and corn, one of which was back of Ironton, Ohio. He was treasurer of Green Township, Ohio, during 1819 and 1820; died 21 February 1837 and his wife died 23 July 1823.

WILLIAM L. BOYNTON, son of Asa and Mary Boynton, was born in Piermont, Grafton County, New Hampshire in 1800, and came with his parents to French Grant, Ohio, in 1810. He was married on 1 January 1822 to Nancy Feurt, was one of the first white inhabitants of Scioto County, Ohio, having come to Alexandria shortly after it was laid out.

Children of William F. Boynton and Nancy Feurt:
i   Mary, m. Doctor Mussey.
ii   Cynthia, m. (1) Samuel Skelton; m. (2) Alva Jaynes.
iii   Peter, m. Eliza J. Cadot.
iv   James
v   Henry, lived at Powellsville, Ohio.
vi   Asa
vii   William who went to Florida. He was Justice of Peace from 1844-1847; was
            Commissioner of Scioto County, Ohio from 1840-1846. d. 12 July 1870.

PETER FEURT BOYNTON was born near Franklin Furnace, Ohio, 17 October 1822. He offered his services to his country at the outbreak of the Civil War but was rejected on account of a crippled hand. He was a trustee of Green Township, Ohio in 1856-7 and in 1858-9, serving two terms. He was a member of the Haverhill, Ohio M.E. Church. He married 10 January 1848 Eliza J. Cadot, dau. of Claudius Cadot.

Children of Peter Feurt Boynton and Eliza J. Cadot:
i   Orin, m. Urania Bush. She m. (2) George M. Clary of Ironton, Ohio.
ii   Asa, of Haverhill, Ohio, m. Margaret Feurt, dau of Henry and Mary A.
            Feurt.
iii   Carrie, m. H. W. Farnham.

WILLIAM SAVILLE, born Mar. 17, 1770, died Jan. 12, 1853
Esther Pool, born Dec. 23, 1777, died Oct. 15, 1798.

They were married Mary 23, 1796.

CHILDREN

William Oliver, born Nov. 7, 1796, died August 28, 1832.
George, born July 28, 1798, died Oct. 20, 1798.

SALLY BYLES LITTLEHALE, born Apr. 30, 1781, died Sept. 13, 1829.

Married WILLIAM SAVILLE Dec. 6, 1804.

CHILDREN

Nathaniel Tucker, born March 25, 1808, died May 28, 1826.
George, born Apr. 3, 1810, died May 25, 1882.
    He married Mary P. Collins, Dec. 25, 1837.
ESTHER, born June 19, 1812, died June 16, 1900.
    She married George W. Somes, Oct. 30, 1842. He died Mar. 13, 1889.
Adeline Trask, born July 15, 1814, died Nov. 28, 1900.
    She married Joseph E. Davis, Dec. 4, 1836.
Charles, born Dec. 12, 1816, died Mar. 10, 1906.
    He married Abigail O. Marchant, Oct. 29, 1846. She died Jan. 14, 1851.
Richard Littlehale, born Jan. 22, 1819, died Jan. 25, 1897.
    He married (1) Mary Byam on May 5, 1844. She died August 9, 1844.
    He married (2) Harriotte Johnson Hovey, Oct. 29, 1846. She died
        June 21, 1902.
Arria, born Dec. 21, 1821, died June 1, 1901.
    She married James Hovey Apr. 30, 1846. He died March 26, 1889.
Edgar, born Mar. 14, 1825, died Nov. 12, 1826.
Sarah Byles, born Aug. 31, 1827, died Aug. 23, 1875.

WILLIAM SAVILLE married for his third wife, Martha Denin Roberts, a widow,
        March 6, 1831. She was born Apr. 11, 1786, died June 16, 1864. There
        were no children by this marriage.

WILLIAM SAVILLE was in early life a school teacher and a trader at Sandy Bay,
which was then a part of Gloucester, but since incorporated as a separate town
under the name of Rockport. Here he married his first wife, Esther Pool,
removing after her death to the "Harbor." Here he resumed his occupation as
teacher and was for some time secretary of the Gloucester Marine Insurance Co.
At a later period he engaged in mercantile business with Benjamin K. Hough under
the name of Hough & Saville. At the dissolution of this firm, March 10, 1826,
he continued the business alone for a time and subsequently formed a co-
partnership with his nephew, James Saville, under the name of W. & J. Saville.
This firm having been dissolved, William was again without a partner and carried
on the business for some years alone. During all this period of business life
he was frequently employed as administrator upon estates, conveyor of land,
scrivener, etc., and for about twenty years he was annually elected to the
office of town clerk. He also held for many years a commission as Notary
Public.

RICHARD LITTLEHALE SAVILE, born in Gloucester, Jan. 22, 1819. He married Mary Byam, May 5, 1844. She died August 9, 1844. He married for his second wife, Harriotte Johnson Hovey, Oct. 29, 1846.

CHILDREN

Harriotte Johnson, born Oct. 13, 1847, died July 22, 1871.
William, born June 30, 1854.

In March 1833, at the age of 14 years, RICHARD LITTLEHALE SAVILLE entered the office of the "Gloucester Telegraph" as an apprentice at the printing business. In July of the same year he went with his employer, William E. P. Rogers, to Bangor, Me., where he remained about four years working at his trade, most of the time in the office of the "Bangor Courier," a weekly neswpaper, afterward becoming a daily under the name of "Whig and Courier." In October 1837, he removed to Boston, entering the counting room of Littlehale & Co., wholesale grocers, as clerk. Upon the dissolution of that firm he became a partner, January 1, 1844, in the new firm of Kendrick, Trundy & Co., which succeeded them and continued in the business at the same place and under various firm names until January 1, 1870 when he retired from business. On the first of January 1877, he again embarked in the grocery business with his nephew, George H. Somes, under the name of Saville, Somes & Co. From 1844 to 1870 his place of business was at #8 South Market Street, now #46. The firm of Saville, Somes & Co. occupied the two stores on State Street, #268 to #274. William Saville was admitted as a partner in this firm January 2, 1882 and in April 1886, the firm removed to #55 Commercial Street.

EDGAR SAVILLE, youngest son of William and Sally B. Saville, born March 14, 1825, died November 12, 1826. His death was occasioned by falling into a tub of hot water while playing about the kitchen on a washing day.

SARAH BYLES SAVILLE, youngest child of William and Sally B. Saville, born in Gloucester August 31, 1827, died in Chelsea, August 23, 1875.

##

(Excerpts from a paper presented by George Saville, grandson of Jesse Saville, at a Saville Gathering at Annisquam in October, 1863)

". . . We will now turn our attention to JESSE SAVILLE whose nuptials we are here today to celebrate. He married Martha Babson, October 6, 1763, built an addition to the easterly end of his father's house and occupied it. Here were born to them nine children. A portion of his early life was spent at Ipswich where he served an apprenticeship at the tanning business and when he returned he built some vats in what is now known as the tan-yard, and erected there a small building as a tan-house. Here he prosecuted the business of tanning upon a small scale. His occupation in this line was not so great as to prevent him from paying his attention to some extent to the coopering business which he probably learned from his father, making ox bows, scythe snaths, and sundry other small articles of woodenware. He also found time to build cellars and walls for his neighbors, write deeds and other documents, administer upon estates, etc., and to cultivate his own soil, disposing of a part of the proceeds to others.

Notwithstanding this variety of employment he was undoubtedly poor, and his children , as soon as they were large enough for manual labor, were compelled to lend their aid in the maintenance of the family. About the year 1770, impelled probably by his necessities, he was induced to accept official position under the Colonial government in the Revenue Service which brought upon his head the maledictions of the inhabitants, some of whom perpetrated upon his person and property the grossest indignities. (See Babson's History of Gloucester.)

Soon after the Revolutionary War, probably from prudential motives, he removed with his family to New Boston where he remained until the end of the contest when he returned to his old home in Gloucester. As evidence of his straightened circumstances I will relate what my father has told me of his residence at New Boston: "The building the family occupied was an old tumble-down affair, in one end of which sheep were kept, while in the other he could lie in his bed, look through the roof and see the stars. Here it was that my father first commenced school-keeping with a barn for the schoolhouse and the cribs of the cattle the seats for the children."

It is recorded that in 1779 John Saville, second son of Jesse, left home and was never heard from again. He was but 11 years old at the time and his disappearance must have been to his father an added affliction to those he had already been called upon to endure. Soon after the death of his first wife, Jesse Saville married Hannah Dane of Hamilton. That my grandfather had made no considerable progress in the accumulation of this world's goods up to the time of his second marriage is evident from the fact related to me by my father. "When my father was about to be married and was going to Hamilton for his bride, knowing that I had a silver French crown (all the money I had in the world and which I had stored up for a long while) he came to me and told me what he was going to do and requested the loan of the crown for he had not a farthing of his own. I rather reluctantly let him have it. He went to Hamilton on horseback and returned with his new wife upon the crouper, but my money was never repaid."

. . . As first I remember Jesse Saville, he was far advanced in life, being nearly 80 years of age, occupying the first story of the easterly end of the house, his daughter Hannah who had married Timothy Hodgkins living in the rooms above; Mary, her sister, I have but little recollection of except that she married a Mr. Rowell of Sandy Bay and went there to live and died shortly after. Grandfather died March 11, 1823 and his remains were deposited in the old burial place near Hodgkins Cove. I was present with my father and other members of his family at the funeral ceremonies and followed the body to its final resting place. It was a cold, blustering day and just as the procession had started an alarm of fire was raised and looking back we could see the shingles upon the roof of the ell in a blaze, probably from a spark from the chimney. A few minutes detention of the procession, however, saw all safe and it again moved on. . . In his last sickness and when very near the end of his earthly career, my father went to visit him. He inquired for my brother Nathaniel and myself and when informed that we were not there, requested that we might be brought to him that he might lay his hands upon our heads and bless us as did Israel the sons of Joseph. When father returned home he told us that we must start early the next morning for Squam and for what purpose. I thought it strange that father should tell us we must go, for I did not comprehend the significance of our mission. The next morning we were early dressed in our best suits (a very unusual thing when going to grandfather's) and started on our journey. We were led into his bedroom, but were too late. He did not recognize us and, there-fore, we did not receive his blessing. But, though the outward form was wanting, I hope we did not miss it altogether."

THE OLD HOME AT 258 MAIN STREET, GLOUCESTER, MASSACHUSETTS

The house in Gloucester which was the homestead of Richard Littlehale, in which all of his children were born and in which he died, came to him by his wife, Sarah Edgar. She inherited it from her first husband, Henry Edgar, who purchased it from the heirs of John Knowlton, by whom it is supposed to have been built. How old the house was at the time of Mr. Edgar's purchase in 1771 is unknown, but it had probably been occupied by Mr. Knowlton and was sold in consequence of his death and the removal of his widow from the town.

William Saville became the purchaser of this house soon after his marriage with the daughter of Richard Littlehale, December 6, 1804, and occupied it, with a brief interval of absence, until his death. Here all their children (with perhaps a single exception of their son Nathaniel) were born.

It was purchased September 13, 1855 by Mrs. Esther Somes, wife of George W. Somes and daughter of William Saville, and has been occupied by her family from that time to the present (1881).

COPY OF A DEED OF THE EDGAR-LITTLEHALE-SAVILLE-SOMES HOMESTEAD
Spring Street (now Main), Gloucester

FROM THE HEIRS OF JOHN KNOWLTON TO HENRY EDGAR.

Know all men by these presents that I, Jonathan Herrick of Manchester in the County of Essex, yeoman, administrator on the estate of John Knowlton, late of Gloucester, in said County in the Province of the Massachusetts Bay, with the consent of Mary, the widow of said Knowlton, deceased, who hereby resigns and quits her right of dower in the estate hereinafter described, in my said capacity by virtue of an order of the Superior Court of judicature holden at Salem within and for the County of Essex on the 1st Tuesday in November, Anno Domini 1770, in consideration of the sum of 163 pounds, 6 shillings and 8 pence, lawful money paid me by Henry Edgar of Gloucester aforesaid, mariner, the receipt whereof I do acknowledge, do give, grant, sell and convey unto the said Henry Edgar, his heirs and assigns, a certain parcell of land lying near Spring Cove in Gloucester aforesaid in the Harbour, so called, with a dwelling house thereon, lying in two pieces, one on the northerly side of the highway whereon the said dwelling house stands, butted and bounded as follows, viz: beginning by the land of William Dollivar...northwesterly by said Dollivar's land 132 feet to a stake, thence northeasterly 69 feet to another stake, thence southeasterly 108 feet to a stake by the way and thence...southwesterly to the point first mentioned. Also, another piece of land on the southerly side of the way beginning at a stake by the said way, running southwesterly along said way 60 feet to another stake, thence southeasterly to the Cove and a stake 80 feet, thence northeasterly by the Cove about 60 feet, thence northwesterly 80 feet to the point first mentioned...

In witness whereof I, the said Jonathan Herrick, and Mary, the widow of the said John Knowlton...have hereunto set their hands and seals this 15th day of January in the 11th year of His Majesty's reign, 1771.

Signed, sealed and delivered in the presence of us: Daniel Witham, Mary Witham, Nathaniel Lee, Elizabeth Lee.

Signed, Daniel Witham, Justice of the Peace.

WILLIAM MURRAY: AN EARLY IRISH SETTLER OF WEST LYNN

By Helen Gallagher Breen

When my paternal great-great-grandfather William Murray arrived from Ireland in 1836, the Waterhill section of West Lynn was well established. A century before, prominent families had settled by the banks of Strawberry Brook near the main road which led to Boston. Slowly, however, the area became industrialized because of the abundant water supply. (Strawberry Brook has long since been diverted underground.) Tanneries and shoe shops were scattered among the field and orchards.

When the original inhabitants sought greener pastures elsewhere in Lynn, many Irish immigrants were eager to acquire their property. Among them was William Murray who purchased for fifty dollars on March 16, 1843, "a lot of land bounded North by Water Hill ... containing about one acre, more or less, with a half house and shed thereon standing." The parcel was bought from Abigail Tarbox. Abutters' names included Johnson, Breed, Newhall and Cox. Murray's flowing signature contrasts with the mark "X" made by the seller. A year later, Murray added an adjoining piece of "forty rods, more or less" from Thomas B. Newhall for one hundred dollars. Bit by bit, Murray built his domain. A small shoe shop was constructed in the yard. The homestead contained a beautiful orchard. Tradition maintains that Murray was generous with its produce. When streets were cut through the area, Murray Street was named for him.

William Murray was listed in the City Directory of 1840 and in all subsequent records as a "tanner," a trade which employed hundreds of Lynners. The farm supplied food and dairy products for Murray's young family. The 1850 Census lists seven children: Bridget 17, John 15 (born in Ireland), Margaret 13, Maria 11, William 9, Anne 7, and James 4 (born in Lynn). These seven children each had seven children. Such Biblical multiplicity persuaded me to limit my genealogical search to direct lines only. No wonder my father often said that his family was related to "everyone" in West Lynn!

William Murray was destined to play a part in local history. He was one of the founders of St. Mary's, the first Catholic Church in Lynn, during a period of strong anti-Catholic feelings in Massachusetts. These prejudices which had developed throughout the early nineteenth century were inflamed during the late 1840s by the flood tide of Irish immigrants surging into the Boston area to escape the ravages of famine in the old country.

In 1831, Lynn became a mission station of St. Mary's Church in Salem. The first mass in Lynn was celebrated in the home of Lawrence Birney on Waterhill Street on October 22, 1833. Margaret Murray Murphy, William's third child, was the first Catholic baby to be baptized in the city. By 1845, Catholics worshipped in the Town Hall on Lynn Common. Reverend Patrick Strain was appointed pastor. Later, Catholics occupied an abandoned Methodist meeting house on Ash Street (in the present area of Elm and South Streets). Murray and his family were active members of the congregation. These parishioners did not escape the anti-Catholic climate of the times. On the night of May 28, 1859, the Ash Street structure was burned to the ground. Although Father Strain suspected arson, no charges were made.

(Recently, I read Father Strain's diary at the Archives of the Archdiocese of Boston concerning the incident. He named a neighbor, Mark Healey as the culprit. Strain wrote: "Healy always wanted the land and acted like a crazy man about it . . . he has gone to the Bishop . . . he has sworn by God that the Church would be burned down. . . He attemped to maliciously drive my horse away by striking him."

A beautiful Gothic Church was built on South Common Street in 1862. St. Mary's served greater Lynn. A dozen parishes would be carved from her boundaries through the years.

William Murray mortgaged part of his property to help build St. Mary's Church. He was the "straw man" in the purchase of land for St. Mary's Cemetery on Lynnfield Street in 1858. Nativist sentiment was queasy about Catholic burial grounds at this time. The deed for the cemetery purchase, on file at the Archives, named Thomas B. Newhall as the seller, the same person from whom Murray had purchased the Waterhill property in 1842. The parcel was sold to John B. Fitzpatrick, bishop of Boston.

When William Murray died on May 12, 1884, the Lynn Reporter observed:

"William Murray, the first or one of the first settlers of Waterhill, died Sunday at the age of 83. Mr. Murray was of a genial nature and received the appellation of "The Father of Waterhill." He took deep interest in St. Mary's Parish, of which he was one of the original members, contributing largely towards its success. He was held in high regard for his sterling worth."

William's good wife Mary E. Riley preceeded him in death. A perplexing question remains. The family always believed that when Mary was a young girl in Ireland, she had brought food into the bogs for her cousin, John Boyle O'Reilly when he was on the run from the British soldiers before being captured and sent to Dartmoor Prison. Later O'Reilly fled to America, establishing himself in Boston as a poet and the editor of the Pilot. This episode could not have happened because the Murrays were well settled in Lynn when O'Reilly was born in Ireland in 1844. However, the similarity of names suggests a connection. Most likely the young girl who aided O'Reilly was a relative of Mary's whose story was related in a letter sent to the Murrays in Lynn.

While on the subject of letters, one bit of Waterhill apocrypha deserves telling. A member of the Sullivan family, who were Murray's neighbors, wrote home after emigrating that he lived "upstairs" on Waterhill Street, a concept which his relatives on the other side could not understand. They sent a letter back addressed: "Sullivan, Waterhill Street, upstairs, U.S.A." It was received!

William Murray's will, on file at the Salem Probate Court, is a beautiful document inscribed by a clerk before printed forms were widely used. He divided his property equally among his seven children. Five of his offspring and their families were living on the Waterhill "compound." To avoid squabbling, Murray provided "a full right and privilege in and to use the open yard between the houses . . . in the same manner as hitherto enjoyed." The two daughters who did not live in Lynn, Maria Gallagher and Anna McNamara, were given equal shares from the sale of Murray's effects. His brother-in-law, James Riley of Salem, executed the will. Murray left real estate valued at $4504, his personal estate was $764. Quite a substantial amount for a tanner who had provided well for his seven children! Murray's funeral befitted a man in his circumstances. W. C. Chandler was paid $171 for his undertaking services. Other expenses included: a requiem mass, $10; a gown from Mr. Driscoll, $9.78; a floral pillow from Mr. McDowney, $21; and coaches from A. B. Breed, $24. William Murray's funeral was one of the largest ever held in St. Mary's Church.

My father's father was William Gallagher who died in Lynn in 1956 in his eightieth year. He was the son of Maria Murray, William Murray's fourth child, and Patrick Gallagher who came to Lynn from Ireland. Gallagher was a designer of wall paper. The family lived for some time in New York City and also in Roxbury, Massachusetts. My Grandfather, William Gallagher, retained strong ties with his Murray cousins on Waterhill. He married Elizabeth Bowen of Lynn. Her early death from consumption in 1908 was a great sorrow to him. She left six young children of whom my father, Francis Gallagher was the second youngest.

William Gallagher and his wife Elizabeth Bowen were among the founders of Sacred Heart Church in West Lynn in 1894. Both of my father's grandfathers, Patrick Gallagher and Patrick Bowen, served with distinction in the Civil War.

In recent years, my interest in local history has led me to research scores of Essex County figures. To this gallery, I add my paternal grandsire, "The Father of Waterhill." His name will not be found in any history book. Yet, the life of William Murray was a tribute to his family, his church, and the Irish community of West Lynn.

Children of <u>William</u> <u>Gallagher</u> (1868-1956) & <u>Elizabeth</u> <u>Bowen</u> (1868-1908)
(back) Ted, Ella (middle) Alice, <u>Francis</u>, Bill   (bottom) Marie
<u>Francis L. Gallagher</u> (1900-1963) m. <u>Ann Boland</u> (parents of Helen Breen)

ANOTHER ELBRIDGE GERRY

By Marion Gosling

(After reading the two interesting articles in TEG about Elbridge Gerry, I thought your readers might be interested in another Elbridge Gerry)

This Elbridge was born 18 July 1818, and it was claimed that he was the grandson of Elbridge Gerry, the Vice-President. How this can be I do not know as Elbridge Gerry, V.P didn't marry until 1786 at the age of 42. He did have ten children, only three of which were sons; and two of them never married. The third son, Thomas Russell Gerry, born in 1794, married Hannah Goelet, 3 July 1830. Their line is well known as the Goelets were N.Y. society, and through this marriage they were connected with the Livingstons and Harrimans.

But to get back to the other Elbridge, born in 1818 in Massachusetts, . . it is said that after his mother died, his father married again and Elbridge left home, at first going to sea. He is reported to have gone to the far west in 1840 and was employed by Sublet & Bent and afterward by the American Fur Company. He spent a number of years about the North Platt and in Montana trapping and trading. While trapping in the North Laramie Region, he married. "To master an Indian language, marry a dictionary" advised a Mountain Man of long ago. This Elbridge did. He married a Sioux Indian girl. Several children were born of this marriage. Their first child was born in 1843 and named Lizzie. She married Seth Ward, a sutler at Fort Laramie. By 1853, Gerry was carrying on a fairly large trade, and several of his account books are in the library of the Colorado State Historical Society in Denver. Account Book #1 has this on the fly leaf. "E. Gerry his book Boston Mass. born July the 18/1818 age 42 yrs old & 2 months South Fork Platt River K.T. Oct 29/1860" Book 4 gives an inventory of the Indian Trade goods he had on hand on 20 April 1860. In 1860 a Federal Census taker who visited him at Miravalle City on Big Thomspoon Creek 40 miles north of Denver recorded the family as E Gerry age 45 occupation trader value of estate 40000 born Ma.

> Elias Gerry age 17 born Maine
> Henry Gerry age 16 born Mass.
> Mary Gerry age 10 born Nebraska
> Saml Gerry age 8 born Nebraska
> Wm. Gerry age 6 born Nebraska
> Anthony Gerry age 3 born Nebraska

According to this census his wife wasn't living with him. He later married another Sioux woman and had additional children. Gerry had been selling or trading supplies to the new-come gold prospectors who founded Denver. The gold reported at Big Thompson Creek didn't materialize and most of the old trappers moved away. Gerry probably moved at this time to the mouth of Crow Creek. Here on the South Platte about 10 miles east of the site of Greely he developed a fine horse ranch. Later Gerry built a trading post on the south side of the river. This was a stage station on the main road along the river.

In the early sixties when the plains Indians grew hostile towards the whites, Gov. Evans of Colorado needed trustworthy helpers dealing with the red men. He wrote "I found when I came here, a few of the old traders that had come out for the fur companies, long before the white settlers were even here, who

were still living here with their Indian wives. Among these, the man that
became my messenger to the Indians and my interpreter to the Cheyennes and
Arapahoes was Elbridge Gerry, a well-educated man and a grandson of the Elbridge
Gerry of Mass. This E. Gerry was acquainted with all the leading men of the
Arapahoes, Cheyennes & Sioux tribes of Indians and consequently being a very
intelligent man, was a very valuable assistant to me in my negotiations with the
Indians." A commission was appointed to negotiate with the Indians in 1863
which was made up of the Governor and two Indian agents. They hired Gerry to
visit the tribes and try to arrange a meeting between them and the commissioners. In July of 1863 Gerry, with a four-mule team loaded with goods and provisions - furnished by the United States Commissioners as presents - went out to
the head of the Smoky Hill River and tried to induce the Indians to meet the
U.S. Representatives to make a peace treaty. But the Indians said the Buffalo
would last a hundred years and they would not leave their hunting grounds.
Large bands of Indians assembled on the upper Solomon River and from here sent
out raiding parties. The white troops who approached their camp were driven
back. The Indians planned a big attack upon the settlements of the Colorado
frontier. But Elbridge Gerry learned of these plans from his wife's relatives
and made a heroic 65 mile dash to Denver with the news, whereupon the settlers
made preparations for defence. The Indians, learning that their secret was out,
abandoned plans for wholesale attacks. They also learned of Gerry's part in
warning the settlers and took revenge upon him. They visited his ranch and
drove off a large band of horses. The next year they again raided his place on
Crow Creek.

Gerry later submitted to the government a claim for the losses he suffered
during the Indian troubles of 1864 & 1865 which was for $30,600 as follows:

21 Aug 1864 By the Cheyenne Indians for 60 head of horses & mules at $200 each.		$13,200
18 Aug 1865 By the Brule Sioux 21 head of horses at $200		4,000
21 Oct 1865 By Ogalalla Sioux, 88 head of brood mares & young stock at $150 each		13,200

An act for Gerry's relief was passed by Congress and approved by the
President on 10 June 1872. It appropriated $13,200, thus paying the claim for
1864 but not those of 1865. With this money, Gerry built a hotel in the new
town of Evans near Greeley, Colorado. The hotel was still standing in 1953.

Gerry died April 1875 and is buried on a little knoll overlooking the ranch
he developed at the mouth of the Crow Creek. With him is buried his wife, his
son Buster and his son-in-law Seth Ward. Greeley citizens later erected a fence
around his grave, and in the cement head stone wrote "First Permanent White
Settler in Weld County."

An interesting fact about this Elbridge Gerry, received from State
Historical Society of Colorado Library, is that he had a tatoo of a ship on his
arm and remarked that there lay the secret of his life. Seth Ward, his son-in-
law was supposed to have been told the secret, but the knowledge died with him.

##

(Much of this information was taken from an article written by Ann W. Hafen -
Provo, Utah and material from the State Historical Society of Colorado.)

MARY, WIFE OF JOHN[3] BULLOCK

By Marion Anderson

In compiling the genealogy of some of the descendants of Henry[1] Bullock of Salem, Mass., serious inconsistencies were found in published records regarding the identity of Mary, wife of John[3] Bullock (Henry[2-1]). These discrepancies have troubled this writer for some time.

For example, in The History of Salem, by Sidney Perley (II:139), the following information is given:

"John Bullock[3], vintner; injured in fighting the Indians, being made a cripple; became an inn-keeper and brewer; married Mary Maverick Aug. 3, 1681; died 1694; she married secondly Archibald Ferguson of Marblehead in 1697. Children: 1. Elizabeth, born 22 June 1683; 2. John, born April 5, 1686."

The marriage date for John[3] Bullock and Mary (Maverick) plus the birth dates of their children Elizabeth and John are all recorded in the Salem Vital Records (III:163, I:137). John's death date is not on record, however he died intestate and insolvent, with a long list of creditors, circa 21 March 1694/95 when his widow Mary surrendered her dower right to four acres of land in Salem (Essex County Probate File # 3986) No date was found in the Vital Records of Salem or Marblehead for Mary's second marriage to Archibald Ferguson in 1697.

Further, in The History of Salem (I:236 footnote), Perley names the children of Moses Maverick, #8 Mary baptized Sept. 6, 1657; married first John Bullock; second Archibald Ferguson of Marblehead; died 1695. The baptismal date for Mary, daughter of Moses Maverick is recorded in the Salem Vital Records as 6:7:1657, and a Mary Ferguson's death date is recorded in the Marblehead Vital Records as ---- 1695, CR 1 (Vol II; 545).

The issue of Archibald and Mary (Maverick) Ferguson, all baptized in Marblehead are found in the Marblehead Vital Records Vol I:173.

1. Archibald, bpt. 19 Oct 1684, CR 1, d. 26 Oct 1684.
2. James, bpt. 3 Jan 1685/86 CR 1
3. David, bpt. 26 Feb 1687/88 CR 1
4. Archibald, bpt. 11 May 1690 CR 1
5. Mary, bpt. 22 July 1694 CR 1

In the Mayflower Descendant (V:3; July 1903) "Moses Maverick's Will and Inventory and the Settlement of His Estate,"
pp.131-132, The will of Moses Maverick of Marblehead made in January, 1685, names his daughter Mary Ferguson.
pp. 140-141, The final agreement of the heirs of Moses Maverick dated 29 November 1698, names Archibald Ferguson, Trustee in behalf of his children by wife Mary, deceased.

It seems obvious that Mary Bullock couldn't have given birth to two children by John Bullock, one June 1683, and the other 5 April 1686, at almost the same time her first two children by Archibald Ferguson were baptized, one 19 October 1684, the other 3 January 1685/86. Therefore, this writer believes that

Mary, daughter of Moses Maverick, was not the wife of John[3] Bullock, that Mary Maverick married only once and then to Archibald Ferguson.

Evidence has recently been found that appears to indicate that Mary, widow of John[3] Bullock was still alive and still Mary Bullock as late as 14 June 1697, when she sold property in Salem to John Robinson and signed the deed with her mark. However, when the deed was acknowleged 17 January 1697/98 OS (27 January 1698) something usually done by the grantor, it was acknowledged instead by the three original witnesses, Simon Willard, Jeremiah Neale, and Elizar Kezeir (?) who stated they saw Mary sign the deed and they set their hands and seals. This deed Essex County Clerk's Office, Liber 15, leaf 20, seems to suggest that Mary may have died between June 1697 and January 1698.

If, as Perley stated on page 139, Vol. II, History of Salem, Mary Bullock married second in 1697, Archibald Ferguson, it would seem to make sense that she married him as his second wife, and then only for a very short period of time. Who then was Mary, wife of John[3] Bullock?

Unresolved questions:

1. Why did Perly in the History of Salem, (I:236) say that Mary (Maverick) Ferguson, widow of John[3] Bullock and 2nd wife of Archibald Ferguson, died in 1695, then in Vol II; 139, state that Mary (Maverick) Bullock married 2nd in 1697, Archibald Ferguson.

2. Were there two Mary Mavericks?

3. Did Perley and the Salem Vital Records both err in calling Mary (wife of John Bullock) Mary Maverick? To date no other Mary Maverick has been found who logically could have been wife of John[3] Bullock.

4. Could there have been a copyist's error in transcribing Mary's maiden name from the original records which has been perpetuated?

##

MAPS OF NOVA SCOTIA

At the February meeting of ESOG, member Marion Towse showed the group some maps she had obtained for Nova Scotia. She has sent in the following information to answer the many requests she received following the meeting.

These maps, drawn by Ambrose Church between 1865 and 1887, attempted to show the location of all inhabited houses and to indicate the name of the occupant of each. The print is very small but readable. (Use of a magnifying glass is recommended.) The original maps were multicolored whereas the reproductions are black and white.

They are available for all 18 counties of Nova Scotia - each county consists of two Sheets. The cost is $6 per county ($3.00 per sheet). They are available from: Land Registry & Research, Department of Lands and Forests, P.O. Box 698, Halifax, Nova Scotia B3J 2T9. (Note: Must reading for anyone with Nova Scotia roots - "Researching Nova Scotian Ancestry," by Terrance Punch and Cj Stevens in the Oct 1984 NEHG Register.

The Ahnentafel

Ahnentafel of Ruth Emily Ellison, 8 North Lane, Northfield, MA 01360

I	1	Ruth Emily Ellison	1909-	Springfield, VT; Northfield, MA
II	2	Oscar Delos Ellison	1883-1944	Rockingham, Springfield, VT
	3	Mary Egery Allen	1885-1962	Concord, Springfield,, VT
III	4	Delos Ellison	1846-1921	Chester, Rockingham, VT
	5	Addie Philbrick	1854-931	Brewer, ME; Rockingham, VT
	6	William Sylvester Allen	1842-1926	Danville, Concord, Springfield, VT
	7	Louvia Jennet Frye	1848-1922	Concord, Springfield, VT
IV	8	Barney Ellison	1812-1886	Chester, Springfield, VT
	9	Sarah Ann Nash	1817-1868	Springfield, VT
	10	William H. Philbridk	1830-1895	Brewer, ME; New London, CT
	11	Susan Barnes		Brewer, ME
	12	John Gordon Allen	1811-1892	Greensboro, VT; Lowell, MA
	13	Nancy M. Crane	1813-1893	Fitzwilliam, NH; Lowell, MA
	14	Chauncey Frye	1806-1884	Concord, VT
	15	Mary Ann Heywood	1809-1886	Lunenburg, Concord, VT
V	16	John Ellison	1770-1853	Uxbridge, MA; Chester, VT
	17	Jemima Barnes	1784-1832	Chester, VT
	18	Lemuel Nash	1776-1852	Dorchester, MA; Grafton, VT
	19	Anna Mason	1778-1830	New Gloucester, ME
	24	Ethan Allen	1783-1877	Brookfield, MA; Washington, VT; St. Johns, Michigan
	25	Hannah Gordon	1787-1880	Chelsea, VT; St. Johns, Michigan
	26	John Crane	1786-1843	Stoughton, MA; Rindge, NH; Greensboro, VT
	27	Susan Poland	1788-	Winchendon, NH; Greensboro, VT
	28	John Frye, Jr.	1777-1864	Royalston, MA; Concord, VT
	29	Mehitable Brown	1772-1855	Concord, VT
	30	William Heywood	1766-1855	Charlestown, NH; Lunenburg, VT
	31	Mary Egery	1779-1869	Hardwick, MA; Lunenburg, VT
VI	32	John Ellison	1736-	Uxbridge, MA; Chester, VT
	33	Mary Tamplins	1742-	Dighton, MA;
	36	Jonathan Nash	1756	Dorchester, Worcester, MA
	37	Ann Bird		Poland, ME
	38	Ebenezer Mason	1732-1876	New Gloucester, ME
	39	Anna Cleaves	1746-1796	New Gloucester, ME
	48	William Allen, Jr	1752-1841	Bridgewater, MA; Lyme, NH; Craftsbury, VT
	49	Zilpha Gilbert	1755-1836	Brookfield, MA; Lyme, NH; Craftsbury, VT
	50	John Gordon	-1798	Scotland; Antrim, NH; Chelsea, VT
	51	Esther Snow		Antrim, NH; Chelsea, VT

###

Ahnentafel of Margaret Joy Bailey, Box 86, Swans Island, Maine

I	1	Margaret Joy Bailey	1955-	Damariscotta, ME
II	2	Norman Sprague Bailey	1912-	Malden, MA

	3	Margaret Ann Hurley	1928-	Boston, MA
III	4	George M. Bailey	1871-1946	Princeton, ME; Plainville, MA
	5	Jessie Helen Sprague	1892-1958	Swans Island, ME; Plainville, MA
	6	Jeremiah Hurley	1879-1938	Boston, MA
	7	Augusta L. Hanousek	1889-1963	Lawrence, Haverhill, MA
IV	8	James Breen		
	9	Caroline McGlaughlin		
	10	Charles Edwin Sprague	1849-1870	Swans Island, ME
	11	Clara Marie Gott	1853-	Swans Island, ME
	12	John Hurley	1849-	Cork, Ireland
	13	Julia Dovovan		Ireland
	14	Joseph Hanousek	1852-1932	Bohemia, Austria; Boston, MA
	15	Sophia Kinzel	1863-1938	Germany; Boston, MA
V	18	Samuel McGlaughlin		
	19	Hannah Mundee		
	20	David Edwin Sprague	1824-1893	Swans Island, ME
	21	Phebe Toothaker Smith	1829-1898	Swans Island, ME
	22	Ambros Gott	1824-	Swans Island, ME
	23	Sarah Ann Herrick	1824-	Swans Island, ME
	24	Timothy Hurley		Ireland
	25	Johanna Growley		Ireland
VI	40	James T. Sprague	1787-183?	Union, Swans Island, ME
	41	Rebecca Hewes - Elwell		
	42	Benjamin Smith	1794-1872	Swans Island, ME
	43	Marjory Toothaker		Swans Island, ME
	44	John Gott	1777-1840	Swans Island, ME
	45	Ruth Barton		
	46	Kimball Herrick	1802-1887	Sedgewick, Swans Island, ME
	47	Abigail Babson		

##

Ahnentafel of Eleanor Norma Dexter, 150 Barker Hill Drive, Guildford, CT 06437 and 82 Wheeler Street, Gloucester, MA 01930

I	1	Eleanor Norma Dexter	1937-	Gloucester, MA
II	2	Harold Clark Dexter	1909-1978	Gloucester, MA
	3	Eleanor Foster Perkins	1911-	Gloucester, MA
III	4	Brant Mess Dexter	1884-1963	Gloucester, MA
	5	Bessie Douglass Clark	1885-1983	Gloucester, MA
	6	Walter Francis Perkins	1889-1970	Gloucester, MA
	7	Christina Elizabeth Foster	1886-1955	Gloucester, MA
IV	8	Edward Francis Dexter	1860-1912	Gloucester, MA
	9	Ida C. Brant	1860-1884	Gloucester, MA
	10	Albert Center Clark	1859-1933	Gloucester, MA
	11	Laura Brown Doublass	1864-1936	Gloucester, MA
	12	Horace Walter Perkins	1864-1941	Gloucester, MA
	13	Emmeline T. Herrick	1862-1937	Gloucester, MA
	14	Francois Fauchet	1857-1889	Gloucester, MA
	15	Susan Johnson (Gay)	1854-1909	Gloucester, MA
V	16	Samuel Dering Dexter	1816-1899	Gloucester, MA
	17	Tamazine Hoyt	1816-1890	Gloucester, MA
	20	William Bishop Clark	1835-1910	Gloucester, MA
	21	Elizabeth Wood Marr	1838-1924	Gloucester, MA
	22	John Douglass	1833-1905	Gloucester, MA

```
    23   Margaret Pushee             1833-1910  Antigonish, N.S.; Gloucester, MA
    24   Levi Gilvert Perkins        1844-1901  Concord, NH; Gloucester, MA
    25   Mary Sophia Lufkin          1846-1921  Gloucester, MA
    26   Gardner Wilson Herrick      1822-1900  Gloucester, MA
    27   Abbie Ann Lee               1827-1892  Manchester, Gloucester, MA
    28   Jean Fauchet                           St. Malo, France
    29   Mary Dennie                            St. Malo, France
    30   James Johnson                          Cape Breton, N.S.
    31   Isabell MacDonald              -1898
VI  32   William Dexter              1789-1830  Boston, Gloucester, MA
    33   Elizabeth Phillips          1792-1827
    34   Chase Hoyt                  1778-      Amesbury, Gloucester, MA
 _  35   Tamazine Griffin               -1846  Gloucester, MA
    40   Gorham Clark                1805-1886  Rockport, Gloucester, MA
    41   Sarah Allen Plumer Adams    1811-1897  Gloucester, MA
    42   Chester Marr                1813-1887  Georgetown, ME; Gloucester, MA
    43   Elizabeth Wood Green        1814-1889  Gloucester, MA
    44   John Douglass               1806-1860  Gloucester, MA
    45   Nancy Norwood               1809-1852  Gloucester, MA
    46   David Pushee                1796-1866  Antigonish, N.S.; Gloucester, MA
    47   Jennie Baxter               1807-1879  Gloucester, MA
    48   Gilbert Perkins             1820-      Topsfield, MA
    49   Mary Marie Antonette Worden 1825-      Pennsylvania; Topsfield, MA
    50   William Lufkin, Jr.         1822-1893  Gloucester, MA
    51   Sophia Walker Rust          1821-1904  Gloucester, MA
    52   Theophilus Herrick          1787-1863  Gloucester, MA
    53   Dorothy (Dolly) R. Bray     1791-1854  Gloucester, MA
    54   Jacob Lee                              Manchester, MA; Illinois
 _  55   Abigail Lufkin Herrick      1805-1902  Gloucester, Manchester, MA
    60   Edward Johnson
 _  61   Susan MacDonald
```

##

Ahnentafel of James S. Mansfield, M.D., P.O. Box 53, Lincoln Center, MA 01773

```
I    1   James S. Mansfield
II   2   George Rogers Mansfield     1875-1947  Washington, D.C.
     3   Adelaide Claflin            1874-1964  Swarthmore, PA
III  4   Alfred Mansfield            1834-1910  Gloucester, MA
     5   Sarah Jane Hubbard          1844-1928  Holden, Gloucester, MA
     6   Harvey Thacher Claflin      1831-1915  Steubenville, Cleveland, OH
     7   Eliza Fertig Scott          1836-1932  Steubenville, Cleveland, OH
IV   8   Alfred Mansfield            1806-1870  Gloucester, MA
     9   Abigail Somes Davis         1811-1900  Gloucester, MA
    10   Samuel Brigham Hubbard      1812-1885  Holden, MA
    11   Sarah Maria Holmes          1817-1906  W. Boylston, Holden, MA
    12   Harvey Claflin              1802-1876  Attleboro, MA
    13   Ann Tyler Thacher           1806-1897  Attleboro, MA
    14   Dr. James Scott Scott       1800-1881  Washington Co., PA; Greeley, CO
    15   Nancy Hammond               1808-1858  Steubenville, OH
V   16   James Mansfield             1765-1842  Lynn, Gloucester, MA
    17   Susan Murphy                1772-1852  Gloucester, MA
    18   Capt. Elias Davis, Jr.      1783-1863  Gloucester, MA
    19   Abigail Somes               1784-1842  Gloucester, MA
```

	20	Samuel Woodward Hubbard	1783-1840	Holden, MA
	21	Betsy Hubbard	1784-1840	Holden, MA
	22	Thomas Holmes	1788-1848	Londonderry, NH; W. Boylston, MA
	23	Sally Graves	1785-1857	Chesterfield, NH; W. Boylston, MA
	24	Noah Claflin, 3rd	1759-1860	Attleboro, MA
	25	Hannah Richardson	1772-1853	Attleboro, MA
	26	Deacon Peter Thacher	1779-1863	Attleboro, MA
	27	Salona Dunham	1780-1824	Attleboro, MA
	28	William Scott	1765-1854	Chester Co., PA; Washington, OH
	29	Elizabeth Coe	1777-1857	Washington, OH; Cedar Co., Iowa
	30	Henry Hammond	1782-1865	near E. Springfield, OH
	31	Mary Beall		near Columbus, OH
VI	32	Col. John Mansfield	1721-1809	Lynn, MA
	33	Sarah Cheever	1730-1780	Saugus, Lynn, MA
	34	William Murphy	1728-1804	County Cork, Ireland
	35	Anna Low	1750-1832	Beverly, Gloucester, MA
	36	Capt. Elias Davis, Sr.	1756-1821	Gloucester, MA
	37	Lucy Haskell	1764-1847	Gloucester, MA
	38	Capt. Samuel Somes, Sr.	1756-1796	Gloucester, MA
	39	Abigail Bray	1753-1811	Gloucester, MA
	40	Deacon Elisha Hubbard	1744-1814	Holden, MA
	41	Mercy Hubbard	1747-1825	Rutland, Holden, MA
	42	Peter Hubbard	1754-1820	Holden, MA
	43	Phoebe Brigham	1752-1810	Sudbury, Holden, MA
	44	Thomas Holmes	1746-1822	Londonderry, NH
	45	Margaret Patterson	1755-1838	Londonderry, NH
	46	Reuben Graves	1753-1786	Athol, MA
	47	Hannah Kendall	1757-1819	Athol, MA
	48	Noah Claflen, 2d	1735-1825	Attleboro, MA
	49	Keziah Carpenter	1733-1788	Attleboro, MA
	50	Vinton Richardson	1744-1820	Attleboro, MA
	51	Hannah White, 3d	1745-1820	Norton, Attleboro, MA
	52	Deacon Peter Thacher	1753-1814	Attleboro, MA
	53	Noanna Tyler	1754-1816	Attleboro, MA
	54	Capt. Abial Dunham	1740-1820	Attleboro, MA
	55	Mahetabel Knapp	1740-1795	Norton, MA
	56	Patrick Scott	1730-1829	Ireland
	57	Lettice Denny	1734-1786	Ireland
	58	Lt. Ebenezer Coe	1736-	
	59	Eunice Jaggers (Jagger)		
	60	George Hammond	1748-1818	Maryland, Spring, OH
	61	Elizabeth Wells	1758-1830	Maryland
	62	Ninian Beall	1755-1831	Maryland, Brooke Co., W. VA
	63	Ann Maria Stricker	1765-1803	Maryland

##

FORTHCOMING AHNENTAFELS

AUG 85: Gail Hepker, Sarah Koehler, Beatrice Goldsmith, Robert Henderson
NOV 85: Jerry Lovejoy, Dorothy Whitford, William Waite, John Stone
FEB 86: Duncan Chaplin III, Jana Hertz, Denise Lovejoy, R. Wallace Hale
MAY 86: Roger Gorham, Oscar Rogers, Harry Whitford, Jr., Roland Rhoades, Jr.

Tools of the Trade

GENEALOGICAL RESEARCH AT THE BOSTON PUBLIC LIBRARY

By William H. Schoeffler

Part II: Bates Hall and the Social Science Reference Room

The Boston Public Library takes quite seriously its role as one of the leading repositories of knowledge in New England and constantly strives to maintain the academic caliber of its Research Collection. Fortunately for the genealogist, BPL's acquisition policy includes special efforts to obtain local histories and genealogies pertaining to New England. Thanks to this BPL policy, researchers will find an extensive collection of surprisingly strong genealogical value. Last issue we focused on the strengths of the Microtext Department, particularly the primary sources available there. Now our attention shifts to the main reading room in the Library's Research Wing, Bates Hall, and the Social Science Reference Room at its north end.

Bates Hall is the primary access point for the bulk of the BPL Research Collection. Most of these books are kept in closed stacks and must be requested by call slip. The extensive card catalog and new microfilm supplement provide the necessary information to identify books you may wish to request. Usually, requested books are delivered to readers in Bates Hall within about 20-30 minutes, although some materials can be consulted only in the Rare Book Room or another of the special collection rooms (such as Government Documents on the first floor). In addition to the books in closed stacks, BPL has a variety of frequently used books on open shelf reference along the walls in Bates Hall and Social Science Reference Room. A third group of books useful to the genealogical researcher is kept on reserve behind the Social Science Reference Desk, where they can be retrieved more readily for reference use.

Genealogists should be familiar with the open shelf reference collection. It is arranged by Library of Congress call numbers and the Massachusetts local history portion of this collection dominates the wall space in the Social Science Reference Room. A full run of the New England Historical and Genealogical Register is a keystone of this collection, together with the available every-name indexes to the first 50 volumes, and a reprint of Savage's indispensable four-volume Genealogical Dictionary of New England. Across the room is a substantial set of published Massachusetts vital records and some of the most important local histories arranged alphabetically by town (still according to LC call numbers). Many leading county histories for Massachusetts are also kept on the open shelves, as are a number of useful works on Boston.

These obvious sources do not exhaust the open shelf reference volumes. The Social Science Reference Room also has low book cases at the ends of the four reading tables with an expansive collection of the Who's Who series. This includes both the current and historical general editions, as well as a wide variety of special subject and locale editions. The recently issued multi-volume Biographical and Genealogical Master Index, which combines the indexes of several hundred special interest publications, and its current three-volume update are also in these bookcases. Elsewhere in the library, several of the works indexed by this Master Index can be consulted.

Perhaps the most significant items in this Reference Room are two special card catalogs. One covers the family genealogies in the BPL Research Collection and provides two supplemental features not found in the main card catalog: cards for vertical file materials (which include some family association newsletters) and special analytic cards to the genealogies. The second special catalog facilitates heraldic research, because it is a 20,000 entry index to family coats of arms, primarily for Great Britain families.

Researchers should not overlook the cartographic cabinet by the vital records shelves. Here are kept the U.S. Geologic Survey maps for all the New England states, and several other detailed maps of historical interest. Detailed atlases of Boston itself and some of the neighboring towns can be quite helpful for determining where cemeteries are, or where your ancestral homesteads may have been. Next to the NEHGS Register, across the room, stands a collection of reference atlases for the United States and the World, which can be helpful for locations outside New England.

Finally, the open shelves have a number of helpful works on military history, historic American events, a biographical set on all State Governors in American history, and a collection of Writer's Project volumes describing many of the individual United States.

Of course, this collection of history books on the open shelves in Social Science Reference is only a portion of the books one finds in Bates Hall. Researchers will also discover leading encyclopedia sets from the USA, Great Britain, France, Germany, Italy, and the Soviet Union. Genealogical subject matter bears the call letters "CS," and the reference shelves include many "how-to" books, the Philby Passenger List Index series, and principal works on peerage, landed gentry, and the major biographical dictionary sets. Along the Dartmouth Street side of the room are a modest group of shipping reference works and many foreign language dictionaries, for those struggling to read foreign genealogical works. Another useful aid for researchers discovering European origins are the reference histories and

travel guides to several countries. Brief descriptions of many towns and regions can be found in them. Especially valuable here are the early Baedeker Guides for many German locales and other parts of Europe as well. England and Ireland are well represented on the reference shelves, too.

At the other end of Bates Hall, in the Humanities Reference Room, the BPL collection of current telephone books covers most parts of the United States and major foreign cities. These allow researchers to discover residences of modern day cousins, descended from common ancestors. Nearby in Bates Hall are a variety of biographical guides and indexes for contemporary people.

The limited shelf space available for the open shelf reference collection should not dismay the researcher. As this discussion has shown, many works can fit. Still, even more reference works are kept within a few steps of the Social Science Reference Desk in the adjacent stack space. Main card catalog entries marked So., Sci. Ref. are available from this desk if they are not on the open shelves. Although these books must be requested, the usual wait is obviated. Typical of the works kept here are some leading journals in the field, such as the Publications of the Colonial Society of Massachusetts, the Massachusetts Historical Society's Proceedings and Collections, and the Essex Institute Historical Collections. Other works of note include all the printed colony and court records of Massachusetts Bay and Plymouth Colonies, and a typescript index to the Suffolk County Inferior Court records.

These reference materials are just the visible tip of the BPL Research Collection iceberg. Many more itesm are hidden away in the closed stacks, so careful searching through the main card catalog is necessary to make full use of the available resources. BPL's coverage of other parts of the United States for genealogies and local histories is a mixed bag. Some gems are there, especially among the large collection of county histories and assorted local volumes collected over the years, but the breadth of this collection naturally suffers from its admitted bias in favor of New England coverage. However, the Library is justifiably proud of its extensive collection on the British Isles, featuring parish records, visitations, county histories, and antiquarian studies.

To get the most out of the BPL Research Collection, users should not stop their search at the card catalog, and the newly introduced microfilm supplement. It is often fruitful to inspect the subject entries in the massive thousand volume New York Public Library Dictionary Catalog. These black volumes fill much of the shelf space in the second room of the BPL main catalog, where letters N-Z are located. The NYPL catalog has many more analytic cards than does the BPL's own catalog, and these are frequently useful for identifying articles of interest in the journals that BPL does hold.

Even if BPL does not have the book or journal you need for your research, this should not deter you. Inter-Library Loan can obtain the book for you from other libraries around the country. Check with the librarians at the Catalog Information Desk for details and the necessary request forms. In this way, you should be able to consult any book you can find in the bibliographies or the National Union Catalog, which is available in the Humanities Reference Room. Do not overlook BPL's membership in the Boston Library Consortium, either. This is a group of some of the leading university libraries in the metropolitan area. By common agreement, they have split up the task of collecting current serials of specialized subject matter, thereby broadening the total coverage without unnecessary duplication of collections. Information about these serials is available on a microfiche union list of serials at the catalog information desk.

One final suggestion will help you get the most out of the research hours you may have available. Once a book has been delivered to your seat from the stacks, you can have it placed on reserve in your name for up to three days at the general request desk, thus avoiding delivery delays on subsequent visits. This can be quite useful for researchers who plan their work around lunch hours, when the delivery time eats into the precious hour.

Additonal Notes. Microtext Department

1) In describing the difference between the federal and state versions of the Boston Passenger Arrival lists, one important detail should be mentioned. The card index created from the state lists is available at the State Archives and can be consulted there.

2) The section describing the "Other Atlantic Ports" passenger lists and the "Supplemental Index" may have been misleading. Several Massachusetts ports are included on the passenger lists film, but Boston is not among them. However, some Boston lists are referred to in the index. The same is true from Philadelphia and New Orleans.

3) One significant collection in the Microtext Department was overlooked. Microfilming Corporation of America has been compiling a fiche collection of significant genealogies and local histories. These are described in a 3-part inventory called "Genealogy and Local History" which BPL has bound in 2 volumes. This lists 560 genealogies, 1230 local histories and 265 published primary sources. All were selected for filming by a distinguished panel of nationally reputed genealogists, and the Microtext Department has the entire series. Several unusual sources are included, and the collection is especially strong on Pennsylvania and Virginia, two areas BPL has not concentrated upon in the past. This microfilming program will continue to add to its collection.

FAMILY ORGANIZATIONS

(A list compiled by Jimmy Goodwin, who writes "Every year around the U.S. are
thousands of Family Organization Reunions. Here are a few that TEG readers
  might be interested in." A few additional Organizations have been added)

ADAMS FAMILY, descendants of Col. John Emery & Sara (Moody) Adams. 1st Sun. Aug.
    Contact: Mrs. Ralph Ebbott, 409 Birchwood Ave., White Bear Lake, MN 55110
ALLEY/ALLY/ALLEE FAMILY. A Family Newsletter: "Allee's All Around" is publis-
    hed by Ginger Rae Allee, P.O. Box 347, Friendswood, TX 77546.
ALLEN FAMILY, Desc. of Wallace Enoch & Mary Jane (McCracken). Ann. Meet. Aug.
    Contact: Howard F. Allen, Box 283, Epping, NH 03042.
BALDWIN FAMILY 75th Reunion was Aug 5, 1984.
    Contact: Edward Matthews, 51 Crest View Drive, Rochester, NY 14625.
CHADBOURNE FAMILY ASSOCIATION
    Box 907, Chadbourne's Ridge, North Waterborough, Maine 04061.
COOLEY FAMILY
    Contact: Mildred Colley, 160 Middle Neck Road, Great Neck, NY 11021.
GOODWIN FAMILY ASSOCIATION, desc. of Daniel of Kittery, ME. 1st Sat in Aug.
    Contact: Mrs. Alice B. Sharp, 13430 Mirella St., Pensacola, FL 32507.
HILDRETH FAMILY
    Contact: Barbara Parkhurst, 7 Overlook Drive, Chelmsford, ME 01824.
HILLS FAMILY
    Contact: Hazel Hills, Rte 2, Box 30, Warren, ME 04864.
HOLT ASSOCIATION OF AMERICA Annual Picnic Meeting Newbury Sat. 15 June 1985,
    350the year of the arrival of Nicholas Holt in Newbury.
    Contact: Melvin L. Holt, Sec/Treas., P.O. Box 112, Candia, NH 03034.
KALLOCH FAMILY
    Contact: Hazel Mills, Rte 2, Box 30 Warren, Maine 04864.
KELSEY KINDRED OF AMERICA
    Contact: Grace Benoit, Sec., 28 Cascade Ct., Stamford, CT 06903.
LIBBY FAMILY - 80th Reunion 22 Sept 1984
    Contact: Steve Libby, Libby Road, West Newfield, ME 04095.
LINDER FAMILY
    Contact: J. Kenneth Linder, Star Rt., Box 364, Walker, MN 56484.
MARSTON FAMILY
    Contact: Mrs. Philip Marston, 6 Emerald Acres, Barrington, NH 03825.
NICKERSON FAMILY ASSOCIATION
    Contact: Jacqui Oakes, R.F.D. #1, Harwich, MA 02645.
ODIORNE FAMILY
    Contact: Barbara O. MacGregor, 25 Farragut Rd., Swamscott, MA 01907.
PAYSON-FOLGER 102nd FAMILY REUNION, 1984
    Contact: Ruth Folger Goff, R.F.D. #1, East Corinth, ME 04427
SANBORN FAMILY, desc. of John & William Sanborn. Assoc. reorganized 1983.
    President: George Freeman Sanborn, Jr.
    Contact: Elizabeth A. Sanborn, Sec., P.O. Box 185, Candia, NH 03034.
RALPH SMITH FAMILY ASSOCIATION Meets September in Nahant.
    (For details, contact Mrs. Corinne Witham, 55 Eastern Ave., Gloucester, MA.
SULLIVAN FAMILY - desc. of Edmund & Delina Sullivan.
    Contact: Mary Leone, 145 George Circle, Vallejo, CA 94590.
WING FAMILY aSSOCIATION
    Contact: Curtis C. Wing, 17 Sandbar Lane, brewster, MA 02631.
WITHAM FAMILY ORGANIZATION
    Contact: Miss Minnie Witham, Rte 2, Plymouth, NH 03264.

Miscellaneous Notes

MASSACHUSETTS STATE ARCHIVES are scheduled to move to Columbia Point in July. The move will take about 2 months. BIG NEWS is they will be open Saturdays 10-3 starting September. A new 12-page booklet (free) called "Researching your Family's History at the State Archives" is now available.

NATIONAL ARCHIVES - BOSTON BRANCH is the new official title of the agency at 380 Trapelo Road, Waltham 02154. They now have the new Soundex Index to New England Naturalization-Petition Records, 1791 - 1906. Ask to see M-1299 for the correct film numbers. All of the actual records are not at Waltham, but the Index will tell you where to find them. The Boston Branch has also received the 3800 microfilm rolls of Revolutionary War Pension and Bounty Land Warrants and Military Service Records. Pension & bounty land warrants are arranged alphabetically by surname; the military records are arranged by unit.

> **WARNING** A confusion to out-of-staters (and in-staters) is that the National Archives - Boston Branch is in Waltham and the Boston Stake of the Church of Jesus Christ of Latter Day Saints (Mormon) is in Weston!

IGI INDEX - NEW ISSUE The International Genealogical Index, which contains 81 million names is now available at Mormon Stake branches. This edition is an increase of 13 million names on microfiche. Hours of service for the Boston Stake Branch (at Weston) are Tuesday 7-9; Thursday 9-3; 7-9; Saturday 9-3.

COLOR COPIES A color-Xerox machine is available at Duprin Copy Center, 14 Henshaw St., Woburn, MA 01801 - just off Rte 128. (Color-Xerox is very suitable for duplicating family photos) 8:30-5:30 Mon-Fri; Sat 9-1. Call 935-4214.

CIVIL WAR INDEX A microfiche copy of the 1890 Massachusetts Census Index of Civil War Veterans or their Widows has been received by the Lynnfield Library. Bryan Lee Dilts is the compiler & it was published in 1985. It can be purchased from Index Publishing, P.O. Box 11476-U, Salt Lake City, UT 84147. The cloth book has 222 pages & costs $52; the microfiche (2 fiche) costs $5.00! The index shows name, state, county, locale, enumerator's district. That info can be used to find original census entry and additional info, if provided, including rank, company, regiment or vessel. A total of 66,317 entries are in the index.

NEW BRUNSWICK The Saint John Branch, New Brunswick Genealogical Society will sponsor a Workshop August 3 - 5. Write to the Society at P.O. Box 3813, Station "B," Saint John, N.B. E2M 5C2, Canada.

GENEALOGISTS HANDBOOK FOR NEW ENGLAND RESEARCH is now being revised by Marcia Wiswall/Lindberg. The new edition should be ready mid-June with all the corrections and additions. Orders will be handled only through the New England Historic Genealogical Society, 101 Newbury St., Boston 02116. Their publication department, under the guidance of Edward Hanson, will publish the book. Price has not been announced as yet.

(Thanks to Rose Morrison, editor of the Newsletter of the National Archives - Boston Branch, and to The Massachusetts Genealogical Council Newsletter (Alicia Williams, Editor) for many items included here)

Our Readers Write

TUFTS/JEFTS Enclosed is further info on Peter Tufts/Peter Jefts and Mary Pierce (TEG, May '84) that might be of interest to your readers. It is from "Tufts Kinsman," newsletter of the Tufts Kinsman Association.

"MARY (PIERCE) TUFTS SPOKE HER PIECE - PAID THE PRICE. Among the amusing incidents of the past, is a case in law, tried in 1660 and copied from the court files of Middlesex County. Peter Tufts, the immigrant of Malden, had whipped and severely abused a man in his employ, who went to his nearest neighbors, James Barrett and William Ludington, told his tale, and wept like a child. For this abuse Tufts was prosecuted, the case was tried, Barrett and Ludington appearing in court as evidence in behalf of the injured man; the case was decided against Tufts. This led Mrs. Mary Tufts, wife of Peter, in her indignation towards Barrett and Ludington to utter these words, viz: "That none spake against her husband at the court, but the skimes of the country, and liars, and them that did not care what they said." For the utterance of these words she was brought before the court and tried for slander, and convicted; here follows the result of the trial. 'The jury brought in their verdict, finding for the plaintiffs damages, ten shillings a peece and an acknowledgement to be made by the defendant at Malden, upon the Lord's day in the afternoon, within the space of thirty days next ensuing, and to be after the public exercise is ended, before the congregation depart manner following viz. in these words. "That whereas I, Mary Tufts am legally convicted of slandering and wronging James Barrett and William Ludington or any other person whom my words might reflect upon by speaking rashly, irregularly and sinfully. I am heartily sorry and do desire to be humbled for the same, and in case of none observance to do as above is promised either to pay ye said ten shillings a peece or making each acknowledgments both for manner and time, the jury do find that ye deff't shall pay unto the plff's fifty shillings a peece and cost of court thirty-one shillings and two pence."'

If persons were thus delt with at the present day, it would give a quietus to many a gossiping and slanderous tongue.",

(John Alley Robbins, Jr., 49 South Front Street, Richmond, ME 04357)

TUFTS KINSMEN, is a publication of the TUFTS KINSMEN ASSOCIATION, Post Office Box 571, Dedham, MA 02025-0571. Subscription $6 per year. $2 per issue. (includes membership in the organization).

###

GERRY In the February issue the discussion of the Geary (etc.) family is of special interest to me. On page 31, #10 Thomas[4] Geary of Stoneham appears "to have removed from Stoneham in later life." I believe that this may be the Geary family of Lancaster and Bolton, Worcester County and I'm especially concerned with Thomas' daughter Keziah. Do you have any further sources of research about them? Keziah Goss of Lancaster m. 21 Feb 1765 Joshua Church of Lancaster. I have never been able to find a Keziah Goss to fit except for Keziah Cary of Lancaster who m. 11 July 1754 (Bolton VR) Ephraim Goss of Bolton. I believe that Ephraim died while serving in the French and Indian War and after two sons were born, Ephraim and Elihu Goss."

(Betty Lou Morris, 96 South Wilson Boulevard, Mount Clemens, Michigan 48043)

Answer: It appears from research to date that Keziah Geary, daughter of Thomas Geary of Stoneham, was the Keziah who married Ephraim Goss. All the children of this family removed to Lancaster, Mass. and married there. More research is now being conducted on the Gearys of the Lancastrian towns, and this research will be published soon in a forthcoming issue of TEG.

##

CAVANAGH I am seeking the Cavanagh family of Edward Isle, Canada. In the thirties and forties Lotta Cavanagh Rice Dunham (Mrs. Melvin A) born May 1891 was working on this line. She at that time resided on Church Lane, Burlington, MA. I am hoping that someone might be working on this line or know what happened to Mrs. Dunham's work.

(Nathalie Siegel, 3869 Lafayette St., Riverside, CA 92503)

##

SPILLER Recent queries and other contacts have brought to light work done and work in progress on the SPILLER family and their connections:
FAMILY HISTORIES IN REPOSITORIES:
   "One Line of the Spiller Family," compiled by Eleanor V. Spiller, 1984.
      copy at Beverly Historical Society. Collateral lines - Cleaves,
      Standley, Ober, Waite.
   "John Spiller and Rebecca Day, His Wife of Ipswich, Mass. and Raymond,
      Maine" compiled by Charles F. Adams, 1957. Copy at Maine Historical
      Society. Collateral lines: Day, Hodgkins, Barton.
   "Genealogical History of Amos L. and Edith Winslow Spiller" compiled by
      Nellie Davis Spiller, 1976. (Actually a family history) Allied
      families: Bryant, Dole, Hodgkins, Manning, Small, Smith Gliddings.
   "Meredith Spiller, His Story and His Descendants" compiled by Wayne
      Spiller, 1975. Many midwestern & Texas surnames. Copy at St. Louis,
      Missouri Public Library.
   "Fragments of Spiller Family History and Genealogy" compiled by Wayne
      Spiller, 1978. Pub. by University Microfilms, Ann Arbor, Michigan.
WORK IN PROGRESS:
   "Progeny of Patriarch Henry Spiller of Ipswich" Researcher Eleanor Spiller
   "Spiller, Pulcifer, Noyes connections" Researcher June Lawson of Orange, MA
   "Spiller, Tripp, Strout, Mayo, Dyer connections" Researcher Rosalind
      Conley of Banning, California.
(Eleanor V. Spiller, 13 Trask St., Danvers, MA 01923)

##

ADDENDA TO GILES COREY Cleaves progeny in "One Line of the Spiller Family and in "William Cleaves of Beverly Genealogy" in progress:
   Giles Corey's daughters -- Deliverance & Henry Crosby: Child: Henry, b.
      14 May 1684 Salem. Elizabeth & John Moulton - Children: Margaret, m.
   Ebenezer Aborn; Elizabeth; John; Miriam; Abigail m. John Burton.
(Eleanor V. Spiller, 13 Trask St., Danvers, MA 01923)

##

Would like to correspond with people working on these lines--from Massachusetts:
THAPPING, TAPPIN, TOPPIN, THAPPIN (Essex Co. Ipswich, Wenham; Marlborouth)
NEWTON from around any area of Mass. (Marlborough, Belchertown, Ashfield)

MORSE Groton, Watertown & Ipswich, Ja.   GREEN Malden
WITT Lynn & Marlborough, Mass.   HILLS Malden & Newbury
MATHEWS md in 1713, Lynn to Witt.   UPHAM Malden & Leicester, MA
LOKER Marlborough   WOOD Malden
LARKIN Charlestown   KITCHEN Salem
SHATTUCK Watertown   GRAFTON Salem
PIERCE Watertown   HUNN Boston, Salem
BAKER m in Lynn? in 1676 to WITT   WALKER Salem
VINTON of Woburn & Lynn   HEATHERED who m. WALKER
LARCUM Ipswich, Wenham.   VINTON of Woburn & Lynn
CASWELL of Easton, Bridgewater, Taunton area

(Mrs. Emma Jean Smith, Rte 1, Box 21, Rocky Hills Ranch, Grass Valley, OR 97029)

###

PASSAMUCKETT   In October 1633, John Winthrop, Jr. was "at Passamuckett." This
was just before he commenced the settlement of Ipswich, Mass. in March 1634.
Where is Passamuckett? It is not found in the "Historical Data - Counties,
Cities & Towns of Massachusetts."

SAWYER HILL BURYING GROUND, NEWBURYPORT Does anyone know the location of the
plot plan of the Sawyer Hill Burying Ground in Newburyport? The superintendent
of the Belleville Cemetery in Newburyport does not know.

(Barbara Washburn, 496 Highland Avenue. So. Portland, ME 04106)

###

DISSERTATIONS RELATING TO MAINE HISTORY The current issue of Maine History News
includes a select list of theses and dissertaticnas relating to Maine history,
completed at the U. of Maine in Orono between 1917-1983. The list was compiled
by Stanley R. Howe, PhD.   Some sample entries appear below:

The Swedish People in Northern Maine by Charlotte M. Lenentine, 1950.
Chapters in the History of Unity, Maine by James Berry Vickery, 1950.
The French Canadian Community in Waterville, Maine, by Joseph Fecteau, 1952.
Chapters in the Early History of the Town of Cape Elizabeth, by William
    Barnes Jordan, 1953.
A Social History of Machias, Maine from 1800 to 1900, by Agnes Arline Gray,
    1954.
The Jesuits in Maine, by Peter Gordan Gowing, 1955.
An Investigation of the Mill Development of Arroostook County, by Maple Ismay
    Percival, 1939.
A History of Woolwich, Maine from Discovery to 1860, by Martha Evelyn Leeman,
    1948.
The Social History of Portland, Maine from 1840 to 1860, by Rosella Adeline
    Loveitt, 1940.
Chapters in the Social and Economic History of Thomaston, by Francis Peter
    Lynch, 1955.

    Would it not be great if some TEG writer would undertake a similar project,
compiling a list of the dissertations and theses submitted to various
Massachusetts universities which relate to Essex County history?
                    (David A. Nichols, Box 76, Lincolnville, ME 04849)

Society News

FORTHCOMING MEETINGS

May 18   Saturday, Centre Church, Lynnfield. (Todd Hall - downstairs)
         Social Hour: 12:00. Lecture promptly at 1:00
         Speaker: Richard Trask, Archivist, Town of Danvers, Mass.
         Topic: Mr. Trask will talk about his experiences as Historical Con-
         sultant for the TV Docudrama, "Three Sovereigns for Sarah."

SUMMER RECESS - JUNE, JULY, AUGUST - TIME FOR TRAVEL - TIME FOR RESEARCH

Sept 21 Saturday, Centre Church, Lynnfield. (Todd Hall)
         Social Hour: 12:00. **ENTERTAINMENT** 1:00. Scottish dancers.
         Speaker: David Curtis Dearborn, F.A.S.G., Ref. Librarian at NEHGS.
         Topic: Tracing your Scottish roots.

REPORTS OF PREVIOUS MEETINGS, by Helen P. Bosworth

MARCH 16, 1985. With the wearin' o' the green and hearin' the piper's tunes
(Susanne Gagnon, flutist), the spirit of St. Patrick brought out more than the
105 seating capacity on a mild, sunny day. Thus a number of late comers turned
to the Genealogy Room to "do a bit o' diggin' in the old sod." (Seems we've
outgrown the Meeting House). To compliment the Irish theme, our Wakefield
colleens brought shamrock cookies, Irish bread, tiny cupcakes capped with green,
and Elinor Sproul, chairlady, created a lovely fresh flower arrangement.
     Domenique Pickett, an affiliate at Northeastern University, gave an
interesting insight into the work being done in conjunction with THE PILOT
(Irish newspaper founded in 1829 by Benedickt Fitzpatrick), its history and
projects - past, present, future. Our main speaker, Ruth Ann Harris, Professor
of History at the University, spoke on "The Irish in New England;" - the
hardships and famine that invoked the early migration trend to New England; the
ups and downs families encountered as they settled in Boston and opened doors to
the where and how of a vast amount of Irish research material available in and
around our local area.

April 20 Workday - an invigorating spring day; a rewarding day for 53 members
who took advantage of our workday at the Haverhill Public Library when the "off-
limit" stacks are open to ESOG as their special guests. I believe some arrived
for breakfast and would have stayed for supper had not the library closed at
5:30. It was a pleasure to meet so many new members among our regular attendees
from Maine and New Hampshire, as well as local. I bet now that the trail has
been blazed and they've seen the many stacks loaded with all kinds of material
to delve into they'll be frequent visitors along with us oldies. Each spring
Bob and Fran Balmer, Delaware, get Essex fever and come up for a meeting or two
and it's always a fun time to see them again. Surprise of the day came around
mid-morning when Barbara Boucot, new member, "flew" in from Oregon to join us.
Our host Gregory Laing (assisted by Dorothea Hart) acquainted new comers with
the collection and spoke about the recent acquisitions. Whispering became
exciting as members found common ancestors and heads got together puzzling out
relationships. It's a joy to be a member of such a friendly "family."

Queries

BAKER/ROW
Need anc Mary BAKER who m 5th parish Gloucester 11 Jan 1759 John Row, Jr.

DIXEY/VICKERY
Need anc Martha DIXEY bpt 28 Aug 1763 Marblehead & Knott VICKERY bpt 19 July 1761 who were m (int) 12 Nov 1783 Marblehead.

ELLIOTT/GROVES (La GRO, LEGRO)
Need anc William & Anna ELLIOTT whose dau Anna b 30 Sep 1710 Beverly & m 27 July 1733 Ipswich Peter GROVES. Name GROVES also shown as La GRO, LEGRO, etc. Was this a Huguenot fam?

STRICKLAND/WOODBURY/WARREN
Need anc Allen STRICKLAND m 2 Oct 1788 in Beverly Sarah WOODBURY b 8 May 1765 dau of Samuel & Mary (WARREN) WOODBURY.

WILLIAMS/COOK
Need anc Mary WILLIAMS b 18 Oct 1786 Beverly m 29 May 1806 Wenham James COOK of Salem.

WOOD/BLASHFIELD/MORGAN
Need anc Joseph WOOD "2nd" m 26 June 1760 Beverly Mercy BLASHFIELD b 24 May 1740 dau Henry & Mary (MORGAN) BLASHFIELD. Mrs. Constance HANSCOM, 200 Orchard St., Belmont, MA 02178.

****

WELLS
Seek info, w, ch of Jonathan WELLS of Ipswich, MA b ca 1731. Served in Col. Moses LITTLE's 17th & 12th Reg't. Need proof he was at Boston Tea Party. Any info appreciated. Mrs. Caroline BARRETT, 5069 Maple Ave., Oscoda, MI 48750.

****

FRENCH/EDWARDS/CLAGGETT
Need par of Parker Hardin FRENCH b ca 1824 in KY; m/1 Lucretia EDWARDS; m/2 Rebecca CLAGGETT ca 1873 poss in Philadelphia; d NY 19 June 1878. Bur in Alton, IL

CLAGGETT/MORRILL
Need proof of b of Rebecca CLAGGETT dau of Rev. William CLAGGETT & w Sara MORRILL. Believe b. Ludlow, VT 10 July 1830.

MITCHELL/CLAGGETT/MCQUESTEN
Need par Y anc of Lettice MITCHELL b 1742 dau of Dr. MITCHELL of Portsmouth, NH; m/1 Wyseman CLAGGETT; m/2 Simon MCQUESTEN.

NAHOR/MCQUESTEN
Need par & anc of Margaret NAHOR b 25 May 1738 dau of James NAHOR; m William MCQUESTEN of Litchfield, NH 13 June 1756. Marian TOWSE, 7 Congress St., Stoneham, MA 02180.

****

CLARK/SMITH
Seeking info anc Abigail CLARK b ca 1711; m Henry SMITH, Jr. ca 1731; d 1747 Walpole, MA. Ch Abigail b 1732, Hannah b 1737, Henry & John b 1735/6, Meriah b 1740, Amos b ca 1743, Sarah b ca 1746. They liv Medfield & Walpole, MA.

LANE
Seeking info anc Mary LANE b ca 1735; m Daniel LANE 1761 of Gloucester, MA. Ch Mary b 1762, Daniel b 1763, Judith b 1765, James b 1767, Giddings b 1770, Elias b 1772, Lydia b 1774, Peter b 1776. Moved to New Gloucester, ME 1770.

LORD/SWIFT
Seeking info anc Mary LORD b ca 1783
NH; m 6 Apr 1805 Wayne, ME Elnathan
SWIFT of Wareham, MA. Ch Enoch b 1805,
Hasadiah b 1807, Mary b 1808, Betsey b
1810, Dean b 1812, Rebecca b 1814,
Rufus b 1816, Elnathan b 1818, Sarah
b 1822.

PALMER/CLOUGH
Seeking info anc Susanna PALMER b 7 Dec
1789; m July 1809 James S. CLOUGH; d
1834 Readfield, ME. Ch Henry c. b
1809, James, Jr. b 1811, Susanne P. b
1819, Elbridge G. b 1821, Lydia b 1827,
Thomas M. b 1830, Florence M. b 1834.

RICHARDS/TRAIN/ROLLINS
Seeking info & anc Hulday (RICHARDS)
TRAIN b 1784 MA; m/2 Josiah ROLLINS of
Newcastle, ME ca 1807; d 15 Sept 1850
Hallowell, ME. Ch William A. b 1808,
Mary b 1810, Betsey b 1812, Sarah b
1815, Hannah b 1817, Lucinda b 1820,
Lucy A. b 1823, Frances b 1826, Caro-
line b 1829.

TUCKER/CLOUGH
Seeking info anc Elizabeth B. TUCKER b
9 May 1812 Raymond, NH; dau of John
TUCKER; m 20 Oct 1835 Henry C. CLOUGH;
d 16 Sep 1892 Readfield, ME. Ch Isaac
H. b 1837, Sarah E. b 1839, John T. b
1842, George W. b 1844, Susan J. b
1849.

WHEELOCK/GILMAN
Seeking info & anc Catherine WHEELOCK b
1802 MA; m Bela GILMAN; d 7 May 1869
Mt. Vernon, ME. Ch Nathaniel b 1828,
Charles E. b 1833, Henry H. b 1836,
Lewis E. b 1840, Mary Ellen b 1844.
Mary A WILHELM, 28 Western Ave. Essex,
MA 01929

****

BRAMAN/BRIGHAM/GROUT
Dr. Amasa BRAMAN b 1766, d Millbury,
MA 4 Oct 1830 ae 64; m Sutton, MA 19
Feb 1793 Mary Polly BRIGHAM dau of
Moses & Mehitabel (GROUT) BRIGHAM.
Want par of Amasa BRAMAN, poss Taunton
or Providence.

BURBANK/GIBBS
Elijah BURBANK b 26 Mar 1736, d 26 Sept
1813 of Sutton, MA; m 21 Nov 1782 Elizabeth GIBBS b 1765, d 1831 ae 66.
Want her par.

DELANO/TURNER/SPRAGUE
Jonathan DELANO, 2nd, b Duxbury, MA 3
Nov 1701, d Duxbury, MA 1744 or 1745;
m Rochester, MA 3 Dec 1736, as his 2nd
w Elizabeth (TURNER) SPRAGUE b 4 July
1699, d Apr 1780, wid of Micah SPRAGUE.
Want her par.

DREW/ROSE
Charles DREW b Duxbury, MA 3 Apr 1769,
d. Duxbury, MA 4 Feb 1858; m/1 Marsh-
field, MA 5 Jan 1794 Betsey ROSE b 16
Apr 1769, d Duxbury, MA 9 Apr 1808.
Want her par.

GORHAM/DUNKS
Seth GORHAM b Fairfield, CT 18 Jan
1782, d Rutland, VT 29 Aug 1852; m/1
Amelia DUNKS b Danbury, CT 29 Mar 1763,
d 17 Oct 1841. Want her par.

KELLOGG/MILLER
Joseph KELLOGG b Hatfield, MA 18 June
1696 d Hebron, CT ca 1765; m 23 Oct
1717 Abigail MILLER of Colchester, VT.
Wand her par.

NEWMAN/ORN(E)/JOHNSON
Benjamin NEWMAN b Ipswich (?), MA 13
Aug 1766, d Newburyport (?), MA 26 Apr
1827; m/2 6 Jan 1799 Hannah ORN(E) b
1765, d 12 Feb 1842. Their dau Hannah m
Jeremiah JOHNSON of Newburyport &
Portsmouth. Want anc Hannah ORN(E).

PEARSON/GREEN
Jeremiah PEARSON b Lynn, MA 20 Dec 1715
d Newburyport, MA 29 Nov 1797; m Hampton Falls, NH 2 Nov 1738 Mary GREEN.
Want her dts & par.

STETSON/CROSSETT
Robert STETSON b 29 June 1772 d 2 Oct
1841, of Hardwick, MA; m Pelham, MA 17
Feb 1795 Isa CROSSETT b 4 Oct 1773, d
25 June 1827. Want her par.

STETSON/TURNER
Robert STETSON, Jr. b 3 Sep 1710 d

Hanover, MA 27 Feb 1768; m Pembroke,
MA 23 Nov 1738 Hannah TURNER b poss
Pembroke, MA, d Sylvester, MA 1801/2.
Want her par. Roger B. GORHAM, 2
Hackmatack Dr. Scarborough, ME 04074.

****

KNAPP/WESTCOTT/HUSTED/SHERWOOD
Sarah KNAPP b ca 1674 prob Greenwich,
CT, dau of Moses & Abigail (WESTCOTT)
m "Samuel HUSTED." Samuel HUSTED b ca
1665 prob Greenwich, s of Angell &
Rebecca (SHERWOOD) m "Sarah KNAPP."
Are these the same Samuel & Sarah?

WESCOTT/KNAPP
Abigail WESCOTT b ca 1647, dau of
Richard & Joan, m 1668 Moses KNAPP b ca
1645 Stamford, CT, d 1756 Peekskill NY.
Need all data Abigail, Richard & Joan.
Dorothy BRANSON, 797 S. James Rd. #14,
Columbus, OH 43227.

****

CLAY
Need bdt & bp of Richard CLAY of Biddeford, ME in 1735. He d 27 Sept 1801
in Buxton, ME.

GRAFFAM/SWETT
Wish ddt & dpl of Mary (SWETT) GRAFFAM,
4th w of Caleb GRAFFAM of Windham and
Gorham, ME; m 14 Nov 1817.

GREEN/GRANT
Need all dates & anc of Betsy GREEN,
w/o James GRANT b 1718 in Berwick, ME.

LOMBARD/GRANT
Would like ddt & dpl of Solomon LOM-
BARD, Jr. & w Lydia (GRANT), poss in
Gorham, ME area.

LOMBARD/HAMLIN
Desire to corr with anyone doing
research or having info on LOMBARDS
of Cape Cod, MA and Gorham, ME. I
have tin-types of Richard LOMBARD & w
Temperance HAMLIN that I would like
positively identified if poss.

MAYBERRY/GRAFFAM
Desire ddt & dpl of Charity (MAYBERRY)

GRAFFAM w/o Enoch GRAFFAM of Windham
& Raymond, ME. He d 1827 in Raymond,
ME.

MITCHELL/LARRABEE
Need dt & anc of Lydia MITCHELL m 24
Oct 1765 William LARRABEE as his 2nd/w;
both of Scarboro, ME.

PENNELL/CLAY
Rachel PENNELL b 25 Nov 1721 w/o
Richard CLAY, was b in Gloucester, MA.
Where & when did she die?

PERVIERE/PHILBRICK
Need anc of Abigail PERVIERE, b 16 Oct
1672, Rye, NH; m James PHILBRICK 21
May 1801 of Hampton, NH.

PIERCE/BELCHER
Desire all info for Mary PIERCE b 24
Jan 1732 prob in Milton, MA. Was 2nd/w
of Elijah BELCHER of Braintree, MA.
Was she dau of William PIERCE of Fal-
mouth, ME?

RIDEOUT/LORD/SEAVEY
Was Lydia RIDEOUT who m Jeremiah LORD
24 Dec 1804 in Kennebunkport, the dau
of Abraham & Molly (SEAVEY) RIDEOUT
of Kennebunkport, ME/

SWETT/HALE
Stephen SWETT b 26 Feb 1738 Newbury, MA;
m 30 Mar 1758 Elizabeth HALE b 1 Mar
1740 Newbury, MA. Would like ddt &
dpl for both. Merle G. GRAFFAM, P.O.
Box 587, Houlton, ME 04730.

****

BARBER/WHITE
Need anc of Mary (Polly) BARBER b West
Newton, MA 6 July 1773; m Ebenezer
WHITE 7 June 1794; d in Whitinsville,
MA 2 Nov 1855.

ELDRED/SMITH
Wish info on par, bdt, bp of Catherine
ELDRED; m Frederick SMITH b ca 1810
prob CT.

SMITH/HANCHETT
Wish info on anc of Augustus Phineas
SMITH b 30 Mar 1805 prob CT; m Eliza

Ann HANCHETT 26 Aug 1833 in Milton, NY.

WHITE
Need bet, bp & anc of Ebenezer WHITE
in Hallowell, ME in 1806. Richard
DONOVAN, Sr. Wymore, NE 68466.

****

RING/STANDISH
Need ch of Andrew RING & Zerviah
STANDISH, bdts & spouses. Especially
interested in s Batchelder RING.

WILL
Wish par & dt J. M. WILL who ma
Harriett ----, 11 Jan 1846 at Methuen,
MA. Mrs. Ida KRETSCHMAR, Route 3, Box
359, Canton, NY 13617.

****

DAVIS/SHEPARD
Seeking sib & anc of Levi DAVIS b 19
Oct 1764 at Epsom (Plaistow?) NH; s of
Ezekiel DAVIS & Martha ----; m Hannah
SHEPARD of Saco, ME. Also seeking VRs
of par. Corr welcome.

SHEPARD/DAVIS
Hannah SHEPARD b ca 1760 at Saco, ME
m Levi DAVIS. Seeking par, anc, pl
of m & dt.

PIKE/PERLEY
Thomas PIKE b Sep 1700 at Newbury, MA
m Lois PERLEY Aug 1727 at Boxford, MA.
Who were par?

MURPHY/CONNORS
Wish w & ch of James F. MURPHY b 1860
in Ireland, s of Lawrence MURPHY & Ann
CONNORS. Liv at N. Andover, MA ca
1820 - 1911; d 9 Aug 1911.

REILLY/CONNORS
Seeking any ch of Henry Patrick
REILLY b 14 Aug 1873 at N. Andover,
MA; m Mary Ellen CONNORS at Lawrence,
MA 4 Mar 1895 and d Lawrence, MA 31
Jan 1935. John R. REILLY, 19 Allen
St., Gloucester, MA 01930.

****

COLBY/ASH/GEORGE
Seek par of wid Sarah (ASH) COLBY who m
John Swaddock GEORGE ca 1759. They
res in Haverhill, MA.

GIDDINGS (GILLINGS)/LUNT
Seek anc Sarah GIDDINGS (GILLINGS) who
m Samuel Allen LUNT in Newburyport, MA
16 Jan 1793.

NICHOLS/GEORGE
Seek bdt & par of Thomas NICHOLS who
m Mary GEORGE 16 Jan 1780 at Haverhill.
MA. Donal B. STEVENS, 25 Gardner
Terr., Delmar, NY 12054.

****

ELLIS/SANDERS/DODGE/DURHAM/BYROM/
SMALLEY/GUNN/CUNNINGHAM
Need par Betsey ELLIS m John SANDERS
res Swanville, ME bur Greenlawn Cem.
Swanville, ME. Ch: John L. m Eliza-
beth DODGE of Searsport, ME; Caroline
m William N. DURHAM; Sarah Elizabeth
m W. BYROM of Thomaston, ME; Henry
m/1 Mrs. Ellen J. SMALLEY, m/2 C. M.
GUNN; Fred Nathaniel d 16 yrs; Permit
Porter m Rebecca A. CUNNINGHAM of
Swanville, ME. Irene Sanders Johnson,
Rt #1, Box 10 Searsport Ave., Belfast,
ME 04915.

****

NASH/SHAW
Need forbears & fam bpl of Joseph NASH,
Sgt RevW of Braintree, MA; bpt 12 Nov
1726, m 16 Dec 1746 Susannah SHAW b 3
Mar 1726 So. Weymouth, MA, later in
Pleasant R./Columbia, MA/ME. Is
Francis his grfa as NEHGR 1900 vol
LIV p 404 states? Barbara MANNING,
148 Boiling Springs Circle, Southern
Pines, NC 28387.

****

TURNER COLBY
Seek par William TURNER who ca 1740
sett Candia, NH with w Sarah COLBY.

TURNER/GOODRIDGE
Seek par William TURNER who m Joanna
GOODRIDGE 30 Mar 1732 at Newbury, MA.

Clayton R. ADAMS, 6 Laurel Road,
Brunsiwck, ME 04011.

****

ALDRICH/RIVERS
Seek par pbl & bdt, ca 1826 for Albert
J. (?) ALDRICH, whaler of New Bedford,
who m 18 Nov 1854 Elizabeth Amelia
RIVERS in Thomaston, ME; d 19 July 1862
at camp opposite Vicksburg, MS; had 3
ch. Edward O. HAHN, 20 Gleason St.,
Thomaston, ME 04861.

****

HERRICK
Who was Andrew HERRICK b 1722 and said
by some to be bur Cranberry Isles, ME?
I assume he is the one of the name at
Louisburg.

HERRICK
Who was Nathaniel HERRICK b 24 Aug
1753 & liv Bluehill, ME? Was he
an unlisted s of Samuel?

SAWYER/CARTER/JONES
The w of Benjamin SAWYER has appeared
as Phebe CARTER, yet, elsewhere she
shows as Phebe JONES. Who was she?
They res Wilmington, Woburn & Danvers,
MA and on Sawyers Island, Boothbay, ME.
Elizabeth C. WESCOTT, RFD 2, Box 920,
Apt 202, Bucksport, ME 04416.

****

COLLIER/PRENCE/BROWING
Mary COLLIER dau of William & Jane
(CLARK) bpt 18 Feb 1611/2 was 2nd w of
Gov Thomas PRENCE. Is this the same
Mary COLLIER who m Malachi BROWNING
was mo of Susannah & Daniel BROWNING &
d 7 Sep 1672? Nancy HAYWARD, 17 Draper
Dr., Wilmington, MA 01887.

****

CADY/DOWNEY
Seek info Honora CADY b ca 1816 Ireland; d Boston; m Patrick DOWNEY Boston (Roxbury) s Thomas J. DOWNEY b 2
Mar 1839 Boston, d 8 Oct 1922 Boston.

FAGAN/O'DONNELL
Seek par Mary Ann FAGAN b ca 1820 d 9
Feb 1842; m Dennis O'DONNELL; bur St.
Augustine's Cem., Dorchester; dau Julia
A. b 13 Oct 1838 Boston, d 13 Jan 1901
Boston. Leonard SWANSON, 20 Webber
Ave., Beverly, MA 01915.

****

BACHILER (BATCHELDER)/MERCER/PRYAULX
Nathaniel BACHILER (BATCHELDER) s of
Rev Stephen BACHILER b ca 1590 m Hes-
ter MERCER. How are MERCER & PRYAULX
fam of Southampton, Eng. connected to
Hester?

BLAKE/DALTON
Need dts & anc both Jasper BLAKE b ca
1614 Wimbotsham Co., Norfolk, Eng &
w Deborah DALTON.

BROOKIN(G)/WALFORD/SANBORN
William BROOKIN(G) b ca 1629, sent by
Mason to his plantation, m Mary WALFORD
dau of Thomas. Did William have a
previous w named Judith SANBORN?

BROWN/MOULTON/TRUE/MORRILL
Thomas BROWN of Kensington, NH s of
Ebenezer BROWN & Sobriety MOULTON of
Hampton, NH, m Hannah TRUE. Was Hannah
dau of Benjamin TRUE of Salisbury who m
26 Dec 1717 Judith MORRILL of Salisbury?

CHAMBERLAIN
Need anc of Experience ----, w of Jacob
CHAMBERLAIN b 18 Jan 1657/8 Billerica,
MA s of William & w Revecca. Also need
name of Rebecca's par.

COLE/BENNET/SPENCER/PHIPS/GOULD/ANDREWS
Need info & anc Rebecca COLE bpt 12
July 1696 Rowley, MA as "Rebeka COLE,
Mrs. Bennett's child." Mrs. BENNETT
was Rebecca SPENCER (dau of Roger);
2nd w Dr. David BENNETT & sis of Mary
w of Sir William PHIPS. Rebecca COLE
m/1 Henry GOULD; m/2 Thomas ANDREWS.

GREEN/WHEELER/COOK
Was Thomas GREEN of Malden, MA who m/1
Elizabeth ----; m/2 1659 Frances, wid
Isaac WHEELER & Richard COOK; and d 19

Dec 1667, the Thomas GREEN bpt 13 May 1599 Gillingham, Co. Dorset, s of Richard & Mary GREEN?

SEARS (SEERES)/HILTON/DOWNER
Need anc & dts both Thomas SEARS (SEERES) & w Mary HILTON alias DOWNER, m 11 Dec 1656 Newbury, MA.

TILLY(e)/HILLIER/HUCKINS(HUGGINS)/SARGENT
Hugh TILLY(E) (also called HILLIER) came 1629 on "Lion's Whelp" to Salem. Rem to Yarmouth & Barnstable. Wife Rose m/2 3 Nov 1648 Nocett, MA to Thomas HUCKINS (HUGGINS). Hugh & Rose par of Deborah b 1643 Barnstable m John SARGENT; and of Samuel b 1646. Need anc of Hugh & Rose.

VIGER/CUMMINGS/DIXON
Need anc & dts Joseph VIGER b France (?) & w Mary CUMMINGS b P.E.I.; par of Anne VIGER b ca 1812 prob Charlottstown, P.E.I. who m William DIXON & had ch bpt at St. Dunstan's Church, Charlottstown 1833-40. Anne Merrill GOULETTE, R.R.3, Box 120, Dexter, ME 04930.

##############################

DARLING/KEEZER
Need anc of William DARLING of Kirkland, ME m int 8 July 1838 to Mary Ann KEEZER.

GODSOE/KEAZER
Wish par of both James E. GODSOE & his w Rhoda E. KEAZER m 23 Jan 1837 Charleston, ME.

LEIGHTON/KEAZER
Desire bp, dpl of Joseph J. LEIGHTON m ca 1850 Clarissa D. KEAZER who d 29 Aug 1853 ae 21.

PACKARD/KEAZER
Seek anc of Silas PACKARD of Charleston, ME m int 10 July 1841 to Susan KEAZER of Charleston.

SMITH/KEAZER
Who were par of Henry J. SMITH of Kenduskeag, ME who m 1 Jan 1866 Clara H.

KEEZER of Hudson, ME? Leon KEYSER, Apt #12, 1350 Forest Ave., Portland, ME 04103.

##############################

BISHOP/ESTES/KENNEY
Need par & VR for John BISHOP fa of Lydia who m Caleb ESTES 1769 Hanover, MA. Caleb & Lydia both d Durham, ME. One John BISHOP m Ann KENNEY at Salem, MA 1726. Could these be the par?

CROSS/WYMAN/FALL
Mary CROSS b 1760 m Francis WYMAN 1769 Vassalboro, ME. Was she nee FALL, wid CROSS?

FISK/BABCOCK
Seek info Asa FISK, early settler Augusta, ME who m Susanna; their dau Sarah b 1751 "in Providence" m 1781 Augusta, ME Henry BABCOCK b 1750 Roxbury, MA.

GROVES
William GROVES b Brunswick, ME 1790 d Carmel, ME bef 1860. Was he a desc of Nicholas LaGroves who came to Beverly, MA 1667?

GROVES/YORK
Patience m William GROVES at East Pond Plt., ME 1828. Was she nee York or wid York?

OSBORN
Where did Isaac & Ephraim OSBORN of Winslow, ME come from? One source says Long Island, NY.

WYMAN
Need maiden name & background for Love who m William WYMAN at Falmouth or Pownalborough, ME ca 1750. Clair E. WYMAN, Sawyers Crossing Rd., Box 27, West Swanzey, NH 03469.

##############################

> **PLEASE USE ONLY 3 X 5 CARDS!!!**
> **ONLY ONE SURNAME PER CARD!!!**
>
> (Include your name and address on the bottom right-hand corner of each card!!)

The Essex Genealogist

VOLUME 5, NUMBER 3   AUGUST 1985

CONTENTS

THE ESSEX GENEALOGIST is published quarterly: February, May, August,
& November for $10 per year, by the Essex Society of Genealogists,
Lynnfield Public Library, 18 Summer Street, Lynnfield, MA 01940.
Second Class Postage paid at Lynnfield, MA 01940. ISSN: 0279-067X.
USPS: 591-350. POSTMASTER: Send address changes to ESOG, Lynnfield
Public Library, 18 Summer Street, Lynnfield, MA 01940

Letter from the Editor

We are pleased to announce that the publication of TEG is becoming a well-integrated group effort. Starting with this issue, we are adding two new assistants to our editorial staff: Beverly Johnson of Peabody, and Eleanor Spiller of Danvers.

Beverly has long been our advisor on computer technology, having acquired her expertise through her job at Addison Wesley Publishing Company. Now she has offered to share the task of typing (or keying) articles for TEG. The disc she prepares is handed over to me to be run off on my "letter-quality" NEC printer, so that the jornal will be uniform in its final appearance. Two articles and all of the queries were prepared by Beverly for this issue.

Eleanor Spiller answered my request for someone to transcribe taped lectures. It was she who prepared Roger Joslyn's article on Census records that appears in this issue. Eleanor also wrote the articles on the "Darling/Fewkes Papers" and "Augustine Heard" that appear on pages 140-147. These articles about Ipswich prompted me to prepare a companion piece on the Ipswich Historical Society. As our regular readers know, in each August issue, we run a feature article on an Essex County Historical Society. Special Features published to date have been Andover in 1982, Newburyport in 1983, and Beverly last year. To assist me in preparing the Ipswich article for this issue, I called upon our "writer-in-residence," Helen Breen. Together we spent a morning in Ipswich talking with Mary Conley, the current motivator of the Ipswich Society, and keeper of its manuscript collection. Helen's account appears on page 137.

Helen Breen has been a member of the Editorial Staff for several years now, and many of her articles have appeared in previous issues of TEG as well as in many local newspapers. Her travels this summer also took her to the Governor's office at the State House, with ESOG President, Ernestine June Rose. (See account on page 159.)

We were especially pleased that Dr. David L. Greene of Demorest, Georgia submitted the article on Sarah Martin. Dr. Greene is Chairman of the Humanities Division, Piedmont College, a Fellow of the American Society of Genealogists, and Associate Editor of The American Genealogist. His cover letter, in which he enclosed an order for TEG, stated: "I subscribed to the first two volumes of TEG, and have regretted since that I failed to continue. Much of my own research has been in Essex County."

Our thanks are also extended to Bob Canney, Walter McIntosh, Arlene Skehan and Danny D. Smith for their contributions; to Lyman Tucker for his art work on heraldry; to Sid Russell for his fine poetry which has appeared in every issue of TEG since the second issue, May 1981; and to Ludovine Hamilton and Katherine Little for their work on the queries.

Of course we must not overlook the continuing work being done by the faithful 18-member collating staff. Under the organization of Helen Bosworth and George Worth, that group is of vital importance to our publication.

If TEG is to continue as a viable genealogical journal, it is important that a broad base of assistants be developed. From the beginning of the Society and the journal, it has concerned us that too much was being handled by too few. We are finally establishing that broad base that bodes well for continuity and growth.

As one of my teachers, many years ago, used to say: "Many hands make light work!"

Marcia Wiswall/Lindberg

TEG Feature Article

GETTING THE MOST OUT OF CENSUS RECORDS

By Roger D. Joslyn, C.G., F.A.S.G.

(A lecture to ESOG November 1984, Transcribed by Eleanor V. Spiller)

I am glad to see you have a healthy interest in census records. They are my favorite genealogical source, and I like to talk about them very much. I will start my talk today with a story, to put things in perspective. When I was 12 years old and living in California, I made contact with a woman in upstate New York about finding something on an ancestral line named SMITH. She charged $5, sent abstracts from Federal and New York State census records on my particular Smith family. Over the years, I developed those particular Smiths but not very far back. One day, after moving to Boston and while working for a client, I was going through the 1860 Federal census that included that town of my Smiths in upstate New York. I paused when I reached a particular family of Charles G. Smith, and saw that, in addition to Charles G., his wife and three daughters, there were two persons not named Smith; namely, Calvin Eastman and Mary (presumably his wife by her age). I made an abstract, took it home, and compared it with the information sent to me years before. Sure enough, the lady had not included the names of the Eastmans on her report to me. Further comparison indicated that Mary "Eastman" was likely the Mary "Smith" listed in 1850 and 1855. On the basis of that information, I was able to find descendants of that couple in Pennsylvania, who not only had pictures of those ancestors I'd never seen, but also provided the necessary clues to complete the tracing of Charles G. Smith and his wife Ruth Sherman's ancestries.

That story points out two things: one, the beneficial use of census records as a genealogical research tool; and two, the necessity of carefully done abstracts.

For our purposes this afternoon, I'm going to confine my talk to the United States Federal Census. Other countries have censuses too but we will not discuss those today. Censuses have a long and interesting history. They were taken mostly for taxation, the counting of people for representation, military strength, and so forth. Although we have censuses for American Colonial times, the first well-known one was the 1790 census taken to determine representation in Congress and the country's military strength. It gives the number of males above 16, the number of females, etc. The census was not created for genealogical purposes, and when you become frustrated, you should keep this in mind.

An interesting overview of the history of the census is in A Century of Population Growth, so I'll not detail that here. Knowing what was expected of the census takers sometimes helps to understand why a record seems wrong or why it is put together in a certain way. I hope to tell you what census records do exist, where they exist, what they contain, and how to find and use the records.

We all should know Federal census records exist from 1790 and have been taken every ten years. From a mere five columns in 1790, we now have very detailed schedules, as those of you who made out the 1980 census can attest. Most researchers have available to them the 1790-1910 population schedules.

Other schedules were prepared, such as for agricultural information, which can be helpful in learning the number of livestock and the wealth of an individual farmer or his family. Also, censuses by individual States were taken in non-decennial years. The Federal Government also took censuses in off-years, particularly in the territories. Some of these censuses were taken to determine if there were enough people to admit a territory as a state. California was done in 1850 and recounted in 1852.

The 1890 Federal census was, indeed, as we've heard, destroyed by a fire in 1921 in Washington, D.C. There are portions of schedules which do survive - three microfilm reels plus two reels of index, none of which survives for New England. Those extant may be seen at the National Archives - Boston Branch at 380 Trapelo Road, Waltham, Mass.

Where do census records exist? They are at the National Archives in Washington D.C., and most are in their original forms. They used to be on open shelves, but because of the huge number of people using them, they were deteriorating. The books are now inaccessible and everything is on microfilm. Many of the census films are hard to read because of poor originals or poor filming techniques. Those using records in the last decade know that the Federal Archives did improve them by refilming 1850 and 1870. You should be aware that everything on film of the Federal census does not necessarily mean that something wasn't missed, because it was. In 1885, Cherry County of Nebraska Territory was not filmed. Ward Two of Baltimore 1860 is not complete. You would need to go to D.C. to search books for the rest. A lot of things are filmed out of sequence - perhaps the fault of the filmer or the person binding the pages. There are no book copies of the 1880 census in the National Archives because they were returned to the states after microfilming.

The National Archives Branch at Waltham has the 1790 through the 1910 censuses on microfilm. The Census Bureau published the 1790 census in book form and the rest of the censuses up through 1850 have been indexed by independent companies. A few later censuses have also been indexed. Waltham also has the special 1890 census for veterans of the Civil War, or widows of veterans. The 1890 veterans schedule exists for only one-half of the country (part of KY, then alphabetically, LA through WY and Washington, D.C.). Waltham is the only Branch to have a set of these 1890 veterans films.

It's also good to know that originals, or hard copies of the census are in D.C. There were two copies of the 1830 and 1840 census made. There is the Federal copy and a copy in the states (often in the county). If you compare these, the information may differ some and you could have the answer to your problem. The 1850, 1860 and 1870 censuses had three copies. One went to D.C., one to the Secretary of State/Territory, and one to the respective county court. If you cannot go to Waltham, some other places that have censuses in this area are New England Historic Genealogical Society at 101 Newbury Street in Boston, Boston Public Library, and other public libraries with genealogical collections. Throughout New England, the state libraries have copies of their own state's original copies of the 1840 through the 1870 schedules.

There used to be Interlibrary Loan from the Regional Archives Centers, but the task became too overburdening, and now a private firm in Maryland has the franchise to loan the censes films for a fee. (Census Microfilm Rental Program, P.O. Box 2940, Hyattsville, MD 20784. Films may be ordered only through libraries, or a participating genealogical society. Basic rental $2.25 per film.)

The State censuses are similar to the Federal ones and should not be overlooked. They might fill in gaps in your research. They might just give you a change of residence or occupation or correction of nickname to Christian names. There are Massachusetts State censuses for 1855 and 1865 in the State Archives. Rhode Island and New York have very useful State censuses. New York 1855 not only asked name, color, sex, and age, but also relationship to the head of the household, county of birth (if in N.Y.), whether a native or naturalized voter, and if an owner of land. Also asked was length of residence in the community, from which you can learn approximately when a family or person came to town. Studying ages may indicate a second marriage, especially when relationships are given. Rhode Island has State censuses for 1865, 1875, 1885, 1895, 1905, 1915 available but not all in the same place.

Accelerated Indexing, Inc. of Salt Lake City, Utah, has produced computerized indexes of the Federal Census for all states through 1850 and are working on later years. In many cases, the computer data-entry people have missed entries or incorrectly entered them.

Some census pages have more than one page number. The National Archives stamped consecutive numbers on pages. Others may have been written earlier or later. Indexers may have followed either. This is something to keep in mind. They did not index all of the names either. They did index head of household and persons with different surnames in the household, and there are duplicates of census indexes. Ohio had indexes before AIS got started, then AIS created their own. Try to consult both, as you may find the name you want in one and not the other. 1800 New York has three different indexes by three different people.

A major mix-up occured with the 1850 New York State Census index. For half the towns in Westchester County, someone used the 1860 roll. If you buy the 1850 Virginia Index, you also get all or part of the 1850 Maine index!

Use your imagination for spelling of surnames. Don't just expect exact or close spellings; some can be very far afield. Look for other family members or neighbors in succeeding censuses. You might just zero in on a family or certain person that way. You might have to go back several times to find someone on a census often missed on the first search. Make sure of and use the different indexes (duplicates). Make complete abstracts. There are census abstract forms, if you think they would be helpful to you. There is some good biographical information on censuses. You can tell the value of real estate and estimate whether the ancestor was landed or perhaps dirt-poor. Also, this indicates whether you might get additional information on a deed. Knowing a person's occupation, or if he was blind, deaf, or dumb is sometimes helpful.

The 1870 census was the first Federal census to ask about citizenship. This helps narrow the search for naturalization records. In 1880, relationships and the birthplace of parents were given. The 1865 Rhode Island and New York State censuses gave information about those who served in the Civil War. The 1900 and 1910 censuses gave the year of immigration and citizenship status.

It is helpful to look at the birthplaces of neighbors to see their place of origin - especially the older people. Don't rely too heavily on ages. I'm always suspicious of them. Often oldsters moved in with the children or younger siblings. You might find a great-grandfather in one of those households. Be aware that the Irish did not seem to know their ages. This is evident with other groups, but not to the same degree; i.e.: there seems to be a different date for every record. Sometimes you get a bonus, such as the county of birth or city or occupation. In 1860, Ward Two of Boston, I once found in the occupation column following the name of a woman in the family - "second wife." Ages can give clues as to whether a wife is the mother of the children. In 1900, sometimes you find the enumerator put down the day in addition to the required month and year of birth.

Mortality schedules listed deaths for the year preceding the census day only. Some mortality schedules have been indexed. In 1820 there was a column for males age 16-18, obviously to determine military strength. Census takers did not seem to know how to use the column since preceeding it was a grouping for ages 10-16 and after it a column for 16-20. The column rather became a potpourri.

There are official census days. For 1830-1900 it was June first, and in 1910 it was April first. If the census taker did not get to a house until September, he was supposed to give the household as it was on the census day, so a birth or a new boarder in August should not have been shown. But sometimes, it may have been, and you have a bonus. Some enumerators did not get to a house until nine months after the official census day.

Don't just collect information and write it down. Dig into it! Think it through! Remember, the census is no more reliable than all the other genealogical sources, but it can be important in making the record linkage and putting the proverbial "flesh on the bones."

As author Val Greenwood said: "Research on no American genealogical problem is complete until all pertinent census schedules have been searched." (p. 139)

* *

A Century of Population Growth From the First Census of the United States to the Twelfth 1790 - 1900 (Washington, D.C., 1909; reprint ed., Baltimore, 1969). (Genealogical Publishing Company)

Val D. Greenwood, The Researcher's guide to American Genealogy (Baltimore, 1975), 139-187, 188-201. (Genealogical Publishing Company)

Keith Schlesinger and Peggy Tuck Sinko, "Urban Finding Aid for Manuscript Census Searches," National Genealogical Society Quarterly, 69 (1981): 171-180.

Henry J. Dubester, State Censuses (Washington, D.C., 1948; reprint ed., Knightstown, Ind., 1975). (The Bookmark)

\#

Roger D. Joslyn, C.G., F.A.S.G., a native of Sacramento, California, now a resident of Tenafly, New Jersey, is a Professional Genealogist. He was Compiler and Editor of Vital Records of Charlestown, Mass., Vol. I (Vol. 2 is in progress), and has contributed to many scholarly journals. He is currently at work on the families of Benchley, Cotton, Farley, McLeish, Tarr and others.

Crest and Shield

By Lyman O. Tucker

ALLEN

FORTITER·GERIT·CRUCEM

BROWN(E)

NEL·TIMEO·NEL·SPERNO

ARMS: Sable, a cross potent Or.

CREST: A nag's head erased emerging
         out of a ducal crown Or.

MOTTO: "He bravely supports the cross"

****

Andrew, Lynn, MA 1642; Andover, Ip-
   swich 1658; d. Andover 24 Oct 1670
Charles, Strawberry Bank, Portsmouth,
   N.H., 1657
George, Lynn 1635; Weymouth, 1637; d.
   2 May 1648 at Sandwich
Robert (Allyn), Salem, 1636; Manches-
   ter, MA 1648; New London, CT 1674, d.
   there by 20 Sept 1683. (Brother of
   William (Allen) below.
Walter, Newbury, 1640; Watertown, 1642
William, Gloucester, 1624; Salem 1626;
   d. Manchester, MA 10 May 1678;
   (Brother of Robert above)

ARMS: In pale argent and sable, a
         double-headed eagle displayed.

CREST: In pale argent and sable, an
         eagle displayed.

MOTTO: "By fortitude and Fidelity"

****

Rev Chad Browne came on "Martin" 1638
   Providence, R.I. to Lynn, MA, etc.
Edward to Ipswich 1637; d. there 1660
James, Newburyport 1652; Salem, 1664;
   d. there 3 Sept 1676; a glazier.
John, came on "Lion" 1632; d. at
   Watertown, 20 June 1637
John (Browne) came to Plymouth 1634;
   rem to Swansea, then Rehoboth; d.
   there 10 Apr 1662; a Magistrate.
John (Browne), Salem 1637. Died by
   24 Nov 1684. Mariner; merchant.
Thomas, Lynn 1653; Groton, 1663; d. at
   Lynn 28 Aug 1693; turner; Constable

117

It Happened in Essex County

THE GREAT NEWBURYPORT CONFLAGRATION OF 1811

By WALTER H. McINTOSH

Present descendants of early 19th Century Newburyport and Newbury residents may not fully comprehend the disaster which took place there in the Spring of 1811, when a blustery fire destroyed much of the business district, and the private homes intermingled there. It was that part of Newburyport downtown and along the river, whose fine brick buildings were constructed right after the fire, and in recent years have been renovated and restored, to make the town a credit to its present day inhabitants and increasingly a tourist's Mecca for those interested in early New England history and architecture.

In a letter to the Columbian Centinel, a Boston newspaper of that time, Mr. E. W. Allen of Newburyport, described the streets affected, and the property owners who were the unlucky ones suffering in the disaster. The letter contains what amounts to a census of the business people of the time, as well as of those who owned residences in the area. The letter follows:

Newburyport, 2 June, 1811

"Dear Sirs:

I have the disagreeable task to call your attention to a scene which defies description. A destructive conflagration has laid waste this town. On Friday night last, about half past nine o'clock, a fire broke out in a block of stables, back of Market square, to the westward, which burnt til 6 o'clock next morning, and consumed about 250 buildings in the centre of the town; the wind was high from the westward.

A list of the sufferers I send you. Excepting the range under the Town Hall, there is scarcely an English goods store remaining. All the West side of Cornhill and State street, to the Market, both sides of Middle street, half way through; the whole of Centre street, both sides; almost the whole of Liberty street, both sides, and on both sides of Water street, including all the stores on the wharves, down to Marquand's wharf, are laid in ashes. The Post Office, 4 printing offices, the Baptist meeting house, 2 insurance offices, Blunt's and the Phoenix buildings are in ruins. The town exhibits truly a melancholy appearance. Perhaps $2,000,000. would not place it in the situation it was before. Many have lost their all.

LIST OF SUFFERERS

State Street, North Side: Arthur Gilman's store, English goods; Paul Noyes, do; Dudley Porter's, do; Pierce & Gordon's, do; Moses Kimball's, do; Francis Somerby's, do; Joseph D. Pike, tailor; Paul Bishop, do; William Francis, hair dresser; Stetson's tavern; Post Office; Phoenix Insurance office; Custom House; Joseph Jackman's store; P. Bagley & Sons' auction office; Moses Osgood's store; Jonathan Coolidge's, do; Joseph Hooper's crockery; David Fairman, engraver; Howard Robinson's house; F. Little & Co.'s printing office; Samuel P. Stevens' hardware store; John Chickering, English goods; Thomas & Whipple's bookstore; Benjamin Lord, tailor.

Market Square, South-west Side: Edward Tappan, English goods; John Peabody, do; Daniel Balch, watchmaker; Timothy Webb's bookstore; James Locke, English goods; Ephraim Titcomb, W.I. goods; Enoch Plummer, Jr., do; Daniel Smith, Apothecary; Nathan Follansbee, W.I. goods; Joseph Jackman's tavern; John O'Brien's attorney office.

State Street, South Side: John Knowlton, cabinet-maker, house and shop; Osgood and Brackett's shoestore; Samuel Clement's house and barn; Jonathan Woodman, jeweler; D. N. Dole, do; John Fitz, saddler; Obadiah Pearson, tailor; Nathaniel Newman, hair dresser; Gilman White, crockery ware; Moses Cole, painter.

Middle Street, South-west Side: Perley Tenney, W.I. goods; E & S Dole, cabinet and chair makers; Mrs. Baldwin's house; Joseph Noyes' house and shop; Woodbridge Noyes' stable; Deacon Abbot's house; Abbot & McAllister's, chair makers; Hugh & Thomas Prichard, 2 houses and store; Capt. Denny's house, occupied by Rev. Mr. Peak; Gilman White's house.

Essex Street, North-east Side: Stephen Greely's shoe store; John Colby, painter; Samuel Mansur, house and barn; N. H. Wright's printing office.

Middle Street, North-east Side: Mrs. Johnson's house; Jeremiah Young's 2 houses and store; Mrs. Stickney's house and barn; Mrs. Moulton's house; Mr. Perkins, saddler; Henry Bolt's house; Nicholas Pierce's house and barn; Samuel Bachelor's house; Mrs. Nelledge's shop; Samuel Noyes house and barn; Hannah Bradbury's house; Nicholas Tracy's house; Thomas Dodge's house and shop; Edward & D. Little's large block of buildings occupied by D. W. Jones, English goods; W. & J. Gilman's printing office of the Newburyport Herald; Nathan Ames office, shoemaker; E. Little & Co.

Market Square, South-east Side: James Kimball, English goods; E. Little & Co.'s house and bookstore; Enoch Pike, tailor; Francis Todd, English goods; Samuel H. Foster's house, store, and barn; Joseph Hervey, tailor; John Jenkin's house; Anthony Smith, hardware; Aaron Davis, apothecary; Union Marine & Fire Insurance Company; Dr. Bradstreet's house; Enoch Plummer's store; Moses Moody's grocery; Thomas Hale's hat store; Joshua Greenleaf's chandlery and back store.

Water Street, South-west Side: Three new stores, unoccupied, owned by Abner Wood and Joshua Greenleaf; Timothy Ford's house and stores, occupied by Mrs. Greenleaf and others; Mrs. Tappan's house and store; B. Tappan, founder; A. Wheeler, grocer; John Greenough's house and shop; Mrs. Gerrish's house and shop; Eben Greenleaf's house; Joseph Tappan's house; Abraham Jackson's house, stores, and barn; Moses Clark's house; Mrs. Prince's house; Thomas Lord, hatter; David Moody's malt house and barn.

Water Street, North-east Side: Joseph Marquand's house; range of stores, wharf, etc.; N. Catter's house and store; William Boardman's store; Enoch Tappan's shop; Mrs. Seaward's boarding house; B. Appleton's hatter's shop; Mrs. Atwood's house; range of stores, etc., occupied by B. G. Sweetser, grocer, M. Hart; Union Tavern, etc.; Hannah Jewett's house and shop, occupied by Pingry & Foster's shoe store; Abraham Jackson's range of stores on the wharf; Mrs. Harrod's house and store; Joseph O'Brien's house and stores on the wharf; William Titcomb's house and stores; Joseph Edwards, grocer; range of stores on Boardman wharf, occupied by. J. Odiorne, B. G. Boardman, and Amos Tappan; Andrew Palmer's house; Humphrey Cook's hat store; Joseph David's house; William Watkin's house and 2 stores; William Bailey, grocer; John Wood, do; Daniel Burnham's, do; Samuel Brown's store; Peter LeBreton's store; A. & E. Wheelwright, 2 stores; sail loft, occupied by J. Stanwood, and rigging loft of T. Pritchard; Z. Cook's store; one store unoccupied; Robert Didge's store. The latter is the range of brick stores on Ferry wharf.

Centre Street, entirely burnt: Samuel Clothier's house and barn; Samuel Wheeler's bake-house, and house; Thomas Boardman's house; Richard Pike's house and barn unoccupied; Enoch C. Tappan's house and barn; Mrs. Roger's house, occupied by three families; Isaac Stone's house and barn, occupied by Capt. Warner; Eleazer Johnson's house, occupied by Elias Pike and Mr. Moore; Joseph Stanwood's house occupied by Capt. Dawset; William Boardman's house; Theodore Pearson's house, bake-house, etc.; Mrs. Johnson's house occupied by B. Appleton; Edward Rand's house and barn; E. C. Beal's house.

Liberty Street, South-west Side: Mrs. Emerson's house; Joshua Greenleaf's house and barn; New Baptist meeting house; William Stickney, 2 houses; Ezekiel Prince's 2 houses and 2 barns, occupied by himself and E. W. Allen. Besides the foregoing, there are many other small building burnt.

The fire was seen in Boston, and plainly seen in Attleboro by passengers in the Providence mail stage. The inhabitants of Newburyport town meeting, 31st inst. offered their sincere acknowledgements of gratitude for the friendly assistance received during the fire, to the citizens of Newbury, Salisbury, Amesbury, Rowley, Haverhill, Ipswich, Topsfield, Beverly, Danvers, Salem, and several towns in New Hampshire. We do not learn that any person was killed during the congflagration.

Yours &c.

E. E. Allen "

###

AN EARLY CASE OF CHILD ABUSE

By Arlene M. Skehan, Pittston, Maine

Excerpts from the Records and Files of the Quarterly Courts of Essex County

Court held at Ipswich, 13 (9 m) 1649, by adjournment. Thomas Cooke to be whipped or fined for his abuse of the ministry and magistrates and going into the woods at unseasonable time of night, carrying fire and liquors with him.

Thomas Cooke presented for saying Mr. Norton taught what was false and also for reproaching the ordinance of baptism, saying that if he had children he would not have them so played the fools withal. Witnesses - Mr. Bartholomew and Joseph Medcalf. William Varney bound for him.

Joseph Fowler, Thomas Cook, Thomas Scott and two of the sons (John and Thomas) of Richard Kimball presented for going into the woods, shouting and singing, taking fire and liquors with them, all being at unseasonable time in the night and occasioning their wives and some others to go out and search therein.

Court held at Salem 29 (12 m) 1649 (-50). Thomas Cooke, sometimes of Ipswich, fined for being overtaken with drink.

Court held at Ipswich, 26 (1m) 1650. Joseph Laughton (Langton in index) & Willm Rayner fined for excessive drinking. For the quart of wine stolen to pay 4s. to Mr. Baker beside the other quart, for which Laugton said he paid Mr. Baker. Thomas Fiske & Thomas White said that Joseph Langton said that John Baker owed him 2 or 3 quarts of wine. - (Waste Book)

Court held at Salem, 17 (7m) 1650. Joseph Armitage of Lin fined 5 pounds for allowing Thomas Cooke to drink in his house, being so drunk when he came out that he fell down. Witnesses: John Chadduck, William Edmunds & Capt. Bridges. The latter siad he found Cooke at William Edmunds' house & he confessed that he had drunk wine at Armitage's house. Armitage testified "he saw the said Cooke not well but distempered at Lin brdige & that he was often with him ad Edmund's house." Continued.

Rachell, wife of Thomas Cooke deceased, someties "inhabiting at Ipswich, brought in an inventory of the estate of her late husbnad. She was appointed administratrix. (Vol. I: 194, 196)

Court at Salem, 1 (5 m) 1652. Joseph Langton presented for evil usuage of a little child of his wife. Lt. Samuel Apleton & John Whipple being feoffes in trust & bound to prosecute him. The child was ordered to continue to live with his grandfather William Varney, and his grandmother, until next Ipswich court.

26 (4m) 1652. Disposition of -----, sworn before Samuel Symonds, that Joseph Langton whipped the child to make it quiet and upon deponents asking why he used such a sticky rod, the small branches being worn off, said Langton whipped the child again. The child had to lie upon staw having but a piece of sail cloth or some such material in the cradle & deponent saw water running down into the room underneath where the child lodged. He could not recall if the child had a pillow (Vol. I: 223-225; 257-8).

Records of the Governor & Company of the Massachusetts Bay in New England, Vol. IV, Part II, p. 8. 22 May 1661. In the case of Rachell Langton, or Verney, the Court judgeth it mute to declare, that she is free from her late husband, Joseph Langton.

Thus we have an early case of alcoholism, death by mis-adventure, child abuse, and divorce.

Rachel was the daughter of Bridget (----) Parsons, the second (?) wife of William Varney. She married:

(1) Thomas Cook;
(2) Joseph Langton;
(3) at Gloucester (17: 8m : 1660) 10 June 1661 William V⁺ncen(t).

Research in Progress

BEGINNER TO SEMI-PRO

By Robert Sayward Canney

Not long after my wife and I were married, her brother received an inquiry from a man who was researching their family. Her brother replied with the known information and shortly afterwards received an eleven-generation lineage for their family branch - back to 1631 - to JAMES NUTE of Dover, NH. He gave us a copy and it was interesting to note that we were the third CANNEY-NUTE marriage - 11th, 7th and 3rd generations.

After about 10 years of wondering - I thought it would be nice to trace my lineage. I thought that I must be connected somehow with THOMAS (1) CANNEY of Dover, New Hampshire (1631). But where should I start? I knew only my great-grandfather's name; JOHN L. CANNEY. As you can understand, this was a very common first name. My great-grandmother was HANORA HELEN (HASKELL). Her family left the Dover area to settle in Kansas during the 1860s. My father died in 1928; my grandfather in 1946. I had no one that I could question. I did have one aunt who was raised in Kansas - she went to Kansas with my great-grandmother about 1910. All she knew was that JOHN L. CANNEY disappeared in the 1890s and my grandfather never talked about the CANNEYS

Like anyone else just starting out, I checked with the Vital Statistics in Concord, NH. Death Record - NONE! Marriage record - yes, but no parents listed. Birth records - NONE! What next? I remembered that my grandfather had an aunt who lived in Somersworth, New Hampshire, and had died when I was young. Her name was Sarah Bugbee. So I went back to Concord to the Vital Statistics Department. Death record - NONE! Marriage record - yes, but no parents listed. Her maiden name was listed as "WOODMAN." How was she an aunt? Wait - this was her second marriage! I asked questions. I was told to check the "Brides Index." This I did. There it was! SARAH CANNEY married John Woodman. Her parents were listed. JAMES M. CANNEY and Lydia O. (Sherburne) CANNEY. So this was my JOHN L. CANNEY's parents. I had my first real step. But who was JAMES M. CANNEY?

My wife and I returned to Concord and copied every CANNEY Birth, Marriage (including Brides), Death and Divorce record on file from the beginning to 1939. With this large volume of data, I started putting the many families together. I also visited the county court houses in Strafford, Carroll and Rockingham Counties. I copied every CANNEY Probate Record, Deed and Name Change. At the library in Dover, New Hampshire, I got a listing of all New Hampshire men in the Revolutionary War, the War of 1812, and the Civil War. I sent to Washington, D.C. and got copies of Military Records, Pension Records and Land Grants. With all this added information I was able to put more families together.

During my research I learned that sometimes my name was spelled "KENNEY" in the old records. But this is a bona fide surname. I had to be careful.

While scanning old town maps (1872), I found a KENNEY in Nottingham, New Hampshire. My wife and I located the old home and stopped to talk to the people living there. They were very nice and told us of the old cemetery up in the woods. Lo and behold, the stones were marked "CANNEY." There was Lydia (Sherbourn) CANNEY. Also others, including MOSES CANNEY. I had him in my family sheets. Now I had the information that I started out to find three years earlier. I might add that during these first three years I spent about 1500 hours for each of these three years researching and compiling all the data I had collected.

One thing to note. My wife's ancester JAMES (1) NUTE and my THOMAS (1) CANNEY came to Dover, New Hampshire from England on the same ship in 1631. They were Puritans. My wife is an 11th generation NUTE and I am an 11th generation CANNEY.

I now had so much data on the CANNEYs, why not continue and complete the research on the whole CANNEY family. Checking all the old town maps, I noted all the towns that contained CANNEYS or KENNEYS. Then I checked the Census records for these towns. I got new information to connect more families. Also I found old cemetery locations that contained CANNEYS. I also sent to Salt Lake City and got the records of the CANNEYS that they had. More bits and pieces were added to my files. At the library in Dover, New Hampshire, they had copies of old newspapers from 1797 to 1900. That was over 5,000 newspapers. This took me three winters to read through all of them. Some more bits and pieces were added to my files. I was one of the last ones to read these old newspapers. I persuaded the library to put them on microfilm as some were pretty badly worn.

Also at Dover, they have the records of the Quakers from 1720. Many CANNEYS were Quakers in the 4th, 5th and 6th generations. More bits and pieces! Quakers were quiet people - no military men or statesmen. It was difficult to find any mention of them in historical records. I had access to between 30 to 40 telephone directories from all over the United States. I found about 80 CANNEYS. I wrote to each one and received replies from about 30. I also got leads to about 20 more. They all sent data to me. One letter leads to another. Over a three year period, I must have written more than 500 letters and got many bits and pieces.

I made up pamphlets from my collection of more than 300 family sheets. These pamphlets contain 10 or 11 generations of any particular family. I sent out over 250 of these pamphlets to all who answered my letters. Even today (10 years later) I get letters from a cousin of someone who did not answer one of my letters back then. Most of my data has come from records available in New Hampshire. I started researching records in Maine about two years ago. This year I started researching Massachusetts records. Again I am adding bits and pieces.

I believe my great-grandfather may have died in Massachusetts between 1935 and 1940. He was born about 1851. My line is very thin - about as thin as you can get. 11th generation - only one son; 10th generation - only one son; 9th generation - only one son; 8th generation - only one son; 7th generation - only one son. My wife and I have only one son, so for six generations there has been ony one son to carry on this line. It must be noted, that when I started, my goal was to find my line. In the process, I did not record the children of the female CANNEYS. The project to research the whole CANNEY family will never be complete. This is unfortunate. To go back in the records to find the children of the female CANNEYS would be a project in itself.

During all the years of research, I haven't found anywhere that someone else had done any in-depth research of the CANNEY family. One great disappointment comes to mind. When my wife and I joined the Piscataqua Pioneers, I found there were some members (now dead) that had CANNEY papers. When I asked to have a copy of them, I was given some disturbing news. In the 1930s an elderly member took these papers to write an article. During the time the member had these papers, he or she died. The family didn't know the importance of the papers and they were destroyed. What a loss!

This project has been very frustrating. Trying to research all alone is most difficult, and a project of this magnitude requires many people. While researching some old records of the early settlers, I noted an historical item. When the Pilgrims landed at Plymouth in 1620, they almost starved that first winter. They sent for food in order to survive. Where did they send for food? To England? Wrong. There wasn't time. It would take months for a round trip to England. They sent to Pemaquid, Maine, where the Puritans had settled about 1607. It is a fact that they were building ships at Pemaquid before the Pilgrims came to Plymouth. How come we did not learn this in school??? While reading the old newspapers of Dover, New Hampshire, I read about Davy Crockett. He was defeated for his second term to Congress. The reporter thought it was good to be rid of this drunkard. WHAT??? Our national hero? Did this defeat lead to his going to the Alamo? Probably!

##

THE CANNEY PROFILES - "350 YEARS"

THOMAS CANNEY AND HIS DESCENDANTS

THOMAS[1] CANNEY was born in 1600, possibly in Okehampton, England. He married first, Mary Loome, who was born about 1613. His second wife is unknown. He married third, before 1655, Jane -----. A search of English records does not show any Canneys living in England at this time. There is found the family of CANNE. Contained in the Index of Wills for Deanery of Totes there is listed:

NICHOLAS CANNE, resident Okehampton, Co, Devon. Will proved in 1587.
JOHN CANNE, resident Okehampton, Co. Devon. Will proved in 1614.

It would appear that this was the same family.

THOMAS[1] CANNEY came to America sometime prior to 1631. The exact date is not known because a fire in 1648 destroyed most of the old Dover records. He was brought to this country by Edward Hilton to settle in Capt. John Mason's "Laconia Patent." He landed at what is now known as Newington, N.H., and moved to Dover Neck in 1634. Dover Neck is across the river from Newington and is now known as Dover Point, which is part of Dover, N.H.

Thomas Canney and Elder William Wentworth were joint proprietors of the Fresh Creek Saw Mill and timber lands. Elder William Wentworth's wife was Elizabeth CANNEY and may have been a sister of Thomas. Thomas took a lot of Capt. Wiggans in 1634, and also had grants of land in 1652 and 1656. He signed the Dover Combination in 1640. He served on the Grand Jury in 1643 and 1656, and he was taxed from 1648 to 1668. He served as Constable in 1648; was described as a "wicked man" when he supported Parson Reynor during the time that the Quaker women were so troublesome. Thomas kept the women locked in his home.

He was a Freeman in 1653, and served as Selectman of Dover in 1658. He moved to York, Maine in 1671 but later returned.

On August 8, 1655, "Jane, wife of Thomas Canney, was presented for beating her husband, her daughter and her son-in-law Jeremy Tibbetts." A Court Record on June 26, 1660 shows that "Thomas Canney brought suit against Thomas Crowley for slandering his minor daughter Phebe." On June 26, 1661, another Court Record shows "Thomas Canney of Dover desireing the Court to free him from Common Training by reason he hath lost his eyesight." It was granted him. On Oct. 22, 1677 he signed a Petition to the King of England. He signed with an "X" because of his blindness.

Throughout the early records we find the name spelled various ways: CANEY, CANIE, CANNE, CANNEY, CANNY, CENNEY, KANNEY, KENNEY, KENNY. In the Dover area these were all the same family.

Children of Thomas Canney:
- i   Mary, b. ca 1637 in Dover, N.H.; m. (1) ca 1655 in Dover, Jeremiah Tibbetts, b. 1631, d. 1677 in Dover, son of Henry & Elizabeth (Austin) Tibbetts; m. (2) Nathaniel Loomis; d. 7 July 1706 in Dover.
- 2   ii   Thomas (see below)
- iii   Hannah, b. 1641 in Dover; m. Henry Hobbs. He d. bef. 18 Apr 1720. She d. after 18 Apr 1720.
- iv   Joseph, b. ca 1643 in Dover; m. (1) bef. 1669 Mary ----; m. (2) 25 Dec 1670 in Dover, Mary Clements, b. 12 Dec 1651 in Haverhill, Mass., dau of Counsellor Job and Margaret (Dummer) Clements; m. (3) Mary Dam, b. 4 Sep 1651 in Dover, dau. of Deacon John & Elizabeth (Pomfret) Dam. Joseph died 17 Nov 1690 in Dover, N.H.
- v   Phebe, b. ca 1647 in Dover.
- vi   Jane, b. ca 1655 in Dover; m. Matthew Austin.

THOMAS² CANNEY was born about 1639 in Dover, N.H. He married 3 October 1666 Sarah Taylor, born about 1647 in Hampton, N.H., died 23 Dec 1707 in Boston, Mass., the daughter of Anthony and Phillipi Taylor. Thomas died 15 May 1677 in Dover.

Children of Thomas Canney and Sarah Taylor:
- 3   i   Richard (possible son) (see below)
- ii   Sarah, b. 3 Aug 1667 in Dover; m. 1687 Thomas Roberts, Jr.
- iii   Martha, b. 5 Feb 1669 in Dover; m. 30 June 1687 in Dover, Benjamin Nason, son of Richard & Sarah (Baker?) Nason; d. bef. 27 Dec 1708.
- iv   Mary, b. 17 Jan 1671 in Dover; m. 18 Apr 1687 in Dover John Twombly, son of Ralph & Elizabeth Twombly.
- v   Lydia, b. 26 Aug 1673 in Dover; m. Tobias Hanson; d. bef 1698.
- vi   Thomas, b. 1 Nov 1675 in Dover; m. 1696 Grace Hartford, dau. of William Hartford. Thomas died in 1707.
- vii   Samuel, b. 24 May 1677 in Dover; m. 15 Mar 1698/9 Sarah (Hackett) Rankin, widow of Joseph Rankin. He was discharged from His Majesty's sevice at Capt. Gerrish's Garrison on 6 Dec 1695. Samuel died in 1735.

RICHARD[3] CANNEY, possible son of Thomas[2] Canney and Sarah Taylor, was born about 1665. He married 15 August 1687 in Dover, N.H. Deborah Stokes, baptized 18 Feb 1727/8, dau. of Isaac Stokes. Richard was under command of Capt. James Davis from 15 May 1712 to 12 October 1712. He was also on a scouting party in 1712 under Capt. Tibbetts. He lived in Dover and moved to the Great Island where he died.

Children of Richard Canney and Deborah Stokes:
4   i   Ichabod (see below)
    ii   Richard, b. ---; m. 19 Oct 1729 Rebecca Otis, b. 11 May 1695,
            dau. of Richard & Susannah (Hussey) Otis. Richard died
            26 Mar 1770.
    iii   James, b. ---; m. Mary Tuttle, b. 7 Jan 1697/8, dau. of Ensign
            John & Judith (Otis) Tuttle. James was a wealthy landowner
            in Somersworth, N.H.
    iv   John (possible son), b. ---; m. Hulda Stanyan, dau. of James
            & Ann (Partridge) Stanyan. They lived in Hampton, N.H.
            John died prior to 1742.
    v   a possible daughter who m. ----Waldron & had son Richard
            Kenney Waldron, b. 1719; m. Mary Clark, dau. of Abraham
            & Anna Clark.

ICHABOD[4] CANNEY, son of Richard Canney and Deborah Stokes, was born 26 June 1705. He married 19 Oct 1729 in Hampton, N.H. Susanna Stanyan, dau. of James and Ann (Partridge - widow of William Partridge) Stanyan. Ichabod was a Selectman of Madbury, N.H. in 1756/7, 1760, 1763-1774. He died (will) 1774 in Dover, N.H.

Children of Ichabod Canney and Susanna Stanyan:
5   i   Isaac (see below)
    ii   Moses, b. 23 July 1745; m. 30 Nov 1768 in Kittery, Maine,
            Hannah Sawyer, b. 6 Dec 1748, dau. of Moses & Hulda (Hill)
            Sawyer. Moses died 21 July 1792.
    iii   Deborah, b. ---; m. 26 Jan 1774 in Dover, Thomas Varney, who
            d. 11 Aug 1796, **son of Ebenezer & Elizabeth Varney.**
            Deborah died 7 Nov 1788.
    iv   Sarah, married and died before 1774.
    v   Susannah, possibly married John Wingate of Rochester, N.H. on
            1 Mar 1784 in Dover.
    vi   Anne, possibly married Joseph Perkins in Dec. 1779 in Madbury.

ISAAC[5] CANNEY, son of Ichabod Canney and Susanna Stanyan, married 2 May 1764 Sarah Daniels, daughter of Jacob and Charity Daniels. He was a Selectman of Madbury, N.H. in 1775 and 1776. He died in March of 1828.

Children of Isaac Canney and Sarah Daniels:
    i   Daniel (possible son), was b. in Feb 1768 in Madbury, N.H.;
            m. (1) Elizabeth Berry; m. (2) 12 Nov 1812 Sarah Nelson of
            Portsmouth, N.H., b. ca 1770. Daniel d. Feb 1846 in
            Farmington, N.H.
    ii   Ichabod (possible son), b. ca 1770 in Madbury, N.H. (1850
            census); m. 12 Jan 1792 in Barrington, N.H. Sarah Hanson,
            who was b. in Dover, dau. of Stephen & Mary (Austin)
            Hanson. Icahbod died 13 Jan 1855 in Dover, N.H.

iii   Jacob, b. 20 Feb 1776 in Madbury, N.H.; m. (1) 10 Apr 1805 in
        Barrington, N.H. Sarah J. Jenness, b. 1781, d. 1844. He
        m. (2) Sarah H. ----, b. 1783, d. 1851. Jacob died 8 Dec
        1857 in Barnstead, N.H.
iv   John, b. 5 Jan 1779 in Madbury; m. 15 Nov 1798 in Madbury
        Elizabeth Woodhouse, b. 2 Feb 1773, d. 10 Aug 1860. John
        d. 1 June 1867.
v   Moses (possible son), was born in Madbury; m. 4 July 1799 in
        Rochester, N.H. Susanna Perkins or Abigail Tibbetts.
6   vi   Samuel (see below)
vii   Susanna, m. 17 Aug 1792 Enock Clark of Barnstead, N.H.
viii Francis S. (possible son), was born in Barrington, N.H.; m.
        28 Mar 1811 in Barrington, Deborah Nutter of Rochester.

SAMUEL[6] CANNEY, son of Isaac Canney and Sarah Daniels, was born between 1780 and
1784 in Barrington, N.H. (1810, 1830 census). He married 2 June 1806 in
Barrington, Olive Ayers, who was born between 1780 and 1784. Samuel died 1848.

    Children of Samuel Canney and Olive Ayers:
        i   Charles, b. between 1794 and 1800 (1810 census); m. ca 1845
                Emma Edes. He moved to Bangor, Maine & d. ca 1902.
    7   ii   Isaac (see below)
        iii   Sarah, b. 8 Feb 1809 in Madbury, N.H.; m. 25 Dec 1836 in Bar-
                rington, N.H. Sampson B. Locke, b. 17 June 1811, d. 31 July
                1863, son of John & Mary (Dame) Locke. Sarah d. 23 Sept.
                1879 in Barrington, N.H.
        iv   Aaron, b. Apr 1822 in Madbury, N.H.; m. (1) 1 Jan 1851 in
                Dover, N.H. Nancy T. Demeritt, b. 2 Dec 1813, d. 7 Dec
                1872, dau. of Eli & Sally Demeritt; m. (2) 18 Sept 1877 in
                Durham, N.H. Hannah C. Hanson, b. 1832, dau. of Samuel &
                Clarissa Hanson. Aaron d. 29 Jan 1879 in Madbury, N.H.
        v   John, b. 24 July 1827 in Madbury; m. (1) Betsy Ann Tirrell,
                b. 1834, d. 25 June 1855; m. (2) Aug 1858 Susan Frances
                Sargent, b. 13 Nov 1836, dau. of Nathan & Mehitable (Brown)
                Sargent. John d. in 1897 in So. Franklin, Mass.
        vi   a daughter, b. between 1794 and 1800 (1810 census).
        vii   Jacob, b. ca 1799; m. 30 Nov 1825 in Strafford, N.H. Betsey
                Foss, b. ca 1796; d. 31 July 1895 in Strafford. Jacob d.
                30 Mar 1830 in Strafford, N.H.
        viii Samuel, b. ca 1815; m. 2 Dec 1844 in Dover, N.H. Hannah Bodge,
                b. ca 1805; d. 27 Nov 1882 in Dover, N.H.

ISAAC[7] CANNEY, son of Samuel Canney and Olive Ayers, was born 21 March 1807 in
Madbury, N.H. He married 26 September 1830 in Somersworth, N.H. Elizabeth
Cator, who was born 23 July 1811 in Barrington, N.H.; d. 3 Oct 1903 in Dover
N.H.; daughter of John and Mary (Gorver) Cator. Isaac died 12 January 1883 in
Dover, N.H.

    Children of Isaac Canney and Elizabeth Cator:
        i   Charles E., b. ca 1833 in Barrington, N.H.; m. (1) 30 Jan 1849
                Almira E. Frazier, b. 1830. He m. (2) 10 Mar 1858 in
                Dover, N.H. Elizabeth C. Kimball. (Will 1863)
        ii   George F., b. 18 Feb 1836; m. (1) Margaret E. Caswell?, b.
                1838, d. 6 Aug 1880; m. (2) 10 Nov 1881 in Dover, N.H.
                Margaret Hannah Babb, b. 1831, d. 27 May 1900, dau. of

Isaac & Lucinder (Leighton) Babb. George d. 6 Jan 1914.
         iii   Olive S., b. ca 1841.
8   iv   John W. (see below)

JOHN W.[8] CANNEY, son of Isaac Canney and Elizabeth Cator, was born 16 December
1845 in Barrington, N.H. He married 13 Mar 1869 in Dover, N.H. Cynthia A.
Huntoon, who was born 1 Nov 1850 and died 1 March 1922 in Pepperell, Mass.,
daughter of George W. and Malvina (Drew) Huntoon. John died 24 January 1923 in
Dover, N.H.

    Children of John W. Canney and Cynthia A. Huntoon:
         i   ?
9   ii   Lyman, b. 24 June 1869; m. 25 Sept 1889 Grace H. Frost, b.
               28 Oct 1865; d. 11 Nov 1932 in Pepperell, Mass., dau of
               Marcells and Susan Melissa (Tuttle) Frost. Lyman died
               1924 in Dover, N.H.

###

THE AMERICAN ANCESTRY OF ELTHEA PRINCE WILLETT,
WIFE OF ELBRIDGE WILLS

     In January I completed the identification of the American ances-
tors of my great-great-grandmother - the first instance within my own
ancestry of completing a one-sixteenth segment of my total American
Ancestry on back to the "first-comers" in that great migration to the
Massachusetts Bay Colony in the early 17th century. On the negative
side, it means that I still have fifteen great-great-grandparents to
complete. So my job as genealogist is still far from complete!

     The enclosed pedigree charts show for the most part the American
ancestry of my great-great-great grandparents. In summary, Moses[6]
Millett (1793-1866) is my great-great-great grandfather (No. 38 in my
ancestry) and his wife was Rhoda Prince (1794-1866). His parents as
well as hers were from New Gloucester, Maine. Moses and Rhoda were
born in Poland, Maine but lived most of their lives in Minot, Maine.
Otherwise, all their ancestry is 100% Essex County, Mass. (Gloucester,
Ipswich, Beverly, Salem, Newbury, Salisbury, and Amesbury). Their
daughter Elthea Prince Millett (1834-1893) married Elbridge Wills
(1829-1907) and they lived in Turner, Maine. Their daughter Rhoda A.
Wills (1860-1938) married Isaiah W. Smith (1859-1925) and they lived in
Gardiner, Maine being the parents of my paternal grandfather Fred L.
Smith (1894-1959).

          Danny D. Smith, R.F.D. #5A, Box 306, Gardiner, Maine 04345

(1793-1866) of Minot, Maine

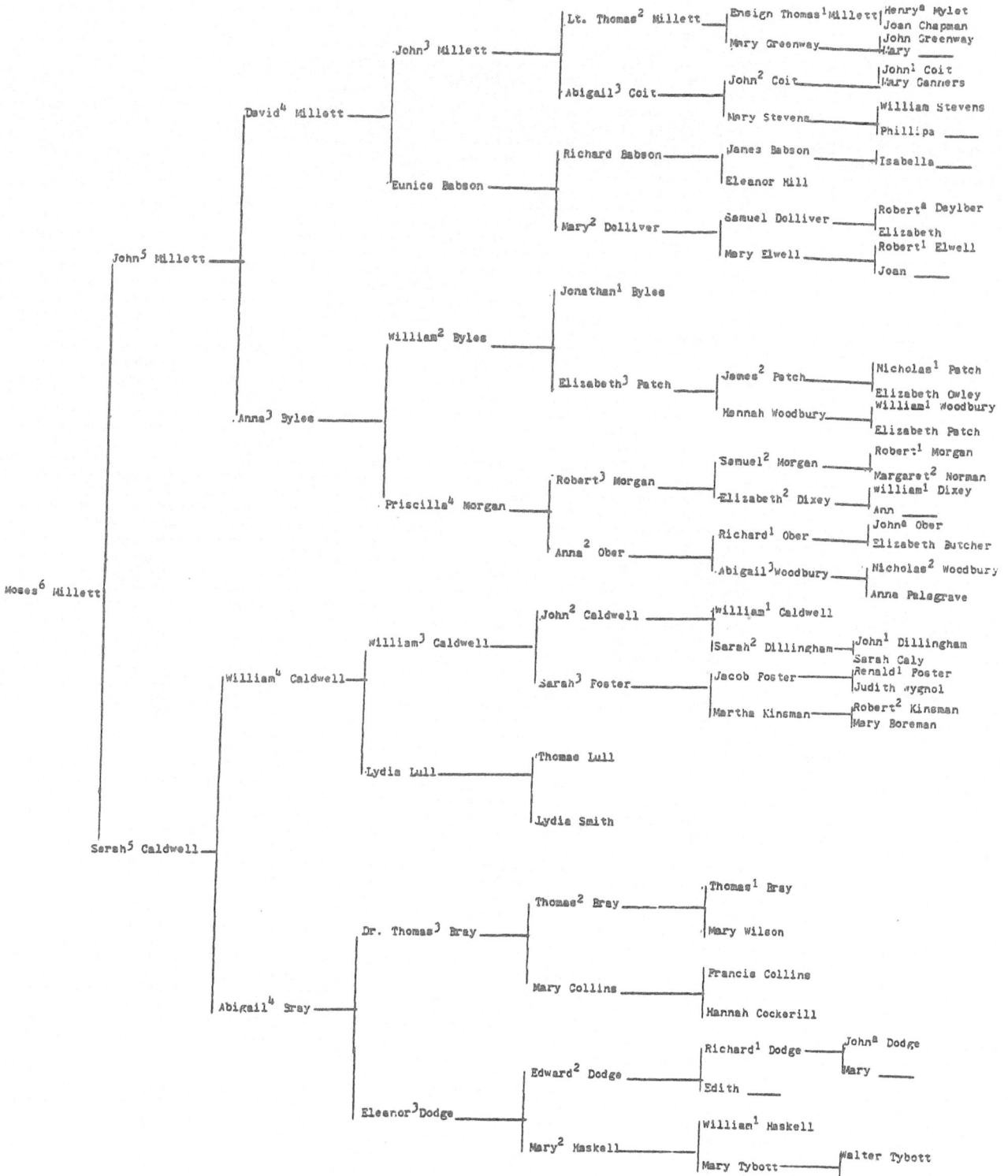

Moses⁶ Millett

John⁵ Millett

David⁴ Millett

John³ Millett

Lt. Thomas² Millett
- Ensign Thomas¹ Millett
  - Henry⁸ Mylet
  - Joan Chapman
- Mary Greenway
  - John Greenway
  - Mary

Abigail³ Coit
- John² Coit
  - John¹ Coit
  - Mary Ganners
- Mary Stevens
  - William Stevens
  - Phillipa ____

Eunice Babson

Richard Babson
- James Babson
  - Isabella ____
- Eleanor Hill

Mary² Dolliver
- Samuel Dolliver
  - Robert⁸ Daylber
  - Elizabeth
- Mary Elwell
  - Robert¹ Elwell
  - Joan ____

Anna³ Byles

William² Byles

Jonathan¹ Byles

Elizabeth³ Patch
- James² Patch
  - Nicholas¹ Patch
  - Elizabeth Owley
- Hannah Woodbury
  - William¹ Woodbury
  - Elizabeth Patch

Priscilla⁴ Morgan

Robert³ Morgan
- Samuel² Morgan
  - Robert¹ Morgan
  - Margaret² Norman
- Elizabeth² Dixey
  - William¹ Dixey
  - Ann ____

Anna² Ober
- Richard¹ Ober
  - John⁸ Ober
  - Elizabeth Butcher
- Abigail³ Woodbury
  - Nicholas² Woodbury
  - Anna Palsgrave

Sarah⁵ Caldwell

William⁴ Caldwell

William³ Caldwell

John² Caldwell
- William¹ Caldwell
- Sarah² Dillingham
  - John¹ Dillingham
  - Sarah Caly

Sarah³ Foster
- Jacob Foster
  - Renald¹ Foster
  - Judith Wygnol
- Martha Kinsman
  - Robert² Kinsman
  - Mary Boreman

Lydia Lull

Thomas Lull

Lydia Smith

Abigail⁴ Bray

Dr. Thomas³ Bray

Thomas² Bray
- Thomas¹ Bray
- Mary Wilson

Mary Collins
- Francis Collins
- Hannah Cockerill

Eleanor³ Dodge

Edward² Dodge
- Richard¹ Dodge
  - John⁸ Dodge
  - Mary ____
- Edith ____

Mary² Haskell
- William¹ Haskell
- Mary Tybott
  - Walter Tybott

129

(1794-1866) of Minot, Maine

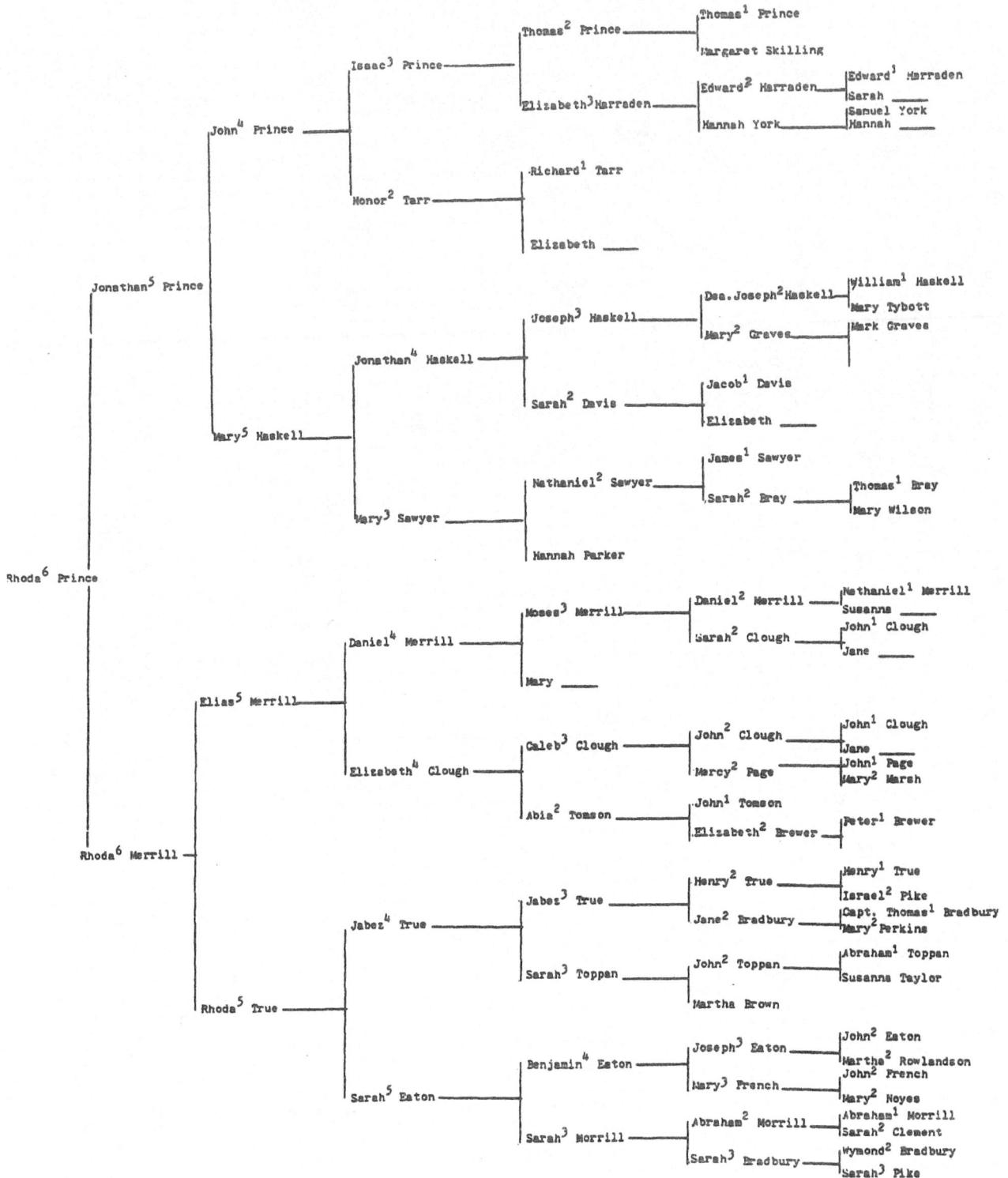

```
Rhoda⁶ Prince
│
├── Jonathan⁵ Prince
│   │
│   ├── John⁴ Prince
│   │   │
│   │   ├── Isaac³ Prince
│   │   │   │
│   │   │   ├── Thomas² Prince
│   │   │   │   ├── Thomas¹ Prince
│   │   │   │   └── Margaret Skilling
│   │   │   │
│   │   │   └── Elizabeth³ Harraden
│   │   │       ├── Edward² Harraden
│   │   │       │   ├── Edward¹ Harraden
│   │   │       │   └── Sarah ____
│   │   │       └── Hannah York
│   │   │           ├── Samuel York
│   │   │           └── Hannah ____
│   │   │
│   │   └── Honor² Tarr
│   │       ├── Richard¹ Tarr
│   │       └── Elizabeth ____
│   │
│   └── Mary⁵ Haskell
│       │
│       ├── Jonathan⁴ Haskell
│       │   │
│       │   ├── Joseph³ Haskell
│       │   │   ├── Dea. Joseph² Haskell
│       │   │   │   ├── William¹ Haskell
│       │   │   │   └── Mary Tybott
│       │   │   └── Mary² Graves
│       │   │       └── Mark Graves
│       │   │
│       │   └── Sarah² Davis
│       │       ├── Jacob¹ Davis
│       │       └── Elizabeth ____
│       │
│       └── Mary³ Sawyer
│           │
│           ├── Nathaniel² Sawyer
│           │   ├── James¹ Sawyer
│           │   └── Sarah² Bray
│           │       ├── Thomas¹ Bray
│           │       └── Mary Wilson
│           │
│           └── Hannah Parker
│
└── Rhoda⁶ Merrill
    │
    ├── Elias⁵ Merrill
    │   │
    │   ├── Daniel⁴ Merrill
    │   │   │
    │   │   ├── Moses³ Merrill
    │   │   │   ├── Daniel² Merrill
    │   │   │   │   ├── Nathaniel¹ Merrill
    │   │   │   │   └── Susanna ____
    │   │   │   └── Sarah² Clough
    │   │   │       ├── John¹ Clough
    │   │   │       └── Jane ____
    │   │   │
    │   │   └── Mary ____
    │   │
    │   └── Elizabeth⁴ Clough
    │       │
    │       ├── Caleb³ Clough
    │       │   ├── John² Clough
    │       │   │   ├── John¹ Clough
    │       │   │   └── Jane ____
    │       │   └── Mercy² Page
    │       │       ├── John¹ Page
    │       │       └── Mary² Marsh
    │       │
    │       └── Abia² Tomson
    │           ├── John¹ Tomson
    │           └── Elizabeth² Brewer
    │               └── Peter¹ Brewer
    │
    └── Rhoda⁵ True
        │
        ├── Jabez⁴ True
        │   │
        │   ├── Jabez³ True
        │   │   ├── Henry² True
        │   │   │   ├── Henry¹ True
        │   │   │   └── Israel² Pike
        │   │   └── Jane² Bradbury
        │   │       ├── Capt. Thomas¹ Bradbury
        │   │       └── Mary² Perkins
        │   │
        │   └── Sarah³ Toppan
        │       ├── John² Toppan
        │       │   ├── Abraham¹ Toppan
        │       │   └── Susanna Taylor
        │       └── Martha Brown
        │
        └── Sarah⁵ Eaton
            │
            ├── Benjamin⁴ Eaton
            │   ├── Joseph³ Eaton
            │   │   ├── John² Eaton
            │   │   └── Martha² Rowlandson
            │   └── Mary³ French
            │       ├── John² French
            │       └── Mary² Noyes
            │
            └── Sarah³ Morrill
                ├── Abraham² Morrill
                │   ├── Abraham¹ Morrill
                │   └── Sarah² Clement
                └── Sarah³ Bradbury
                    ├── Wymond² Bradbury
                    └── Sarah³ Pike
```

A SAMPLER TELLS THE STORY

By Marcia Wiswall Lindberg

Nathan Mudge, my fourth great-grandfather, had two wives and sixteen children - and I descend from his first wife, Hannah Ingalls. I was not particularly interested in his second wife, whom <u>Mudge</u> <u>Memorials</u> gives as "Elizabeth Burrill, widow of Shubael," and when I received a query years ago asking if I knew who she was, I replied in the negative.

Then, several months ago, in a fine example of genealogists helping one another, Warren Falls of Lynn told me there was a "Mudge" sampler at the Lynn Historical Society. Would I like a photograph of it? "Yes, indeed," I replied. "I would love it!" Reproduced on page 132, this touching needlework of 10-year-old Lydia Mudge tells the whole story.

Nathan's second wife, "widow Burrill," had been married not just once, but twice before, and had had two children by each of her first two husbands. Born Elizabeth Baker (16 July 1765), she married (1) Peter Granger (b. 15 Oct 1755; d. 2 July 1786) and had Charles Granger (b. 22 Sept 1782), and Elizabeth Granger (b. 2 Apr 1785). She married (2) Shubel Burrill (b. 7 Sept 1754; d. 6 Oct 1793); and had Alden Burrill (b. 5 May 1789; d. 2 Feb 1806); and Shubel Burrill (b. 28 Aug 1791; d. 1 Oct 1801). She married (3) Nathan Mudge and had nine more children. Nathan and Elizabeth, between them, had <u>20 children</u>. In those days, children had to learn to adapt to step-parents without benefit of all the "How-to books" we have today!

After the excitement of "finding" this beautiful sampler abated, I wondered if it would have been possible to have pieced this family puzzle together using only the Lynn VRs to 1850. And, indeed, it would have! By matching the four Burrill males who married "Elizabeths" (in the right time frames) with the deaths of those Burrill males, only one died early enough for Elizabeth to marry Nathan Mudge - Shubel Burrill who married Elizabeth Granger. The "code" beside this marriage is given as "P.R. 16" - and that reference, given in the front of the VRs is: "Record from sampler now in possession of Mary E. Walter of Chicago!" Once that has been discovered, a look at Granger births yields no Elizabeth of correct age. <u>But</u>, if one were careful enough to consider another possible marriage, the Granger marriages show only one record with "P.R. 16" beside it - Peter Granger to Elizabeth Baker! Thus the story could be traced without seeing the sampler itself. The births of Peter Granger and Elizabeth Baker, however, do not appear to have occurred in Lynn. No record of their parents has been found and the <u>Genealogy</u> <u>of</u> <u>the</u> <u>Descendants</u> <u>of</u> <u>Edward</u> <u>Baker</u> <u>of</u> <u>Lynn</u>, by Nelson M. Baker, does not help. If any readers know the parentage of these two, I would be interested in that information.

I was also interested to call Faith Magoun, Director of the Lynn Historical Society, to see if she had a record of the doner of this particular sampler. Her record did not give the doner - so I pointed out the credit in the Lynn VRs.

All this "Monday morning quarterbacking" is fine, but few of us would take the time and trouble to work these puzzles out. Lydia Mudge's sampler makes it so much easier. Young Lydia died, according to an added bit of stitchery on the sampler, in 1822 at the tender age of 19, but she left behind an exquisite piece of needlework for all to enjoy.

MUDGE SAMPLER - THE FAMILY OF NATHAN MUDGE OF LYNN

Embroidered at Lynn, 2 September 1813, by Lydia Mudge, age 10

(Sampler owned by Lynn Historical Society - Photograph by Warren Falls)

OTHER FAMILY REGISTERS FROM SAMPLERS AT LYNN HISTORICAL SOCIETY

(Submitted by Faith Magoun)

ATWILL/INGALLS   Sampler LHS #3342

(emboidered by Betsy F. Attwill, aged 10, July 11th, 1814)

Mr. John D. Attwill, born May 7, 1771; married Nov 18, 1794, Miss Martha Ingalls, b. March 2, 1778.

Chidren's Names	Births	Deaths
Martha Attwill	March 20, 1797	July 3, 1817
Nelson R. Attwill	September 1, 1798	
John D. Attwill	May 1, 1800	
Mary Attwill	April 25, 1802	
Betsy F. Attwill	Feb. 4, 1804	
Alfred Attwill	January 29, 1806	
Gustavus Attwill	May 22, 1808	
Edwin Attwill	August 7, 1810	
Richard J. Attwill	July 17, 1812	
William A. Attwill	March 22, 1814	
Jacob Attwill	March 26, 1816	April 4, 1816
Joseph W. Attwill	July 2, 1817	
Benjamin E. Attwill	July 3, 1817	

(Note: last 2 appear to be twins born, presumably, around midnight!)

###

ALLEY/BUFFUM   Sampler LHS #23

(Wrought by Hannah Alley, 1826, age 12 years, Lynn)

Mr. John Alley was born Jan 14, 1777. Miss Mercy Buffum was born April 6, 1779

Names	Births	Deaths
Caleb B Alley	born Sep 29 1801	
Daniel Alley	born Nov 24 1804	
Jonathan Alley	born Jan 10 1807	Died Aug 17 1814
John Alley	born Aug 8 1809	Died Sep 12 1809
Peace B. Alley	born Oct 19 1810	
Hannah Alley	born Aug 29 1812	Died Oct 26 1813
Hannah Alley	born Feb 10 1814	
Jonathan Alley	born Aug 3 1816	
John B. Alley	born Jan 7 1817	
Anna Alley	born April 9 1818	
Sarah Alley	born Oct 17 1819	
Mary B. Alley	born April 20 1822	
Catherine Alley	born March 21 1824	Died Sep 23 1824

##

HALL/HANSON   Sampler LHS #4921

(Wrought by Mary Ann Hall, 1835)

Paul Hall, born July 31 1798 married Oct 12 1820 Huldah Hanson, born Oct 31 1799

Their Progeny
Augustus H. Hall	born July 12 1821	
Amos B. Hall	born Dec 7 1822	
Edward R. Hall	born Aug 7 1824	Died Sept 9 1823
Phinelia El Hall	born Nov 9 1825	
Mary A. M. Hall	born April 3 1827	
George E. Hall	born Dec 17 1829	

###

HOOD/BREED   Sampler LHS #3036

(Wrought by Content Hood, 1810)

Abner Hood, born 7 Month 26 1733 married 6 Month 11 1783 Keezia Breed, born 8 Month 14 1750 (?)

Abner Hood	born 4 Month 1 1784
Richard Hood	born 3 Month 13 1786
Theodate Hood	born 3 Month 23 1787
Benjamin & Ebenezer Hood	born 4 Month 7 1790
Content Hood	born 2 Month 21 1792

###

NEWHALL/FARRINGTON   Sampler LHS #196

(Hannah Newhall, aged 17, wrought this work, Lynn, June 7th, 1814)

Micajah Newhall, born October 18th, 1756, married 10 June 1779 Joana Farington, born November 16th, 1763.

Children's Names	Births	Deaths
Josiah Newhall	November 10th, 1780	
Nathaniel Newhall	July 2nd, 1782	
Micajah Newhall	July 25th, 1784	
Paul Newhall	February 17th, 1786	
Otis Newhall	January 15th, 1788	
Sarah Newhall	August 17th, 1789	
Ellies Newhall	August 16th, 1791	
Ellies Newhall	March 7th, 1793	
Joanna Newhall	February 8th, 1795	
Hannah Newhall	April 8th, 1797	
Suanna Newhall	October 25th, 1799	June 10, 1802
William F. Newhall	January 13th, 1802	
Lydia Newhall	September 2d, 1804	

###

RAMSDELL/MANSFIELD   Sampler LHS #194

(Wrought by Mary Ramsdell, Lynn)

Mr. Abijah Ramsdell, born Jan 17 1768, married June 30, 1791, Miss Deborah
Mansfield, born June 4, 1768.

Names	Births	Deaths
Daniel S. Ramsdell	April 11 1792	
Sarah Ramsdell	Dec 24 1793	
Mary Ramsdell	Oct 22 1797	Dec 2, 1804
Robert Ramsdell	Aug 3 1800	Aug 12, 1809
Huldah Ramsdell	June 4 1803	Oct 14, 1804
Mary Ramsdell	Oct 4 1805	
Robert Ramsdell	April 6 1812	
Oliver Ramsdell	Nov 12 1815	

****

LOVEJOY/BLANCHARD   Sampler LHS #193

(Wrought by Harriet Lovejoy, 1823, 9 years)

Mr. John Lovejoy was born Dec 16, 1789, married May 30, 1813 Miss Lavina
Blanchard, born Jan 11, 1791.

Names	Births	Deaths
Harriet Lovejoy	March 10, 1814	
Elbridge Lovejoy	May 24 1816	
Charles Lovejoy	July 30 1818	August 28 1819

Sarah L. Larrabee	Nov 11 1836	
Ellen R. Larrabee	March 31 1842	
Charles L. Larrabee	Nov 1 1845	

Mrs. Lavina Lovejoy   Died   August 27 1819 aged 29 years

****

NOURSE/MANSFIELD   Sampler LHS #5443 (badly damaged)

Mr. James Nourse, born Feb 7, 1762, married September 15, 1785, Mrs. Elizabeth
Mansfield, born May 10 1763.

Children's Names	Births	Deaths
John	March 25 1786	
Edmund	April 5 1788	
Lucy	(?) 1790	
Robert	Sept (?) 1792	(?) June 5 1810
Rebekah	Oct 23 1794	
Elizabeth	April 15 (?) 1797	
Mary	March 8 1800	
James	Nov 14 1802	

```
**************************************************
```

ALLEY/TARBOX   Sampler LHS #195

(wrought by Mary Ann Alley, Lynn, October 9th, 1818, aged 10 years)

Mr. Joseph Alley, Jr., born May 6th, 1789, married at Lynn May 3d, 1807 Miss Anna Tarbox, born October 29th, 1789.

Children's Names	Births	Deaths
Mary Ann	born April 6th, 1808	Oct. 30th, 1877
George Warren	born July 27th, 1810	Sept. 27th 1811

Mrs Anna Alley died August 22d 1812.

```
**************************************************
```

JOHNSON/CHADWELL   Sampler LHS #525

(Wrought by Eliza Ann Johnson, 1826, aged 16 years)

Mr. Timothy Johnson, born Dec 30th, 1763; married Nov 15th, 1789, Miss Elizabeth Chadwell, born July 12th, 1769.

Names	Births	Deaths
Lydia Johnson	was born Oct. 31st, 1790	
Timothy Johnson	was born Dec. 30th, 1793	died Nov. 12th 1795
Timothy Johnson	was born Aug. 25th, 1796	
Rufus Johnson	was born Oct. 30th, 1798	
Richard Johnson	was born June 30th, 1805	
Eliza Ann Johnson	was born June 22nd, 1810	

But they shall live again	Then stop the falling tear
Enrobed in bright array	And hush the heaving sigh
Shall take their part in heavenly	And sorrow not for them
strains	they're where
In everlasting day	Eternal joys arise.

```
**************************************************
```

(Note: Most of the above-described samplers had verses embroidered at the bottom similar to the one wrought by Eliza Ann Johnson)

```
**************************************************
```

Special Feature

COLLECTIONS OF THE IPSWICH HISTORICAL SOCIETY

By Helen Breen

"Essex County has more historical societies per square mile than any part of the country," a sage once remarked. And, he may have added, "no two are alike." Genealogists with roots in surrounding towns should contact the appropriate historical societies and inquire about the availability of their papers which may contain valuable data. Perusing such materials is fun, particularly when the experience is combined with lunch and historical sightseeing nearby in the company of a fellow-researcher. Recently Marcia Wiswall Lindberg and I enjoyed such a day while investigating the collections of the Ipswich Historical Society for TEG readers.

Arriving on a muggy July morning at the Ipswich Public Library, we were greeted by Mrs. Penny Gaunt, a friend of Marcia's, who is the Head Librarian. We had a quick tour of the facility which is in the process of renovation. A climate-controlled space in the basement is being prepared to house the historical papers. Delays in the project have resulted from budgetary constraints, a story we all know well.

Then Mrs. Mary Conley, Chairperson of the Historical Commission and a Director of the Ipswich Historical Society, escorted us upstairs in the building to where the historical holdings are kept. Three round tables with four chairs each provide sufficient work space. Large glass book cases along one wall contain about 150 family histories, in addition to the standard fare of regimental histories and works of local interest. Then we got to the heart of the matter, the papers of the Ipswich Historical Society which are locked in four large steel filing cabinets at the far end of the room. Mary explained that since the founding of the Ipswich Historical Society in 1898, hundreds of documents, family papers, enlistments, diaries, accounts, and miscellaneous records have accumulated. When the Mormons microfilmed town records in the late 60s, the Historical Society realized that their own vast holdings badly needed attention. Consequently, the Society, with the cooperation of the Historical Commission, the Public Library, and the town fathers, created an Archives Committee to oversee the restoration and cataloging of the collections. Tom Leavitt of the Textile Museum in North Andover was the original consultant. Important papers were sent to the Northeast Document Center for treatment. A number of grants from the Arts and Humanities Council defrayed some of the costs.

The richness and variety of the collections will intrigue genealogists and historians alike. Mary mentioned a few examples of materials which have attracted the attention of scholars in women's studies. One group of materials includes the directories and accounts of the Ipswich Female Seminary, which drew hundreds of girls to the town from 1826 to 1863, includng Mary Lyon, the founder of Mt. Holyoke College. Another is the diary of a local girl, Mary E. Brown, which recently caught the attention of a researcher from the Radcliffe Library. Giving a charming glimpse into everyday life in the nineteenth century, the account begins: "January 1, 1898. Snowing hard. Otis gone to the ordination. Mother making donuts."

The biggest bonus for genealogists, however, is the eight-drawer card file to the papers by name and date. A small group of dedicated volunteers, headed by the late Ann Durey, spent years combing through these materials listing and cross-referencing every name contained in the documents. Hence, if a person was a witness to a will, his name would be on a separate catalog card with a "see" reference to the appropriate record. As a librarian, Marcia was impressed with this attention to detail. A catalog of the papers by date is also available. Mary modestly admitted that she worked on this task herself for years. Truly a labor of love!

Two examples of catalog cards pulled at random are:
1678   APPLETON, Major Samuel
Dec 28 APPEAL, by Samuel Appleton, Jr. re Saugus Iron Works
                property.
1728   KNOWLTON, Dan
May 22 DEED OF SALE to Dan Calwell
                upland lot #244 at Jeffrey's Neck, Ipswich

Anyone wishing to use the collections of the Ipswich Historical Society should contact the Ipswich Public Library, 25 North Main St. (356-4646). Researchers should call ahead because these irreplaceable documents can be viewed only in the presence of Mary or other qualified volunteers.

###

THE IPSWICH HISTORICAL SOCIETY

The Ipswich Historical Society was organized in 1890 and incorporated in 1898 by Rev. Thomas Franklin Waters, who served as its president until 1919. A local minister, he wrote Ipswich in the Massachusetts Bay Colony one of the finest local histories of the period. The Society has a full lecture series, hosts a Christmas "Open House" at the Heard mansion, and sponsors the famous "Ipswich 17th Century Day" each summer.

Marcia and I toured the Whipple House, home address for the Society, before our library visit. There we enjoyed a pleasant chat with the resident curator, Mrs. Elizabeth Newton. We bought a few booklets for the ESOG collection. Five old publications of the Ipswich Historical Society include:
Thomas Dudley and Simon and Ann Bradstreet (a study of house-lots to determine
    the location of their homes), 1903.
The Old Bay Road from Saltonstall's Brook and Samuel Appleton's Farm. (a
    genealogy of the Ipswich descendants of Samuel Appleton), by Waters, 1907.
Augustine Heard and His Friends, by Waters, 1916.
Two Ipswich Patriots, by Waters, 1929.

Two more recent monographs from the "Essex Institute Historical Collections" are:
John Wise of Ipswich was no Democrat in Politics, by Raymond Stearns, 1961.
Nathaniel Ward: Constitutional Draftsman, by Frederick S. Allis, Jr., with
The Body of Liberties, 1984. The latter was commissioned by the Ipswich Historical Society as part of the 250th Anniversary of the founding of the Town on August 5, 1634.

Marcia and I are grateful to Mrs. Penny Gaunt and Mrs. Mary Conley for welcoming us to Ipswich and inviting us to view their unique collections.

DRAWING OF F.F. REINERT

DRAWING BY FREDERICK P. REINERT

THE WHIPPLE HOUSE — 1640

The John Whipple House built by John Fawn
in 1640 was originally a two story, two room house
— with the steep-pitched, thatched roof and case-
ment windows of the Elizabethan period. By 1642
Elder John Whipple was living here and it was
owned and occupied by successive generations of
his descendants for two hundred years. The east
half was added in 1670 and the lean-to after 1700.

Entering through a charming 17th century
garden with clam-shell walks, the visitor will see
the heavy chamfered oak and tamarack beams, gun-
stock posts, pine panelling with shadow moulding,
clay and brick filled walls and huge fire-places of
the early seventeenth century. Wallace Nutting
called the "Great Room — probably the best in the
country". Its cross summer beam of oak with ogee
moulding is unusually fine.

In 1898 the Ipswich Historical Society bought
and restored the house. Many of the old Ipswich
families have contributed to the furnishings which
are of the seventeenth and eighteenth centuries.

CAPT. AUGUSTINE HEARD.

Capt. Heard was the founder of the Ipswich Free Public Library,
giving the building, 3,000 volumes, and an endowment fund of
$10,000.

139

AUGUSTINE HEARD, THE IPSWICH LIBRARY, and THE DARLING PAPERS

By Eleanor V. Spiller

Augustine Heard, modest philanthropist, was one of thirteen children. His father, John Heard, was a most prosperous merchant of Ipswich, Massachusetts. He was owner of a distillery and ships; he was Coroner, State Senator, Session Justice of the Circuit Court of Common Pleas, Presidential Elector in 1820, and a delegate to the Constitutional Revision Convention. He bought the interest of many returning Ipswich privateersmen and he contributed to the outfitting of the "General Stark" of Gloucester, soon arming and equipping his own brig "John," during the Revolution. Gilbert Stuart painted his portrait.

John Heard married twice. His first wife, Elizabeth Ann Story, who died 26 June 1775, was the daughter of William Story, Esq. They married in October 1766 and had five children; three died young. Sarah Staniford became his second wife on 9 February 1777, and she reared the survivors of his first family. Sally died on 12 September 1795 after the birth of her ninth child, Mary.

Augustine Heard, born 30 March 1785, was the fifth of John and Sally's children. His brothers were illustrious in their own right. Much could be written about John Jr., Daniel S., and Dr. George W. Heard. John and George went to Harvard, but neither Daniel nor Augustine chose to do so. Lack of much information of Charles may indicate a stay-at-homer. Augustine started at Phillips Exeter in 1799. In 1805, when barely twenty years of age he was employed as a supercargo, on one of Ebenezer Francis's ships. Through the years, his astute business/trading acumen took in, in the employ of several merchants, on other trips to Leghorn, Calcutta and various other worldly ports of call. He represented such men as Israel Thorndike of Beverly, and Mr. Pickering Dodge, plus several Boston men whose firms or ships traded throughout the Mediterranean and Far East.

Captain Augustine Heard, following the same call as other men of his family, took out his first vessel in 1812. His past experiences aided him greatly in the pursuance of his duties as chief officer and master mariner. One of his last ships, the "Linten" took him to China. He retired from the active sea life after this trip which started 7 July 1830. His log books are filled with exasperating and memorable experiences.

Thereafter, he and two Forbes brothers went out to Canton to manage the affairs of Russell & Co. - a commission or agency house. Owing to a dispute among the partners of Russell & Co., Augustine soon organized his own firm of Augustine Heard and Co., after 1836. Continuing most successfully in the China trade until the 1870s, the firm's most lucrative years were the early 1850s. The Opium Wars treaties of 1842-1844 liberalized terms in new fields of operations.

By 1855, Augustine (known to the business as Augustine Sr.) was a silent partner in Ipswich. As nephews John, Augustine (Jr. in the business) and Albert F. came of age they became controlling partners in the firm. They set up branch offices in Hong Kong, Shanghai, Foochow, Amoy and Ningpo. Their constituents consisted of many firms in Boston, New York and still others in Australia, Britain, Sitka, Paris, Manila, St. Petersburg, etc. Commodities involved were tea, specie, opium, beche de mer, manufactured goods, indigo, cloves, pepper, rattans and more. At one time, in 1859, Heard & Co. had 27,000 chests (135 pounds per chest) of Malwa opium and 6,000 chests of Patna opium in receiving ships in Shanghai (Woosung).

Augustine Heard gave of his fortune munificently but quietly and unostentatiously. No case of real need was ever laid before him in vain. Among his larger contributions to his community was the fine organ for the new First Church Meeting House built in 1847. His nephew John gave the bell.

The Ipswich Town Report tells us that, during the United States Civil War, "Mr. Augustine Heard, in conjunction with his nephews John, Augustine, Alfred F. and George F. Heard, in June, 1863, placed in the hands of trustees, $10,000 to be applied for the relief of such persons belonging to the town as may suffer from sickness or wounds incurred in the service of their country in the present civil war and for the relief of such persons as may be deprived of support by the loss of relatives engaged in the like service."

In his declining years, Augustine's prime interest was the leaving of a library to the town of his birth. He personally selected the site and the plans, purchased the land, and supervised the building of the edifice. He appointed the Trustees, declared the policy he wished followed, and appointed the first librarian. He provided for an endowment so that the library would be self-supporting forever, and free to all. He provided for 3,000 volumes of English literature, and later his nephews gave money for another 7,000 volumes. Augustine's total legacy totalled over $40,000. He never lived to see the use of his dream by the "common people" whom he wanted to have "literary advantages of the highest order."

Augustine Heard died on the 14th of September 1868 after a short illness. The Ipswich Heard library is, indeed, a monument to his love, intelligence, sagacity and benevolence.

References:
Augustine Heard and Co. 1858-1862 - American Merchants in China, by Stephen C. Lockwood. (Harvard East Asian Monograph)
Augustine Heard and His Friends, by Thomas Franklin Waters.
Augustine Heard Funeral Service, First Parish, 16 Sept. 1868. Eulogy by Rev. J. P. Cowles, Principal of the Ipswich Female Seminary.

##

GENEALOGY OF AUGUSTINE HEARD

Daniel Heard, grandfather of Augustine Heard, was baptized at Ipswich 6/8mo/1717; died Nov 1794. He married at Ipswich 16 April 1741, Mary Dean (Dane) who was baptized at Ipswich 25 June 1721.

Children of Daniel Heard and Mary Dean (Dane), all baptized at Ipswich:
    i   Daniel, bpt. 16 May 1742; d. 14 Dec 1770; m. Elizabeth Knowlton.
 # ii   John (see below)
   iii   Samuel, bpt. 5 Apr 1747.
    iv   Mary, bpt. 9 July 1749.
     v   Nathan, bpt. 22 Sept 1751.
    vi   Samuel, bpt. 6 Jan 1754.

vii   Amos, bpt. 18 Jan 1758; m. Mary Stevens of Durham, NH.
viii   Nathaniel, bpt. 27 Aug 1758; d. 9 Nov 1840; m. Susanna Spiller.
        (12 children)

<u>John</u> <u>Heard</u> was baptized at Ipswich 19 May 1744; died there 11 August 1834. He married, first October 1766, Elizabeth Ann Story. She died 26 June 1775 and John married second, 9 February 1777 Sarah Staniford. Sarah died 12 Sept 1796.

Children of John Heard and Elizabeth Ann Story, all born at Ipswich:
   i   Elizabeth, b. 16 Feb 1771; d. April 1771.
  ii   Elizabeth, b. 15 May 1772; d. 6 July 1773.
 iii   Mary, b. 27 May 1773; d. 9 Oct 1795. Studied music.
  iv   John, b. 12 Jan 1775.

Children of John Heard and Sarah Staniford, all born at Ipswich:
   v   Daniel, b. 3 Dec 1778; d. 13 Dec 1801 at Canton. He was a Partner: Frankford & Heard - mercantile Ship. Sea Capt/supercarge.
  vi   Sarah, b. 3 Aug 1780; d. 22 May 1801.
 vii   Elizabeth, b. 26 Mar 1782; d. 20 June 1805.
viii   Margaret, b. 26 Aug 1783; m. 1807 Dr. Thomas Manning.
  ix   Augustine, b. 30 Mar 1785; d. 14 Sep 1868.
   x   Hannah Staniford, b. 3 June 1789; m. Harvard Prof. Sidney Willard.
  xi   George Washington, b. 1792. Harvard 1812; Medicine, 1815; m. Elizabeth Ann Farley. Children: John, Augustine, Albert Farley, George.
 xii   Mary, b. 24 July 1796.

###

THE FAMILY OF EDWARD CHISTOPHER DARLING

<u>Edward</u> <u>Christopher</u> <u>Darling</u> (Dallin) was born 20 July 1811 at Salem, Mass.; died 24 August 1879, son of Michael C. and Sally (Lee) Darling. He married (1) 21 March 1830 at Lynn, Mary Ann Coleman Orne Alley, born 10 January 1813; daughter of Samuel and Rebecca (Haskell) Alley. Edward married (2) 22 May 1872 at Ipswich, Emma Matilda Fewkes, b. at Ipswich 15 October 1832; daughter of Benjamin and Elizabeth (Smith) Fewkes of Ipswich.

Children of Edward Christopher Darling and Mary Ann Alley (born at Lynn):
   i   Emeline Lee, b. 9 July 1837; m ? Otis Farington.
  ii   Lois Maria, b. 16 Oct 1840 (9 Oct Fam. Bible); d. 16 Mar 1844.
 iii   Margaret Ellen, b. 21 Feb 1843; d. 21 Nov., 1844.
  iv   Ellen (Nell) Margaret, b. 6 May 1845; unmarried.
   v   Francis Turner (twin), b. 2 Feb 1848, (changed name to Ann Elizabeth); m. 29 June 1869 John M. Goodwin.
  vi   Eliza Oliver, (twin), b. 2 Feb 1848.
 vii   Louise Mariah, b. 30 Aug 1851 (Lou, 1851) cor. Union & Pearl Sts. (Fam. Bible)
viii   girl (stillborn)

Children of Edward Christopher Darling and Emma Matilda Fewkes:
  ix   Bessie May, b. 1 May 1873; d. 6 May 1873 (age 6d)
   x   Edward Lee, b. 20 Sept. 1874; m. 10 Aug 1898 Mabelle C. Barker, daughter of George and Charlotte.

"THE DARLING/FEWKES PAPERS" AT THE IPSWICH PUBLIC LIBRARY

This discussion of the compilers of the so-called "Darling Papers Collection" is brief because of omissions, visible errors and discrepancies. The following was gleaned from statements in various letters in the "Darling" volume.

Ernest E. Fewkes, who did most of the major work for the 188 volumes, lived in Bangor, Maine. He was a scientist involved in X-Ray technology and ultimately suffered injury in that field. A letter from "Ed" to "Cousin John" dated 12 January 1940, states: "Ernest is still alive, but has lost about half of each hand with the X-Ray burns." Fewkes started his compilations in the early 1900s as ascertained from other correspondence by him. Again from "Ed" to "Cousin John," a letter of January 1940 states: "I want you to know how much the loan of the papers has been appreciated by me, and Ernest seemed to be very much pleased with the account I sent him." This would certainly indicate Darling was involved in the project a while before Fewkes died although the cover sheet to the Ipswich Library Surname Index states that Darling received the collection after Fewkes died. The date is not given.

Fewkes and Darling were cousins, but the exact connection was not readily ascertained in these papers. Another statement in the 1940 letter indicates there was much to be done on the Fewkes family.

Edward Lee Darling was born in Ipswich on 20 September 1874. He married in Hamilton on 10 August 1898 Mabelle C. Barker, who was born 30 April 1879 at Ipswich. She was the daughter of George F. and Charlotte (Nutting) Barker. Edward was for a time a mailman in Ipswich. In the 1940 letter he advises Cousin John that when he was in the Post Office they preferred not to accept clams for shipment but if packed very well, sometimes would take a chance on the rather expensive Air-Mail. Edward L.'s parents were Edward Christopher and Emma M. (Fewkes) Darling. They were married 22 May 1872 at Ipswich. Edward L. and Bessie May (born and died 1873) were the only children of this union. Edward did, however, have eight half-sisters from his father's first marriage to Mary Ann Coleman Alley of Lynn. Edward Christopher Darling, shoemaker/merchant, publisher of the trade paper "AWL" and Civil War volunteer, was born on 20 July 1811 at Salem, Mass, to Michael Christopher and Sally Lee Darling. He died on the 25th of August 1882 at Ipswich. Michael Christopher Darling was born in Pomporania, Denmark, formerly part of Sweden, although his lineage, thought to be Scotch, is not given. He died the first of July 1816 at Calcutta, India, on the ship "Glide," for which he had been supercargo. His widow married, at Salem, on 4 January 1818, John Deland.

THE DARLING/FEWKES PAPERS comprise 188 volumes of Ipswich vital records compiled from several sources; the printed Massachusetts Vital Records to 1850, personal knowledge, church records and gravestones, and in some instances, letters. The compilations are essentially in family groups, but are far from complete or correct. Taken strictly as an aid, they are helpful, but primary records definitely need to be consulted. Each family surname is in one or more loose-leaf notebooks. The pages are typewritten. Fewkes used black type and Darling made additions in red type. A few volumes have brief biographies and some have informative correspondence. Also included are some English origins with family registers and parish registers.

The Library received the Collection in a seemingly vague and circuitous manner, but it is there, and worthy of consideration. The staff does NOT do research by mail. They are helpful in locating the material and photocopying the material (at 15 cents per page). The Genealogy Room also has the Massachusetts Vital Records volumes to 1850, some local published biographies; genealogies, town histories, various military volumes and more. Although the room is small, the Ipswich Public Library is well worth a visit.

##

DARLING/FEWKES PAPERS SURNAME LIST WITH EARLIEST ASSOCIATED DATES

1774	Abanatha, Elizabeth		1731	Burnham, Soloman
1722	Abbey, Joseph		1788	Burnham, William
1671	Abbott, Arthur		1600s	Butler, William
1661	Adams, William		1600s	Buxton, Anthony
1821	Akerman, Joseph Lord		1721	Caldwell, Aaron
1653	Alley, Hugh		1817	Chapman, Albion
1743	Andrews, Amos		1740	Chapman, Amos
1618	Andrews, John		1760	Chapman, Benjamin
1668	Andrews, Robert		1776	Chapman, David
1776	Andros (Andrews), Mark		1765	Chapman, Dudley
1625	Annable, John		1825	Chapman, Duncan
1586	Appleton, Samuel		1850	Chapman, Ebenezer
1820	Averell, Charles		1600s	Chapman, Edward
1649	Ayers (Ayres), John		1700	Chapman, Edward
1739	Bailey, Amos		1788	Chapman, Ephraim
1634	Baker, John		1819	Chapman, Horace
1687	Balch, Cornelius		1863	Chapman, Howard V.
1682	Balch, Benjamin		1777	Chapman, Ichabod (Ct)
1753	Balch, David 3rd		1651	Chapman, John
	Barber, William		1700	Chapman, John (Ct)
1616	Barker, Robert		mid 1700s	Chapman, John
late 1500s	Batt, Thomas		1767	Chapman, Josiah
1711	Beckford, Benjamin			Chapman, Leeman
1628	Black, Daniel		1600s	Chapman, Michael
1630	Blaney, John		1653	Chapman, Nathaniel
1709	Bools (Bowels), Joseph		1616	Chapman, Ralph
1639	Boardman (Bourman), Dan		1654	Chapman, Samuel
1725	Boardman, Thomas		1642	Chapman, Symon
1601	Bowreman, Thomas		1700	Chapman, Washington
1603	Bradstreet, Simon		1690	Chapman, William
1616	Bragg, Edward		1600	Chappleman, Michael
1628	Brocklebank, Samuel		1635	Chute, James
early 1600s	Brown, John		1600	Clarke, Daniel
1643	Brown, John		1643	Clinton, Lawrence
1815	Brown, Edward		1665	Coates, John
1600s	Brown, Edward		late 1700	Coburn, Stephen
1746	Brown, Jeremiah		1600	Cooke, Henry
1744	Brown, Nathan		1739	Cooke, Henry
early 1700s	Buffington, James		1707	Crane, Silas
1700s	Burnham, John		1612	Cross, Robert
1738	Burnham, John		1695	Cue, Robert
1813	Burnham, Noah		1800	Curtis, William
early 1600	Burnham, Robert		1803	Curtis, Stoddard

1754	Daggett (Doggett), Joseph	1581	Haffield, Richard
1640	Daland, Phillip	1636	Hale, John
1600	Damon, Samuel	1794	Harris, Ephraim
1500s	Dane, John	1732	Harris, Job
	Darling, Christopher	1734	Harris, Edward
1600	Davis, John	1773	Harris, Job
1616	Day, Anthony	1695	Harris, John
1742	Deland, John	1740	Harris, Peter
1580	Denison, William	1570	Harris, Ralph
1630	Dennis, Thomas	1599	Harris, Thomas
1600	Diamond, John	1614	Hart, Isaac
1707	Dodge, Barnabas	1713	Haskell, Mark
1764	Dodge, Ezekial	late 1500s	Haskell, William
1820	Dodge, George	1746	Heard, John Jr.
1766	Dodge, Isaac	1606	Heard, Luke
1580	Dodge, John	1600s	Henderson, John
1770	Dodge, Jonathan, Jr.	1751	Hills, Obadiah
1721	Dodge, Joshua	1800s	Hiscock, David & Henry
1724	Dodge, Peter	1812	Hiscock, Creighton
1670	Dodge, Richard	1600s	Hobbs, Jonathan
1608	Dow, Henry	1796	Hobbs, Josiah H
1576	Dudley, Thomas	1622	Hodgkins, William
1600	Dwonill (Dwinell)	1690s	Homans, Peter
1615	Edwards, Rice	1618	Hovey, Daniel
1600s	Ellsworth, Jeremiah	1796	Howard, Algerman S.
1584	Emmerson, Thomas	1636	Howe, Abraham
1621	Endecott, Thomas	1826	Howe, Nathaniel
1622	Epes, Daniel	1847	Howe, Calvin
1648	Eveleth, Sylvester	1872	Howe, Leonard
1600s	Farley, Michael	1854	Howe, Alfred
1682	Fellows, Jonathan	1693	Howlett, Samuel
1788	Fewkes, Benjamin	1672	Howlett, Thomas
1600s	Fewkes, Henry	1602	Hutchinson, Richard
1821	Fewkes, Thomas	1598	Ingalls, Edmund
1400s	Fiske, Symond	1634	Ingalls, Samuel
1566	Fiske, William	1805	Jewett, Ebenezer
1600s	Flint, Thomas	1643	Jewett, Ezehiell
1600s	Foster, Reginald	1768	Jewett, Joseph
1590	Fowler, Philip	1634	Jewit, Abraham
1600s	French, Thomas	1704	Jones, Nathan
1620	Fuller, John	1700s	Jopplin, Robert
1600s	Gaines, John	1605	Jowett, William
1592	Gardner, Thomas	1741	Kendall, Ephraim
1774	Glidden, William	1640	Kent, John
1823	Glidden, Edward	1595	Killam, Austin
1815	Glidden, John	1754	Kimball, Benjamin
1703	Goodale, John	1807	Kimball, John
1604	Goodale, Robert	1595	Kimball, Richard
1612	Goodhue, William	1709	Kinsman, John
mid 1600s	Goss, Richard	1600s	Kinsman, Robert
1645	Grant, Francis	1760	Kinsman, William
1761	Grant, Thomas	1740	Kneeland, Edward
1720	Greaves, John	1600s	Knoulton, John Tertius
1605	Griffin, Humphrey	1700s	Knowlton, John
1799	Griffin, John Little	1742	Knowlton, Joseph

1553	Knowlton, Richard	1635	Pulsifpher, Benjamin
1804	Knowlton, William	1579	Putnam, John
1651	Lakeman, William	mid 1600s	Quarles, William
1658	Lambert, Daniel	1639	Rindge, Daniel
1634	Lamson, William	1747	Ripley Campbell
1653	Lane, John	1538	Rodgers, John
late 1600s	Leatherland, William	1701	Rogers, Nathaniel
mid 1700s	Lee, John	1740	Rollins, Samuel
1602	Lord, Robert	1744	Rollins, John
1753	Lord, Samuel	1751	Ross, Timothy
1754	Low, David Jr.	1600s	Russell, Robert
mid 1600s	Low, John	1600s	Rust, Henry
1663	Low, Thorndick	mid 1700s	Rutherford, William
1605	Low, Thomas	1700s	Savage, James
1755	Lowe, Aaron Jr.	1594	Scott, Thomas
1643	Lummus, Jonathan	1500s	Shatswell, John
1724	Luscomb, William	1600s	Simonds, William
1875-1936	Manning High Grads	1600s	Small, John
1622	Manning, Richard	1600s	Smith, George & John
1600s	Marshall, Edmund	1600s	Smith, Richard & Thomas
1648	Martin, George	1623	Smith, Robert
1593	Mayhew, Thomas	1600s	Smith, Willima
1665	Metcalfe, Joseph	1656	Souther, John
1602	Moulton, James	1500s	Southwick, Lawrence
1685	Neeland, Philip	1660	Spiller, Henry
1682	Nelson, Joseph	1600s	Stacy, Hugh
1641	Newman, Thomas	1648	Staniford, John
1600s	Newmarch, John	1710	Staniford, Thomas
1599	Nichols, William	1699	Stone, William
mid 1600s	Nutting, John	1614	Story, William
1766	Osborn, Henry	mid 1600s	Sutton, Richard
1770	Osborn, William	1626	Swan, Richard
1807	Patch, John	1626	Swab, Robert
1740	Patch, Nehemiah	1653	Swasey, John
1678	Patch, Richard	1600s	Sweet, Jabez
1706	Patch, Robert	1633	Symonds, James
1500s	Patch, William	1584	Symonds, Mark
1565	Payne, William	1595	Symonds, Samuel
mid 1600s	Pederick, John	1700s	Symonds, Thomas
1610	Pengry, Moses	1634	Tapley, Gilbert
1699	Perkins, Joseph	1656	Tarbox, John
1806	Perkins, True	1801	Tenny, John
1495	Perkyns, William	1832	Tenny, Silas
1583	Philbrick, Thomas	1814	Thurston, Brown
1692	Philbrook, Jonathan	1704	Todd, Joseph
1600s	Phippen, David		Towne, John
1644	Pickard, John	1587	Trask, William
1663	Pickard, Samuel	1637	Treadwell, Thomas
1701	Pool, Caleb	1500s	Tuttle, John
1667	Pool, John	1653	Urin, William
1596	Porter, John	1600s	Wade, Jonathan
1628	Potter, Anthony	1600s	Wainwright, Francis
1746	Potter, John	1500s	Waite, Samuel
1700s	Prichard, Benjamin	1600s	Walton, William
1595	Proctor, John	1615	Warner, John

1637	Warner, William
1777	Water, John
1700s	Webber, Edward
1605	Wells, Thomas
1600s	Willcomb, Zeccheus
mid 1500s	Whipple, Matthew
1727	Whipple, Stephen
1600s	White, Thomas
1615	Whitmore (Wetmore), T.
1500s	Woodberry, Johannes
1741	Woodberry, Obadiah
1589	Woodbury, William
mid 1600s	Yell, John
1605	Younglove, Samuel

IPSWICH FREE PUBLIC LIBRARY.

##

HISTORICAL SOCIETIES (AND MUSEUMS) IN ESSEX COUNTY

(Arranged in order of size of membership)

Name	Membership	Employees		Volunteers
Peabody Museum (Salem)	2,500	28 (full time)	15 (part time)	150
Essex Institute (Salem)	1,156	26	20	64
Gloucester Historical Society	880	2	3	20
Newburyport Historical Society	780	3	3	
Marblehead Historical Society	650	1	2	80
Wenham Historical Society	650	1	3	70
Andover Historical Society	500	1	1	30
Haverhill Historical Society	500	2	2	
Lowell Historical Society	500			12
Lowell Museum	500	2	2	40
Manchester Historical Society	458		2	25
Beverly Historical Society	450	1		25
North Andover Historical Society	450		2	30
Topsfield Historical Society	450			25
Ipswich Historical Society	350	1	1	25
Lynn Historical Society	350	2	3	30
Danvers Historical Society	300	1		9
Lynnfield Historical Society	250			
Swampscott Historical Society	210			
Saugus Historical Society	150		2	
Reading Historical Society	125			10
Peabody Historical Society	120			15
North Reading Historical Society	92			15

(Data obtained from Historical Societies in the United States and Canada by the American Association of Historical Societies. 1984 edition.)

Book News

(Acquisitions between August 1984 and July 1985 - Lynnfield Public Library - Headquarters of ESOG. For earlier lists, see August issues of TEG)

FAMILY HISTORIES

ABBOTT   Descendants of George Abbott of Rowley, Mass. (Abbott) Repr. 1984
ADAMS   A Gen. Hist. of Henry Adams of Braintree, Mass. (Adams) Repr. 1984
ADAMS   A Gen. Hist. of Robert Adams of Newbury, Mass. (Adams) Repr. 1984
BAKER   Genealogy of the Descendants of Edward Baker of Lynn, Mass.
            (Baker) 1867
BAILEY   Bailey Genealogy: James, John, Thomas & their Descendants. (Bailey)
            Repr. 1984
BATCHELDER Batchelder/Batcheler Genealogy; Descendants of Rev. Stephen Bacheller
            (Pierce) Repr. 1985
BATTS/   Lineal Descendants of Christopher & Ann (Bayton) Batt, or the Ances-
  BATES   try of Maria Wentworth Bates, 1983. (Carpenter) (in binder)
CHADWELL   Chadwell Family; Descendants of Thomas Chadwell who settled at Lynn,
            Massachusetts, 1637. (Wiswall) 1983
COAN   Coan Genealogy 1697-1982. (Fulton) 1983
COBB   Early History and Genealogy of the Cobb Family in New England. 2 vols
            (Cobb) (Copy of typescript at Maine Hist. Soc.) (in 5 binders)
DOLE   Four Generations of the Descendants of Richard Dole, a First Settler
            of Newbury. (Pramberg) 1984
GOODRIDGE   Goodridge Genealogy. (Goodridge) Repr. 1985
GOODWIN   Early New England Goodwins. 1984. (Goodwin) (Typescript)
GREENLEAF   Genealogy of the Greenleaf Family. (Greenleaf) Repr. 1985
HALEY   Thomas Haley of Winter Harbor & his descendants... (Davis) 1930
HAWKES   Hawkes Family Information... (Hawkes) (3-ring binder)
HOYT   Genealogical History of the Hoyt, Haight & Hight Families. (Hoyt)
            Repr. 1984
JEWETT   History & Genealogy of the Jewett Family of America. 2 vols.
            (Jewett) Repr. 1985
KING   King Family of Suffield, Conn. (King) 1908
LITTLE   Descendants of George Little who came to Newbury in 1640. (Little)
            Repr. 1985
MARSTON   Marston Genealogy. (Marston) Repr. 1985
MORRILL   Morrill Kindred in America...(Smith) Repr. 1985
NOYES   Genealogical Record of Some of the Noyes Descendants of James, Nicho-
            las & Peter Noyes. 2 vol. (Noyes) Repr. 1984
PIERCE   Four Generations of the Descendants of Daniel Pierce of Newbury.
            (Pramberg) 1984
PILLSBURY   Pillsbury Family; being a History of William & Dorothy Pillsbury of
            Newbury. (Pilsbury) Repr. 1984
STOCKMAN/   Stockman/Gallison Ancestral Lines. (Dickson)
STONE   The Oxford Descendants of Gregory Stone of Cambridge, Mass.
            (Stone) 1904
WHEELER   Genealogical & Encyclopedic History of the Wheeler Family in America.
            (Wheeler) Repr. 1985.

CONNECTICUT

CONN Connecticut 1850 Census Index (AIS) 1978
CONN Genealogies of Connecticut Families, from the NEHG Register. 3 vols.
     (Roberts) 1983
GUILFORD Families of Early Guilford, Connecticut. (Talcott) Repr. 1984
MIDDLETOWN Middletown (Conn.) Upper Houses. (Adams) Repr. 1983
SAYBROOK Vital Records of Saybrook Colony, Connecticut.

MAINE

AUGUSTA History of Augusta, Maine (North) Facs. ed., 1981
BELFAST History of the City of Belfast (Williamson & Johnson) Vol II.
     Repr. 1983
BOOTHBAY History of Boothbay, Southport & Boothbay Harbor, Maine. Repr. 1984
CAMDEN Camden/Rockport, Maine: Births, deaths, marriages (Watts & Maresh)
     1985
EMBDEN Embden, Town of Yore (Walker) Repr. 1984
FARMINGTON History of Farmington, Maine (Butler) Repr. 1983
GRAY   History, Records and Recollections of Gray, Maine. Vol. 1. 1978
HERMAN Inscriptions of Cemeteries in Hermon, Maine (Brooks) 1985
INDUSTRY History of Industry, Maine. Repr. 1984
LINCOLN - Lincolnville, Maine: Births, deaths, marriages. (Maresh & Watts)
 VILLE   1985
N.YARMOUTH Old Times in North Yarmouth, Maine. Facs. ed. 1977
PARIS   History of the Town of Paris, Maine (Lapham) Repr. 1983
SACO   Saco Valley Settlements (Ridlon) Repr. 1984
WALDOBORO Index of Proper Names in J. J. Stahl's History of Old Broad Bay &
     Waldoboro.
WELLS   History of Wells and Kennebunk. Repr. 1984
WOODSTOCK History of Woodstock, Maine (Lapham). Repr. 1983

MASSACHUSETTS

BEVERLY Washington's New England Fleet; Beverly's Role in its Origins.
     (Beattie) 1969.
CHARLESTOWN Vital Records of Charlestown (Joslyn) 1984.
COHASSET Genealogies of the Families of Cohasset, MA (Davenport) Repr. 1984
DEERFIELD History of Deerfield, Mass. (Sheldon) Facs. ed. 1972.
FRAMINGHAM History of Framingham, Mass. (Barry) Repr. 1983.
HADLEY History of Hadley, Mass. (Judd) Facs. ed. 1976.
HAMILTON Hamilton Historical Society History.
LAWRENCE Lawrence City Directories; 1861-1881 (Microfiche)
LYNN   Lynn City Directories; 1889/1893/1899.
MARBLEHEAD Founding of Marblehead (Gray) 1984.
MARBLEHEAD History and Traditions of Marblehead (Roads) 1880.
NEWBURY Ould Newbury (Currier) Repr. 1984.
NO. ANDOVER Johnson Landmarks in North Andover (Johnson) 1984.
ORLEANS History of Early Orleans (Barnard) 1975.
PEPPERELL Vital Records of Pepperell (Rice) 1985.
STERLING Vital Records of Sterling, Mass. (Tapley) 1976.
WEYMOUTH Genealogies of Early Families of Weymouth. (Chamberlain) Repr. 1984
YARMOUTH Vital Records of Yarmouth, Mass. (Sherman) 1975.

NEW HAMPSHIRE

HENNIKER   The Only Henniker on Earth. 1980.
STRAFFORD   Abstracts of the Probate Records of Strafford County, N.H. 1771-
              1799. (Evans) 2d ed., 1983.

VERMONT

WAITSFIELD History of the Town of Waitsfield, VT (Jones) 1909.

NEW ENGLAND

Early New England People (Titcomb) Repr. 1984.
Genealogical Research in New England (Crandall) 1984.
True Stories of New England Captives Carried to Canada (Baker) Repr. 1984.

CANADA

NEW   Passamaquoday; Genealogies of West Islaes Families (Barto) 1975.
BRUNSWICK   The First History of New Brunswick (Fisher) Repr. 1980.
NOVA   The Story of Framboise (Cummings) 1984.
SCOTIA   Index to Guysborough Sketches and Other Essays (Koen) 1984.
QUEBEC   Dictionnaire Genealogique de familles du Quebec (Jette) 1985.

MISCELLANEOUS

Directory of Scottish Settlers in North America. (Dobson) 1985.
Trail of the Huguenots; in Europe, the U. S., South Africa; Canada (Reaman)
    1983.
Men who Married Women of the Mayflower (Goodwin) 1984.
Journals of Ashley Bowen (Smith) 2 vols., 1973.
Les Filles du Rois (in French) (Dumas) 1972-1983.
English Origins of New England Families; from the NEHG Register (Roberts)
    1st series, 3 vols., 1984; 2nd series, 3 vols., 1985.
The Famine Immigrants. Vols. IV & V.
Ancestry's Guide to Genealogical Research; Case Studies in American Genealogy.
    (Cerni & Eakle) 1985
Computer Genealogy (Andereck & Pence) 1985.
Mayflower Ancestral Index (Terry) 1981.
Census of Ireland (1861); general alphabetical index to the Townlands & Towns,
    parishes & baronies of Ireland... Repr. 1984.
Genealogical Research: Methods and Sources. Revised ed., 2 vols. 1984/5.

SPECIAL MULTIVOLUME ACQUISITIONS

The New England Historical and Genealogical Register. Vols. 1-50.

New Hampshire State Papers. 40 Vols. (Gift from Lynn Historical Society)

The Ahnentafel

Ahnentafel of Gail L. Brown (Hepker), 405 Radar, Coos Bay, OR 97420

I	1	Gail L. Brown	1949-	Seattle, WA
II	2	Clarence Donald Brown	1930-	Minot, ND
	3	Joan L. Gardner	1930-	Sioux City, IA
III	4	Clarence Revere Brown	1905-1961	Rugby, ND
	5	Loraine M. Westfall	1908-1978	Ida Grove, IA
	6	Eugene Walter Gardner	1906-	Springfield, SD
	7	Louise M. Clement	1910-	Burbank, SD
IV	8	George Washington Brown	1870-	Indiana
	9	Phoebe Bell	1879-	Missouri
	10	Joel Westfall	1870-	Tomway, IA
	11	Mary White	1885-1958	Springfield, IL
	12	Clarence E. Gardner	1875-	Yankton, SD
	13	Katherine F. O'Donnell	1885-	Iowa
	14	Allen B. Clement	1885-1944	Hudson, SD
	15	Elsie Armstrong	1887-	Kansas
V	24	Milton D. Gardner	1837-1922	Rome, NY
	25	Ophelia Brewer	1839-1906	Rome, NY
	26	Mike Bernard O'Donnell	1845-	Castle Reagh, Ireland
	27	Ellen Kiernan	1854-1922	Mt. Holly, NJ
	28	Phillip Henry Bartlett Clement	1847-1895	Boston, MA
	29	Harriet N. Allen	1849-1932	Cherry Creek, NY
	30	Isaac Armstrong	1853-	Ohio
	31	Nellie ------	1862-	Illinois
VI	48	Frederick Gardner	1811-1870	Floyd, NY
	49	Sarah Wiggins	1816-1878	Western, NY
	56	Phillip G. Clement	1812-1851	New Hampshire
	57	Charlotte ----		Vermont
	58	Isaac Allen	1804-1883	Vermont
	59	Sarah Ann Blaisdell	1812-1862	Cherry Creek, NY

※※※

Ahnentafel of Sarah Rose Murray (Koehler), 9 Clinton Road, Melrose, MA 02176

I	1	Sarah Rose Murray	1914-	Utica, NY; Melrose, MA
II	2	John Francis Murray	1884-1929	Williamstown, Utica, NY
	3	Alice Elizabeth Conniff	1887-1976	Vernon Ctr., Utica, NY
III	4	John P. Murray	c1844-1914	Ireland; Eastchester, Port Henry, Williamstown, NY
	5	Catherine Boylan	c1827-1935	? - Conn.; Pt. Henry, Williamstown & Verona Beach, NY
	6	John Conniff	1851-1911	Peterswell, Co. Galway, Ireland; Vernon Center, NY
	7	Anne Quinn	1867-1946	Culdalee, Aclare, Co. Sligo, Ireland; Rome, NY
IV	8	Patrick Murray	c1809-1889	? - Kings Co.?, Ireland; Dundee and Kilmarnock, Scotland; Eastchester, Williamstown, NY

9	Mary Conley		Ireland; Eastchester, Williams-town, NY
10	Michael Boylan	c1824-1908	Ireland; Pt. Henry, Williamstown, NY
11	Catherine Burns	c1827-1895	Co. Monaghan, Ireland; ? Conn.; Port Henry, NY
12	Peter Conniff	c1806	Peterswell, Co. Galway, Ireland
13	Sarah Shaughnessy	c1808-1978	Co. Clare, Peterswell, Ireland; Westmoreland, NY
14	Mark Quinn		Culdalee, Aclare, Co. Sligo, Ire.
15	Norah O'Hare		Culdalee, Aclare, Co. Sligo, Ire.
V 16	Timothy Murray		Ireland
_17	Elizabeth ----		Ireland
20	Patrick Boyland		Ireland
21	Mary Clancy		Ireland
22	Thomas Burns		Co. Monaghan, Ireland
23	Ann Conley		Co. Monaghan, Ireland
_24	John Conniff		Co. Galway, Ireland
26	Francis Shaughnessy		Co. Clare, Ireland
27	Elizabeth Welden		England, Co. Clare, Ireland
28	Mark Quinn		Culdalee, Aclare, Co. Sligo, Ire.
29	Catherine Gallagher		Culdalee, Aclare, Co. Sligo, Ire.
30	John O'Hara		Co. Slige, Ireland
31	Norah Leonard		Co. Sligo, Ireland

###

Ahnentafel of Beatrice Marsh (Goldsmith), 119 Jersey St., Marblehead, MA 01945

I 1	Beatrice Marsh	1903-	Lynn, Marblehead, MA
II 2	Charles Wallace Marsh	1872-1942	Chelsea, Lynn, Marblehead, MA
3	Lotta Alley	1878-1908	Lynn, MA
III 4	George Warren Marsh	1835-1900	Boston, Chelsea, MA
5	Mary Louisa Rice	1837-1896	Dorchester, Chelsea, MA
6	Charles Otis Alley	1834-1894	Newburyport, Lynn, MA
7	Elizabeth Chase (Huse) Janvrin	1838-1915	Newburyport, Lynn, MA
IV 8	Warren Marsh	1808-1867	Windsor, ME; Boston, MA
9	Lucy Hubbard	ca1813-1836	Boston, MA ?
10	Peter Adam Rice	-1838	Germany; Dorchester, MA
11	Annie Margaret Hooper		Germany; Dorchester, MA; Boothbay, ME
12	Joseph Alley	1804-1880	Kennebunk, ME; Newburyport, MA
13	Lucy Backman Knowles	1809-1882	Newburyport, MA
14	Joseph Adams Janvrin, Jr.	1811-	Lost at sea, Newburyport, MA
15	Elizabeth Ladd	1813-1894	Newbury, Lynn, MA
16	Isaac Marsh III	1775-1839	Gilmanton, NH; Windsor, ME
_17	Mary (Polly) W. Choate	1779-1859	Whitefield, Windsor, ME
24	Josiah Otis Alley		Kennebunk, ME
25	Nancy G----		Kennebunk, ME; Isle of Jersey, France
—			
28	Joseph Adams Janvrin, Sr.	1786-1944	Newbury, MA
29	Joanna Thurlow (Thurla)	1790-1863	Newbury, MA
30	Capt. Daniel Ladd	1777-1806	Haverhill, NH; Newbury, MA

	31	Elizabeth Huse	1785-1863	Newbury, MA
VI	32	Isaac Marsh II	-1807	Gilmanton, NH
	33	"Old Lady Marsh"	-1815	Gilmanton, NH
	34	Abraham Choate	1732-1800	Ipswich, MA; Whitefield, ME
	35	Sarah Potter	bpt 1736-1800	Whitefield, ME
##	36	Capt. John Hubbard	(married 1714 at Boston)	
	37	Elizabeth Peck Gooch		

- - - - - - - - - - - - - - - - - - - -

Note: John and Elizabeth Hubbard were the parents of Tuttle Hubbard (Boston 1720 - ca1804) who involved the family in the French Spoilation Claims. During Pres. Coolidge's administration, Charles W. Marsh (listed above) received his share of the estate of Tuttle Hubbard. (That I know - I was there!) I cannot find documentary proof. Lucy Hubbard (No. 9 above) seems a likely link, but who is Lucy? No one answers my queries!

##

Ahnentafel of Robert F. Henderson, 62 Summer Avenue, Reading, MA 01867

I	1	Robert Fisher Henderson	1923-	Chagrin Falls, OH
II	2	Lloyd Fisher Henderson	1892-1964	Chagrin Falls, OH; Reading, MA
	3	Evangeline Fay Wright	1898-1971	Indianapolis, IN; Concord, NH
III	4	Hugh Goudy Henderson	1866-1922	Orange Twp, OH; Tulsa, OK
	5	Ada Mary Fisher	1867-1930	Chagrin Falls, OH
	6	Walter Clarence Wright	1878-1941	Rush Co., IN; Cleveland, OH
	7	Amy Bertha Davidson	1880-1962	Marion Co., IN; Cuyahoga Co., OH
IV	8	Ira Henderson	1843-1927	Orange Twp, OH; Bradenton, FL
	9	Talitha Bailey	1847-1932	Geagua Co., OH
	10	Thomas Jefferson Fisher	1830-1893	Chagrin Falls, OH
	11	Harriett Amelia Lovejoy	1840-1908	Newbury, Chagrin Falls, OH
	12	George Harvey Wright	1850-1903	Fayette Co., Indianapolis, IN
	13	Sarah Margaret McBride	1853-1935	Rush Co., Indianapolis, IN
	14	James David Davidson	1849-1928	Jafferson Co., Indianapolis, IN
	15	Bertha Elizabeth Weber	1857-1922	Port Chester, NY; Indianapolis, IN
V	16	James Henderson	1809-1892	Columbia Co., NY; Orange Twp, OH
	17	Sarah Maria Traver	1816-1899	Claverack, NY; Orange Twp, OH
	18	James Iddo Bailey	1818-1900	Trumbull Co., Chagrin Falls, OH
	19	Elizabeth Williams	1822-1886	Oneida Co., NY; Chagrin Falls, OH
	20	James Fisher	1792-1834	Stoughton, MA; Orange Twp, OH
	21	Mercy Litch	1807-1857	Irasburg, VT; Chagrin Falls, OH
	22	William Lovejoy	1809-1843	Hollis, NH; Geagua Co., OH
	23	Mary Ober	1808-1891	Hollis, NH; Geagua Co., OH
	24	Harvey Wright	1820-1906	Centerville, OH; Indianapolis, IN
	25	Delila Stephen	1827-1913	Fayette Co., Rush Co., IN
	26	Joseph McBride	1830-	Rush Co., IN
	27	Mary Ann Saunders	1832-1903	Butler Co., OH; Rush Co., IN
	28	James Davidson	1812-	Indiana
	29	Maria Talbott	1815-1850	; Jefferson Co., IN
	30	Henry Yost Weber	1830-1872	Hesse Nassau; Indianapolis, IN
	31	Katherine Wilhelmina Hild	1834-1912	Hesse Nassau; Indianapolis, IN
VI	32	Ira Handerson	1782-1850	Amherst, MA; Orange Twp, OH
	33	Elizabeth Hopp	1779-1844	Livingston, NY; Orange Twp, OH
	34	Hanry J. Traver	1771-	Rhinebeck, NY
	35	Elizabeth Caspar	1772-	
	36	Iddo Bailey	1773-1838	Haddam, CT; Geagua Co., OH

37	Mary ----	1775-1855	? CT; Gaegua Co., OH
38	John Williams	1800-aft. 1850	Wales; Gaegua Co., OH
39	Betsey ----	1800-aft. 1850	Wales; Gaegua Co., OH
40	Abel Fisher	1767-1831	Stoughton, MA; Newbury, OH
41	Deborah White	1772-1802	Dedham, Canton, MA
42	Caleb Litch	1773-1818	Walpole, NH; Cuyahoga Co., OH
43	Mercy Dean	1778-aft. 1850	? CT; Geagua Co., OH
44	William Nevins Lovejoy	1785-1813	Hollis, NH; Sackett's Harbor, NY
45	Susanna Rideout	1784-	Hollis, NH; ?
46	Zechariah Ober	1775-1862	Tewksbury, MA; Geagua Co., OH
47	Abigail Hardy	1775-1858	Hollis, NH; Geagua Co., OH
48	Dan Wright, Jr.	1790-1861	Orange Co., VT; Rush Co., IN
49	Catherine Reeder	1800-1866	Hamilton Co, OH; Rush Co., IN
50	Thomas G. Stephen	1796-1867	? PA; Fayette Co., IN
51	Hannah Sutton	1805-1864	? OH; Fayette Co., IN
52	David McBride	1797-1865	? KY; Rush Co., IN
53	Susanna Reed	1794-1872	? MD; Rush Co., IN
54	Joseph Saunders	1799-1848	Fayette Co., PA; Rush Co., IN
55	Mary Dine	1806-aft. 1889	Butler Co., OH; Rush Co., IN
56	Andrew Davidson	1789-1866	Scotland; Jefferson Co., IN
57	Isabella Hay	1792-1826	Scotland; Jefferson Co., IN
58	Daniel Talbott	1779-bef. 1840	Spottsylvania, VA; Jefferson Co., IN
59	Elizabeth Paris		
60	Henry Weber	1805-	Hesse Nassau
61	--- Hecker		Hesse Nassau
62	Augustus Hild	1806-aft. 1880	Hesse Nassau; Indianapolis, IN
63	Anna Katherine Weber	1815-1881	Hesse Nassau; Indianapolis, IN

###

MASSACHUSETTS GENEALOGICAL COUNCIL

ANNUAL MEETING AND WORKSHOP SEPTEMBER 7TH

The 1985 Annual Meeting and Workshop of the Massachusetts Genealogical Council has been scheduled for September
7th at the Knights of Columbus Hall in Auburn, Mass.

Speakers at the workshop will include Martha Clark, who
will describe the new Massachusetts State Archives, which is
scheduled to open about that time, and John Fipphen, who will
speak on research in Worcester County. A third speaker will
be announced later. The Program Committee is searching for a
speaker who can cover the western Massachusetts area and
would welcome suggestions.

Program Chairman for the Massachusetts Genealogical
Council is Ann S. Lainhart, 13 Sachem Street, Boston, MA
02120. To support the MGC and its work, send annual dues of
$7.50 to Treasurer Helen F. Bosworth, 37 Main St., Saugus, MA
01906.

Our Readers Write

THE MARTINS OF SALISBURY, AMESBURY, AND IPSWICH: A Response to "Martin-Durkee Connections" and "Susanna (North) Martin". . .

The May 1985 issue of The Essex Genealogist contains two articles by Bernice B. Gunderson: "Martin-Durkee Connections" (5:74-77) and "Susanna (North) Martin - Another Salem Witch" (5:77-79), both reprinted from The Durkee Family Newsletter. These articles contained a number of problems which I have already addressed in "George Martin of Ipswich" (The American Genealogist [TAG], 56[1980]:155-59) and in "Salem Witches III: Susanna Martin" (TAG, 58[1982]:193-204, 59[1983]:11-22). Here I shall provide a few corrections to and comments on the material in The Essex Genealogist; for more complete discussions, readers should consult the TAG articles.

I. The Parentage of Susanna (North) Martin

The article in TEG states that Susanna (North) Martin was a daughter of Richard and Ursala North of Salisbury. Susanna was, in fact, a daughter of Richard North by an unknown earlier wife. In 1916, David W. Hoyt concluded that all Richard North's children were probably by a previous marriage (Old Families of Salisbury and Amesbury, 3:993). The evidence that changes Hoyt's probability into a certainty is found in the discussion of the complicated litigation over the wills of Richard and Ursala North (TAG, 58:196-99). One of the many documents filed in the case when it reached the Court of Assistants in 1673/4 was a statement by George and Susanna Martin in which they called Ursala a stepmother without the right to dispose of her husband's property (Court Files #1334, Suffolk Co. Courthouse, Boston). Thus, when Ursala North made "my grand child Mary Winslo [i.e. Mary (Jones) Winsley] the wife of Nathaniel winslo" her chief heir, she was actually naming a step-grandchild (Probate Records of Essex County, 2:223-4; the will was executed 19 May 1668 and probated on 11 2m [Apr.] 1671; the inventory was taken on 15 Mar. 1670[/1]).

II. Hannah ——, First Wife of George Martin of Salisbury and Amesbury

The TEG article states that the first wife of George[1] Martin of Salisbury and Amesbury was "Hannah (possibly Green)" and that she died in 1646. Hannah is named explicitly in only one record: that for the birth of her daughter, also named Hannah, in Salisbury, 1 12m [Feb.] 1643 [probably 1643/4]. We also know that she must have died before 11 Aug. 1646 when her husband married Susanna North in Salisbury. Certainly Hannah (-----) Martin died between the birth of her daugher and her husband's second marriage, but I know of no reason to narrow further the time of her death to 1646.

Some descendants have written me that the first wife of George[1] Martin was Hannah Green. I have been able to find no contemporary authority for this statement, and I am inclined to think that it is a confusion based upon the second edition (1935) of Elliot Burnham Watson and Alven Martyn Smith, George Martin of Salisbury, Mass. and His Descendants (this is the title of the first edition [South Pasadena, Cal., 1929]. The copy of the second edition at the New England Historic Genealogical Society lacks a title page, although the cover supplied by the NEHGS says "Martin Family--A.M. Smith--1935." Both editions are mimeographed). The second edition states that the first wife of George Martin of Ipswich (who Watson and Smith presumed was a son of George of Salisbury and Amesbury) was "Hannah -----" and adds that "It is thought she was the daughter of Judge Henry Green, b. as early as 1620 and went to Hampton, N.H. a few years after its settlement" (p. 13). Two highly reliable works, the Genealogical Dictionary of Maine and New Hampshire, pp. 285-86, and Gerald Faulkner Shepard and Donald Lines Jacobus, Shepard Families of New England, 3:330, state that Hannah, daughter of Judge Henry Green, married first, 5 June 1676, John Acey of Rowley, and second, before 1698, John Shepard of Rowley. If these conclusions are correct--and there seems no reason to doubt them--Hannah, daughter of Judge Henry Green, could not have married either George Martin. I have seen no contemporary evidence that provides even a first name for the first wife of George Martin of Ipswich.

III.   The Death of George Martin of Salisbury and Amesbury

The TEG article gives no death date for George[1] Martin of Amesbury. In TAG, 58:200, I show that he died in the month between 15 Mar. 1685/6, when he acknowledged a deed, and 15 2m [Apr.] 1686, when the inventory of his estate was taken (Old Norfolk Co. Deeds, 3:2:348; Essex Co. Probate #17890).

IV   George Martin of Ipswich

Since the publication of the Martin genealogy in 1929, many descendants have accepted its conclusion that George Martin of Ipswich was a son of George[1] and Susanna (North) Martin of Salisbury and Amesbury. This conclusion is stated as a fact in the TEG article. The 1929 genealogy presents the following evidence for the presumed filiation: 1) the birth of George, son of George and Susanna Martin, in Salisbury on 21 8m [Oct.] 1648, 2) the fact that Salisbury and Ipswich are near each other, and 3) the death of George Martin in Ipswich on 14 Apr. 1734, aged 86. The Martin genealogy states that the age at death corresponds exactly with the birth record, an incorrect conclusion since the George Martin born in Salisbury in Oct. 1648 would not have been 86 until Oct. 1734. But, given the frequent inaccuracies in ages in early records, we can agree that, if there were no other evidence, the birth and death records could refer to the same man.

There is other evidence, however, and a full consideration of it leads to the conclusion that George Martin of Ipswich was not a son of George and Susanna (North) Martin and that the George Martin born in Oct. 1648 died, probably without issue, before 19 Jan. 1683/4, when George[1] Martin of Amesbury executed his will without mentioning his son George (Essex Co. Probate #17890). Such an omission is not in itself proof that the son had died earlier. All experienced genealogists realize that the usual reason for omitting a living child from a will is that that child had already received his or her portion of the estate. In this case, however, that explanation will not work. The will names wife Susanna, son William (to inherit all the estate after Susannah's death or remarriage except for ₤5 to grandson John Hadlock), and leaves five shillings each to "natural [i.e. not adopted or children by marriage] Children" Richard Martin, John Martin, Hanna[h] Wathen, Hester Gimson [i.e. Jameson], Jane Hadley, and Abigail Hadlock. The only way to interpret the token sums left to all the children but William is that they had already received their portions. The ommission of the son George must mean that he was dead or that he had offended his father so deeply that he was not left even the token sum. If the latter were true, it is unlikely that his father would have neglected to say so in his will. And in this case, we can point out that he did give his son Richard a token sum, even though Richard had been presented before the Quarterly Court at Salisbury in October 1669 "for abusing his father and throwing him down, taking away his clothes and holding up an axe against him..." (Records and Files of the Quarterly Courts of Essex County... 4:186). Finally, I have found no evidence in land or court records of any association between the Martins of Salisbury and Amesbury and those of Ipswich.

Since we lack both a death record for the George Martin born in Salisbury in 1648 and evidence of the parentage of George Martin of Ipswich, we cannot say absolutely that the two Georges were different. But the preponderance of evidence is that George Martin of Ipswich was not a son of George and Susanna (North) Martin. Certainly the burden of proof is on those who believe that he was, and any new evidence should be much stronger than that presented by the 1929 genealogy.

What then was the origin of George Martin of Ipswich? The compilers of the 1929 genealogy do not seem to have considered the possibility that he was an immigrant. In Nov. 1679, Mr. John Barton, "chirurgion," sued Nicholas Manning at Salem Quarterly Court for two shillings six pence for each passenger who had come on the ship Hannah and Elizabeth, which had apparently arrived in Salem the previous September. The passenger list, which was submitted in evidence, includes "George Martine and his wife" (Records and Files, 7:302-5). George Martin's first child was born in Ipswich on 17 Sept. 1680, a year after the Hannah and Elizabeth had arrived.

David L. Greene, Ph. D., F.A.S.G., C.G., P.O. Box 398, Demorest, GA 30535

##

ANOTHER PATRIOT OF THE BOSTON TEA PARTY. . .

I have another name to add to the list of Patriots who threw the British tea into Boston Harbor, 16 December 1773. The article about them was in the May '85 issue of "TEG."

Williamson's "The History of the City of Belfast, Maine" (I:92-3), has an article about JOHN COCHRAN, one of the early settlers of Belfast, who came there in May, 1770. He was a native of Boston. Williamson writes: "The monument erected to his memory in Grove Cemetery, bears the following inscription: 'He was one of the Memorable Tea Party at Boston, Dec. 16, 1773.'" I have seen his stone. It is on the right side as you enter the front gate, not far from the front, in the oldest part of the cemetery. Grove Cemetery is beside Rte 3, which connects Belfast to Augusta, Maine.

In the same May issue, I read with interest the article on Susanna Martin, who is one of my ancestors.

I doubt if many people know that JOHN ALDEN was accused, tried, and imprisoned as a witch. His family had moved from Plymouth, Mass. to Duxbury, Mass. about 1630. They helped him escape from jail and hid him until the trials were over. John Alden then went to court to have the false charges against him dropped.

Irene Sanders Johnson, Searsport Ave. Rte 1, Box 10, Belfast, Maine 04915

Society News

FORTHCOMING MEETINGS - ESSEX SOCIETY OF GENEALOGISTS

September 21   Todd Hall - Centre Congregational Church - Lynnfield
Saturday   Social Hour: 12 - 1 Members with Scottish ancestry are
                        requested to wear their tartans.
                    ENTERTAINMENT: 12:30 - 1 SCOTTISH DANCERS OF SALEM
                    SPEAKER: DAVID C. DEARBORN, F.A.S.G., Ref. Libr., NEHGS
                    Topic: "Researching Scottish Ancestors"
                    (Note: Fee for this meeting: $1 members; $1.50 non-members)

October 19   Todd Hall - Centre Congregational Church - Lynnfield
Saturday   Social Hour: 12 - 1
                    SPEAKER: THEODORE CHASE, "New England Gravestones"

November 16   Todd Hall - Centre Congregational Church - Lynnfield
Saturday   Social Hour: 12 - 1
                    SPEAKER: DAVID A. NICHOLS, "Recent and New Resources for
                        Genealogical Research in Maine and Massachusetts"

GOVERNOR DUKAKIS PROCLAIMS FAMILY HISTORY WEEK IN MASSACHUSETTS

(Photography courtesy of "Nexus" - Newsletter of NEHGS)

A DATE WITH THE GOVERNOR

By Helen Breen

On Tuesday, May 14, June Rose and I visited the State House to witness Governor Dukakis sign a proclamation declaring May 12-19, 1985 as "Family Week in Massachusetts." Such invitations are few. Consequently, June's boss at Long's Jewelry and my principal at Lynn Tech gave us time off to attend. Even the Lynn Superintendent of schools encouraged me to participate. ("Teachers need good press," he said.)

The day was overcast, but our spirits were not dampened. On our way, we stopped at the Boston Athenaeum at 10 1/2 Beacon Street. There we trod quietly on oriental rugs among the old volumes, marble busts, leather arm chairs, and greenery where we communed briefly with the ghoses of the past.

Being early, we had time to tour the State House. When we passed by the Senate gallery, we were greeted warmly by Senator Walter Boverini of Lynn (a former Lynn teacher) who also represents Lynnfield. He gave us a glimpse of the Senate chambers and wished us well in our genealogical endeavors. We had arranged to meet with our Representative Richard Tisei. Richard, a handsome 22-year-old graduate of Lynnfield High, and a resident of Wakefield, is one of the youngest to serve in the General Court in the Bay State's history. We sat "up front" in the House with him while we watched the day's proceedings. After saying "good-bye" to our elected officials, we went to the Governor's outer office where many genealogists were gathering. Several were old friends of ESOG, as you can see from the photograph. The Chief Executive's schedule is tight and many groups preceded and followed our 1:45 appointment. When we entered his private office, however, His Excellency extended a hearty welcome and quipped with us as we assembled for the signing of the document and picture taking.

Family history adds to the body of the state's history, Dukakis believes. Publicizing the resources of our public libraries, archives, and historical societies strengthens our tourist industry. "Massachusetts Homecoming" is a theme which the Governor and his aides will be developing in thie coming year. The search for "roots" fits nicely into the whole picture. On behalf of the ESOG, our gracious President, June Rose, presented the Governor with copies of TEG. With a boyish grin, he replied, "Can I really keep them? Thank you so much!"

After all the excitement, June, Rose Morrison and I retired to the comfort of a nearby Brighams to discuss the events of the day.

Pictured with the Governor at left: Joseph Guertin, Pres. Berkshire Family History Association; Dr. Ralph Crandall, Dir., NEHGS; Rose Morrison, Vice Pres., Plymouth County Genealogists; Helen Breen, ESOG; David Robertson, Past Pres., MSOG; Marie Daley, Pres., TIARA; Shirley Barnes, Pres., Concord Gen. Round Table; James Nesbit, Pres. of MSOG; Ernestine June Rose, Pres., ESOG; Sheila Fitzpatrick, Pres. of Middlesex Chapter, MSOG; & Robert Starrett, Pres., MGC.

Miscellaneous Notes

GENEALOGISTS HANDBOOK FOR NEW ENGLAND RESEARCH, 2ND EDITION is now ready. To order, send $9 to: Sales Department, New England Historic Genealogical Society, 101 Newbury St., Boston, MA 02116. Copies may also be purchased at the Lynnfield Public Library. This edition contains more than 200 corrections and additions, and has colored state dividers. Cost includes postage & handling.

ASSOCIATION OF ONE-NAME STUDIES. Genealogists and groups in the U.S. & Canada spend hundreds of hours working on surname lines of interest. Often this intensive research is a duplication of work conducted previously or concurrently by others. The Association of One-Name Studies has been established to prevent duplication & to coordinate efforts. Registered researchers are encouraged to meet the requirements to become a formally constituted one-name society, such as extracting all entries of the surname from the public records of all states and Canada. To register your surname with the Association for One-Name Studies, send $3 to the Association at 57 West South Temple, Suite 751, P.O. Box 11980, Salt Lake City, UT 84101. To subscribe to the Association's register of surnames, a quarterly newsletter, send $10 to the above address. (From "Nexus," II:3; June, 1985; p. 58/9)

HISTORIC COOKBOOK To raise "matching funds" for a grant from the National Endowment for the Humanities, the New England Historic Genealogical Society is proposing to publish an Historic Cookbook. "Memorable" recipies and every-day recipes found in handwritten cookbooks and Grandma's memory are being requested. Send suggestions and recipes to Alice Ledogar, NEHGS, 101 Newbury St., Boston, MA 02116. Please use "TB" & "Tsp" abbreviations, give approx. temperatures and times, and PLEASE double-check recipe before mailing. (June "Nexus," p. 70)

CORRECTION OF ERROR The ESSEX INSTITUTE in Salem is _not open on Saturdays_. Summer hours are Mon - Fri 9 - 5; Winter hours (after 1 Nov): Tues - Fri 9 - 5.

FAMILY NEWSLETTERS - Thinking of starting one? "The typical Family Newsletter is composed of ten sheets of 8 1/2 X 11 paper, printed both sides, stapled on left side; appears quarterly, costs $10/yr; & has 200 subscribers. Queries are usually free. There is no paid advertising. It survives on subscriptions & donations; is non-profit & usually short of money. To save money, editors do everything possible - writing, typing, designing pages, photographs & captions, collating, stapling & stuffing envelopes. Only actual printing is usually done outside the house. 250 copies of a 24-page letter costs $315 (Canadian)." It is suggested that the newsletter be listed in Hilborn's Family Newsletter Directory c/o Robin Hilborn, 42 Sources Blvd., Pointe Claire, Quebec H9S 2H9, Canada. (From The Genealogical Helper, May-June 1985; p. 8)

ANN LAINHART SPECIAL "or how female researchers can eliminate the 'where shall I leave my money, keys, etc. while I search the shelves' problem. Ann Lainhart solved the problem by making a skirt with two large pockets - these hold her money, keys, etc. At Jordan Marsh, there are "Katie Brooke" skirts - all colors and sizes - all with two big pockets, button down & snap fronts. I think Ann Lainhart should receive a commission on this idea!" (from Rose Morrison's Newsletter of the National Archives - Boston Branch)

Queries

CHAMBERLAIN/BRIDGES
Seek anc & info on John CHAMBERLAIN who m Sarah BRIDGES 26 APR 1753 at Hopkinton, MA and sett in Holliston, MA

HOOKER/HILLIARD
Seek anc & info on both Henry HOOKER and Elizabeth HILLIARD m 13 Aug 1708, Boston & were in Medfield, MA by 1713.

LARKIN
Seek anc & info on John LARKIN & w Leah, par of Thomas LARKIN b 22 JAN 1803, Mount Vernon, ME

WASHBURN/FLAGG
Seek bp & bdt of Sally FLAGG who m Samuel WASHBURN 18 June 1810 at Framingham, MA. Also dp & ddt for both.

WASHBURN/WOODCOCK
Seek bp & bdt for James WASHBURN who m Mary WOODCOCK 10 Oct 1839 at Sherburn, MA; also ddt & dp for both. Need names & dt for ch. Sybil L. DANIELS, 25 West St.,Salem, NH 03079

BACON/KNOWLES
See par & dts for Elizabeth BACON who m 25 Apr 1717 at Windham, CT Nathaniel KNOWLES of Eastham, MA

BROWN/PRESCOTT
Wish par & dts for Abigial BROWN who m 28 Dec 1759 Micah PRESCOTT of Epping, NH

ELWELL/KNOWLES
Wish dts & par of Sarah ELWELL who m int 27 Dec 1754, Falmouth, ME Samuel KNOWLES. He was b 1733 at Provincetown, MA

SAVELL/NOYES
Seek par & dts for Deborah SAVELL who m 1741 John NOYES of Newbury, MA. Pauline H. Keene, Pitcher Rd. Box 519, Belfast, ME 04915

MORTON/COOPER/CARPENTER/WRIGHT
Acc to George Morton & Some of his Descendants, by Allen - Ephraim MORTON s of George, m 18-28 Nov 1644 his cousin Ann COOPER, dau of John COOPER of Scituate, MA & Priscilla (CARPENTER) WRIGHT wid of William WRIGHT. Savage says John COOPER m 1634 Priscilla, wid of WRIGHT & d without ch. Could Ann be dau of William & Priscilla? David DOBSON, 8 Burnham St. # 12, S. Portland, ME 04106

HAWKINS
See info on Charles HAWKINS b 1856, New York City (or State) to William & Fannie d 1879 Dover, NH.

MARSONS/HARRIS
Seek info on early MA MARSONS. Samuel, a brewer in Boston being the earliest m Elizabeth HARRIS 10 June 1731.

WITHAM/TAYLER
Seek par of Joseph WITHAM m Catherine TAYLER 1842 Somersworth, NH. She was from Wells-Ogunquit, ME area. The liv Dover, NH. Brian TAPSCOTT, 154 Indigo Hill Rd., Somersworth, NH 03878

MERRETT/SANDIN
Was Mary SANDIN who m Nicholas MERRETT of Marblehead in 1636 related to Arthur SANDIN at Marblehead at same time? Winnifred PIERCE, 211 McCotter Dr., Ann Arbor, MI 48103

CLAYTON
Need bp & par Charles D. CLAYTON b 31 Oct 1830 Eng. The 1870 ME Cen shows him as farmer in Dedham, ME but mov to Cotuit, MA. Need par of w Mary b 10 Oct 1832 in Cotuitport, MA.

CLAYTON
Wish corr with desc.Charles D. CLAYTON & w Mary, liv in Cotuitport; 5 ch b there; Annie E. b 19 Apr 1859; Charles D. b 28 Sep 1861; Laura B. b 13 Nov 1863; Charles D. b 29 Oct 1865, and Mary H. b 18 May 1868. Mrs. W. F. WINSLOW, 36 Bodge St., South Portland, ME 04106

###########################

BURRILL/WHITING
Searching anc Esther Foss BURRILL b 23 Jan 1818, Corinna, ME. m 1839 Philander WHITING b Newport, ME. Her par Josiah & Hannah (-----) b MA ?. Bur Rutland Rd. Cem. NO. Newport, ME

CURTIS/LANCASTER
Need anc Sarah CURTIS b 22 Feb 1760 where? dau of John & Mary (-----) CURTIS prob b MA. Sarah m David LANCASTER b 22 May 1758 Woolwich, ME

SWETT(SWEATT)/SMITH/BUTTS
Searching for Jacob SWETT & w Abigail SMITH prob b MA par of Jacob, Jr. b 29 July 1811, Salem or Strong, ME d 14 Mar 1784, New Portland, ME m 1833 Mary BUTTS, b 18 Nov 1813.
Postage & copy fees refunded. Mrs. Janice W. PHELPS, 1300 Shetter Ave. #30, Jacksonville Beach, FL 32250

###########################

HARRINGTON/CONNER
Seeking par & bp Elisha HARRINGTON, b 1776 MA. Rem to MI 1806. M Susanna CONNER 1807, d 5 Nov 1848 Macomb Co. MI. Doris M. AMSBURY, 320 Jones St., Mt. Clemens, MI 48043

###########################

ARNOLD/PEAKE/SMITH
Stephen ARNOLD b Eng 22 Dec 1622 d Pawtuxet, RI 15 Nov 1699 s of William & Christian (PEAKE), m Providence 24 Nov 1646 Sarah SMITH b 1629 d Pawtuxet 15 Apr 1713, dau of Edward of Newport Desire mo of Sarah.

BURNAP/MILLER/BROWNE
Robert BURNAP b 1627 d 1695 Reading, MA s of Robert & Ann(Agnes) (MILLER), m 28 May 1662 2/w Sarah BROWNE. Des par VR of Sarah.

CARGILL/ARNOLD/BOVEE/ROCKWELL
Daniel CARGILL b Cumberland, RI 17 Sept 1773 s of James & Dorcas (ARNOLD) m 1801 Elizabeth BOVEE. Son Preston m Gainesville, NY 1830 Electa ROCKWELL. Desire par Elizabeth, info BOVEE fam.

EDWARDS/SWEET
David EDWARDS d Boston, MA 1 Oct 1696, m there 1676 Mary Sweet dau of John & Susanna. Four ch b there bet 1676-1687. Were there others? Des par bdt David.

GROVER
Stephen GROVER b ca 1658 d Charlestown, MA 22 Oct 1694, s of Thomas & Elizabeth M there 1680 Sarah. Des par Sarah & Elizabeth.

WARREN/HILDRETH/SPALDING
Jacob WARREN bpt Chelmsford, MA 8.12m 1673, d Plainfield, CT 3 Sep 1727 s of Jacob & Mary (HILDRETH), m ca 1690 Sarah (1667-1759). Dau Sarah m Josiah SPALDING. Des par VR 1st Sarah. Mrs. Margaret S. ROSE, 2011-20th Street, Portsmouth, OH 45662

###########################

BAILEY
Need anc Benjamin Webster BAILEY b 2 Mar 1790 Warner, NH Prob. s of Dudley & gson of Deacon BAILEY of Haverhill,MA

BROWN/ROGERS
Need anc Polly BROWN, dau of Josiah who m 23 Apr 1801 Steven ROGERS, prob. Plymouth or Ashland, NH.

CHENEY/WORCESTER
Need anc Mary CHENEY of Newbury, MA, m 29 Jan 1690-1 Francis WORCESTER of

Bradford, MA

DALTON/DORR
Hist. of Warner, NH says papers pertaining to anc of Philemon DALTON of Ipswich were held by B. DALTON DORR of Philadelphia in 1879. Do they still exist, and if so, who has them?

DAVIS
Francis DAVIS of Amesbury, MA brought from Wales a cane which has remained in the fam for centuries. Waldo DAVIS of Lima, OH had it in 1964. Who has it now?

DUDLEY
Need surname & anc of Elizabeth 3/d w of Samuel DUDLEY, s of Gov. Thomas of Exeter, NH.

FULLER
Need surname & anc of Mary, w of John FULLER, b 27 Mar 1679, Hampton, NH.

GILMORE/STEWART/FRENCH
Need info on David GILMORE who m Mary STEWART 4 June 1772 Haverhill, MA. Later res. Warner, NH. Also seeking desc of their ch; Mitchell b 1773; John b 1775; Margaret, b 1777, m Beman FRENCH.

GORDON/ROGERS
Need anc Mary Ladd GORDON, b 9 July 1801 Pittsfield, NH, m 25 Oct 1827 Charles ROGERS of Plymouth, NH.

HALL
Need w & anc of Richard HALL b 20 Sep 1729, Tewksbury, MA.

ROGERS/FOSTER
Need anc Elizabeth ROGERS, who m 17 Nov 1719 Moses FOSTER of Boxford, MA d 2 Oct 1729 Andover, MA

McCLURE/STEWART
Need anc Mary McCLURE m 31 Jan 1784 John STEWART in Haverhill, MA

NOYES/CUTTING
Need info on Nicholas & Mary (CUTTING) NOYES. Res Newbury, MA early 1600's.

PARRATT/WORCESTER/MARSH
Need anc Elizabeth PARRATT d 9 May 1690 Haverhill, MA m/1 Samuel WORCESTER, m/2 Onesiphorus MARSH.

STEWART
Need Irish anc of John STEWART d 6 Nov 1784 Haverhill, MA. Bailey ROGERS, 10018 Regency Ct., Cincinnati, OH 45239.

****

BOURNE/HOLMES
Need bdt & mdt Thomas BOURNE of Kent, Eng & Marshfield, MA. m Elizabeth HOLMES (bur Marshfield 18 July 1660) Seeking her par.

BROOKS/VINING
Need bdt & par Mehitable BROOKS of Abington, m there Benjamin VINING 22 Oct 1761.

BURRELL/TUTTLE
Need par bdt, bp Anna BURRELL m James TUTTLE at Chelsea, MA 6 Apr 1721.

CHUBBUCK/MAXIM
Need anc Martha CHUBBUCK b Wareham 1741, m Nathan MAXIM.

CHURCHILL/PONTUS
Need bdt & bp for John CHURCHILL (the immigrant) m Hannah PONTUS.

CHURCHILL/WOOD
Need ddt & pl Benjamin CHURCHILL b Plympton 31 Jan 1728, m Thankful WOOD, liv Middleboro.

HICKS/FREEMAN
Need mdt & pl, ddt & pl Dorcus HICKS dau of Samuel b at Plymouth, m Edmund FREEMAN.

HUTCHINSON/WHEELWRIGHT
Need mdt & pl, ddt & pl, anc Mary HUTCHINSON, dau of Edward, m John WHEELWRIGHT.

PERRY/FREEMAN/PRENCE
Need all data Ezra PERRY, m Rebecca FREEMAN dau of Edmund FREEMAN & Rebecca PRENCE.

163

STANDISH/ALDEN/STURTIVANT
Need m data on Alexander STANDISH & Sarah ALDEN; on Ebenezer STANDISH, & Hannah STURTIVANT; and on Myles STANDISH & Barbara -----.

WATERMAN/SHAW
Need ddt & pl Lydia WATERMAN, dau John & w of Benoni SHAW. Mrs. Ida KRETSCHMAR, Route 3, Box 359, Canton, NY 13617

###########################

CARR/PUTNAM
George CARR of Carr's Island at Salisbury, MA d 1682 Salisbury. When did he come to America? He was in Ipswich, MA 1633. Dau Ann b 1661 m Thomas PUTNAM. They figured prominently in Salem witchcraft hysteria.

CHENEY/POOR
Wish anc Martha CHENEY m Amos POOR bef 1752.

COLE/URIN
Wish anc Rebecca COLE m John URIN prob of Isles of Shoals bef 1715.

HENDERSON/CURRIER
Need anc of Esther HENDERSON m Joshua CURRIER of Isles of Shoals (int) 15 Dec 1744, Ipswich, MA

POOR/CHENEY/CURRIER
Wish anc Amos POOR m Martha CHENEY. Their dau Mary b 20 July 1752 Newbury, MA, m John CURRIER 14 Dec 1772, Newbury, MA.

URIN/COLE/CROCKETT
Wish anc John URIN m Rebecca COLE, their dau Eleanor bpt 25 Sep 1715, m/1 Diamond CURRIER, m/2 Abraham CROCKETT, both of Isles of Shoals. Barbara WASHBURN, 496 Highland Ave., So. Portland, ME 04106

###########################

BARTLETT/MARSHALL/YOUNG
Wish to corr with anyone having info on BARTLETTS of Kingston, Brentwood, NH & Amesbury or Newbury, MA. From immigrant

Richard D., 1647 Newbury, MA to David b 1775, w Dorothy YOUNG, fa Moses F. MARSHALL.

HOLT/KIMBALL
Wish info on Sarah Elizabeth HOLT b 18 Nov 1831 d 3 May 1906; m Nelson KIMBALL. Liv Amesbury, Haverhill, Ward Hill, MA. dau of William HOLT poss of Lawrence, MA.

JOHNSON/MOORE/BURROUGHS
Wish info on Sarah JOHNSON b 15 June 1805 prob Amesbury, MA; m/1 Joseph MOORE, mov to W. Topsham, VT or Waits, River, VT; m/2 _____BURROUGHS. Said to have Mayflower anc. Virginia M. MORTON, 5860 Midnight Pass Road # 26, Sarasota, FL 34242.

###########################

GINNVARIE/ELMER
Need par, bdt, bp, ddt, dpl of Rosamond GINNVARIE, m John ELMER Oct 1669, of Hartford, CT. Helen BURGARD, Rt 2 Box 414, Idaho Falls, ID 83401.

###########################

ALLEN
Need ch Thomas ALLEN of Kittery & Newbury & 2 w (m 1712 & 1723/24). Was Joanna a dau.?

CARTER
Did Edward CARTER b 14 Dec 1719 of Hollis, NH have 2nd w Mary? Did he have a s Michael b 1765; a dau Jane; did his dau Mary marry?

CARTER
Need ch of Edward CARTER all of Hollis, NH; Lucretia (b 1746), Mary (b 1751), Elizabeth (b 1754), Thomas (b 1758), Sarah (b 1762).

COX/CARTER
Need info on Philip COX & w Jane CARTER m Portsmouth 1722.

DERBURN (DEARBORN)
Need names & dts of all ch Jacob DERBURN of Biddeford (m 1739). Have only John bpt 1756.

DYER/CARTER
Who was Jane CARTER int Boston 25 Oct 1769 to Michael DYER?

HASKELL/WESCOTT
Wish info on Mrs. Mary WESCOTT of New Marblehead, ME who m 5 Aug 1750/58 Thomas HASKELL as 3d w.

SMITH/HERRICK
John Smith of Beverly int 23 May 1748 Mrs. Mary HERRICK. Need all ch who, I believe, included Mary & John. Did John b 2 Oct 1785 have a w Betsey HERRICK? Did he have a bro Ebenzer?

WESCOTT
Need all info on Daniel WESCOTT & Maria of Marblehead 1646. Not in printed Marblehead VR. Miss Elizabeth C. WESCOTT, RFD2, Box 920, Apt.202, Bucksport, ME 04416.

****

CLARK
Wish par of Ichabod CLARK b 12 Oct 1777 prob in St. John, NB. Was he junior? Listed in 1800 cen Levant, ME. An older Ichabod is in same cen for Corinth, ME.

MATTHEW/McFADDEN/JORDAN
Want background of Nathaniel MAYHEW who m Mary McFADDEN JORDAN Georgetown, ME 1756 mov to Bangor, ME 1774.

HUSSEY/JAMES/DORE
Need par of James HUSSEY & w Anna, Smithfield, ME early 1800's. Was she dau of John JAMES, Jr. & Lydia DORE?

WALKER/COOMBS
Wish par of Martha WALKER who m Sylvanus COOMBS in Georgetown, ME 15 Jan 1749/50. Mrs. Clair E. WYMAN, Sawyer's Crossing Road, P.O. Box 27, West Swanzey, NH 03469.

****

HAINES/MOULTON
Seek info & par of Joshua HAINES b ca 1755 in Greenland, NH; m Lucy MOULTON of Rye, NH. Was he the same Joshua

HAINES murdered in Haverhill, MA bet 1780-1788?

MERRILL/BARRETT
Seek par & info on Hannah MERRILL d 26 Nov 1839; m Lemuel BARRETT 16 Mar 1826.

SHERBURN/LANG
Need par & info on Sarah SHERBURNE m 1785 to William LANG of Portsmouth, NH b 19 Dec 1759. Gloria KELLEY, 115 E. Lindbergh, Universal City, TX 78148.

****

ANDERSON/BOGART
Need par of Loyalists Jonathan ANDERSON (1742-1809) & w Mary (1748-1829) of Annapolis Co., Nova Scotia, par of Isaac, William, Clara (BOGART) & others; prob from Long Island or Albany, NY area.

McFEE/VAN PELT
John McFEE m 7 Oct 1782 Elinor VAN PELT in Westchester Co., NY; mov Sackville, NB, Can. where they raised a large fam. Need par of both. Mildred L. D'AMBROSIO 25 Pleasant St., No. Reading, MA 01864

****

SAMPSON/FULLERTON
Seek info on Ruth SAMPSON m John FULLERTON at Marshfield 13 Oct 1720. Beverly DOMERATZKY, 18 Oakhurst Road, Beverly, MA 01915.

****

BROWN/FLINT
Need dt par anc of Mary BROWN, m 15 Jan 1717/18 at Concord, MA Thomas FLINT.

EDWARDS/WRIGHT/HARMON
Need dt par anc of Miriam EDWARDS b ca 1718, w of Aaron WRIGHT, s of Joseph & Ruth (HARMON) WRIGHT.

HARMON/WRIGHT
Need dt par anc of Ruth HARMON, m 1704 as 1/w of Joseph WRIGHT of Northampton, MA.

MOODY/WRIGHT/EDWARDS
Need dt par anc of Dorcas MOODY, m Justus WRIGHT (1752-1791), s of Aaron & Miriam (EDWARDS) WRIGHT. Aaron d in Eng.

NURSE/HILL
Need dt par anc of Samuel NURSE, m 21 June 1711 Deborah HILL, both of Charlestown, MA.

SEARLE(S)/MILLER
Need dt, par anc of Enos SEARLE(S) m 3 June 1818 in Westboro, MA. Lucinda MILLER, b 26 Nov 1796 in Westboro, MA.

SPRING/HEWETT
Need dt par anc of Diana B. SPRING, w of Ephraim Gay HEWETT. Believe her par were William SPRING b ca 1767 in MA & Huldah _____ b ca 1771 in MA.

WORSLEY/NASON
Need dt par anc of Sarah WORSLEY m 13 May 1773 in Walpole, MA as 2/w of Thomas NASON b 1730 Ipswich, MA. Douglas A. WENNY, 1124 Windon Dr., Wilmington, DE 19803.

****

ALLE/PILLSBURY/GAVETT
Need dts & anc Sarah ALLE m 18 Jan 1703 Newbury to Daniel PILLSBURY s of Job PILLSBURY & Katherine GAVETT.

CUTTING/MILLER
Need anc & dts Capt. John CUTTING who d 20 Nov 1659 at Newbury, MA. & w Mary _____ who m/2 John MILLER & d Mar 1663 Newbury, MA.

FELLOWS
Need anc of Samuel FELLOWS b ca 1619, d 6 Mar 1697/8 Salisbury, MA & w Ann _____ who d 5 Dec 1684 Salisbury.

HORNE/CLOUGH
Need all dts & info on John HORNE who came 1635 on "Elizabeth" & his w Jane CLOUGH.

KENT
Need anc & info Richard KENT who d 11

June 1765 Newbury, MA & w Hannah ---- who d 10 June 1677 Newbury.

KNIGHT/COFFLEY
Need anc & info on Richard KNIGHT who d 4 Aug 1683 ae 81 Newbury & w Agnes COFFLEY who d 22 Mar 1679 Newbury, MA.

PRATT
Need anc Martha PRATT d 10 May 1747 ae 83 or on 20 Sep 1742 ae 79. She was 2/w of John PRATT b 1655, d 15 Nov 1742 Malden, MA. Need anc of John PRATT poss s of Richard or Phineas.

SCALES/CURTIS
Need anc & dts Sarah ----"of Rowley, MA" m 1712 Matthew SCALES bpt 29 Mar 1685 Rowley, d 24 Apr 1725 Falmouth, ME s of James SCALES & Sarah CURTIS.

VIALL/SARGENT
Need anc & dts Nathaniel VIALL & w Sarah ---- par of Mary VIALL b 23 Aug 1711 Boston, MA, m 29 May 1729 Nathan SARGENT.

WOOD/GATES
Need dts & anc Daniel WOOD d 21 May 1838 Waterford, ME & w Bethia GATES. Anne M. GOULETTE, R.R.3 Box 120, Dexter, ME 04930.

****

The Essex Genealogist

VOLUME 5, NUMBER 4   NOVEMBER 1985

CONTENTS

THE ESSEX GENEALOGIST is published quarterly: February,
May, August & November for $10 per year, by the Essex Soci-
ety of Genealogists, Lynnfield Public Library, 18 Summer
Street, Lynnfield, MA 01940. Second Class Postage paid
at Lynnfield, MA 01940. ISSN: 0279-067X USPS: 591-350
POSTMASTER: Send address changes to ESOG, Lynnfield Public Library, 18 Summer Street, Lynnfield, MA 01940.

Letter from the Editor

Our Feature Article this issue deals with a subject that should interest all of us - the "Pitfalls of Genealogical Research." We appreciate Milton Rubincam's generosity in reviewing and correcting the typescript of his lecture, which was delivered at "Hist Gen" in 1974. The subject is as timely today as ever. Our thanks are also extended to Eleanor Spiller who performed the arduous task of transcription.

We hope our readers will enjoy the four related articles on that fascinating segment of American History - the California Gold Rush. Helen Breen's general article on Lynn men who were bitten by the gold bug first appeared in the Daily Evening Item of Lynn. My own article on "David Hewes - Maker of San Francisco," is one I have wanted to write for a long time. Through the Tapley line, David Hewes and I are second cousins four times removed, according to a consanguinity chart.

Philip and Nancy Lord Graves' article on "49er" Isaiah Graves arrived at a propitious moment and it seemed fitting to include it here. Then Effingham Humphrey wrote to see if there would be interest in his "Massachusetts Men who appear in Tuoloumne County, California in 1856." We were pleased to publish the list since it tied in so nicely with the theme of this issue. Mr. Humphrey's list of New Hampshire men in Tuolemne County appeared in New Hampshire History Magazine.

Mary Koen's article on indexing is sure to strike a responsive chord in anyone who has attempted this difficult task. We continue to encourage indexing projects and hope Mary's article does not discourage such ventures. Certainly Burrill Stallard's monumental index of the 1850 U.S. Census for Essex County stands as a record achievement.

Once again, we are indebted to Beverly Johnson of Peabody who prepared four of the articles on her word processor.

We are sorry to report that our Query Editors are retiring after ten "untiring" years of editing queries and providing annual indexes for them. Our sincere thanks are extended to Ludovine Hamilton and Kay Little for a job splendidly done.

This, then, concludes Volume V of the Essex Genealogist. We are hoping to prepare a complete index to Volumes One through Five during the next year. This will probably be in the form of a single volume that will be offered as an additional item - separate from the journal subscription. We welcome any comments, suggestions or offers of assistance.

Marcia Wiswall Lindberg

****

RULES FOR SUBMITTING ARTICLES TO TEG

1. Articles should be typed and properly documented according to the MLA Handbook, Cite Your Sources, or a similar written manual.

2. Articles should have some relation to Essex County or to general genealogical research. Families or groups who migrated to or from Essex County would be suitable subjects.

3. TEG reserves the right to accept or reject any article.

5. TEG does not assume responsibility for the content of articles printed.

****

PITFALLS IN GENEALOGICAL RESEARCH

By Milton Rubincam, F.A.S.G.

(Typescript of a lecture held at New England Historic Genealogical Society;
Transcribed by Eleanor V. Spiller)

Those of you who are experienced in genealogy will relive with me some of
the pitfalls in Genealogical Research and those just starting may very well wonder
what you're getting into when I describe some of these pitfalls.

PITFALL # 1 - "Sanctity of the Printed Word"

Now, you all know that everything you see in print must be true - otherwise it
would not be in print. Dr. Jean Stephenson, remembered as Dean of American
Genealogists for many years, used to begin her lectures by "I don't believe a
thing I see in print." Since I've seen so much, I wanted to get up and say
"thanks." I quite agree. I don't believe anything I see in print either -
especially when there are errors accepted in my own research.

In 1902, a gentleman named O. B. Leonard, who had the reputation at that time
of being a very careful and good genealogist, wrote an article in which he said a
man by the name of Jonathan Smalley was born in 1683, and married a girl named
Sarah Fitz-Randolph. Now, in New Jersey genealogy, to marry a Fitz-Randolph was
really something. It is one of the few families with proven lineage back to the
very early medieval period of English history. Its accuracy has been attested to
by such authorities in England as Sir Anthony Wagner and in this country by John
Insley Coddington, F.A.S.G., one of our top genealogists. But the marriage of
Jonathan Smalley to Sarah Fitz-Randolph had a meaning other than English medieval
and royal ancestry, because Sarah Fitz-Randolph, through her mother, was a descendant of Edward Fuller, a Mayflower passenger. You know what the Mayflower means
here in New England and also the rest of the country. Consequently, thousands of
Jonathan Smalley descendants dashed madly to join the Mayflower Society. They
succeeded in 1902 because it was printed and was therefore believed to be true.

Mr. Leonard first published his article on the Smalley-Fitz-Randolph families
in a newspaper, and he reprinted the story in the proceedings of the New Jersey
Historical Society. So, that means it came out in a scholarly work of New Jersey
history which then devoted a lot of its issues to genealogy. Since it was accepted by the Editors of the New Jersey Historical Society, of course it was true,
and so it continued to be repeated by Orra Eugene Monnette, a genealogist, in his
volume First Settlers of Piscataway and Woodbridge, Olde East New Jersey. Anyone
who knows anything of Mr. Monnette knows he accepted anything. It was repeated by
Lewis Fitz-Randolph in his "Fitz-Randolph Traditions," which does not have a good
reputation today, but in his day, no doubt did. It was repeated several times
more by other compilers. All these publications followed Leonard's article of
1902.

Then a friend of mine, Lewis D. Cook, a competent Philadelphia genealogist,
looked into the matter. He looked for source material to verify the marriage and
he finally found a family Bible which Mr. Leonard knew about but did not bother to

look at. This Bible was owned by David Smalley, who was born in 1776, grandson of Jonathan and Sarah Smalley, and in it he says "my grandfather Jonathan Smalley married Sarah Bird." Now I must admit that Bird is a long way from Fitz-Randolph. There is a possibility that the name should be Birdsall. It happens that in that part of New Jersey (Middlesex County), there were Bird and Birdsall families. The family Bible records shows that there was a syllable after Bird but the page was torn there. Mr. Cook published his findings in the Genealogical Magazine of New Jersey but no one believed him. Why should they? All those other works outnumbered Cook's.

In recent years, the Mayflower Society began its magnificent five-generation project in which they began to examine the genealogies of the families of those who came over on the Mayflower. They were determined to throw out all family traditions, legends and untrue statements and depend only on documentary evidence, and finally they took up the family of Jonathan Smalley and Sarah Fitz-Randolph. Three referees were appointed (I was one) to examine the records. They sent all the documentation to me. The only reputable document was the "incriminating" family Bible giving the Smalley-Bird marriage. Leonard had nothing substantial on which to base his article. I wrote to the Chairman of the Five-Generation Project in which I rejected the Leonard unsubstantiated claim. The other two referees, Dr. Gilbert H. Doane and Kenneth Richards, Archivist of New Jersey, voted the same. No one else may now join on the marriage of Jonathan Smalley and Sarah Fitz-Randolph.

There is a sequel to the story. I went to Newark to the New Jersey Historical Society on research of my own, and while there discovered that they had the original O. B. Leonard papers, carefully arranged by family files. I immediately seized the Smalley-Fitz-Randolph files, went through it avidly, and found that the whole claim was based on a letter from a lady saying "I think my ancestor Jonathan Smalley must have married Sarah Fitz-Randolph, who was descended from Edward Fuller, the Mayflower passenger." But I found out something else, too. In 1889, 13 years before Leonard published, a man named Smalley had published his ancestry in another newspaper, and he had the family Bible before him and he stated, Jonathan Smalley married Sarah Bird. When he read Mr. Leonard's article, he sent him the evidence and asked him to retract his erroneous information. Leonard refused. All those years the same story has been rehashed.

This has been a long-winded story, but I've done it with a purpose - to show you no matter how many times a statement has been made in print, it does not necessarily mean it is true. You have to take it with a grain of salt. You must try and prove it with documentary evidence, if at all possible.

PITFALL # 2 - "Families of the same or similar surnames who lived in the same community were probably related."

There is a Bates family in Georgia. They have long claimed descent from Clement H. Bates, the Massachusetts immigrant. Clement Bates' family became rather famous in this part of the country. There is no proof whatsoever to connect the Clement Bates family of Massachusetts and the Bates families of Georgia. True, there were migrations from Massachusetts to Georgia. Some of the families could be descended from Clement Bates, but some also could be descended from a John Bates who was an early settler in Virginia and did move south into Georgia. When you look at the meaning of Bates, it is a common name. It means, son of Bartholomew, so that there are thousands of Bates families in England and America who have no connections with one another. A friend of mine who was an authority on Pennsylvania Germans, saw a Pennsylvaniia German in everybody. He tried to make their name sound like it even if it didn't. My office assistant in the Department of Commerce, had the surname "Bean." In Pennsylvania, a similar sounding name is spelled "Biehn." When my friend came to the office to visit, I introduced him to my assistant. He immediately said "Ah, Biehn! Your family must be of German origin." She replied "No, we are of Scottish origin. It was originally "MacBean." My friend was greatly disappointed that he couldn't find a Pennsylvania German at every desk in my office. This illustrates that you can not jump to conclusions.

Another problem, still in connection with names, is that of translation from one language to another. You may think you are of English ancestry if your name is Carpenter, but don't be surprised if a good genealogist finds out that your ancestors were originally named Zimmerman, which means Carpenter. In Pennsylvania, the Lancaster County family Carpenter was originally Zimmerman. Their ancestors settled in an English-speaking area where people had difficulty with Zimmerman, so the family changed it themselves to the more easily pronounceable English equivalent - Carpenter. In Louisiana, where we have the LeNoir family (French for Black), their genealogist traced them back to a German named Schwartz (German for Black).

According to Donald Lines Jacobus, the foremost American genealogist, there is in Connecticut a family named Banks, but would you believe, the name was originally Oysterberk, or Osterberg in Germany. In the next generation, the children dropped the oyster and became just Burke. Now that's Irish. They changed nationalities rapidly. In the next generation, to distinguish themselves from other Burkes they changed the name to O'Burke, thus definitely making themselves Irish. Then, in the course of time and for unknown reasons, the name became Banks, thus implying an English origin!

In Orangeburg, South Carolina we have a family named Jennings, which is English. Their ancestor was an Italian named Zennini. The name posed a pronunciation problem for South Carolininas so the immigrant changed or adopted the name Jennings. I've seen documentary evidence where he called himself John Zennings and not too long after it simply became Jennings. And here's another for you. Dr. Emmison, an English archivist, was approached by a man named Whitbread. He'd gotten his ancestors back to 1600 and he wanted to know how to go back further. He thought he'd searched everything, all conceivable documents. Emmison thought for a moment and said "Try Blancpain." (Bad Franch, correctly it should be pain blanc - white bread.) When the researcher went back to the documents he found that the Whitbread family had used the French form 'Blancpain' down to 1550-1600. Being too much even for Englishmen, it was changed to Whitebread/Whitbread. So when dealing with surnames, use your imagination, but not too much so you go too far astray. The origin could be German, French, etc. You must think of all possibilities.

PITFALL # 3 - "Family Tradition"

Donald L. Jacobus, in one of his articles, has said, "Tradition is a chronic deceiver." It may be true or it may be false. It must be proven. It isn't necessarily true because your honest Aunt Susie told you about it. In my own family, I had a wonderful tradition told to me by my uncle. The Rubincam family was of noble origin. What else! We were French Protestants and soldiers, shedding our blood on the battlefield for the Catholic kings who persecuted us! Our name was Rubinchamp, which my uncle interpreted as "red field" or "field of blood." When I became proficient in doing research and could read French and German, I found that our name was not Rubinchamp but German Rubenkanp, we were not soldiers but Reformed preachers, and instead of our name meaning "red field" it means "turnip field."

PITFALL # 4 "The three brothers tradition"

You've all heard of the three brothers tradition. Almost every family has a tradition that the family was started by three brothers. After all, they had the same name; they settled in the same community. That is not necessarily true. There may have been no relationship whatsoever. Yet, many a genealogy based on that tradition is erroneously compiled. I saw one, that was absolutely amazing! These three brothers came over separately; one on the Mayflower; the second in 1650, and the third brother came over just in time to participate in the Revolutionary War!

Let me tell you of two traditions that have been verified. One is the ancestry of George Andrew Moriarty, Jr., our late distinguished member of the American Society of Genealogists, and the other involves one of my wife's families. This I verified myself. You have all heard of the distinguished Crowninshield family of Salem, Massachusetts. It was founded by a German, Dr. Johann Kaspar Richter von Kroninschildt, a beautiful aristocratic name for someone from peasant stock. A tradition, in the Crowninshield (Anglicized) family was that Dr. von K had studied at the University of Leipzig, now in the Soviet zone of East Germany, and was expelled because he fought a duel. He eventually studied medicine and came to America and won fame, fortune and a distinguished place in Salem. Mr. Moriarty wanted to find out what the exact story was, and through research he did. Briefly, the story is this. Doctor von Kroninschildt was not Kroninschildt at all, but Richter. Why he called himself von Kroninschildt we do not know. He could have adopted a coat of arms with a crown and shield or he could have lived in a house, inn, maybe a tavern known as the Crown and Shield - something of that sort. His father was Kasper Richter, who went to Leipzig University; was indeed expelled, reason unknown. He took up with a girl whom he did not bother to marry, but they had a son and that son was later Dr. Johann Kasper Richter von Crowninshield of Salem, Massachusetts. Now, there is a thread of truth in this, but the expulsion from college was not the Salem doctor, but his father.

Now, the other story involves the Cadwalader family of Philadelphia, my wife's mother's family. They had lived in Indiana for well over a century, and had long had the tradition of descent from General John Cadwalader, of considerable Revolutionary War distinction. The alleged daughter of the general was named Sarah. She married a man named Henry Parry, of Pittsburg. It was their son who went to Indiana and from whom my wife descended. I found that General John Cadwalader was married twice. The first marriage was to an heiress, by whom he had three daughters - none Sarah. He married a second time and had a daughter who was not named Sarah. In 1948, while on business in Pittsburg, I found more information on the Parry-Cadwalader situation. I found a deed, dated 1804. A considerable piece of property, in Allegheny was deeded by a couple named Archibald and Elizabeth McCall to Henry Parry and wife Sarah. He specified, rather unusual, that the property was to go to the heirs of Sarah only. That meant that if Sarah died and Henry remarried, the children by the second wife were not to enter into receipt of any of the McCall property. Interesting even more was the identity (I knew through prior research) of Elizabeth McCall. She was the second daughter of General Cadwalader, by his first wife. This meant that Sarah Parry was something special to the McCalls and Cadwaladers. I looked into the family of

John's brother, Colonel Lambert Cadwalader, thinking she might have been a cousin of Elizabeth through him. It was not until a few years later, in Philadelphia, when I found and went through a file on the Cadwalader family archives (100,000 pieces of paper but fortunately divided into sections), I jumped on the General John section. He did indeed have a daughter named Sarah, but not by either wife. In 1776, a hired girl, Ann Dingwell, figured prominently in his papers. She was nurse for his youngest daughter, Maria, by his first wife. He took her to his estate in Kent county - obviously to get her away from his severe Quaker mother who did not approve of her military son's affair. They had a daughter Sarah. That girl was baptised at Christ Church. Recorded was the mother, Ann Dingwell. The name of the father was missing. What clinched it was that General John made five wills. In the first four of these wills he left inheritance to "Sarah, daughter of Ann Dingwell." When Ann got married he referred to her as "Sarah, daughter of Ann Dingwell, nurse to my daughter Maria." Each time he wrote about Sarah he identified her with Ann and it connected with the child of the baptismal register. Then, in his last will, he left a handsome bequest without naming her but just said "daughter of Ann, who was nurse to my daughter Maria, etc." Another clincher was the letter I found, written 1804, from a General Samuel Ringgold who was connected with Maria Cadwalader. He wrote to Archibald McCall in Philadelphia saying "Thursday last week there came to the door a carriage from which stepped a well-dressed young man and woman. They presented a letter of introduction in which it appears that "Mrs. Parry is the natural daughter of our deceased father-in-law. They are going to Philadelphia to see you. They are going on to Trenton to see Tom (later Major General) Cadwalader. Please see what you can do for them." This accounted for the considerable landed estate deeded two years later. This was another case where good research turned up the truth.

PITFALL # 5 - "Titles"

Titles often followed English precedent and the researcher should be familiar with what they connote. Today people of the proper sex are all called "Mr., Mrs., or Miss," or the unflattering "Ms." In the 17th and 18th century, this was not the case. If a man was called "Mister," it was because he was a gentleman; he owned property; he probably had a coat of arms; he was in the upper social stratum. A lady was called "Mrs." if she was of the upper social class also. She was not necessarily married, because "Mrs." is the abbreviation of "mistress" which in the 17th and 18th centuries was applied both to married and unmarried women. She could have been an unmarried gentlewoman who enjoyed the best society could offer; sat in the front pew of the church, etc. Here in New England is the only place we have the term "goodman" and "goodwife." She was often referred to as "Goody." They were substantial farmer stock. They were not of the gentle class nor were they aristocrats, but they usually owned considerable property. "Yeoman" and "husbandman" are words for plain farmer. One day a student came to me and said "Mr. Rubincam, I'm going to examine Navy Department records for my ancestor. I found a record that describes him as a 'yeoman' and that's a naval rating." I hastily suggested she search land records instead, as "yeoman" is also a farmer. "Esquire" was a man of the upper social class, probably an official, perhaps a member of the Provincial assembly or a Judge. Esquire designates his class. Then there are the terms "senior, junior, first, second, third," etc. You will find people of the same name and same place and time are designated with these distinctions. It does not necessarily mean that John Smith, Jr. is the son of John Smith, Sr. It does not mean they were related at all - not uncle and nephew - not cousins. It means simply there were two people of the same name and different ages, and to designate them for reference, they were "senior" and "junior." If there were more than two then we find "3rd" etc. to tell them apart.

Donald Lines Jacobus tells a story of the Robinson family in Connecticut in which there were five men so designated. When one died, the "slot" was filled by the proper one moving into that designation. "Uncle," "nephew" and "cousin" are interchangeable in early records. I have an ancestor who appointed his cousin as executor of his will. The man was not his cousin at all but his nephew. The same man referred to his uncle as cousin.

Then we come to that troublesome word, "nepos." It means grandson, in Latin. In more recent generations, it has been corrupted to nephew, but comes from "Nepos." John Frederick Dorman, a distinguished Virginia genealogist, published an interesting article on a Farish family of Virginia. He gave a beautiful example of the use of "nepos." He abstracted the will of John Hay of Augusta County, Virginia. In this will, John Hay left a bequest to "my nephew John Hay, my nephew William Hay, my Nephew Rebecca Hay, my nephew Rebecca Guines, my nephew William Guines, etc. When the researcher checked up on these relationships not one of these persons was a niece or nephew. They were the testator's grandchildren. The same applies to "son" and "daughter." "Son" could be "step-son" or "son-in-law" or adopted son. Daughter ditto. "Brother" and "sister" also meant other than today's usage. It could be "step-brother," "half-brother," "brother-in-law," brother in a lodge or church. The same is true of "sister." A will may read to my "brother-in-law" which may turn out to be not husband of a sister or brother of his wife, but a half-brother; a brother "in-law" - same mother and different father.

Then we come to the word "alias." This could signify illegitimacy or assumption of a name for inheritance. An historic example is the following. Oliver Cromwell, Lord Protector of England, in the male line, was a Williams. His ancestor Richard Williams had married the sister of Thomas Cromwell, minister of Henry VIII. The Cromwell estate would pass to the Williams children on condition that the Cromwell name be added to Williams. So they called themselves "Williams alias Cromwell" for a few generations until they became just "Cromwell," dropping the Williams entirely - hence "Oliver Cromwell."

Now what can we make of the will of George Kirby of Hereford, England, made in 1609, when he said he was "crazy." Well, I looked at Noah Webster's first dictionary which came out in 1806. In the 17th, 18th and 19th centuries, when a man said he was "crazy" it meant he was "sick" or "ill," of "feeble constitution." This was the original meaning of "crazy." So when you look at these words in wills, deeds and church records, etc., you must do a great deal of thinking to see what they actually mean. Do they really mean what we would interpret as the meaning?

PITFALL # 6 - "Chronology"

Dates are all important. Many a false genealogy has been built up because the compiler did not pay any attention at all to dates. He may have had a child born two years after the mother died. There are such cases in print. Sometimes in order to claim a distinguished family it has been more convenient to disregard dates. In 1922, a genealogy of the Haines family of New Jersey came out in which they showed that Richard Haines, the founder of the New Jersey family, who died at sea in 1682, was the son of Rev. John Haynes of Essex, England and grandson of John Haynes, Governor of Connecticut, one of the most distinguished families of New England. This was a beautiful ancestry (and a descendant believed it) because Governor Haynes' wife, Mabel Harlakendon, was of noble ancestry. I used to plaster my bedroom walls as a boy with lovely charts of my royal ancestry. Later, I discovered the facts of life relative to genealogy. It was impossible for Richard Haines to have been Gov. Haynes' grandson. It is true that Gov. Haynes' son Rev. John went back to England after graduating from Harvard, became a minister, had a son named Richard. But it was not _my_ Richard Haines, who was the grandson. Two reasons. His alleged grandmother, Mabel, would have been 21 years old when her grandson was born, and he would have had to be born the same year as his father. I could go on with many other examples.

PITFALL # 7 - "Lack of careful research"

Tuttle is a famous family in New England and there is a branch in New Jersey. I became interested in Samuel Tuttle of Morristown, New Jersey. If I believed all I saw in print, he was a bigamist; raised two families within a few miles of one another at the same time. What did I discover? There were two men, Samuel Tuttle and Samuel Tuthill, both of Morris County, both born in 1724, neighbors to each other, witnessed each other's deeds, and the brother of my Samuel Tuttle married the sister-in-law of Samuel Tuthill! You can readily see why the Tuttle-Tuthill genealogists were easily confused. I was completely bewildered until I discovered that my Samuel had moved away from Morristown, where the other Samuel lived, and settled at Hanover, in Morris County, where I picked him up in the Hanover church registers.

Let me tell you about the case of Job Whipple, a Rhode Islander in the 17th century. According to Arnold's Vital Record of Rhode Island, Job Whipple was the son of John Whipple and born in Providence 25 December 1690. It had to be true, it was in print. My friend, H. Minot Pitman, when called on to investigate the Whipple family, made some startling discoveries. Job was not the son of John. He was not born December 1690 and not in Providence. Mr. Pitman did what everyone should do. He examined the original book of births, marriages and deaths of Providence. He found an entry made November 1719 of information given to the town clerk by Job Whipple himself. It was not reported by his parents. At this time he was a married man with children of his own. It was duly entered into the record of Providence. The original records searched of John Whipple and his wife Lydia, showed nowhere a son Job among the children. To make a long story short, a record of his apprenticeship (1696) was found, showing that Job Liddeason, son of Lydia, wife of John Whipple, was apprenticed to John Sayles of Providence. It is apparent that Job was not the son of John Whipple, but of his wife Lydia (nee Hoar) by another connection.

Other genealogical pitfalls could be mentioned, but those discussed are sufficient to show the care which one must exercise in pursuing one's researches.

* *

Milton Rubincam is a native of Philadelphia and now lives in Hyattsville, Maryland. A graduate of Temple University, and American University at Washington, D.C., he is a Certified Genealogist and one of the most noted genealogists in the United States today. He retired in 1972 from the U. S. Department of Commerce. Mr. Rubincam is a well-known lecturer and belongs to numerous genealogical and honorable societies. His publications include Genealogical Research: Methods and Sources, Vol. I and many articles in scholarly genealogical journals. He is Editor of the National Genealogical Society Quarterly.

Crest and Shield

By Lyman O. Tucker

PIERCE, PEIRCE, PEARCE

ARMS: Argent, a fesse hummette gules
        between three ravens rising,
        sable.

CREST: A dove proper, holding an olive
        branch in its beak vert.

MOTTO: "He said and he did"

****

The Dictionary of the Ancestral Heads
of New England Families, by Frank R.
Holmes, lists 32 Pierce, Peirce, Pearce
"heads of families." On this list are
10 Johns, 5 Williams, and 2 Georges,
Richards, Roberts and Thomases. Only 3
were of Essex County: Daniel, blacksmith, Watertown, 1634, rem. to Newbury 1638; John, husbandman, freeman,
Gloucester, 1651; Thomas, Gloucester,
before 1651. 9 Pierces are listed "of
Boston," 4 "of Charlestown," 3 "of
Watertown."

PRATT

ARMS: Gules, and eagle Or.

CREST: An eagle Or.

MOTTO: "The Flowering Meadows Smile"

****

"Holmes" lists 19 Pratt "heads of
families." On the list are 3 Johns,
2 Samuels, and 2 Williams. Five settled in Connecticut and Rhode Island,
and the rest in Massachusetts:
Abraham, Phineas and Richard settled
in Charlestown; Ephraim, John, Joseph,
Micah, Samuel, Thomas and William settled in Weymouth; another John settled
in Dorchester; Joshua settled in Medfield; Matthew settled in Rehoboth,
and Thomas settled in Framingham.

THE FIRST RECORDED MURDER IN GLOUCESTER

By DONALD DOLIBER

The first documented murder in the town of Gloucester took place around the year 1772. The alleged murderer was Samuel Plummer, the son of a highly respected physician, and was a most unlikely person to commit the "sin of Cain". Samuel Plummer, the son of Dr. David Plummer and Hannah Moody, was born on 23 July 1752. As a young man he attended Governor Dummer Academy. He was admitted to Harvard College in 1767/68. Throughout his entire matriculation, only one black mark was recorded against Plummer - "a fine for defacing a library book." He was graduated with the Class of 1771 and received both AB and AM degrees.

After returning home, young Plummer entered an apprenticeship with his father who "resided near Poles' Hill at Riverdale." As a physician, David Plummer showed great promise and was well liked by the town. Soon, however, the community gossips' tales upset the Plummer house. A black female slave in that house began to show the early signs of being pregnant. Samuel Plummer was whispered as the perpetrator of the outrageous deed.

As the time of delivery approached, the stories grew more vicious. The Plummer household was under a great deal of stress. One evening the servant girl failed to return home from her chores. She had been sent to bring the cows back from pasture. An immediate search for her was initiated.

Her mutilated body was found in the pasture. A well-placed fatal wound had inflicted a quick death. A more careful investigation uncovered a bloody sword in a fissure of ledge near the body. The weapon was identified as owned by the elder Dr. Plummer.

No further discoveries or legal action followed as the weeks passed from the time of the murder. The town hummed with gossip and rumors. The finger of accusation was pointed at David Plummer. Social ostracism affected the practice of the Plummers. One day David Plummer disappeared without a trace. The community interpreted this hasty removal as a clear sign of guilt. For a short period of time the stories continued and then the town settled back to normalcy.

Some thirty years had passed when one day a stranger stepped down from the stagecoach at Lowe's Tavern. The old men who lounged in the sun near the depot wondered who had come to Gloucester. The mysterious character registered at the tavern for one evening and then wandered through the town. David Plummer had come home. He made himself known to only one man - his cousin. The relative informed him of the births, marriages and deaths that had transpired over the thirty year span. The next morning he disappeared as quickly and as quietly as he had years before. No mention of the murder or of his innocence or guilt had taken place.

Nothing more was seen of him. It was rumored that his death occurred in 1815. Thus the chapter on the first murder in Goucester was closed forever.

DID YOU LOSE AN ANCESTOR DURING THE GOLD RUSH?

By Helen Breen

GOLD IN CALIFORNIA!!!! The discovery of this precious metal at Sutter's Mill in January 1848 started the most exciting chapter in American history. News of the find spread like prairie fire throughout the region. Soon the tidings reached "the States." Hundreds of thousands of '49'ers headed for the Golden Gate. The millennium was at hand! The argonauts who pursued the Golden Fleece in ancient legend rose again and started for the gold fields. The saga had the qualities of an epic - the arduous journey, the elusive quest, and the weary return. For many it would end in death and disappointment. The event was among the best chronicled in the American experience. Every newspaper in the country published accounts from the Coast. Relatives valued and preserved letters from their kin in California. Finally, many adventurers recorded their trips in diaries. Even men who would not normally keep journals, realized that this episode was the most significant of their lives. Hence, it must be written down.

Through his research, the genealogist becomes a demographer. The migrating patterns of his lines often mirror national trends. Perusing the following sources will give us an understanding of our forefathers (or their lost brothers) who participated in the Gold Rush in the middle of the nineteenth century.

\#   \#   \#   \#   \#   \#   \#   \#   \#   \#   \#

1. Jackson, Donald Dale. GOLD DUST. New York: Alfred A. Knof, 1980.

GOLD DUST is a sparkling account of the Gold Rush from this treasure's heady discovery to "the morning after." Prospectors and traders reached the coast of California from three directions: around the Horn, across the Isthmus of Panama, and overland. Each approach brought expense, danger, disease, and infuriating delay. (The first trans-continental railroad would not be completed for twenty years.)

The well-known dangers of rounding the Horn were increased by the use of less than sea-worthy vessels pressed into service to accomodate the hoards anxious to get to the mines. Some ships drifted to the shores of Africa on the downward leg and across to Hawaii on the Pacific approach in order to get the right winds. Scurvey, seasickness, and boredom were inevitable on every voyage.

The Isthmus route was the fastest, hence the most expensive. After sailing to Panama and being ferried up the Char-gres River, the travelers then faced a wearisome overland trek before reaching Panama City. Once there, thousands found that the steamer promised to carry them to Sacramento or San Francisco was often delayed or dangerously overcrowded. Added cost was always involved.

These routes were above the means of the ordinary person. Therefore, the majority of those who went by boat had some money and usually considerable education. But the greatest number of "49ers" (and those who followed in the early 50's) went overland. The exuberant hopes of these pioneers were cruelly crushed. The endless prairies led to torturous mountain ranges and river crossings. The trail was littered with heirlooms and provisions too heavy to carry. Horse and mule carcasses proved that the abundant forage was not sufficient for the thousands of animals used by the emigrants to the gold fields.

Whether by land or by sea, exposure to the extremes of temperature and the constant threat of cholera were suffered by all who journeyed to the Coast.

Still, thousands made the trip, met success of failure, experienced muscle-breaking toil, and lived to tell the tale. Most were satisfied in the end if they broke even and survived.

Gold Dust introduces an array of colorful gamblers, miners, preachers, operators, fancy women, saints and sinners. Mr. Jackson's skillful use of primary sources (the kind that genealogists love to find) provides immediacy and excitment.

In passing, he mentions a note of local interest:

"In Lynn, Massachusetts, the fifty-two members of the Lynn Sagamore and Califor-nia Mining and Trading Company donned full-dress uniforms for their leave-taking: dark gray suits and caps trimmed with silver lace, hunting boots, rifles, swords, life preservers, and a brace of pistols per man." p. 143-144.

We can only wonder how our proud forefathers from Essex County looked when they got there!

*   *   *   *   *   *   *

2. Breed, Warren Mudge, "The California Gold Discovery of 1849." The Register of the Lynn Historical Society 23 (September 1, 1926): 3-35.

This paper, read before the Lynn Historical Society on November 14, 1918, gives a panoramic view of the Gold Rush with emphasis on the experiences of Lynners who participated. From examining old newspapers, Mr. Breed provided a list of 176 men and 2 women who left Lynn for the Coast in 1849. That ratio, by the way, was typical. The exodus was decidedly masculine. Observers agreed that much of the disorder and drunkeness which developed among the miners and traders resulted from lack of feminine influence and company! For many Lynners, the experiment was a sobering one:

Isial Graves: "This gold fever is one of the most precious humbugs that was

ever conceived. They brought out the frame of a house twenty by thirty-two, one and a half stories. They raised and boarded it, and rented it for $555.00 a month. ...Have been to the mines but was sick all the ten weeks. I hardly know what I shall do this winter. Thousands of emigrants pouring in all the time."

Alonzo Kendrick: "I would willingly exchange all my prospects of California gold for one look at home and the green fields of Lynn."

Edwin H. Tarbox: "If you know of any one coming out here expecting to get rich immediately, just assure him for me that there are hundreds of men working for their board alone here, and many others anxious to get the same chance... Those men who have families, and are living comfortably at home, I would caution to look well at both sides of the question before they start for California." (p. 28).

However, memories of the experiences sweetened with time. Most returned to their families and businesses in Lynn. A large number became enthusiastic members of the Society of California Pioneers. Over a fine wine and dinner these survivors loved to reminisce about the high point of their lives-- the Gold Rush of '49!

*   *   *   *   *   *   *

3. Richardson, Katherine W. "The Gold Seekers: The Story of the LaGrange and the California Pioneers of New England." Essex Institute Historical Collections 115 (Spring, 1979): 73-122.

Ships from Salem, Massachusetts were among the first to set out for California after gold was discovered. In March, 1849, the Salem and California Mining and Trading Company left the city on the bark LaGrange with 65 passengers and crew, most of whom were shareholders in the company. The Salem Gazette of March 17, 1849, anticipated their success: "Acting as a band of brothers, bound to pull together under any circumstances, and to act in harmony with one another, we predict a pleasant and prosperous journey." (p. 75)

These prospectors, representing every trade and profession, had assembled from the heart of Essex County: Salem, Danvers, Beverly, Lynn, Gloucester, Manchester, Rockport, Newburyport, and Middleton. Their names and occupations are given. (p. 78-79) Carrying provisions for two years, the LaGrange chartered a course around the Horn. Many men on board kept diaries to pass away the time. The accounts of Nathan Delap, Asa E. Kitfield, Henry Tuttle, and Augustus Harrington found their way into the archives of the Essex Institute where the author, Mrs. Richardson, uncovered them. She is the managing editor of the Collections. From these journals, she reconstruc-ted the entire adventure. Like thousands of others who pursued the dream of instant riches, their expectations were soon tempered by the realities of the long journey and the hardships of toiling in the gold fields.

The crewmen of the LaGrange who returned to Salem also joined the Society of California Pioneers. Wisely, they decided to donate to the Essex Institute all memorabilia of their excursion, including badges, albums, scrapbooks, and the four journals. Mrs. Richardson's informative article ends with a useful bibliography. Gold Dust provides an overview and the Lynn Historical and Essex Institute articles give a close range look at our ancestors, whether lost or accounted for, who took part in the Gold Rush. Yours may be among them!

THE U.S. CENSUS - DR. HILLERETH - AND IBM

In the mid 1880s, it became apparent to Dr. Herman Hillereth, who was the Director of the U.S. Census Bureau, that the 1880 Census would not be completed until after 1890 with the method they were using at the time. To avoid a collapse of the entire work, Dr. Hillereth invented first a punch paper tape and then a punch card that could carry data and be processed by machines. He invented two basic machines; one machine could sort cards numerically, and the other could count (tabulate) them. By assigning numeric values to states, counties, etc., the data could be quickly sorted and counted by machine.

The 1890 census was the first to be "machine processed" and was completed in approximately one-third of the time it took to do the 1880 census despite an increase in population from 50 million to 62 million. Dr. Hillereth, realizing the value of his new machines, left the Census Bureau to form the Tabulating Machine Co. This company rented machines to the government and to industry. It became IBM.

In 1900 James Powers succeeded Dr. Hillereth as Census Bureau Director. He had to rent the Hillereth machines to process the 1900 census. In 1910 James Powers developed his own machines (better, faster, etc.) for processing census data, and in 1911 he left the Bureau to form the Powers Accounting Machine Co. which in 1927 became Remington Rand, Inc. From this point on, both companies rented their machines to business and government. By the mid 1940s, IBM was the dominant company.

(From T. Radamaker, Business Systems. Vol II; submitted by Richard Herlihy)

DAVID HEWES, "MAKER OF SAN FRANCISCO"

By Marcia Wiswall Lindberg

David Hewes is Lynnfield's most famous native son; a man whose long and varied career earned him two epithets - "Maker of San Francisco" and "Giver of the Golden Spike." His rise to prominence from a small-town farm boy in New England to an eminent Californian builder, rancher and railroad man is a true "Horatio Alger" saga, and the strong moral principles learned in his youth influenced his entire career. Early in life he realized the value of education and hard work, and throughout his career he was fearless in taking great risks and courageous in facing total losses.

THE EARLY YEARS David Hewes was born in Lynnfield, Massachusetts on 16 May 1822, the fifth son of ten children of Joel and Ruthe Tapley Hewes. His father was an early convert to Methodism whose all-consuming piety was a strong influence on all of his children. It was Joel Hewes who invited Methodist ministers to preach at Lynnfield and when a small society was formed, he was appointed their class leader and steward. Ruthe Tapley Hewes was a strong and religious woman. When her husband died in 1827, leaving her with eight children ages three to nineteen, Ruthe struggled to maintain her family. David Hewes' autobiography, which is included in Eben Putnam's Joshua Hewes: New England Pioneer, describes his early childhood.

"Every Sunday afternoon, before evening service, it was the custom to call the children into the long family room where, seated on a bench, we were taught the catechism by our mother, and every morning we all united in family worship. My mother had the improvement of her husband's estate as long as she remained a widow, in consideration of her support and education of the children during their minority. Two years after the death of her husband, she married Oliver Swain. . . I was then ten years old; old enough in the opinion of Mr. Swain to be set at tasks about the farm, which would bring ample compensation for my maintenance. Association with my step-father impressed me with the importance of work and industry. I was obliged to rise early and perform work which was equal to two-thirds the work of a man. Later I was "bound out" to my brother-in-law, Benjamin Cox, Jr. . . and received $30 a year for clothing, board and lodging, and six weeks' schooling each year in return for my services until I was seventeen and one-half, when I was to receive my freedom. The last year of my apprenticeship, Mr. Cox gave me 12 weeks' schooling, in recognition of my faithfulness. . . I attended West Reading Academy for two years with certain hours before and after school being devoted to farm work. After this for four years I was with Mr. Allen Rowe, a prosperous merchant and shoe manufacturer in Stoneham with compensation of $12.50 a month with board. Mr. Rowe was of noble characteristics and my

association with him did much to mold my future life as a business man.
But I realized plainly the need of a higher education, and left to attend
Phillips Academy at Andover in 1844. In order to meet my expenses I
undertook part of the care of the buildings of the Abbott Female Semina-
ry. During vacation I sawed wood for the boarding school - but always
succeeded in obtaining a weeks' visit to my mother in Lynnfield. At
commencement, I had a part and was prepared for admittance to Yale."

In order to earn money for his education at Yale, David began taking
subscriptions for a children's magazine called "Peter Parley's Merry Museum," and
his success was phenomenal. His first attempts in the city of Lowell secured for
him one thousand subscriptions in 30 days and netted him $400. (This was in 1848
when most Americans were paid only a few dollars a month.) Eventually he accumulated $3,000, and although the magazine's owner wanted to make him a partner, he
decided instead to invest in the future of the West.

THE MOVE TO CALIFORNIA

"While at Yale my attention was arrested by the accounts published in
the papers regarding California. As there was no building material
prepared in California at that time I thought it a desirable opportunity
to invest my $3,000 in "Peter Naylor's Iron Houses." I went to New York,
purchased the houses which were boxed and shipped to Boston to be reship-
ped on the ship Norfolk on which my cousin and his brother-in-law were to
sail to California via Cape Horn. When my cousin's wife and only child
died, I knew it would utterly unfit him to attend to selling my buil-
dings. So I secured a leave of absence from college to make a trip to
San Francisco via the Isthmus to be there when the ship arrived with my
cousin and my houses. The accomodations were anything but pleasant, the
company of the most miscellaneous character, rough flotsam and jetsam of
the great tide of migration to California, as well as many very nice
people."

In San Francisco, David Hewes' plans were to sell his houses at a great
profit and then return to New England to study medicine or law, but the ship with
his "tin houses" was two months late in arriving. Meanwhile, he traveled to
Sacramento and got a job. When the galvanized iron arrived, he had it shipped to
Sacramento, set up the houses and immediately rented them out for as much per
month as their original cost. He prospered greatly and a year later bought a
large piece of land in the heart of the booming city, where he erected a six-story
building to house his land-office mercantile business. He also built a large
hostelry named the "Queen City Hotel."

LETTERS FROM MOTHER While his interest in real estate and business was great,
David Hewes did not neglect his spiritual needs. Even if he had not been so
inclined, monthly letters from his mother back home in Lynnfield constantly remin-
ded him of the perils that awaited the ungodly.

"My dear son, what matters it whether we leave one dollar or a
million dollars behind us, if we have an interest in Heaven?" "A little
of this world with a clear conscience and a contented mind is far better
than gold or silver." "Oh my son, if you should get rich, but lose that
peace which the world cannot give, awful would be your state."

David Hewes heeded his mother's advice. In his autobiography, his interest
in religion and church are very much in evidence.

> *"During the early months of my first year's residence in Sacramento
> there was no regular school, or place of worship, except poorly construc-
> ted tents of cloth. Theaters, places of amusement, and gambling houses
> were run without any restraint. The first Sunday after my arrival I
> listened to a sermon preached by Rev. J. A. Benton under a large sycamore
> tree. At this time gambling and vice was so noticeable that the press
> took up the matter. With their cooperation, I started a subscription for
> funds to build a church. A committee was appointed of which I was a
> member. We found it not at all difficult to secure sufficient funds to
> erect a very substantial church which would seat from three to five
> hundred people and which was crowded every Sunday. There was a large
> Sabbath school to which I gave a large library. This library I had
> selected before leaving home and had brought with me across the Isthmus,
> knowing what would be required for such a purpose as, while at Andover, I
> had established a Sabbath school at Lawrence, Mass. five years before."*

THE FIRST DISASTER   David Hewes' successful ventures in Sacramento were destined
to be short-lived. For in 1852, he suffered the first of his total losses when
the "great fire" destroyed the entire city. Undaunted, he immediately began to
rebuild his mercantile establishments and his church, but the following year a
second natural disaster struck.

> *"The flood came on the last day of December, the levee broke and six
> feet of water covered Sacramento valley. I, with other merchants, saved
> what goods we could by putting them on board a stern-wheel steamer,
> drawing only about two feet of water. We took our goods to Brighton,
> which was high land, and there we erected tents, and conducted business
> for the next four months. At this time certain rich merchants from San
> Francisco purchased a tract of land, five miles below Sacramento on which
> they attempted to build a city, and solicited our merchants to move to
> the new town site, which they called "Sutterville," offering them corres-
> ponding lots to those they owned in Sacramento. The experiment soon
> failed. During that time the question again arose regarding title to the
> site of Sacramento City. The "Squatters Riots," which created great
> excitement in the California settlements, arose from the attempts of the
> landless and more or less lawless individuals to disregard the title to
> land held under the Spanish grant to John A. Sutter. A small party of
> rioters, headed by a squatter leader, engaged a hastily-gathered law and
> order posse, and several persons were killed and wounded. Disgusted with
> my experiments in Sacramento, and the disputes over titles, I determined
> to go to San Francisco, and on leaving Sacramento, I carried all my
> worldly possessions in a handbag. I reached San Francisco, put up at a
> hotel, and then went out to look about the town."*

His mother wrote from Lynnfield: "I was sorry to hear you had met with a
loss. Well, my son, they that have must lose. I feel so anxious about you. I
read and hear so much about that part of the world where you are. If you don't
die a natural death, I am afraid you will be killed. I do want you to come home.
Be careful, won't you, my son."   "My dear son, when I get a newspaper I don't
stop for anything till I look it over to see if your death was in it." "I want
you to come home and build in Lynnfield."

MAKER OF SAN FRANCISCO   In San Francisco, David made the acquaintance of two men who helped to shape his destiny. Mr. George Amorage owned a lot at the northeast corner of Stockton and O'Farrell streets and was anxious to have it leveled so he could build a house on it for his family. He offered David Hewes the job. Another acquaintance, Mr. James Cunningham was engaged in grading on an extensive scale and had filled lands in New York City, Brooklyn and Boston. When David mentioned his project, Mr. Cunningham advised him to "Pitch in and grade it, Mr.

Hewes: you can do it, and get Chinamen at $2 a day, while you would have to pay an Irishman $4." David followed his advice and that first contract netted him a profit of $600. Soon he had ten and then twenty Chinamen with their shovels and wheelbarrows filling lower portions of the lot. Later James Cunningham sold David fifteen large horses, carts, harnesses and equipment, and for security, David used his "contract" for the grading of Bush Street. He soon paid off the debt of $3000 and became an indepentent contractor. David next purchased Mr. Cunningham's entire grading outfit for $42,000 and began the grading of Market Street where the hill was nearly as high as the Call building in the fall of 1858. He filled in water lots on the south side of Market from Fremont to Stuart and then began filling in the Bay on the north side of Market Street. Continuing in the same way, David leveled the sand hills and filled in lots from First Street, then Second, Third, Fourth, Fifth, etc. to Tenth Street, until Mission Bay was filled in. His track took in about two miles in extent, and this public work earned him the complimentary title of "The Maker of San Francisco."

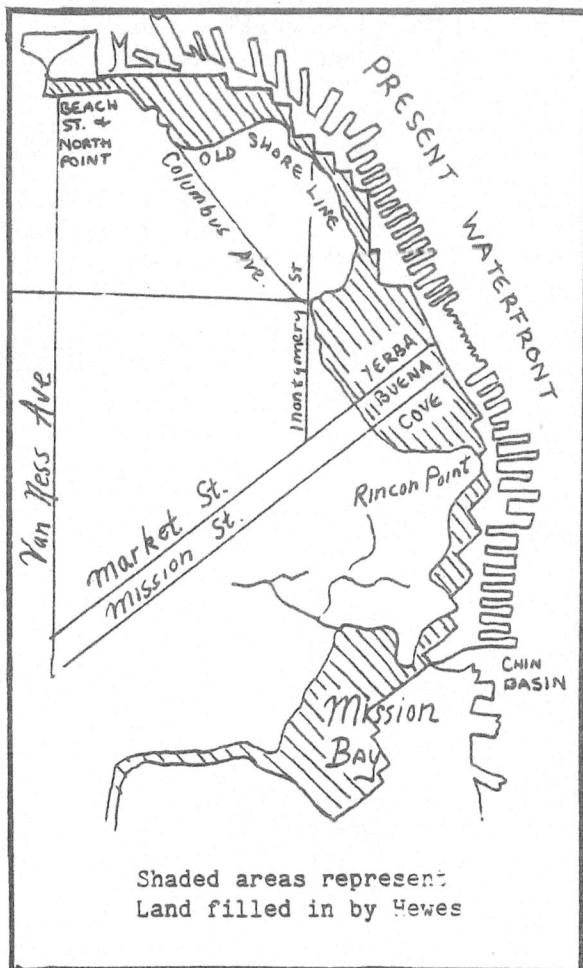

Shaded areas represent Land filled in by Hewes

THE "STEAM PADDY" AND THE "OREGON PONY"

Leo J. Friis, in his David Hewes: More than the Golden Spike, describes the equipment used by Hewes in his work on the hills of San Francisco:

"The acquisition of steam shovels was an important addition to Hewes' equipment as they were capable of scooping up two tons of earth with a single "bite." They were commonly called "steam paddies" because they did the work of the Irish pick and shovel laborer who bore the nickname of "paddy." Hewes referred to himself as a "Steam Paddy and Railroad Contractor" and his early bill heads bore the picture of a steam shovel. He was widely known as "Steam Paddy" Hewes.

To expedite his earth moving operations Hewes later used three locomotives. The first of these was called the "Pioneer," and the second one of greater capacity he named "Pluto." His third locomotive, the "Oregon Pony," was built in 1862 for the Oregon Steam Navigation Company, *and that is believed to be the first railroad locomotive constructed in California. Four years later Hewes purchased it for $1,000 and converted it into a coal burner. The Pony was first used in San Francisco in the sand pits as a switch engine at the head of Fourth Street. When Hewes retired from the earth moving business, he stored his engines in a warehouse where they were damaged by fire. When the Lewis and Clark Exposition of 1905 asked him to loan the Oregon Pony for an exhibit, he had the locomotive repaired at a cost to him of over $2,000 and donated it to the State of Oregon. It now stands in a miniature park across from the Portland railroad station. Hewes retained the other locomotives until 1910 when he presented them to the Golden Gate Park museum in San Francisco."*

TRANSCONTINENTAL RAILROAD   David Hewes was never directly involved with the building of the transcontinental railroad, but was always an ardent supporter of the dream.

Having lived in Sacramento from 1850 to 1853, I was well acquainted with Stanford, Hopkins and Huntington and these merchants very strongly solicited me to join with them in the construction of the Central Pacific Railroad. However, having lost my fortune in Sacramento, and having a well-established business in San Francisco and with no competition, I did not care to risk my prospects for the furture and all my property and become engaged in the proposed railroad enterpries. However, no one had more faith in its speedy completion than myself.

The building of the transcontinental railroad was "magnificent in conception and marvelous in execution." Before it was completed, it took 30 days to travel from New York to San Francisco by way of the Isthmus of Panama. Leland Stanford of California, later Governor, whose wife was sister-in-law of David Hewes, is credited with being the man of the hour. "Without his calm forethought and untiring physical energy the overland railroad would never have been completed." The times were not propitious. The Civil War was raging in the east putting a tremendous strain on the treasury. Nevertheless, President Lincoln signed the bill on the first of July 1862, and on January eigth, 1863, ground was broken at the foot of K street in Sacramento, with Governor Stanford officiating at the ceremony. The race was on, and there followed some marvelous feats of track-laying.

"The Union Pacific laid six miles in one day. The Central Pacific laid seven. The Union Pacific surpassed this by half a mile, etc. A wager of $10,000 was laid by Mr. Durant of the Union Pacific that the Central Pacific could not lay ten miles in one day, but the feat was accomplished on the 29th of April 1869 between sunrise and sunset. No such feat of railroad-building had ever been known. Four thousand men were constantly employed who handled in this one day 25,800 cross-ties, 3,520 rails, 55,000 spikes, 7,040 fish-plates, and 14,000 bolts weighing 4,352,000 pounds. It had astonished the scientific and won the admiration of the world. It only remained to lay the last rail for which preparations were made on the 10th of May at Promontory Point in Utah, the place of meeting, eighty miles west of Ogden and 804 miles east of San Francisco. Two lengths of rail had been left by each road for the final ceremony. The day was pleasant and residents of Salt Lake valley began to gather early. When everything was ready the engines of the two roads moved forward until only ninety feet apart."

GIVER OF THE GOLDEN SPIKE   Robin Lamson, in The Man Who Gave the Golden Spike, describes a scene between David Hewes and Governor Sanford at this time:

> *"When at last the transcontinental railway was on the eve of completion, Governor Stanford was telling David Hewes of his plans to drive the last spike with appropriate ceremony. 'I suppose,' said Hewes, with an ironical smile, 'that the Comstock millionaires of Nevada have donated a couple of solid silver rails for uniting the two railroads?' 'You suppose too well,' answered Stanford. 'They've offered us nothing of the sort.' David Hewes then opened his mouth - and his heart. 'The completion of the overland railway,' he declared, 'is the greatest event in the history of California since the discovery of gold. I want to contribute a last crosstie of California laurel and a last spike of pure Mother Lode gold for the ceremony in Utah. Will you accept it?' Replied the Governor. 'You bet we will!' David Hewes carried $400 worth of virgin gold nuggets to his jewelers, and the Last Spike was cast and engraved and then carried in its velvet box to its immortal hour at Promontory Point."*

Actually, the solid gold spike was too soft to be driven, so it was dropped into a hole already bored into the hardwood tie, and then symbolically tapped by the gandy-dancer's hammer. A long rough slug of gold attached to the tip of the last spike was broken off and made into souvenir rings for Stanford, Oakes Ames, President Ulysses S. Grant and William H. Seward. The original last spike is now the property of Stanford University.

In the meantime preparations had been made for the entire country to participate in the historic moment. And it was David Hewes who made the arrangements. In his autobiography, he describes his activities.

> *"I suggested to Leland Stanford the plan of attaching a wire to throw over the company's telegraph line, thus connecting with the Golden Spike, and have it operated like a telegraph instrument, so that signals for the firing of heavy guns by electricity could be produced. I consulted with officers of the Western Union Telegraph Co. and with General Ord (commanding on the Pacific Coast) with regard to the matter. He obtained permission from Washington to connect the telegraph wires with the parapet guns in the fort at Fort Point."*

The celebration went off as planned. At 2:27 P.M. Promontory Point said to the people congregated in the various telegraph offices: "Almost ready. Hats off, prayer is being offered." A silence for the prayer ensued. At 2:40 the bell tapped again and the Point said: "We have got done praying. The spike is about to be presented. All ready now, the spike will be driven." One, two, three, the signal; another pause, and the lightning came flashing eastward, vibrating over 2,400 miles between the junction of the two roads and Washington. At 2:41 P.M., Promontory Point wired a single word - "DONE!" - making this the shortest telegraphic message on record.

WAS HEWES AT THE CEREMONY?   Mr. Friis thinks that it was "probable" that David Hewes did not attend the ceremony, because "if he had, he would have said so in his autobiography." An argument that he was at the ceremony is based on the fact that his likeness appears in the famous painting by Thomas Hill called "Driving the Last Spike." Hill spent four years on the canvas under the misapprehension

misapprehension that Leland Stanford had commissioned it. When it was finished, Stanford refused to pay for it, denied he had ordered it, and objected to its portrayal of seventy railroad officials of whom only a few were present. Therefore, Hewes portrait in that painting does not prove he was at the ceremony.

PROMONTORY POINT, UTAH   Today Promontory Point is a National Park in Utah where two replicas of the original steam engines perform daily as they did on that historic date over 100 years ago.   Betsy and Dean Williams, who are members of ESOG and former Lynnfield residents, recently visited the Park and were delighted to hear the lecturer tell about the Golden Spike. During the question and answer period, Betsy asked if the name David Hewes was significant. The lecturer "lighted up and began a lengthy discourse on David Hewes." Betsy had to tell him that they were from the birthplace of David Hewes and that they bought their land there from the Hewes estate. The Ranger later presented the Williams with a copy of a booklet on David Hewes from which parts of this article were culled.

A TRIP EAST   In August following the completion of the railroad, after an absence of twenty years, David Hewes decided to travel east. His purpose was two-fold; he wanted to visit his old family home in Lynnfield, and he planned to seek medical advice in Boston. For many years he had suffered with a facial skin disease called "epithelioma." Unfortunately the doctors in Boston were unable to help him and he returned to California in 1869, accompanied by eighteen relatives and friends who then became permanent residents of that state. The following year, 1870, still sorely troubled by his disease, he traveled to Vienna to consult with two specialists there. This time the treatment was successful although extremely painful. He took with him his brother Charles and his sister Ruthe and her husband, and his nephew Granville. After his cure, they traveled the continent and the British Isles, returning to California in 1872.

In 1874 David Hewes undertook a new venture, constructing and reconstructing a line of rail for the Seattle Coal Company of which he was principle stockholder. The work included building tramways, a barge to carry the coal, a railway across the isthmus between Lakes Union and Washington, and facilities for loading steamships. The situation at Seattle, however, was unsatisfactory to him. He discovered that unfair contracts had been made in his absence and that other stock-holder manipulations had transpired. After the completion of his work, he sold his shares to the Northern Pacific Railroad, later describing the whole Seattle venture as one of the most tryng experiences of his life.

PERSONAL LIFE   Meanwhile, David Hewes personal life was finally being given some attention. In 1865, Mrs. Matilda C. Gray and her daughter visited the Pacific Coast. She and David developed a friendship which culminated in their engagement and marriage at Saratoga Springs in 1875. David was 53 years old. Their wedding trip started by sailing down the Hudson and thence to England with Matilda's sister and daughter. On to the continent, they visited twenty-two countries including Egypt, Palestine, Greece and Italy. Mrs. Hewes stayed in Italy for several months while David, accompanied by his brother-in-law, Dr. Abbott, traveled down the Nile, visited Jerusalem, Jordan, Galilee and Damascus, with Dr. Philip Schaff, a distinguished Biblical scholar. Back in Italy, David and his wife collected many works of art which were eventually given to Stanford University.

On their return from Europe in 1877, Mr. and Mrs. Hewes settled in Oakland where they remained until 1881. Their home became a meeting place for a society devoted to the study of art and literature. When President and Mrs. Hayes came to

Oakland, the Hewes home was selected to entertain them. At this time, also, David Hewes made a brief sortie into the world of politics. He was invited to stand for election to the Oakland Council, and at his wife's urging, he ran and was elected. However, politics was not to his liking and he soon returned to private life.

MOVE TO SOUTHERN CALIFORNIA In 1881 the Hewes removed to Tustin, in southern California hoping to find a more suitable climate for Mrs. Hewes who suffered from bronchial distress. David purchased a ranch of 800 acres and became a rancher in earnest. He planted 500 acres in Malaga grapes, 50 acres of apricots, 50 acres of prunes and ten acres of pears. But before long a disease attacked all the vine-yards of Los Angeles, Orange, and largely Riverside counties. Over the next several years, he lost every plant. His bearing acres that had yielded $400 per acre had been reduced to land worth only $20 to $30 per acer. Meanwhile, Mrs. Hewes health had failed rapidly and she died in January of 1887. David left his ranch with a manager and returned to San Francisco. There, to house his art collection, he built a gallery which was open only to his friends.

On 11 June, 1889, David married as his second wife, Miss Anna M. Lathrop, sister of Governor Stanford's wife. They were married in the Governor's mansion, after which the Governor placed his private car at their disposal for their wedding trip across the continent. They visited Albany, Mrs. Hewes' home, and then traveled to Europe for the remainder of the year. Governor and Mrs. Stanford met them in London where they were entertained by, among others, Mr. Gladstone. When they returned to the United States, they visited David's birthplace at Lynn-field and the first American home of Mrs. Hewes ancestor, Rev. John Lathrop in Scituate. On their return to California, they made their home at the corner of Van Ness and Pacific Avenues. With them lived Mrs. Hewes brother and his daughter who became the "light and joy of their home." But their happiness was of short duration. Mrs. Hewes' health began to decline about the time of the dedication of Leland Stanford, Jr. University and she passed away at San Francisco on 2 August 1892.

David then returned east and spent the fall of 1892 mainly visiting historic sites and scenes of his youth. He attended the funeral of the poet Whittier, and the reunion of the Tapley family in November 1892. He had the Tapley tomb at the corner of Lowell and Chestnut Streets restored, and began collecting material for a genealogy of the Hewes family. When he returned to Los Angeles, he once again became interested in real estate and he built what was known as the Hewes Market. Then after 1900 he returned to his ranch in Tustin. To restore the ranch, he now purchased 50,000 young orange trees. Eventually, he planted 300 acres in lemons, 250 acres in oranges, 75 acres in olives and 30 acres in walnuts. The remaining 720 acres were kept for hay and grain for his stock.

ANOTHER CATASTROPHE In 1906, another catastrophe resulted in the loss of all of David Hewes' buildings in San Fancisco. This was the great earthquake in which so many lost their lives. David was at his ranch in Tustin when he got the news, and in typical Hewes fashion, he sent a cablegram to his relatives in the East, who he feared might be worried:

"Safe; destroyed to-day, build tomorrow!"

He immediately began to plan how to place upon his lot a building which should be a credit to the city. He was 80 years old. The building that he then caused to have built was completed in 1909. It was fourteen stories tall, and was voted by the Trades Union as the best building erected since the earthquake.

David Hewes died in California on July 23, 1915. According to the <u>Santa Ana Blade</u>:

> *"The mind of this well-loved man was clear until forty-eight hours before his death, when a sinking spell seized him. Never faltering and with a smile on his lips, the brave old man awaited the end which came at 10:30 last evening."*

He was ninety-three years old. He left more behind than the Golden Spike connecting the Central Pacific and Union Pacific Railroads. He contributed to the business development of California, helped establish many churches, endowed new universities and supported several philanthropic ventures. His cousin, Harriet Sylvester Tapley, in her <u>Genealogy of the Tapley Family</u>, writes a fitting memorial to this outstanding man.

> *"The vigor and undaunted courage of this life must be apparent to all who read this sketch, yet it but faintly touches on the obstacles which had to be overcome and the disappointments which fell to his lot. He defied the touch of time, both mentally and physically. Yet, not in these characteristics will he be remembered; nor yet in his happy cheerfulness. The greater marvel is the wide extent and number of his benefactions. Through all his life, with a lavish hand he bestowed gifts upon the church, his family and his friends. Among his brothers and sisters, there is not a member who has not had occasion to have loving remembrances of him, and this tender thoughtfulness has been extended even to their children. Wide also is the number of personal friends, whom he has included in his generous giving and loving thought, and wider, possibly greater, in its helpfulness has been the atmosphere of kindness and tender sympathy which has constantly radiated from him to those in need."*

* *

REFERENCES

Friis, Leo H., <u>David Hewes: More than the Golden Spike.</u> Santa Ana, California: Friis-Pioneer Press, 1974.

Lampson, Robin. <u>The Man Who Gave the Golden Spike.</u> Richmond, Calif. : Chimes Press, 1969.

Putnam, Eben. <u>Lieutenant Joshua Hewes: a New England Pioneer.</u> (New York : J. F. Tapley Co.), privately printed, 1913.

Tapley, Harriet Sylvester. <u>Genealogy of the Tapley Family.</u> Danvers, Mass. : (Endicott Press), 1900.

HEWES

Joshua[1] Hewes
b. 1611/12 Royston (Hertford) Eng.
came to Boston 1633
d. 25 Jan 1675/6
m. (1) Mary Goldstone. 3 children

Joshua[2] Hewes
b. Roxbury 25 May 1644
d. Boston 30 Oct 1706
m. Hannah Norden. 7 children

Samuel[3] Hewes
b. Boston 8 Sep 1677
d. Antigua bef. 1720
m. Hannah Johnson. 5 children

Joshua[4] Hewes
b. Boston ca 1705
Removed to Sherburne 1730
m. Hannah -----. 3 prob. children

John[5] Hewes (prob. son of above)
b. 13 July 1741
d. Lynnfield 14 Feb 1817
m. Anna Wellman. 8 children

Col. Joel[6] Hewes
b. Lynnfield 30 Dec 1786
d. Lynnfield 18 Dec 1827
m. Ruthe Tapley

TAPLEY

Gilbert[1] Tapley
b. 1634 Marldon Parish, Eng.
to Beverly bef. 1665, Setl. Salem
d. Salem, 17 Apr 1714
m. Tomasine (Tamsin) ----. 3 children

Gilbert[2] Tapley, Jr.
b. Salem 26 Aug 1665
d. Salem 1710
m. (1) Lydia Small. 4 children

Joseph[3] Tapley
b. Salem 30 July 1691
d. bef. 1739
m. Margaret Masury. 4 children

Lt. Gilbert[4] Tapley
b. Salem 6 May 1722
d. Danvers 6 May 1806
m. (1) Phebe Putnam. 8 children

Joseph[5] Tapley
b. Danvers 10 Apr 1756
d. Lynnfield 11 Mar 1820
m. (1) Mary Smith. 12 children

Ruthe[5] Tapley
b. Lynnfield 1 Apr 1791
d. Lynnfield 13 Sep 1852
m. Joel Hewes

RUTHE TAPLEY HEWES

"Few women have equalled the vigorous womanhood of Ruthe Tapley, wife of Col. Joel Hewes and afterward of Oliver Swain. She was a bride at seventeen and a widow at thirty-six, having had ten children. She was an energetic, progressive woman, who did not wait until the necessity came, but was forehanded, doing the work for the fall in the summer and always in advance. She found time to be a teacher in the Sunday school and an officer in the sewing circle and a neighbor, whose advice was constantly sought. She was a promoter of Methodist interests in Lynnfield and a remarkable class-leader. First and always in her thought was the spiritual welfare of her children. She was also interested in their secular education, giving all her children the benefit of the public schools and sending Ruthe to the Academy at West Reading and Lucy to the Charlestown Female Seminary. She had a kind, loving heart and excellent judgment. Her son Daivd Hewes had her life sized portrait painted after her death with the open Bible in her lap and this picture hangs by the side of her son in the Anna Lathrop Memorial Room in the Museum of Stanford University."

ISAIAH GRAVES - FORTY NINER

By Philip and Nancy Lord Graves

Isaiah Graves was born November 21, 1826, in Lynn, Mass., son of Samuel and Anna (Ireson) Graves. He was educated in the public schools of Lynn and the Phillips Academy in Andover. News of the "California Gold Rush" appealed to him far more than farming and shoe cutting and he decided (as did several young men of Lynn) to pursue the lure of adventure. So Isaiah, along with two local friends, Eugene B. and Amos M. Attwell (of Woodend, Lynn), bought passage to "The Golden Gate." The obligation required $200 from each adventurer and the promise to relinquish their wages for seven months after arrival in California-- or a minimum of another $200 each. In return they would be provided with the necessary supplies, food, and medical care. The agreement was signed by the three from Lynn and by Ezra Foster, James Briant, and George Foster, owners of the Brig Sterling. They sailed out of Beverly, Mass. January 1, 1849, travelling around Cape Horn--a treacherous voyage of six months and 25,000 miles--arriving in San Francisco on July 1, 1849.

For the next seven years, Isaiah wandered around the gold fields and elsewhere following his quest. He was at first awed by what he found but later seemed to develop home-sickness and sometimes even disillusionment. The letters he wrote home to his father and brother in Lynn were saved and some time later were copied and distributed among immediate family members (descendants). Where the originals are today, we do not know.

As a point of explanation, the Susan Ann that Isaiah expressed such concern for in almost every letter was his sister (of ill health) who eventually passed away before his return. The Susan Ann mentioned with a lighter air was his sweetheart.

Isaiah returned to Lynn via the Isthmus of Panama in 1856, not much richer than when he left and in 1857 married Susan Ann Emerton. Settled to some extent, he pursued the shoe business for several years and later the grocery business, being one of the founders of the Franklin Grocery Company. His adventures were now political. An active Democrat, he attended the primary conventions, once even serving as a delegate to the National Convention in New York. Locally he was twice elected to the Lynn Common Council, in 1870 and 1871. In 1872 he was a member of the Board of Alderman under Mayor Bubier.

In 1885 Isaiah inherited from his father, Samuel, large tracts of land--most of which had been in the Graves family since the first Samuel settled in Lynn (Saugus) before 1635--in what was commonly called "Gravesend" (Lynn). The tax records show that at one time he was the largest individual property owner in the city.

A self-styled historian and avid reader, Isaiah was also well aware of his heritage. A Charter member of the Lynn Historical Society, he also provided verification for most of the Graves listed in the Vital Records of Lynn, published by the Essex Institute. Some examples of where further information on the Graves family of Lynn may be found are: History of New England: 1630-1649 by John Winthrop; History of Lynn by Alonzo Lewis; and The Register of the Lynn Historical Society for the year 1909.

Isaiah died December 31, 1909 at age 83 years, 1 month, 10 days and his wife, Susan Ann, followed January 4, 1910 at age 73 years, 3 days. Although eight (possibly nine) children were born of this marriage, only three survived Isaiah and Susan Ann: Edwin Johnson Graves (wife, Julia Abbie Nichols); Samuel Albert Graves (wife Alice M. Brown); and Mary Annie [called Annie M.] (husband, Otis S. Ramsdell).

One major puzzle remains to be solved. Upon Isaiah's return to Lynn he continued his association with his "mining buddies" and became actively involved with two other organizations not previously mentioned" The Associations of California Pioneers of '49 and the New England Association of California Pioneers, serving as a director in the latter. We have a piece of a newspaper clipping concerning the annual meeting of The Society of California Pioneers of '49 which had been held at the Hotel Pemberton, Hull, Mass. At that time, according to this clipping, the President of the Society was Samuel Snow of Cambridge, and membership numbered 155 with the average age being 70 years, 6 months. Unfortunately, whoever saved the article did not save the whole article, the name of the newspaper, or the date, but we believe it was written circa 1895-1901.

Does anyone know anything about either of these organization for "Old '49ers" or where we might find some information on them? It may be possible that once all membership passed on, the organizations died.

# # # # # # # # # # # # # # #

LETTERS WRITTEN BY ISAIAH GRAVES FROM CALIFORNIA

San Francisco. July 1, 1849
Dear Father, I arrived here the first, after a long and tedious passage... I will give you some particulars. The first night out we had a N.E. gale with a severe snow storm. I did not get much sleep, the noise of the tramping of the men made a long night besides I felt squirmish, but was not sick enough to vomit, nor have I lost a meal's victuals since I have been aboard. When I came on deck in the morning the land had disappeared and the Brig was driving madly before the gale under close reefed top sails. This lasted five days. After we crossed the gulf the gale abated to fine weather which continued to near the equator. We crossed the equator 34 days from Beverly in Longitude 30 degrees E., we now had pleasant weather and fresh breeze making nearly two degrees of latitute to Falkland Island. The Brig was old, sails and rigging poor, our crew consisted of but five men before the mast, one of which was taken sick the third day and continued so all the passage, and four boys who came out to work their passage, they were little or no good. under these circumstances the passage was gloomy enough. We were off the Cape fifty days, went as far south as 60 degrees, had gales most every day with snow, rain and sleet, had our starborad bulwark washed off from the main chains to the taffrail. We had now got well to the westward of the Cape in the fine pleasant weather of the Pacific, crossed the equator the second time 145 days from port. When we got inthe Latitude of our port we were 1000 miles to the westward of our port. ... We arrived here Sunday July 1st. As the steamer sails tomorrow, and the mail closes today at 12 o'clock, I cannot give you many particulars. ... There are 150 sails of vessels here, mostly foreigners. I have enjoyed good health all the passage. The Attwells are well.

Mormon Island, Aug. 10, 1849
My Dear Father, I left San Francisco on the 6th of July in the Brig that I came from home in, for Sacramento. When we arrived there we found the town to consist

of about a dozen tents, it looked more like a military camp than a town. I started for the mines with Eugene and Amos, we had proceeded five miles when Amos became sun struck and died. We were obliged to go back to the vessel and stop almost a fortnight. When we started again we were obliged to walk, as there were nothing but ox teams to carry baggage... I think this country is the most barren the sun shines upon. The people raise nothing and you can get no vegetables but a few potatoes. We are obliged to live on flour, water, salt pork, tea and coffee, and that without milk, as we cannot pay so much as it sells for. We lie upon the ground under a tent. This gold fever is one of the most precious humbugs that was ever got up, thousands of men have been deceived by it. You will see doctors, lawyers and ministers working side by side on the river. Those that come out here expecting to get gold without labor are very much disappointed. it is very hard work. The most of it is taken from the banks of the river. The dirt is exceedingly hard so that it is impossible to use a shovel without a pick...

Mormon Island, Aug. 10, 1849
My Dear Brother, I will try to give you some sort of a description of San Francisco... There are not more than twenty frame houses in the place, the rest are tents. Nearly all the places of business are tents.... There is no law and very little crime... I never saw so much gambling, you may see a hundred of thousand dollars on the table at one time, most of it gold.

Sacramento, Nov. 19, 1949
Dear Father, ...I have been to the mines but was sick almost all the time I was there, which was 10 weeks. I had the fever ague, dysentery and scurvy. I have now got better and am able to go to work. I hardly know what I shall do this winter. I had made arrangements to go to the mines with the Essex Co. The weather there has been so rainy that the roads are now impassable. Provisions are very high... Real Estate is very high. We brought out the frame of a house, it is 20 X 32, not finished. It has been rented out as is... for $550 per month. None of the buildings here are lathed and plastered, they are lined with cotton cloth which is nailed around the building to the studs.

Sacramento, Mar. 30th, 1850
Dear Father, ... There are thousands of emigrants pouring in every day from almost all countries, and gold continues to be found, but there are so many to work the mines that a single person can not make so much as he could...

Nevada, July 15th, 1850
Dear Father, ... When I wrote you my last letter, I left Sacramento for this place. Nevada is situated on a large creek running into the Yuba River, 80 miles above Sacramento City. The mines in this vicinity have been very rich but they are nearly worked out. They were discovered last fall...Claims on gold run have been sold as high as $14,000 for 120 feet. The miners make laws to define the limits of claims, in some localities 30 feet are allowed to each man, in other 60 ft. He places some tools on the claim and these tools will hold the claim for ten days, if at the expiration of that time he does not come to work on it, some other person may go to work on it and he drives him off of it. A man is not allowed more than one claim at a time, should he have two, any person that chooses may go on to the one that he is not at work on and hold it. This is what is called jumping a claim. When I came up here most of the claims were taken up, but I secceeded in getting one on Big Deer Creek.... We then prospected it and found it would not pay to work it, so after losing nearly a thousand dollars each in time and money, we were obliged to abandon it. I now intend to leave this place for Feather River, 100 miles from here and 400 miles north from San Francisco...

Nevada, Sept 21st, 1850
Dear Father, ... I have received no letters or heard from home since January last. I hope you will write soon. I want to hear from home, and to hear that you are well, and Samuel and Susan Ann, and Aunt Mary, and Grandfather and Grandmother, to hear how you get along farming, how business is, in fact all the news you can get....

Nevada, Nov. 29, 1850
Dear Father, ... I see by the papers, for I occasionally get one, that California is admitted into the Union. I don't see why Congress delayed it so long... I suppose yesterday was Thanksgiving Day in the old Bay State, and while you were feasting on roast Turkeys and plum puddings, I had bread, meat and coffee which I cooked myself. Such is life in California. A man must do his cooking, washing and mending... You need not worry for me. I am with a young man from Ill. We have a very good log cabin and I think we shall pass a pleasant winter....

Nevada, Jan 19th, 1851
Dear Brother, ...California is not half the country to make money in it was one year ago, the mines are not as good, business of all kinds is very dull and wages are low, the country is full of people, a great many of them are not making more than their board and clothes, about one in a thousand are getting rich...

Canyon Creek, New Georgetown, Oct. 12th, 1851
Dear Father, ... I have spent nearly all the season in running about in search of diggens. I left Nevada City in May for the Feather River, but found the diggens to be very limited...I left for the southern mines...the American River, and after prospecting for two or three days I pushed on to the Consunnes, I had no better luck there. I then tried the Mequeleme and Calevarns with no better success. Then I came up here, bought into a claim with some Missourians, and I have been doing a little something ever since. ... the chances of making a fortune in the mines is every day growing smaller.

French Corral, April 14, 1852
Dear Father, ... I have been mining here (French Corral) some three months and have done very well. My diggens are now nearly worked out. I hope to stay this summer, it is not very profitable to be running about in this country as I have found by my own experience.

French Corral, Sept. 5th, 1852
Dear Father, ... I received a copy of the Boston Journal of July 5th, containing the death of my sister, can this be true! O my God I cannot realize it..I cannot believe it...surely you would have written...I cannot think that her I loved so fondly is no more. O write to me that she is well and ease my painful mind...

French Corral, Cal., Feb 14, 1853
Dear Father, ... I am still at work here and doing something towards getting home. I have very good health and I think that the climate agrees with me. This is a fine country for cattle and stock of all kinds. For a man to settle here with his family and go to farming I think there can be no better country in with world, the soil is rich and very productive...

San Francisco, Cal., Jan 26, 1854
Dear Brother... Business is very dull here now, and has been since I have been here. There have been some failures and more are looked for.

(Continued on page 222)

"GONE WEST" – MASSACHUSETTS MEN IN CALIFORNIA, 1856

By Effingham P. Humphrey, Jr., F.U.G.A.

A phrase that occurs occasionally in genealogies during the pre-Civil War period is, "Left home when a young man and was never heard from again." These men often went to sea, to the "big city," and, especially in the 1849-60 period, to California as part of the Gold Rush.

Some of this latter group can be identified in the Index to the 1850 Census of the State of California, by Alan P. Bowman (Baltimore, 1972). This census (the count was taken in 1850 and into the Spring of 1851) gave not only the name of the individual but also his age and state of origin.

Equally helpful, though for a limited area, is the later Miners & Business Men's Directory. For the Year Commencing January 1st, 1856. Embracing a General Directory of the Citizens of Tuolumne, and portions of Calaveras, Stanislaus and San Joaquin Counties. Together with the Mining Laws of Each District, a Description of the Different Camps, and Other Interesting Statistical matter, by Heckendorn & Wilson (Columbia: Printed at the Clipper Office, Fulton St., Near Main. 1856.).

This small pamphlet, in the Rare Book Room of the New York Public library, consists of 104 pages, plus paper covers, four pages of advertising, a title page, and a view of Columbia - one of the richest and most important settlements in the Mother Lode. The brief preface disclaims completeness and accuracy because of the lack of cooperation in certain mining camps, and states "we have not given over one-eight (sic) part of the population."

Nonetheless, several thousand names, with occupations and states of origin, are included, listed by town, mining camp, or district. The names of the men from Massachusetts (either born there or previous residents) are presented as shown in the pamphlet, under their respective location.

Tuolumne County, one of the original 27 counties of California, was organized on 18 February 1850, and the County Seat in 1856 was Sonora. it lies at the southern end of the gold mining area, and the three other counties mentioned are neighboring areas to the west and north.

Grateful acknowledgement for valuable assistance is made to Carlo M. De Ferrari, Tuolumne County Historian, Sonora.

* *

All spellings and punctuations are as in the original.

If any readers have any questions about names, Mr. Humphrey will be glad to answer them provided a SASE is provided.

* *

Mr. Effingham P. Humphrey, Jr., F.U.G.A.
228 Booth Lane, Haverford, PA 19041

COLUMBIA DISTRICT

Abbott, J.M., Paper Hanger
Bailey, E., Miner
Baldwin, D.S., Flour Dealer
Bartlett, F., Livery Stable
Battel, A.J., Miner
Bennett, G., Miner
Blass, F.E., Miner
Blood, C., Butcher
Bonney, O., Carpenter (Clerk, Ohio)
Bridges, F.M., Miner
Briggs, E.A., Miner
Briggs, S.A., Miner
Brown, J., Mienr
Burt, J.P., Miner
Burbank, E.L., Miner
Carew, S., Miner
Cavis, J.M., Attorney
Church, L., Miner
Church, E.S., Miner
Colby, F., Miner
Daley, F., Miner
Daley, T., Miner
Dampatcher, J., Miner
Donnell & Parson, Merchants
Duchow, J.C., Editor
Duchow, W., Printer
Dun, T., Miner
Ellis, F., Miner
Fish, H.L. Carpenter
Fisher, H., Miner
Fitzgerald (n.i.), Miner
Flanders, C.A., Miner
Fletcher, J.L., Miner
Fuller, L., Carpernter
Gale, C.A., Miner
Gallijan, T., Miner
Gibbs, C., Physician
Glover, B.S., Steward
Goding, E., Miner
Harrington, J., Miner
Haley, T., Miner
Hathaway, E., Miner
Haworth, H., MIner
Harlow, J., Miner
Hoag, J., Miner
Kelly, O., Miner
McDoneld, H.H., Gentleman
McDoneld, B., Ranchero
Mitchell, J.E., Miner
Mitchell, J., Miner
Millard, G., Miner
Miller, W. A., Miner
Northy, ----, Hotel Keeper

Nye, S.F., Carpenter
Osgood, H., Miner
Parsons, C.A., Merchant
Parker, B. D., Miner
Pickens, A., Miner
Pratt, F. B., Carpenter
Preble, C.E., Miner
Railey, T., Miner
Richards, S.S., Miner
Richmond, J., Miner
Roman, T., Miner
Ross, A.H., Miner
Sampson, B.C., Carpenter
Sargent, C.H., Miner
Sheppard, J.H., Miner
Skinner, E.S., Miner
Smith, D.F., Miner
Sprague, A., Miner
Staples, E.H., Watch-maker
Steinfelter, (n.i.), Miner
Taylor, C., Miner
Tuck, J.W., Miner
Tucker, S.P., Miner
Underwood, W.R., Miner
Weed, A., Miner
White, H.K., Saloon
Wilcomb, D., Butcher
Woodbury, G.W., Teamster

SONORA

Bruce, Chs., Baker
Bruce, W., Baker
Harrington, C.F., Painer
Lull, E., Clerk
Moulton, B.F., Hydraulic Ditch
Morehouse, W.P., Agt. Wells Fargo & Co.
Murphey, S., Hydraulic Ditch
McCarthy, D.O., Livery Stable
Nye, A., Lumberman
Nye, A.R., Lumberman
Pitts, A., Jeweler
Raymond, R.S., Clerk
Rutherford, C., Paint Store
Rutherford, F., Paint Store
Thomas, L., Merchant
Thomas, J., Carpenter
Thompson, (n.i.), Carpenter
Walker, J.B., Wagon Maker

JAMESTOWN

Ammidon, M., Miner
Bradford, Wm., Carpenter
Brown, J.D., Clerk

Bush, C., Miner
Chase, R.C., Miner
Clark, W.J., Miner
Coburn, G.D., Miner
Coburn, A.W., Miner
Dagle, J., Livery Stable
Gookin, G.D., Baker
Gray, H.C., Miner
Hallock, R.L., Miner
Hesney, R., Miner
Hogan, P., Miner
Holmes, E.R., Miner
Kelley, M., Miner
Keith, H., Miner
Lamb, A., Miner
Latimer, J.B., Millright (sic)
Long, W.H., Miner
McCool, J., Miner
Poor, G.P., Gold Spring Cottage
Poor, H.G., Miner
Randall, J.H., Miner
Roberts, J.W., Butcher
Ward, M., Miner
White, C., Tinsmith

SHAW'S FLAT

Bayley, C.W., Merchant
Collingwood, G., Miner
Covington, L., Miner
Cushing, A., Miner
Cushman, G.H., Miner
Finney, P., Miner
Getchell, E., Miner
Haskins, G.H., Miner
Holbrook, F.W., Miner
Holmes, S.R., Miner
Howland, L.L., Miner
Lynde, N., Miner
Mann, H.S., Miner
Merritt, M.B., Miner
Orcutt, S.S., Miner
Pachard, N., <Miner
Pierce, M., Miner
Rainer, J., Miner
Recard, I.W., Miner
Renfield, L., Miner
Rosefelt, M., Miner
Sampson, J.A., Miner
Shaw, J., Miner
Snyder, J., Miner
Stetson, J.B., Constable
Stetson, C., Miner
Wellington, E., Merchant
White, S., Miner

Whitman, F.B., Miner

SPRINGFIELD

Andrews, C., Miner
Benwar, C., Miner
Bride, R., Miner
Brown, H., Miner
Brown, W.H., Miner
Colson, W.P., Carpenter
Cowan, J.H., Miner
Dunn, P., Miner
Ervin, W., Miner
Fennessey, E., Miner
Feny, H., Miner
Fuller, M.J., Miner
Gardiner, C., Miner
Gifford, J.R., Miner
Glover, A.B., Hotel Keeper
Hamblin, T., Miner
Higgins, ----, Miner
Hodges, G.Z., Hotel Keeper
Holbrook, H., Gentleman
Holbrook, M.D., Miner
Holbrook, ----, Miner
Homer, J., Miner
Honey, Calvin, Carpenter
Hosmer, Josiah, Miner
Kattan, G.W., Miner
Knight, A.Y., Miner
Mann, G.H., Miner
Mathison, F., Miner
Morehouse, G.W., Miner
Orcutt, L.S., Miner
Parker, J.H., Dairyman
Patter, T., Miner
Peleggiflora, ----, Miner
Phillips, F.W., Miner
Phillips, F.M., Miner
Rimmee, G., Miner
Sanburn, T.D., Butcher
Sargent, C.H., Miner
Sherbourne, A.S., Miner
Smith, J., Miner
Stott, J., Hotel Keeper
Thayer, E.L., Miner
Walker, W.H., Miner
Whiting, L.C. Miner
Whitcomb, H., Miner

GOLD SPRINGS

Brunson, J., Miner
Curtain, J., Miner
Esterbrook, J.E., Miner

Healey, J.C., Miner
Keith, J.W., Miner
Kelly, J., MIner
Kelly, P., Miner
Kight & Brother, Miner (sic)
Munroe, H.S., Dairyman
Rice, ----, Miner
Wright, C.S., Miner

YANKEE HILL

Cox, J., Miner
Daessy, M., Miner
Dresser, B., Miner
Johnson, E.C., Miner
Jones, J.W., Miner
Johns, T.W., Miner
Kidder, J.T., Miner
Lewis, C., Miner
Massey, S., Miner
Pope, R.P.S., Miner
Rogers, C., Miner
Smith, T.R., Dairyman
Stevens, C.B., Miner

SAW MILL FLAT

Culling, C.C., Miner
Dow, Wm., Miner
Edwards, Dan'l, Miner
Frazier, John, Miner
Henry, Joseph, Miner
Folbrook, Fred, Miner
Houghton, S.B., Dairyman
Whiting, Geo. A., Miner

BROWN'S FLAT

Bowen, John, Miner
Burt, W.A., Miner
Cassady, James, Miner
Collins, George, Miner
Elms, J.O., Miner
Erving, Wm., Miner
Henry, Thomas, Miner
Henesy, D., Miner
Lambird, P.M., Miner
Lounger, John B., Miner
Prasasa, F.A., Miner
Quintan, ----, miner
Ripner, E.A., Miner
Sellea, B.G., Miner
Snail, C.W., Miner
Taber, F., Miner
Windgarterner, G., Miner

MONTEZUMA

Anderson, C.F., Miner
Baldwin, John, Miner
Cushman, C.C., Miner
Danvis, Robt., Miner (name smudged)
Doyle, P.H., Miner
Forden, M., Miner
Forden, P., Miner
Heirman, P., Miner
Hickey, Pat, Miner
Horgan, J., Miner
Kenney, ---- , Miner
Kerigan, M., Miner
Klutts, J.C., Miner
Maynard, J., Miner
Murphey, John, Miner
Power, Pat, Miner
Reynolds, C., Miner
Waterman, C., Miner
Whitford, Wm., Miner
Whipper, J.P., Miner

CHINESE CAMP

Baxter, R., Miner
Brimhall, (n.i.), Carpenter
Castleberg, (n.i.), Miner
Cutting, C., Miner
Cutting, D., Miner
Daley, J., Miner
Le Shure, W.C., Miner
Morris, D., School Teacher
Sleepmann, H., Miner
Tuckwell, G., Carriage Maker

JACKSONVILLE

Barnes, R., Miner
Chields, G., Miner
Church, H., Miner
Gafley, T., Miner
Garner, P.G., Miner
Hallahan, T.H., Miner
Keene, Alonzo, Miner
Kingsley, S.B., Hotel Keeper
Thomas, E.S., Carpenter
Tucker, T.J., Miner

POVERTY HILL

Aderaft, Wm.H., Miner
Andrews, J.E., Miner
Green, Wm., Miner
Harriman, ----, Miner

Hussey, J.W., Miner
Johnson, N., Miner
Leonard, H.N., Miner
Morison, W.A., Miner
Moore, P.C., Miner
McDonough, T., Miner
Peterson, H., Miner
Phipps, John, Miner
Richard, Charles, Miner
Souther, A.F., Miner
Tilly, H., Miner
Todd, G.L., Miner
Tredick, W.A., Miner

BELVIDERE FLAT

Hughes, J., Miner
Richardson, (n.i.), Miner
Crosby, E.M., Miner
Griner, ----, Miner
Howard, J.A., Miner

ALGERINE

Bryner, John, Miner

WOOD'S CROSSING

Quimby, A., Miner

CAMP SECO

Gleason, Geo., Ditchman
Midbury, P., Teamster
Whitehouse, W., Miner

CURTISVILLE

Fuller, J.A., Miner
Fuller, W.H., Miner
Fuller, Jas., Jr., Miner
Goodnow, S., Miner
Kern, T., Miner

STEVEN'S BAR

Dalton, H.N., Miner

OHIO DISTRICT

Bohan, P., Miner
Clark, P., Miner
Mulvany, E., Miner
McDonald, J., Miner
McMahon, ----, Miner

McGerr, M., Miner
McElheny, R.D., Hotel Keeper
Nugent, N., Miner
Rourke, M., Miner
Wellington, J.K., Miner

BIG OAK FLAT & GAROTE DIRECTORY

Chafee, F.A., Miner
Chamberlain, J.P., Miner
Colman, Thos., Miner
Fisher, J.G., Miner
Godfrey, J.F., Miner
Heron, John, Miner
Holland, Andrew, Miner
Hollis, A.J., Miner
Hussey, Andrew, Miner
Kinnel, John, Miner
Lincoln, B., Miner
Oneil, Andrew, Miner
Perrin, Otis, Jr., Hotel Keeper
Shears, S., Miner
Sprague, J., Carpenter
Ward, G.H., Miner

Crocker, A.S., Miner
Watson, G.W., Boot Maker

LA GRANGE

Calhoun, Samuel, Miner
Calhoun, R., Miner
Calhoun, Wm.B., Miner
Carter, J.M., Restaurant
Clapp, Gosham, Merchant
Esaw, Peter, miner
Henfield, John, Miner
Holmes, W.C., Carpenter
King, G.W., Physician
Moody, Chas., Miner
McDonald, George, Miner
Richardson, J.A., Expressman
Russell, Edward, Miner
Russell, Geo., Miner
White, A.G., Physician
White, A.C., Carpenter

MURPHEY'S CAMP

Bond, E. Miner
Carpenter, G.A., Miner
Crispin, Wm., Grocer
Dowling, James, Miner

Faxon, F., Merchant
Faxon, J., Merchant
Genter, J.H., Miner
McCalgin, M., Miner
Parker, G.W.H., Miner

DOUGLASS' FLAT

Hunt, C.A., Miner

CARSON'S

Land, J., Miner

FRENCH CREEK

Blackburn, J., Miner

SANDOMINGO CREEK

Foster, G., Miner

KNIGHT'S FERRY

Fisher, Z., Stage Proprietor
Johnson, Joseph C., Miner
Peck, W.H., Miner
Perry, Curtis E., Miner
Ward, Patrick, Miner

COLUMBIA

Beauvais, A.B., Miner
Davis, R.E., Painter
Hildebrand, M., United States
   Bakery
Stone, M.W., Miner

SONORA

Mills, Albert, Miner
Orcutt, J.G., Miner
Salter, F., Furniture
   Ware-rooms
Shaw, John, Druggist
Scott, John, Baker
Townsend, D., Printer

TABLE MOUNTAIN

Keith W., Miner
Nourse, J.E., Miner

SALVADA

Holtze, C., Miner
Spinney, Jacob, Miner

KELLER'S FERRY

Johnson, Daniel, Miner
Jordan, A.K., Painter

BUENA VISTA

Field, N.M., Miner
Field, E.A., Miner

(Miscellaneous list at end)

Colson, M.A., Jackson, Miner
Gates, A.H., Humbug Hill, Miner
Grant, W.H., Empire Diggins, Miner
Hunt, E.B., Oak Shade, Miner
Harris, J., Ohio Diggins, Miner
McNaughton, J., Reynold's Ferry, Lumberman
Lindsay, Thos., Abbey's Ferry, Miner
Loring, J.M., Abbey's Ferry, Ferryman
Packard, H.A., Roach's Camp, Miner
Sanborne, J.C., Empire Diggings, miner
Steele, J.S., Empire Diggings, Miner
Vickery, J., Reynold's Ferry, Butcher
Young, N.S., Humbug Hill, Miner

###############################

Note: A ditchman was employed to walk the lines of the hydraulic ditches serving the mines, chec them for breakage and water stealing, and collect the fees for the water which was sold at so much a "miner's inch" - the price usually being whatever the market would bear.

CENSUS INDEXING - NOT ALL FUN AND GAMES

By Mary Elizabeth Koen

"How did I get into this?" That is a question one might not find too difficult to answer. The real problem is when you begin asking yourself, "How do I get out of it?"

If you have spent long hours searching through microfilm records of Census data, you know the joy of suddenly finding a familiar name and information on a family member. The tired eyes, "crick" in the neck and tedium are also all too familiar. So often we know exactly the names we expect fo find in Census records. Fine, they are either there or they are not. But when you have exhausted yourself and have "finished" only to discover there is another family name you did not know at the time, you may be faced with the horrible prospect of painstakingly searching through the same records a second, or even a third time. After a few such experiences, I felt impelled to do something about some Census records with which I was working.

Several years ago, complete frustration at not being able to find what I wanted in an unindexed book of historical and genealogical significance started me on my course of becoming an "indexer." The first project, completed in October 1984, resulted in my Index to Guysborough Sketches and Other Essays of A. C. Jost, a two part "Name" and "General" Index of 137 pages. It took some time to finish the job, spread over a three-year period, being done in the old-fashioned way with 12,000 3 X 5 cards, instead of the splendor of a computer. It is something of a monument to endurance. Like the definition of a lexicographer, the indexer also deserves recognition as a "harmless drudge."

That is how I got involved in my second and third efforts at indexing. While I had survived the endurance contest, now something new was added. Working as I had from printed material in a book, little did I realize the more difficult task ahead of me just to be able to "read." The "Index for the Census of Nova Scotia 1860-1861" I chose to do was "Heads of Households, Consolidated Listing for Guysborough County." It was not my first inspection of the microfilm records for that Census, when I started the task of doing "the whole thing" for Guysborough County. I merely used a different source and a new location when, instead of the Mormon records, I requested the Lynnfield Library to obtain an Inter-Library Loan from the Public Archives of Canada, at Ottawa, Ontario. That resulted in practically living in the Genealogy Room at the Library from the 14th until the 26th of November 1983. During that period, I managed to copy the data from the 56 abstracts covering the 11 Polling Districts for Guysborough County, plus some other more extensive age/sex distributions for selected family names. Since the microfilm had to be returned I had no second chance to review it, and decisions had to be made immediately. Following the sessions at Lynnfield Library, there was the work required to transfer the data to 3 X 5 cards for alphabetizing and typing in book form. This was done in leisurely fashion over the following year.

"Once bitten twice shy" is an old adage that still serves well. By now I had become interested in the 1858 Census of Nova Scotia. I also had learned that there was a microfilm printer at the Salem Public Library. Again the Inter-Library Loan System served me well. I reviewed the microfilms from the Public Archives of Canada, selected the portions covering Guysborough County, Nova Scotia, and made photocopies of the pertinent sections. My troubles were not over at this point, however. Despite using intense light and high magnification, some names were still extremely difficult to decipher. Old-fashioned handwriting was problem enough, but, coupled with faded ink and partially photographed or obliterated sections, the schedules for some districts became a real horror to transcribe. Fortunately, the first areas I worked on were well-written and reasonably legible. Had I not completed a goodly portion I might have been less reluctant to "give up." And that is when I decided the only solution was to pay a visit to the Public Archives of Nova Scotia to see if the problems could be solved.

In July I finished the 1860 Census just in time to take a copy of it to present to the Public Archives at Halifax. That was my introduction to the Acting Archivist Allan C. Dunlop, who immediately made available to me the original Census documents. After three days of comparing data from the Census with my own records, I was satisfied that the verification was as good as it was possible for me to make. In a few extreme cases I consulted with the Archivist in residence, Philip L. Hartling, whose knowledge of local names and expertise in reading old manuscripts helped solve problems of identification.

Since I got back from Nova Scotia in August, I have completed the manuscript for "1838 Census of Nova Scotia, Consolidated Index of Heads of Guysborough County Families." The name and occupation of the "Head of Family" is given, as well as family composition statistics, by sex in three age groupings: Under 6; Under 14; Over 14; and in Total.

It is easy to understand how I got involved in Census Indexing. Now, as to getting out of it, that is not so easy. It is insidious the way a few words from a fellow genealogist will encourage further efforts. Making new friends with common interests, finding a relative or two among the purchasers or just a kind word of "thanks" for making life easier has its effect. Requests to purchase unfinished books, no questions asked, is the "tops."

Should I do the 1817 or the 1870 Census of Nova Scotia next?

IMPORTANT NOTICE

Starting in 1986, Send Queries to:

Query Editor
ESOG

C/O Lynnfield Public Library
18 Summer Street
Lynnfield, MA 01940

The Ahnentafel

I	1	Jerry Hersey Lovejoy	1952-	Milford, MA
II	2	Jerry Hersey Lovejoy, Sr.	1927-	Gardner, MA
	3	Constance Lea Bolduc	1930-	Cambridge, MA
III	4	Harry Cleveland Lovejoy	1888-1946	Claremont, NH; Milford, MA
	5	Harriet Adeline Hersey	1902-1964	Meriden, NH; Bellingham, MA
	6	Arthur Joseph Bolduc, Sr.	1908-1948	Cambridge, MA
	7	Mabel Constnace Rogan	1905-1970	Cambridge, Milford, MA
IV	8	Edgar Eugene Lovejoy	1861-1934	Claremont, NH
	9	Cora Minnie Hastings	1864-1947	Charleston, Claremont, NH
	10	Charles Sumner Hersey, Sr.	1867-1957	Meriden, Hillsboro, NH
	11	Carrie Belle Fadden	1871-1953	Manchester, Hillsboro, NH
	12	Raoul Bolduc	1862-1938	Quebec, CAN; Cambridge, MA
	13	Lea Cantin	1875-1918	St. Pierre, CAN; Brighton, MA
	14	Thomas F. Rogan	1871-1942	Ennis Crone, IRE; Cambridge, MA
	15	Winifred Lydon	1875-1955	Spiddal, Galway, IRE; Cambridge, MA
V	16	John Eugene Lovejoy	1819-1898	Unity, Claremont, NH
	17	Ellen Maria Deane	1842-1914	Walpole, Claremont, NH
	18	John (M.?) Hastings	ca 1840	Charleston, NH
	20	Stephen Hersey, Jr.	1822-1900	Grafton, Lebanon, NH
	21	Caroline M. Thompson	1828-1893	Plympton, MA; Plainfield, NH
	22	James Fadden	1831-1917	Canton, MA; Meriden, NH
	23	Mehitable Dean	1844-1914	Hartland, VT; Meriden, NH
	24	Marcel Bolduc	ca 1830-	St. Joachim, CAN
	25	Marie Tremblay	ca 1830-	Baie St. Paul, Quebec, CAN
	26	Joseph Cantin	ca 1850-	St. Pierre, Ile d'Orleans, CAN
	27	Elizabeth Adeline Leclerc	ca 1850-	St. Pierre, Ile d'Orleans, CAN
	28	Robert Rogan	ca 1850-	Ennis Crone, Co. Sligo, IRE
	29	Anne McDermott	ca 1850-	Ennis Crone, Co. Sligo, IRE
	30	John Lydon	ca 1850-	Spiddal, Co. Galway, IRE
	31	Mary Curran	ca 1850-	Spiddal, Co. Galway, IRE
VI	32	Nathan Lovejoy	1784-1841	Andover, MA; Claremont, NH
	33	Abigail Tarr	1790-1852	Danvers, MA; Claremont, NH
	34	Horace R. Deane	1811-	VT; Claremont, NH
	35	Carrie Scribner	1811-	NH; Claremont, NH
	40	Stephen Hersey, Sr.	1783-1870	Newbury, Grantham, NH
	41	Betsey Bowley	1790-1858	? - Grantham, NH
	42	Jacob Thompson	1782-1856	Halifax, Plympton, MA
	43	Esther Shaw	1790-1832	Middleboro, Plympton, MA
	44	Nathaniel Fadden	1806-	Canton, MA
	45	Lovina Wood	ca 1810-	
	46	David Dean	1814-1897	Stanbridge, Quebec; Plainfield, NH
	47	Caroline Beers	1824-1887	Hartland, VT; Plainfield, NH
	48	Antoine Bolduc	ca 1800-	Baie St. Paul, Quebec, CAN
	49	Lucille Cote	ca 1800-	Baie St. Paul, Quebec, CAN
	50	Francois Tremblay	ca 1800-	Baie St. Paul, Quebec, CAN
	51	Felicite Gagnon	ca 1800-	Baie St. Paul, Quebec, CAN
	52	Augustin Cantin	ca 1820-	St. Pierre, Ile d'Orleans, CAN

53	Domithilde Beaudoin	1821-	Repetigny, L'Assumption, CAN
54	Pierre Leclerc	ca 1815-	St. Pierre, Ile d'Orleans, CAN
55	Genevieve Gourdeau	ca 1820-	St. Pierre, Ile d'Orleans, CAN

\#

Ahnentafel of Dorothy Wentzel (Whitford), P.O. Box 282, Rutland, VT 05701

I	1	Dorothy Louize Wentzel	1925-	Melrose, MA
II	2	Raymond Earle Wentzel	1902-1980	Melrose, MA; Rutland, VT
	3	Edna Rosamond Woods	1901-	Malden, MA
III	4	Ethelbert Ellison Wentzell	1879-1944	Hopewell Cape, N.B.; Wakefield, MA
	5	Louisa Clark Keith	1875-1943	Boston, Melrose, MA
	6	Edward Melven Woods	1874-1946	Yarmouth Co., N.S.; Medford, MA
	7	Lillian Estelle Milberry	1874-1903	Advocate Harbor, N.S.; Malden, MA
IV	8	George Gilbert Wentzell	1859-1935	Milton, N.S.; Melrose, MA
	9	Orinda Christopher	1856-1902	Hopewell Cape, N.B.; Melrose, MA
	10	George Chester Keith	1845-	Boston, MA
	11	Emma Clark Wales	1836-1897	Newton Lower Falls, Boston, MA
	12	Robert Wentworth Woods	1847-1903	Kemptville, N.S.; Malden, MA
	13	Ann (Anngeline) Hamilton	1849-1906	Forest Glen, N.S.; Malden, MA
	15	Rosamond D. Morris	1841-1898	Advocate Harbor, Advocate, N.S.
	14	William Henry Milberry	1809-	
V	16	James Frederick Wentzell	1832-1896	Charleston, Milton, N.S.
	17	Lucy Ann Oickle	1835-1910	Lunenburg Co., Milton, N.S.
	18	Joseiah Christopher	1826-1903?	Alma, Hopewell Cape, N.B.
	19	Margaret Alexander	1831-	Scotland, Apple River, N.S.
	20	Martin Keith	1819-1861	Casheen, IRE; So. Boston, MA
	21	Mary Elizabeth Elliott	1826-1904	So. Thomaston, ME; Holliston, MA
	22	Nathaniel Wales, Jr.	1802-1873	Newton Lower Falls, Saugus, MA
	23	Catherine Clark	1814-1891	Needham, Saugus, MA
	24	John Woods	1804-1878	New Plymouth, Kemptville, N.S.
	25	Elizabeth Morton	1807-1873	New Plymouth, Kemptville, N.S.
	26	Daniel Hamilton	1823-1903	Yarmouth Co., Forest Glen, N.S.
	27	Anna Kavanagh	1819-1911	Canaan, Forest Glen, N.S.
	30	John K. Morris	1816-	Advocate Harbor, Advocate, N.S.
	31	Barbara Mills	1817-	Advocate Harbor, Advocate, N.S.
VI	32	Conrad Wentzel	1788-1817	Sentry, Lunenburg Co., N.S.
	33	Anna Mary Glatienberg		Lunenburg Co., Queens Co., N.S.
	34	Johann George Eichel		
	35	Elizabeth Weagle		
	36	Collins Jackson		
		Christopher	1798-	Portsmouth, NH; Alma, Harvey, N.B.
	37	Orinda Stevens	ca 1799-	Alma, Harvey, Hopewell Cape, N.B.
	40	John Keefe		Ireland; Rochester, NY
	41	Bridget ------		
	42	Ambrose Elliott	ca 1778-1807	England; So. Thomaston, ME
	43	Sarah Choate		
	44	Nathaniel Wales	1778-1864	Watertown, Newton Lower Falls, MA
	45	Sally Mills	1776-1802	Needham, Newton Lower Falls, MA
	46	Lewis Clark	1785-1829	Needham, MA
	47	Hannah Kingsbury	1788-1865	Needham, MA
	48	John Woods		; Yarmouth Co., N.S.
	49	Mary (Rapp) Kenton, Sims		; Yarmouth Co., N.S.
	50	Archibald Morton		; Yarmouth Co., N.S.

```
     51   Mary Hendestead                                      ; Yarmouth Co., N.S.
     52   David Hamilton            ca 1793-1846  Argyle, Tusket, N.S.
     53   Mary Gavel                                 Tusket, N.S.
     54   Simon Kavanagh               1790-1870  Ireland; Gavelton, Yarmouth, N.S.
    _55   Sarah Hurlburt                                 Yarmouth, N.S.
     60   Randall (Randolph) Morris  1790-1875  Parrsboro, Advocate Harbor, N.S.
     61   Lois Knowlton                1789-1871  Halfway River, Advocate, N.S.
```

##

Ahnentafel of William Henry Waite, 1 Hedgerow Place, Wilmington, DE 19807

```
I    1   William Henry Waite        1909-         Boston, Wakefld, MA; NY; OH; PA; DE
II   2   Marcus Warren Waite        1882-1968  Calais, Woodbury, VT; Boston,
                                                          Wakefield, MA
     3   Lillian Violet Kemp        1891-         Boston, Wakefield, MA
III  4   William Henry Waite        1854-1915  Calais, Woodbury, VT
     5   Florence Rich Leonard      1856-1944  Calais, Woodbury, VT; Wakefield, MA
     6   William Henry Kemp         1867-1902  Nahant, Boston, MA
     7   Cora Olive Stone           1859-1949  Kennebunkport, ME; Boston,
                                                          Wakefield, MA
IV   8   Marcus Swain Wait          1827-1911  Windsor, Stowe, Montpelier,
                                                          Calais, VT
     9   Mary Ann Parker            1824-1913  Groton, Montpelier, Calais, VT
    10   Joseph Warren Leonard      1828-1905  Calais, VT
    11   Dolly Ann Rich             1830-1900  Calais, VT
    12   William Henry Kemp         1838-1919  Harpswell, ME; Nahant, MA
    13   Cornelia Ann Johnson       1840-1916  Harpswell, ME; Nahant, MA
    14   John Littlefield Stone     1829-1901  Kennebunkport, ME
    15   Lavinia Marie King         1836-1920  Yarmouth, M.S.; Kennebunkport,
                                                          Berwick, ME
V   16   Richard Waite #            1784-1854  Windsor, Stowe, VT
         (Cook Mayflower line)
    17   Elizabeth Bishop           1786-1858  Windsor, Stowe, VT
    18   Nathan Parker              1791-1862  Lyman, NH; Groton, Calais, VT
    19   Eliza Chamberlain          1796-1882  Newbury, VT; Lyman, NH; Groton,
                                                          Calais, VT
    20   Gilbert Leonard            1794-1842  Taunton, MA; Calais, VT
    21   Elfrida Wheelock           1800-1880  Calais, VT
    22   Samuel Rich                1797-1856  North Montpelier, Calais, VT
    23   Dolly Davis                1800-1841  East Montpelier, Calais, VT
    24   John Kemp                  1797-1859  Harpswell, ME
    25   Almira Sinnett             1804-1892  Harpswell, ME
    26   Joseph Johnson             1788-1866  Harpswell, ME
    27   Susan Foster                  -1881  Thomaston, Harpswell, ME
    28   John Stone                 1789-1858  Arundel, Kennebunkport, ME
   _29   Olive Littlefield          1798-1854  Arundel, Kennebunkport, ME
VI 32   Richard Wait               1745-1823  Sudbury, Brookfield, MA; Windsor, VT
    33   Susanna Allen *            1750-1798  Bridgewater, Brookfield, MA;
                                                          Windsor, VT
    34   Levi Bishop                1759-1837  Union, CT; Windsor, VT
    35   Elizabeth Grandy           1760-1799  Reading, Windsor, VT
    36   Isaac Parker               1763-1851  Lyman, NH
    37   Esther Fisk                            Lyman, NH
    38   Rodolphus Chamberlain                 Newbury, Ryegate, VT; Bath, NH;
```

39	Betsey Grant	-1798	Newbury, VT
40	Gilbert Leonard	-1801	Taunton, MA
41	Polly Gerry	1772-1861	Taunton, MA; Calais, VT; Taunton, MA
42	Abijah Wheelock	1764-1846	Charlton, MA; Calais, VT
43	Lois Nichols	1764-1847	Oxford, Charlton, MA; Calais, VT
44	Samuel Rich	1769-1826	Sutton, MA; North Montpelier, VT
45	Margaret McCloud	-1850	Londonderry, NH; No. Montpelier, VT
46	Nathaniel Davis	1769-1843	Dudley, MA; East Montpelier, VT
47	Dolly Davis	1773-1809	Oxford, MA; East Montpelier, VT
48	Timothy Kemp	1770-1822	Harpswell, ME
49	Hannah Snow	1772-1861	Harpswell, ME
	(Hopkins Mayflower line)		
50	Stephen Sinnett	1765-1844	Harpswell, ME
51	Hannah Bailey Merryman	1769-1843	Harpswell, ME
52	David Johnson	1755-1839	Harpswell, ME
53	Jane Roduck	1761-1832	Harpswell, ME
54	Eben Foster		Thomaston, ME
55	Susannah Kennedy		Thomaston, ME
56	Dudley Stone	1755-1827	Arundel, Kennebunkport, ME
57	Hannah Perkins		Arundel, Kennebunkport, ME
58	Benjamin Littlefield	1758-1835	Arundel, Kennebunkport, ME
59	Hannah Proctor	1769-1866	Arundel, Kennebunkport, ME

##

Ahnentafel of John Stone, g.g.grandfather of William H. Waite

I	1	John Stone	1789-1858	Arundel, Kennebunkport, ME
II	2	Dudley Stone	1755-1827	Arundel, Kennebunkport, ME
	3	Hannah Perkins		Arundel, Kennebunkport, ME
III	4	Jonathan Stone	1730-1799	Beverly, MA; Arundel, ME
	5	Hannah Griffin	-1759	Beverly, MA; Arundel, ME; Beverly, MA
	6	Eliphalet Perkins	-1776	Arundel, Portland, ME
	7	Mary Perkins	1728-1802	Arundel, ME
IV	8	Jonathan Stone	bpt 1702-1750	Beverly, MA; Arundel, ME
	9	Hannah Lovet	bpt 1695-	Beverly, MA; Arundel, ME
	12	Thomas Perkins	1700-1752	Greenland, NH; Arundel, ME
	13	Lydia Harding		Arundel, ME
	14	Thomas Perkins	1681-1761	Topsfield, MA; Arundel, ME
	15	Mary Wildes	bpt 1692-1742	Topsfield, MA; Arundel, ME
V	16	Nehemiah Stone	bpt 1670-1732	Beverly, MA
	17	Lydia Hart	1672-1733	Salem, Beverly, MA
	18	Simon Lovet	bpt 1668-	Beverly, MA
	19	Annis Swetland		Beverly, MA
	24	Thomas Perkins	-1741	Greenland, NH; Arundel, ME
	26	Stephen Harding	-1747	Wells, Arundel, ME
	27	Abigail Littlefield	ca 1680-1747	Wells, Arundel, ME
	28	Elisha Perkins	ca 1654-1741	Topsfield, MA
	29	Catherine Towne	1662-1714	Salem, Topsfield, MA
	30	Ephraim Wildes	1665-1725	Topsfield, MA
	31	Mary Howlett	1672-1758	Topsfield, MA
VI	32	John Stone	ca 1622-1691	England; Salem, Beverly, MA
	33	Abigail Dixey	bpt 1636-1703	Salem, Beverly, MA

34	Jonathan Hart	bef 1721	Marblehead, Salem, MA
35	Lydia Neale	bpt 1650-1681	Salem, MA
_36	John Lovet		Beverly, MA
_48	Thomas Perkins		Scarborough, ME; Greenland, NH
52	Israel Harding		Providence, RI; Wells, ME
53	Lydia Gooch		Wells, ME
54	James Littlefield		Arundel, ME
55	Katherine Heard		Arundel, ME
56	Thomas Perkins	1622-1686	England; Ipswich, Topsfield, MA
57	Phebe Gould	1620-	England; Topsfield, MA
58	Jacob Town	bpt 1632-1704	England; Salem, Topsfield, MA
59	Catherine Symonds		Salem, Topsfield, MA
60	John Wildes	-1705	England; Ipswich, Topsfield, MA
61	Sarah Averill *	-1692	Ipswich, Topsfield, MA
	(Hanged as a witch, July 19, 1692)		
62	Samuel Howlett		Topsfield, MA
63	Sarah Clark		Topsfield, MA

###

Our Readers Write

"I was interested in the Article on the Canney family in the August issue of TEG. My grandfather's mother was Elizabeth Canney born March 10, 1799 in Strafford, N.H. She married Smith Peary (now Perry) of Strafford. I would like to write to Bob Canney. Would you send me his address? He might be interested in the photograph I have of Henry Canney taken by a photographer in Dover, N.H. Henry was a cousin to my grandfather, John Hill Perry. I also have a picture of the house that Smith Peary built, and where he and Elizabeth Canney lived, and brought up their family. I would be happy to share the Perry genealogy with him, which shows the children of Smith Peary and Elizabeth Canney."

Irene Sanders Johnson, Searsport Ave. Rt. #1, Box 10, Belfast, Maine 04915

(Bob Canney's address is: Robert S. Canney, Box 1057, Berwick, Maine 03901)

# # # # # # # # # # # # # # # # # #

"Volunteers are needed in many places and I would like to add my plea to members of Essex County to consider volunteering at the Nationarl Archives and Records Service - Boston Branch at Waltham and/or the Massachusetts Vital Records Office at 150 Tremont Street. Volunteers not only help to maintain longer hours of service at these important offices, but it also gives genealogists a time to do some personal research on their own. There are now sixteen names on the list of potential volunteers for 150 Tremont Street. Many also volunteer at both the State and National Archives. Three days of volunteerism isn't too much since both State 'jobs' are for only half a day each."

Rose Buckman Morrison, 75 Hemingway St. Apt. 203, Winchester, MA 01890

# # # # # # # # # # # # # # # # # #

Miscellaneous Notes

SELECTIVE SERVICE RECORDS: When the United States became involved in World War I in 1917, <u>all</u> males between the ages of 18 and 45 were required to register for the draft. More than 24 million of these selective service records are on file at the National Archives and Records Center in East Point, Georgia. They are filed by state and then by draft board. The registration form was completed by the individual himself, who may have been born as early as 1872, and it may supply important information regarding parents, spouse, date of birth and place of birth. In order to request a copy of one of the selective service records, you must supply the full name of the person and the city and/or county in which they were living at the time of registration. If your relative resided in one of the following cities, you must also supply an exact street address, which is available from a 1917 city directory:

Albany, NY	Kansas City, MO	Philadelphia, PA
Atlanta, GA	Los Angeles, CA	Pittsburgh, PA
Baltimore, MD	Louisville, KY	Providence, RI
Boston, MA	Luzerne County, PA	St. Louis, MO
Buffalo, NY	Milwaukee, WI	St. Paul, MN
Chicago, IL	Minneapolis, MN	San Francisco, CA
Cincinnati, OH	Newark, NJ	Seattle, WA
Cleveland, OH	New Orleans, LA	Syracuse, NY
Indianapolis, IN	New York City, NY	Washington, DC
Jersey City, NJ		

Requests may be made to General Services Administration-Region 4, Federal Archives and Records Center, 1559 St. Joseph Ave., East Pont, GA 30344. A check for $5.00 made out to the National Archives Trust Fund Board must accompany each request.

...Whittier Area Gen. Soc. Newsletter, Vol. 4, No. 1, June 1984, p. 4
(Submitted by Sid Russell)

NATIONAL ARCHIVES - BOSTON BRANCH - CLARIFICATION OF HOLDINGS

1. <u>Census Records</u>: All Federal Censuses for all states (1890 destroyed by fire) Soundex Index (on microfilm) for 1880, 1900 & part of 1910 (only 21 states, and not Massachustts)

2. <u>Naturalization Records</u> only prior to 1906.
   A Name <u>Index</u> (on microfilm) of <u>all</u> naturalizations 1790-1906.
   <u>Original Records</u> for <u>Federal Courts</u> (U.S. District Courts and U.S. Circuit Courts)

3. <u>Passenger Arrival Records</u>
   Most are in Washington D.C. NARS - BOSTON does have <u>some</u> lists for Boston, New Bedford and some others.

4. <u>Revolutionary War Pension, Bounty Land Warrants, and Service Records</u>
   Copies of records (on microfilm) of all those who served in the Rev. War.

5. <u>War of 1812</u>
   <u>Index only</u> (on microfilm) of Volunteer Soldiers of War of 1812.

AVAILABILITY OF CANADIAN CENSUS RETURNS   Three reels at a time may be borrowed for use by any library or other institution which possesses a 35MM microfilm reader and participates in the Interlibrary Loan arrangement. Requests for loans must be submitted by the borrowing institution on authorized forms to the:

Public Archives of Canada
395 Wellington Street
Ottawa, Ontario, Canada, K1A ON3

Microfilm copies of most census records may be purchased. Returns prior to 1851 give only the names of heads of households and the total numbers in each household.   ...Bill Stevens, 39 Dexter St., Peabody, MA 01960

AID FOR QUEBEC RESEARCH A new genealogical research center for U.S. searchers having problems in searching their ancestral roots in the Province of Quebec, Canada, is the Institute de Recherches Les Sources Du Passe Enr., B.P. 1293, Trois-Rivieres, Quebec, Canada, G9A 5L2. The Institute will search printed sources such as marriage indexes, Vital Records, Church or Census Records. Send for fees and details. Despite the French name, the services would be given in English.   ...advertising flyer

---

SOME NUMBERS All 50 states of the USA and all Canadian provinces except Yukon and Northwest Territory have at least one genealogical society. During 1982-1984 there were some 150 new societies formed. The total number of societies is now near 1500. The National Genealogical Society is the largest - ahead of the New England Historical and Genealogical Society with 6900 members. There are 23 societies having 1,000 or more members. Independent Periodicals published now number 200.   ...Genealogy Digest, Summer 1985

BEATRICE BAYLEY GETS HER "COME-UPPANCE" IN WISCONSIN   On 26 July 1985 Judge Richard W. Bardwell of the Dane County, Wisconsin, Circuit Court, found Beatrice Bayley, Inc. "guilty of untrue, deceptive and misleading solicitation" in connection with the sale of its "family heritage books," in violation of a consent judgment issued by the court in 1980, and ordered a forfeiture of $1,500. In addition, the judge set forth a series of guidelines with which Beatrice Bayley must comply in the future in making solicitation to prospective customers in Wisconsin. Beatrice Bayley Schneider and her son, Kurt Schneider, were defense witnesses. Under cross examination, she testified that the family heritage books are identical except for the names listed in each book, that those names are assembled from auto license registrations, telephone books, social security lists, and city directories, and that the lists do not include deceased family members or female family members who have married.   ...NGS Newsletter

---

PILGRIMS BROUGHT RARE EYE AILMENT   The Mayflower may have carried the gene of a rare eye disease to America, says Dr. Gordon Klintworth, research director of the Duke University Eye Center in Durham, North Carolina. Klintworth has traced the family trees of four victims of macular corneal dystrophy to Pilgrim father William Brewster. The disease, which usually requires a corneal transplant to correct, is hereditary and found primarily in rural North Carolina and Virginia. Both parents must carry the gene for it to be transmitted to their child.
           ...Newsclipping submitted by Beverly Domeratzky, Beverly, Mass.

Society News

FORTHCOMING MEETINGS

November 16   Saturday, Todd Hall, Centre Congregational Church, Lynnfield
              Social Hour 12:00. Lecture promptly at 1:00
              Speaker: Hon. David A. Nichols, of Lincolnville, Maine
              Topic: "What's New in Northern New England Genealogy"

December 21   Saturday, Todd Hall, Centre Congregational Church, Lynnfield
              12:00 - Traditional Covered Dish Luncheon
              (details will be announced in ESOG Newsletter)
              Program: Members' "Show and Tell"

January 18   Saturday, Lynnfield Public Library
              9 - 5. All day work meeting
              1:00 P.M. Used Book Auction

February 15   Saturday, Todd Hall, Centre Congregational Church
              12:00 - Social Hour. Lecture promptly at 1:00
              Speaker: Bob Marcotte of Peabody, Mass.
              Topic: "Lincoln's Boots - How they turned up in Lynn"

REPORTS OF PREVIOUS MEETINGS

DAVID
DEAR-
BORN:
SCOTTISH
FAMILY
RESEARCH
One hundred and ten people attended ESOG's opening meeting on 19 September at the Centre Congregational Church in Lynnfield. Joining the regulars were members from western Massachusetts, New Hampshire, Maine, Florida, Arizona, and even a guest from England. The Scottish theme of the day was reflected in the refreshments which included a Dundee Cake. President Ernestine June Rose encouraged members to join the "McDiddit" clan by writing a biographical sketch of an ancestor. She awarded ribbons to those who already "did it!" These sketches will be bound and placed in the genealogy room. The Salem Country Dancers - four ladies and four gentlemen, all members of the worldwide Royal Scottish Country Dance Society, performed traditional country dancing. Professional teacher Sally Dee, and narrator Jim Anderson, led the group. The speaker of the day was David Curtis Dearborn, F.A.S.G., noted lecturer from NEHGS and member of ESOG. He gave a brief outline of Scottish history, its interaction with America, and provided detailed suggestions for Scottish family research. His lecture will appear in a future issue of TEG.

HELEN
BREEN:
THE
LOWELL
FAMILY
Bee Dalton's refreshment committee provided a compliment to brown-bag lunches during the social hour, which was attended by members Paula Owen and Nick Marks from California. Nick presented the Society with an enlarged and detailed map of the Danvers (Salem Village) "witchcraft" area, which is now on display in the genealogy room - along with his ten-generation fan chart. Speaker of the day was ESOG's Helen Breen, who presented a most enjoyable illustrated lecture on the Lowell family of Massachusetts. Watch for it in a future issue of TEG.

Queries

GUIDELINES FOR SUBMITTING QUERIES

Readers may submit free queries. No query to
exceed 50 words. No limit on number of queries.
Ask specific questions re parentage, birthplace,
marriage, children, etc. Use identifying detail
such as name, date, or place. *Type* or *print* on 3 x
5 card. Use abbreviations listed at end of
February Query section. Deadlines for queries:
Jan 1, Apr 1, July 1, Oct 1. Send queries to:
Ludovine Hamilton/Katherine Little, 77 Edgehill
Rd, Lynn, MA 01904.

HARRIS/NICHOLSON
Seek par & dts for Samuel HARRIS m
Elizabeth NICHOLSON 20 Oct 1715
Marblehead, MA

GREEN/TUCKER
Seek par & dts for Peter GREEN &
Charity TUCKER who m in Marblehead,
MA 11 Apr 1712.

MULLETT/RUSSELL
Seek par & dts for Thomas MULLETT who
m 30 July 1780 Mrs. Abigail RUSSELL in
Marblehead. She d 14 Jan 1829 in
Marblehead.

ROADS(ROSE)/GREEN
Seek par & dts for Elizabeth ROADS who m
Samuel H. GREEN of Marblehead, MA 17
Nov 1767.

STANLEY/CHARDER
Seek par & dts for Sands STANLEY m 1
Oct 1724 to Mary CHARDER in Marblehead,
MA

WASHBURN/LE BARON
seek info on Elizabeth Washburn of
Middleboro, MA m 9 May 1781 to James
LE BARON. Mrs. Mary E. Lenth, RFD #1,
Box 78J, Essex, CT 06426

#############################

ALLEN/HAMER/GREEN/DANE/ROGERS
Seek anc of Charity ALLEN m Josiah
(Jessie) HAMER poss dau of Lt. William
ALLEN (d 1794 PA) & Rebecca GREEN.
Dau Mary E. HAMER b ca 1802 m Daniel
Harris DANE, Livingston Co., NY, d
Framington, MN. Effy ALLEN (prob sis)
m 1783 Robert ROGERS.

ARCHAMBEAU/TORIQUE/MCNUTT/FENN
Seek anc Catherine ARCHAMBEAU b 1840
Hannibel, MO, dau of Joseph & Catherine
TORIQUE. Sis? bro? M/1 ----- MCNUTT,
m/2 ----- FENN.

DANE(DAINE,DAIN)/HARRIS
Seek anc of Abiah HARRIS 1/w Lemuel
DANE b 1775 Norwich, CT, d Wenham, CT.
Had Daniel Harris DANE m Mary Ellen
HAMER & had dau Nancy; 2d/w Abigail
WIGHT DANE wid Nathan. Rem. to VT.

FROST/HILL/BREED
Which William FROST (Capt) came from
Sanford, ME to Groton, VT. d on his
farm 1835, ae 65, m Berwick, ME Lydia
Breed HILL dau of Joseph HILL & Mary
BREED.

FROST/BREED/HILL/KIMBALL/COTTON/
WITCHER/GARY
Seek anc Capt William FROST of Sanford,
ME rem to Groton, VT 1732 m Lydia Breed
HILL dau of Joseph HILL. Dau Mary Breed
FROST m ---- KIMBALL & dau Lydia Minerva
m ---- COTTON. Foxwell WITCHER & Capt
Ephraim GARY also m daus of Joseph HILL.

HAMER/LYON/ALLEN
Seek anc Charity ALLEN m Josiah HAMER b
1779 Westmoreland, PA s/o Capt Thomas
HAMER b 1740 & Eleanor LYON b 1750.
Charity ALLEN rel Ethan ALLEN.

IVES/HOTCHKISS/FENN/HART
Seek anc Lois IVES b 1777 CT, dau John
IVES & Lois HOTCHKISS of New Haven.
Did John IVES have 2 w? Did she name
sons Norman & Ira FENN after HARTS?
She m Gamailiel FENN II 1798 s of
Gamaliel FENN I of Waterbury, CT.

IVES/MORGAN/HOTCHKISS
Seek info John IVES b 1748 New Haven,
m/1 Lois HOTCHKISS, m/2 ----? son of
Isaac IVES b 1721 & Lydia HOTCHKISS #2
Henry HOTCHKISS. Wish res & 2d/w. Dau
Lois IVES m Gamaliel FENN II.

TORIQUE/ARCHAMBEAU/PEPIN
Seek anc Catherine TORIQUE mo of
Catherine ARCHAMBEAU. Mo b 23 Feb 1806
St. Genevieve, MO, dau of Pasqual
(Pierre) TORIQUE b 1751 Belme, Spain,

& Catherine ARCHAMBEAU. Fa Charles 1770 St. Anne, Canada m Teresa Celeste PEPIN 1804.

WILLIAMS/LINCOLN/MERWIN/LEAVENS
Seek anc Esther WILLIAMS b 1744 Killingly, OH d 1828 Zanesville, OH, m John LEAVENS III b 1734, d Middleton, OH; dau Frances b 1769 m Joseph LINCOLN b 1760 Scituate, MA 9 1804 Marietta, OH. Had dau Susan, b 1791, m Elijah Bottom MERWIN. Dianne Kimball Knoblock, 1349 Comstock Ave., Los Angeles, CA 90024.

****

KIMBALL/PERKINS
Seek info on Samuel KIMBALL b ca 1790 Kittery, ME & his w Abigail PERKINS b 1807 Kittery, ME, d 26 Oct 1891, Charlestown, MA dau of John & Ann PERKINS of Kittery, ME. Samuel & Abigail were the par of Thomas Albert KIMBALL b 30 July 1854, Charlestown, Ma. Mrs. Elizabeth HALEY, 19 Dean Rd., Reading, MA 01867.

****

BROWN/BUTLER
Need par & 1st/h Ruth BROWN who had dau Ruth BROWN by 1st/h then m John BUTLER 10 Oct 1714, 1st CH, Stonington, CT. Ruth's 1st/h prob Lynn, MA BROWN. Which of these: Samuel, oldest s of Thomas Jr., Jonothan, 5th s of Thomas, Sr., E. Ebenezer, 7th s of Thomas, Sr., Joseph, 2d s of Thomas Sr. & 2nd/w

BUTLER
Daniel BUTLER poss from Sandwich, Barnstable, MA prior 1700, m Margaret _____, later settl. Saconitt Pt. area, RI, d June 1718. Will N. London, CT (probate 17 June 1718) Their pars? Other VR? Jewett B. BUTLER, 13156 Stillwater Rd., Waterport, NY 14571.

****

BRACKETT/WYMAN/MARSTON
Did Love BRACKETT m William WYMAN ca 1755 at Falmouth or Pownalborough, ME? Samuel & Lydia (MARSTON) BRACKETT had a dau Love b at New Castle, NH 18 Apr

1727. Love & William named a dau Lydia.

WYMAN/OSBORN/BROWN
DAR records say Lydia Wyman m 1788, as his 3d/w Ephraim OSBORN, Sr. of Winslow, ME. In 1780 he m Sarah BROWN. Who was w/1?

YORK/GILES/GROVES
Solomon YORK & Patience GILES, both of Norwood, NH m there 20 Aug 1809. Did she, as wid YORK, m William GROVES at East Pond Plantation, ME 13 Nov 1828? Mrs. Clair E. Wyman, Sawyer's Crossing Rd., P.O. Box 27, West Swanzey, NH 03469.

****

CLARK/WITTAM
Seek par of Redigon CLARK b 1626, m to Peter WITTAM in Boston 17 June 1652. Nancy C. HAYWARD, 17 Draper Dr., Wilmington, MA 01887.

****

DOUGHTY/ROBINSON
Need anc of James DOUGHTY & of Mary ROBINSON who m 10 Apr 1707 Hampton, NH.

EMERSON/BRAY
Need anc Mary EMERSON who m Thomas BRAY 23 Dec 1686. Res. Gloucester, MA.

EMERY/MURCH
Need anc Deborah EMERY of Biddeford, ME who m 28 Feb 1760 Samuel MURCH of Gorham, ME.

HAINES/YOUNG
Need anc Eleanor HAINES who m 23 Apr 1696 Matthew YOUNG.

MATTHEWS
Need anc w & ch of John MATTHEWS who was in New Boston (now Gray) ME as early as 1760.

PERKINS
Need proof that John PERKINS b 14 May 1693 was s of Luke PERKINS b 1649 & 2d/w Sarah -----.

PERKINS/PACKARD/WILLIAMS
Need proof that Anne PERKINS who m
Reuben PACKARD, Bridgewater, MA was
dau of John PERKINS & Abigail WILLIAMS
b 4 Mar 1737 Ipswich. Miss Katherine
W. Trickey, 158 Parkview Ave., Bangor,
ME 04401

##################################

FARRAR/FISH
Mercy FARRAR m Jireh FISH 7 Dec 1767
Dartmouth, MA. Who were they? Res
Lee, ME.

FRENCH
Humphrey FRENCH & Abigail ---- had ch
in Salem, MA 1693-1707. Who were
Humphrey & Abigail?

FRENCH/BURTON
Who was Margaret FRENCH, b 1 July 1764
Salem, MA m Simon BURTON 1787 Sutton,
MA?

HUME/SIMPSON
John HUME (1733-1802) in Rev War from
MA, & Eleanor ---- had dau Eleanor b
1764 who m Reuben SIMPSON 1787 Winslow,
ME. Have been told he came from VA &
liv aft 1802. Need HUME info.

JACKSON/TUPPER
Joseph William JACKSON of Litchfield,
ME m Abigail TUPPER 17 Feb 1763 Nan-
tucket, MA. TUPPER Gen. & Hist. of
Litchfield disgree about who their ch
were. Help. Does TUPPER Fam. Ass'n,
once in Beverly, MA still exist?

LEACH/KNOWLTON
Ezekiel KNOWLTON b 1679 Ipswich or
Manchester, MA m Sarah LEACH 29 Jan
1698. Who was she?

MORRILL/FRENCH/JOY
Need proof that Sarah MORRILL who m
Stephen FRENCH 20 Feb 1794 Salisbury,
MA was dau of Sgt. Abraham & Sarah JOY.

MUDGRIDGE (MORGRAGE, MORGRIDGE)
Compiling a gen. One branch liv in
Newbury, MA ca 1700. Want info & will
share info.

POORE/NOYES
Who was Mary Poore who m John NOYES 23
Nov 1668 Newbury, MA?

SAFFORD/HASKELL
Did John SAFFORD b ca 1709 Ipswich, MA m
Mayflower desc Martha HASKELL & res in
Harvard, MA?

TRASK/WHITE
John TRASK & Penelope WHITE had s
William 27 July 1729 Bridgewater, MA.
Need info on TRASK & WHITE fam.

WHITE/THAYER
Susanna WHITE dau of Samuel & Anna, b
12 Mar 1689 Weymouth, MA m Richard
THAYER in Braintree. Need info on
Samuel & Anna. Roland RHOADES, Jr.
RFD 1 Box 152, Sanford, ME 04073.

##################################

CONNER
Wish info Jemima ---- b ca 1784, d
1820, bur Sheffield, VT, 1st/w of
Benjamin CONNER.

CONNER/LOCKS
Wish info Thankful Ingalls Weeks LOCKS,
1793-1876, bur Brooks Cem., St. Albans
Bay, VT, 2d/w of Benjamin CONNER.

EVANS/CONNER/WEAVER
Anna EVANS b ca 1760 d aft 1838 (where)
m 23 Oct 1780 Joseph CONNER in Ports-
mouth, NH. Was she dau of David & Anna
(WEAVER) EVANS m 29 Nov 1745 in
Freetown, NH?

MARTIN/TODD
Who was Mary MARTIN b ca 1755, d 1831, m
Samuel TODD, Rev War soldier in Rowley,
MA, bur St. Albans Bay, VT Brooks Cem.
Ch Polly, Sally, Betsey, Abigail, Jane
& Samuel, Jr. Jane Kaskela, 6 Jessica
Pl., Whitesboro, NY 13492.

##################################

ELDRIDGE/TOURTELOTTE
Seek par, dts for Joseph ELDRIDGE who
m Anna (Amy) TOURTELOTTE 5 May 1819
Brewer, ME. Norma L. ANDREWS, 14
Leonard St., Gloucester, MA 01930.

ALEXANDER/SEELEY

Need info Charles L. ALEXANDER b France, d ca 1862 Coast of Africa. Info also re w Margaret J. SEELEY b 1833 Nova Scotia (1850 Census). Three s went to orphanage 1862. Then "bound out to their majority." Reunited Salem 1884 per clipping from Boston Sunday Globe 13 Apr 1884.

DAY/MATCHET

Wish anc Anthony DAY (per Hist. of Gloucester) b 1616, to Gloucester ca 1645, m Susanna perhaps Susan MATCHET. Has this been proved? Any other info re Susanna.

DODD/LUNDGREN

Elizabeth DODD, b ca 1804 MA m 11 Sept 1828 Salem, Nils Peter LUNDGREN b 10 Feb 1794 Trelleborg, Sweden. Need all info re Elizabeth - bdt, ddt, par, sib, etc.

STONE/LUNDGREN

Need anc Benjamin F. STONE b 6 Jan 1815, Salem, MA, d 22 June 1892 Salem, m 6 June 1851 Salem Hellen E. LUNDGREN m cert states fa Benjamin F. STONE. Who was mo? Helen H. DREW, RR #1, Box 216, Hollis Ctr., ME 04042

ALLEY

Nathan ALLEY (1752-1832) m Mary ALLEY (1755-1836). Twelve ch b Lynn, MA bet 1778 & 1798. Need par & anc of Nathan & Mary. Will exch all info.

ALLEY/WILEY(WILLEY)

Micajah ALLEY b 15 Feb 1786 Lynn, MA m 1807 Dorcas WILEY b ca 1786, NH. Four ch b Lynn bet 1809 & 1820. Need bp, par & anc of Dorcas.

FIELD/BLAKE

Moses FIELD m Anna BLAKE, res Freeport, Cumberland Co., ME. Ch b Freeport: Eunice 1797, Ezra 1799, John 1801, Jonathan 1803, Hannah 1805/6, William 1807, Zacharia, Almira. Need all info on Moses & Anna. Carol Ann Hamilton,

1529 Eucalyptus Hill Road, #4, Santa Barbara, CA 93013.

ELLINGWOOD/ROWLANDSON/ROBSON

Ralph ELLINGWOOD m Martha ROBSON ROW-LANDSON 19 Aug 1691, Marblehead, MA. Need bdt, ddt, locs & par of Martha. Was her maiden name ROBSON or ROWLAND-SON?

KENNEY/SMITH

Hannah KENNEY b 30 June 1786, MA, m Joseph SMITH. Need par, sib, mdt, ddt and pls.

SMITH/ALLEN

Job SMITH m Sarah ALLEN 22 Oct 1750, Beverly, MA. Eleven ch. Need Sarah's par, bdt, ddt & locs.

SMITH/FOSTER/STONE/LOVERING/GOODHUE

Bible recs show Job SMITH, Jr. m Elizabeth FOSTER, Hannah STONE, Esther LOVE-RING, and Anna GOODHUE, order unk. Joseph s of Job b 4 Oct 1774. Who was Joseph's mo? Need mdt, ddt & pl for all wives.

SMITH/KENNEY

Joseph SMITH b 4 Oct 1774 Beverly, MA m/1 Elizabeth ---- m/2 Hannah KENNEY, Beverly, MA. 18 ch - 9 each w. Youngest, Esdras b 1 Sep 1829, Langdon, Sullivan Co., NH. Need mdt, pl each w, ddt pl for all. Mrs. Betty L. MILLS, 17860 Crescent Court, S.V.L. Box 7013, Victorville, CA 92392.

EMMONS/SHACKLEY

John EMMONS Jr b ca 1765 Lyman, ME m Huldah SHACKLEY (of Wells, ME) int 3 Aug 1793, Lyman. Need his ddt & names of their ch.

HOLT

William H. HOLT, Jr., shoe manufacturer b 8 Apr 1840 Lynn, MA left Lynn in 1906 for CA. He remr. & had another ch. Need ddt & 2nd mdt, maiden name of 2nd/w & name of ch.

HOLT/HARRIS
Loammi B. HOLT of Andover, MA m Mary (Polly) HARRIS 12 Jan 1797 at Andover. Need dt & par of Mary, also names of their ch.

MUNGER/DODGE
Reuben S. MUNGER m Mary Ann DODGE 9 Apr 1827 at Northampton, MA d 25 June 1837 Lynn, MA ae 39. Need par & bdt of both.

NEWHALL/LOCKER
Locker NEWHALL s of Jacob NEWHALL & Abigail LOCKER was b Lynn, MA 12 Nov 1708, m Sarah ----. Need dts for both & maiden name & par of Sarah.

NEWHALL/MAKEPIECE
Jacob NEWHALL s of Jacob Landlord NEW-HALL b 1 Nov 1780 Lynn, MA m Abigail MAKEPIECE 22 Sep 1801 in Lynn. Need biographical info on both.

OLIVER/PRATT
William OLIVER m Mary PRATT Jr. of Chelsea, MA 25 July 1771 at Chelsea. Need par & dts on both. Robert J. HOLT, 6 Garten Ter., Asheville, NC 28804.

****

PARKER/GERRET/LUFKIN
Need anc of John PARKER & Lucy GERRET (GARRET) who m 25/26 Feb 1781, Glouces-ter, MA. Were they the par of Andrew Morgan PARKER, b 21/27 Aug 1791 & is he the Andrew PARKER who m Nancy LUFKIN 15 July 1812?

PARSON/PARKER/TAPPAN
Need anc of Angie PARSONS who m George Whitefield PARKER (b 18 Mar 1836, Gloucester, MA, s of Andrew PARKER & Sophia D. TAPPAN). He d 30 Jan 1895; she d 1898.

SARGENT/EAMES/LANE/YOUNG
Need anc of Reuben T. SARGENT (b. NH 1799) m Maria EAMES, sett. Riley Plan-tation, Newry, ME area. Had dau Nancy H who m 18 July 1854 Franklin YOUNG (s of Daniel YOUNG & Hannah LANE of

Gloucester, MA) b 22 July 1827 (Had s Charles Franklin YOUNG)

WOODBURY/DENNEN/YOUNG/FOSTER/MORSE/ MCCLELLAN/RUST
Seek anc of Frank WOODBURY (1855-1941) & w Mary DENNEN (1861-1953) of Lanes-ville, Gloucester, MA. Had foll ch bet 1881-1903: Joseph E; Grace M; Lillian Augusta (1886-1950) 2nd/w of Charles Frank YOUNG; Hazel (RUST); Helen Mae (MORSE); Ruth M. (MCCLELLAN); Ralph F.; & Gladys E. (FOSTER).

YOUNG/YORK/ROBINSON
Need anc of William YOUNG who m Sarah YORK (dau of Joseph YORK & Abigail ROBINSON) in Gloucester, MA in 1725. Mary J. YOUNG, 21 Old Mill Rd., South Berwick, ME 03908.

****

ABBOT, Samuell, 52
ALDEN, Sarah, 164
ALDRICH, Albert J., 109
ALEXANDER, Charles L., 214
ALLE, Sarah, 166
ALLEN, Charity, 211; Effy, 211; Ethan,
    211; Joanna, 164; Sarah, 54, 214;
    Thomas, 164; William, 211
ALLEY, Mary, 214; Micajah, 214; Nathan,
    214
ANDERSON, Clara, 165; Isaac, 165;
    Jonathan, 165; Mary, 165; William,
    165
ANDREWS, Thomas, 55, 109
ANDROSS, Margaret, 54
ANTHONY, John, 52
ARCHAMBEUA, Catherine, 211; Joseph, 211
ARNOLD, Dorcas, 54, 162; Stephen, 162
ASH, Sarah, 108

BABCOCK, Henry, 110
BACHILER, Nathaniel, 109; Stephen, 52,
    109
BACON, Elizabeth, 161
BAILEY, ---- (Deacon), 162; Benjamin
    Webster, 162; Dudley, 162
BAKER, Mary, 105; Mary (Polly), 107
BARRETT, Lemuel, 165
BARTLETT, David, 164; Joseph, 53;
    Richard, 164; Tirzah, 52
BATES, Ann, 52
BEEDLE, Mary Magdelane, 52
BELCHER, Elijah, 107
BELL, Nancy, 52; Isaac, 52; Zephenian,
    52
BENNETT, David, 109
BISHOP, John, 110; Lydia, 110
BLAKE, Anna, 214; Jasper, 109
BLASHFIELD, Henry, 105; Mercy, 105
Bogart, -----, 165
BOVEE, Elizabeth, 54, 162
BRACKETT, Love, 212; Samuel, 212
BRAGG, William, 53
BRAMAN, Amasa, 106
BRAY, Thomas, 212
BREED, Allen, 55; Mary, 211
BREWER, Nellie, 54
BRIDGES, Sarah, 161
BRIGHAM, Mary Polly, 106; Moses, 106
BROOKIN(G), William, 109

BROOKS, Mehitable, 163
BROWN, Abigail, 161; Betsey, 53; E.
    Ebenezer, 212; Ebenezer, 109; Jono-
    than, 212; Joseph, 212; Josiah, 162;
    Mariam, 52; Mary, 165; Polly, 162;
    Ruth, 212; Samuel, 212; Sarah, 212;
    Thomas, 109, 212
BROWNE, Sarah, 162
BROWNING, Daniel, 109; Malachi, 109;
    Susannah, 109
BURBANK, Elijah, 106
BURNAP, Robert, 162
BURRELL, Anna, 163
BURRILL, Esther Foss, 162; Hannah, 162;
    Josiah, 162
BURROUGHS, ----, 164; John, 54
BURTON, Simon, 213
BUSHEY, Angelette, 53
BUTLER, Daniel, 212; John, 212
BUTTS, Mary, 162
BYROM, W. W., 108

CADY, Honora, 109
CARGILL, Daniel, 54, 162; James, 54,
    162; Preston, 162
CARPENTER, Priscilla, 161
CARR, Ann, 164; George, 53, 164
CARTER, Charity, 53; Edward, 164;
    Elizabeth, 164; Jane, 164, 165;
    Lucretia, 164; Mary, 164; Michael,
    164; Phebe, 109; Sarah, 164; Thomas,
    164
CHAMBERLAIN, Experience, 109; Jacob,
    109; John, 161; William, 109
CHAMBERLIN, Elizabeth, 55
CHARDER, Mary, 211
CHASE, Judith, 55
CHENEY, Martha, 164; Mary, 162
CHUBBUCK, Martha, 163
CHURCHILL, Benjamin, 163; John, 163
CLAGGETT, Rebecca, 105; William, 105;
    Wyseman, 105
CLARK, Abigail, 105; Ichabod, 165;
    Jane, 109; Redigon, 212
CLAY, Richard, 107
CLAYTON, Annie E., 162; Charles D.,
    162; Laura B., 162; Mary, 162;
    Mary H., 162

CLOUGH, Elbridge G., 106; Florence M., 106; George W., 106; Henry C., 106; Isaac H., 106; James S., 106; Jane, 106; John T., 106; Lydia, 106; Sarah E., 106; Susan J., 106; Susanne P., 106; Thomas M., 106.
COFFEY, Agnes, 166
COKER, Catherine, 52; Robert, 52
COLBY, Sarah (ASH), 105
COLE, Rebecca, 55, 109, 164
COLLIER, Mary, 109; William, 109
CONNER, Benjamin, 213; Jemima, 213; Joseph, 213; Susanna, 162
CONNORS, Ann, 108; Mary Ellen, 108
COOK, Hannah, 54; James, 105; Richard, 109
COOMBS, Sylvanus, 165
COOPER, Ann, 161; John, 161
COTTON, ----, 211
COX, Philip, 164
CREEL, Elizabeth, 52
CROCKETT, Abraham, 164
CROSS, Mary, 110
CROSSETT, Isa, 106
CUMMINGS, Mary, 55, 110; Rebecca A., 108
CURRIER, Diamond, 164; John, 53, 164; Joseph, 53; Joshua, 164 Mary, 53; William, 53
CURTIS, John, 162; Sarah, 162, 166
CUTTING, John, 166; Mary, 163

DALTON, Deborah, 109; Phiemon, 163
DANE, Abigail (WIGHT), 211; Daniel Harris, 211; Lemuel, 211; Nancy, 211
DARLING Family, 53
DARLING, William, 110
DAVIS, Ezekiel, 108; Francis, 163; Levi, 108; Waldo, 163
DAY, Anthony, 214
DECKER, John, 52; Sarah, 52
DELANO, Jonathan, 106
DENNEN, Mary, 215
DERBURN, Jacob, 164; John, 164
DESPAIN, Solomon, 52
DIXEY, Martha, 105
DIXON, William, 55, 110
DODD, Elizabeth, 214
DODGE, Elizabeth, 108; Mary Ann, 215
DORE, Lydia, 165
DORR, B. Dalton, 163
DOUGHTY, James, 212
DOWNER, Mary, 110
DOWNES, Massey, 54

DOWNEY, Patrick, 109; Thomas J., 109
DREW, Charles, 106
DUDLEY, Elizabeth, 163; Samuel, 163; Thomas, 163
DUNKS, Amelia, 106
DURHAM, William N., 108
DYER, Michael, 165
EAMES, Maria, 215
EDWARDS, David, 162; Lucretia, 105; Miriam, 165, 166
ELDRED, Catherine, 107
ELDRIDGE, Joseph, 213
ELLINGWOOD, Ralph, 214
ELLIOTT, Anna, 105; William, 105
ELLIS, Betsey, 108
ELMER, John, 164
ELWELL, Sarah, 161
EMERSON, Mary, 212; William, 53
EMERY, Deborah, 212
EMMONS, Eunice, 54; John, 214
ESTES, Caleb, 110
EVANS, Anna, 213; David, 213

FAGAN, Julia A., 109; Mary Ann, 109
FALL, Mary, 110
FARRAR, Mercy, 213
FELLOWS, Ann, 166; Salome, 53; Samuel, 166
FENN, ----, 211; Gamailiel, 211; Ira, 211; Norman, 211
FIELD, Almira, 214; Annie, 214; Ezra, 214; Hannah, 214; John, 214; Jonathan, 214; Moses, 214; William, 214; Zacharia, 214
FISH, Jirah, 213
FISK, Asa, 110; Sarah, 110
FLAGG, Sally, 161
FLINT, Alice, 55; Thomas, 165
FOSTER, ----, 215; Betsy, 54; Elizabeth, 214; Moses, 163
FOWLER, Deborah, 54
FREEMAN, Edmund, 163; Rebecca, 163
FRENCH, Abigail, 213; Beman, 163; Humphrey, 213; Margaret, 213; Parker Hardin, 105; Stephen, 213
FROST, Lydia Minerva, 211; Mary Breed, 211; William, 211
FULLER, John, 163; Mary, 163
FULLERTON, John, 165

GARLAND, Josiah, 52; Thomas, 52
GARY, Ephraim, 211
GATES, Bethia, 166
GAVETT, Katherine, 166
GEORGE, John Swaddock, 108; Mary, 108

GERRET, Lucy, 215
GIBBS, Elizabeth, 106
GIDDINGS, Sarah, 108
GILES, Patience, 212
GILMAN, Bela, 106; Charles E., 106;
    Henry H., 106; Lewis E., 106; Mary
    Ellen, 106; Nathaniel, 106
GILMORE, David, 163; John, 163;
    Margaret, 163; Mitchell, 163
GINNVARIE, Rosamond, 164
GODSOE, James E., 110
GOODHUE, Anna, 214
GOODRIDGE, Joanna, 108
GORDON, Mary Ladd, 163
GORHAM, Seth, 106
GOTT, Peter, 54; Samuel, 54;
    Stephen, 54
GOULD, Henry, 55, 109
GRAFFAM, Caleb, 107; Enoch, 107
GRANT, James, 107; Lydia, 107
GREEN, Betsey, 107; Mary, 106, 110;
    Peter, 211; Rebecca, 211; Richard,
    110; Samuel H., 211; Thomas, 109
GROUT, Mehitabel, 106
GROVER, Elizabeth, 162; Stephen, 162;
    Thomas, 162
GROVES, Peter, 105; William, 110, 212
GUNN, C----, M----, 108
GUNTERMAN, Sophia, 52

HAINES, Eleanor, 212; Joshua, 165
HALE, Elizabeth, 107
HALL, Richard, 163
HAMER, Josiah, 211; Mary, 211; Mary
    Ellen, 211; Thomas, 211
HAMLIN, Temperance, 107
HANCHETT, Eliza Ann, 107-8
HARMON, Ruth, 165
HARRINGTON, Elisha, 162
HARRIS, Abiah, 211; Elizabeth, 161;
    Mary (Polly), 215; Samuel, 211
HART, ----, 211
HARVEY, David, 55
HASKELL, Martha, 213; Thomas, 165
HATHORNE, Sara, 52
HAWKINS, Charles, 161; Fannie, 161;
    William, 161
HAYDEN, Phebe, 55
HENDERSON, Esther, 164; Melinda, 54;
    William, 54
HERRICK, Andrew, 109; Betsey, 165;
    Mrs. Mary, 165; Nathaniel, 109;
    Samuel, 109
HEWETT, Ephraim Gay, 166
HICKS, Dorcus, 163; Samuel, 163

HILDRETH, Mary, 54, 162
HILL, Deborah, 166; Joseph, 211;
    Lydia Breed, 211
HILLIARD, Elizabeth, 161
HILLIER, Deborah, 55; Hugh, 55;
    Rose, 55
HILTON, Mary, 110
HODGDON, Caleb, 54; Joel D., 53
HOLBROOK, Alice, 55
HOLMES, Elizabeth, 163
HOLT, Loammi B., 215; Sarah Elizabeth,
    164; William, 164; William H., 214
HOOKER, Henry, 161
HORNE, John, 166
HOTCHKISS, Henry, 211; Lois, 211;
    Lydia, 211
HUCKINS, Thomas, 110
HUME, Eleanor, 213; John, 213
JUSSEY, James, 165
HUSTED, Angell, 107; Samuel, 107
HUTCHINSON, Edward, 163; Mary, 163
HYDE, Samuel, 55

INCHES, Thomas, 54
IVES, Isaac, 211; John, 211; Lois, 211

JACKSON, Joseph William, 213
JAMES, Anna, 165; John, 165
JOHNSON, Jermiah, 106; Sarah, 164
JONES, Anne, 55; Phebe, 109
JORDAN, Francis, 52; Mary, 52; Mary
    (McFadden), 165
JOY, Sarah, 213

KEAZER, Clarissa D., 110; Rhoda E.,
    110; Susan, 110
KEEZER, Clara H., 110; Mary Ann, 110
KELLOGG, Joseph, 106
KENNEY Ann, 110; Hannah, 214
KENT, Richard, 166
KILBURN, Lucy, 54
KIMBALL, ----, 211; John, 52; Nelson,
    164; Samuel, 212; Thomas Albert,
    212
KING, Sarah Elizabeth, 54
KNAPP, Moses, 107; Sarah, 107
KNIGHT, Richard, 166
KNOWLES, Nathaniel, 161; Samuel, 161
KNOWLTON, Ezekiel, 213

LaGROVES, Nicholas, 110
LAMBERT, Jesse, 54; Rachel, 54
LANCASTER, David, 162

LANE, Daniel, 105; Elias, 105; Giddings, 105; Hannah, 215; James, 105; Judith, 105; Lydia, 105; Mary, 105; Peter, 105
LANG, William, 165
LARKIN, John, 161; Thomas, 161
LARRABEE, William, 107
LEACH, Sarah, 213
LEAVENS, Frances, 212; John, 212
LeBARON, James, 211
LEIGHTON, Joseph J., 110
LINCOLN, Joseph, 212; Susan, 212
LOCKER, Abigail, 215
LOCKS, Thankful Ingalls Weeks, 213
LOMBARD FAMILY, 107; Richard, 107; Solomon, 107
LORD, Jeremiah, 107; Mary, 106
LOTT, Sarah, Mrs., 52
LOVERING, Esther, 214
LUFKIN, Nancy, 215
LUNDGREN, Hellen E., 214; Nils Peter, 214
LUNT, Johnson, 54; Samuel, 54; Samuel Allen, 108
LYON, Eleanor, 211

MacMAHON, Elizabeth, 55; Michael, 55
MAKEPIECE, Abigail, 215
MANSFIELD, Lydia, 54; Rebecca, 54
MARSH, Onesiphorus, 163
MARSHALL, Moses F., 164
MARSON, Samuel, 161
MARSTON, Lydia, 212
MARTIN, Mary, 213
MASON, Mrs. Helen, 52; John L., 54
MATCHET, Susanna, 214
MATTHEWS, John, 212
MAXIM, Nathan, 163
MAYBERRY, Charity, 107
MAYHEW, Nathaniel, 165
McCLELLAN, -----, 215
McCLURE, Mary, 163
McDERMOTT, Mary, 55
McFADDEN, Mary, 165
McFEE, John, 165
McNUTT, ----, 211
McQUESTION, Simon, 105; William, 105
MERCER, Hester, 109
MERRETT, Nicholas, 161
MERRIAM, Elizabeth, 55; William, 55
MERRILL, Hannah, 165; Joseph, 55; Richard, 55
MERWIN, Elijah Bottom, 212
MESERVE, Clement, 52

MILLER, Abigail, 106; Ann (Agnes), 162; Frederick, 55; John, 166; Lucinda, 166
MILTON, John, 53
MITCHELL, Lettice, 105; Lydia, 107
MOODY, Dorcas, 166; Mary, 52
MOORE, Joseph, 164; Mariam, 52
MORGAN, Mary, 105
MORRILL, Abraham, 213; Judith, 109; Sara, 105; Sarah, 213
MORSE, -----, 215
MORTON, Ephraim, 161; George, 161
MOTT, Adam, 51; John, 52
MOULTON, Lucy, 165; Sobriety, 109
MUGRIDGE Family, 213
MULLETT, Thomas, 211
MUNGER, Reuben S., 215
MURCH, Samuel, 212
MURPHEY, James F., 108; Lawrence, 108

NAHOR, James, 105; Margaret, 105
NASH, Francis, 108; Joseph, 108
NASON, Thomas, 166
NEWHALL, Jacob, 215; Jacob Landlord, 215; Locker, 215; Sarah, 215
NEWMAN, Benjamin, 106; Hannah, 106
NICHOLAS, Alexander, 54
NICHOLS, Thomas, 108
NICHOLSON, Elizabeth, 211
NOTT, Temperance, 54
NOYES, John, 54, 161, 213; Nicholas, 163
NURSE, Samuel, 166

O'DONNELL, Dennis, 109
OLIVER, William, 215
ORN(E), Hannah, 106
OSBORN, Ephraim, 110, 212; Isaac, 110

PACKARD, Reuben, 213; Silas, 110
PALMER, Susanna, 106
PARKER, Andrew, 215; Andrew Morgan, 215; George Whitefield, 215; John, 215
PARRATT, Elizabeth, 163
PARSONS, Angie, 215; Hannah, 53
PEAKE, Christian, 162
PEARSON, Jeremiah, 106
PENNELL, Rachel, 107
PEPIN, Teresa Celeste, 212
PERKINS, Abigail, 212; Ann, 212; Anne, 213; John, 212, 213; Luke, 212; Sarah, 212
PERLEY, Lois, 108
PERRY, Ezra, 163

PERVIERRE, Abigail, 107
PHILBRICK, James, 107
PHILLIPS, Kezia, 55
PHIPS, William, 109
PICKERING, Elizabeth, 55; John, 55
PIERCE, Mary, 107; William, 107
PIKE, Thomas, 108
PILLSBURY, Daniel, 166; Job, 166;
   Mary, 55
PONTUS, Hannah, 163
POOR, Amos, 164; Mary, 53, 164, 213
POTTER, Susanna, 52
PRATT, John, 166; Martha, 166; Mary,
   215; Phineas, 166; Richard, 166
PRENCE, Rebecca, 163; Thomas, 109
PRESCOTT, Micah, 161
PRESSEY, Judith, 53
PRYAULX Family, 109
PUTNAM, Thomas, 164

REILLY, Henry Patrick, 108
RHOADS, Hannah, 56
RHODES, Henry, 55; John, 56; Samuel, 56
RICH, Robert C., 53
RICHARDS, Huldah, 106
RIDEOUT, Abraham, 107; Lydia, 107
RING, Andrew, 108; Batchelder, 108
RIVERS, Elizabeth Amelia, 109
ROADS, Elizabeth, 211
ROBERTS, Sarah, 54
ROBINSON, Abigail, 215; Mary, 212
ROBSON, Martha, 214
ROCKWELL, Electra, 162; Moses, 54
ROGERS, Charles, 163; Elizabeth, 163;
   Hannah, 55; Robert, 211; Steven,
   162; William, 55
ROLLINS, Betsey, 106; Caroline, 106;
   Frances, 106; Hannah, 106; Josiah,
   106; Lucinda, 106; Lucy A., 106;
   Mary, 106; Sarah, 106; William A.,
   106
ROSE, Betsey, 106
ROW, John, 105
RUSSELL, Abigail, 211; Silas, 55
RUST, ----, 215

SAFFORD, John, 213
SAMPSON, Ruth, 165
SANBORN, Judith, 109
SANDERS, Caroline, 108; Fred Nathaniel,
   108; Henry, 108; John, 108; John
   L., 108; Permit Porter, 108; Sarah
   Elizabeth, 108
SANDIN, Arthur, 161; Mary, 161

SARGENT, John, 55, 110; Nancy H., 215;
   Nathan, 55, 166; Reuben T., 215;
   William, 55
SAVELL, Deborah, 161
SAWYER, Benjamin, 109
SCALES, James, 166; Matthew, 166
SEARLE(S), Enos, 166
SEARS, Thomas, 110
SEAVEY, Molly, 107
SEELEY, Margaret J., 214
SHACKLEY, Huldah, 214
SHAW, Benoni, 164; Susannah, 108
SHEPARD, Hannah, 108
SHERBURNE, Sarah, 165
SHERIDAN, Henry, 55
SHERWOOD, Rebecca, 107
SHILLABER, Hannah, 56
SHIPPEE, MArgaret, 54
SHORES, Sally, 53
SIMPSON, Reuben, 213
SMALLEY, Mrs. Ellen J., 108
SMITH, Abigail, 105, 162; Amos, 105;
   Augustus Phineas, 107; Ebenezer,
   165; Edward, 162; Elizabeth, 214;
   Esdras, 214; Frederick, 107;
   Hannah, 105; Henry, 105; Henry J.,
   110; Job, 214; John, 105, 165;
   Joseph, 214; Mary, 165; Meriah, 105;
   Sarah, 105, 162
SOUTHWICK, William, 54
SPALDING, Josiah, 162
SPAULDING, Rhoda, 54; Sampson, 54
SPENCER, Mary, 109; Rebecca, 109;
   Roger, 109
SPRAGUE, Elizabeth (Turner), 106;
   Micah, 106
SPRING, Diana B., 166; Huldah, 166;
   William, 166
STANDISH, Alexander, 164; Ebenezer,
   164; Myles, 164; Zerviah, 108
STANLEY, Sands, 211
STETSON, Robert, 106
STEWARD, John, 163; Mary, 163
STONE, Benjamin F., 214; Hannah, 214
STRICKLAND, Allen, 105
STURTIVANT, Hannah, 164
SWEET, John, 162; Mary, 162; Susanna,
   162
SWETT, Jacob, 162; Mary, 107;
   Stephen, 107
SWIFT, Betsey, 106; Dean, 106;
   Elnathan, 106; Enoch, 106; Hasadiah,
   106; Mary, 106; Rebecca, 106; Rufus,
   106; Sarah, 106

TAPPAN, Sophia D., 215
TARBELL, Sally, 55
TAYLOR, Catherine, 161
THAYER, Jeremiah, 55; Richard, 213;
    Uriah, 55
TILLY, Deborah, 110; Hugh, 110; Rose,
    110; Samuel, 110
TODD, Abigail, 213; Betsey, 213;
    Elizabeth, 53; Jane, 213; Polly,
    213; Sally, 213; Samuel, 213
TOPPAN, Abigail, 53; John, 53
TORIQUE, Catherine, 211; Pasqual
    (Pierre), 212
TOURTELOTTE, Anne (Amy), 213
TRAIN, Huldah (Richards), 106
TRASK, John, 213; William, 213
TRIPP, Ada B., 55
TRUE, Benjamin, 109; Hannah, 109
TUCKER, Charity, 211; Elizabeth B.,
    106; John, 106
TUPPER, Abigail, 213
TURNER, Elizabeth, 106; Hannah, 107;
    William, 108
TUTTLE, James, 163
URIN, Eleanor, 164; John, 164

VAN PELT, Elinor, 164
VAN VALKENBURG, Francis, 54; Hannah,
    54
VEAZIE, Ann, 55
VEIZEI, Joseph, 55
VIALL, Mary, 55, 166; Nathaniel, 55,
    166
VICKERY, Knott, 105
VIGER, Anne, 110; Joseph, 110
VINING, Benjamin, 163

WALFORD, Thomas, 109; Mary, 109
WALKER, Martha, 165
WALTON, Joseiah, 54; Timothy, 54
WARREN, Jacob, 54, 162; Mary, 105;
    Sarah, 54, 162
WASHBURN, Elizabeth, 211; James, 161;
    Samuel, 161
WATERMAN, John, 164; Lydia, 164
WEARE, Christine, 52
WEAVER, Anna, 213
WELLS, Jonathan, 105
WESTCOTT, Abigail, 107; Daniel, 165;
    Joan, 107; Maria, 165; Mrs. Mary,
    165; Richard, 107
WESTON, Aaron, 53; Jonathan, 53;
    Mary (Molly), 52
WHEELER, Frances, 55, 109; Isaac, 55,
    109; Thomas, 55

WHEELOCK, Catherine, 106
WHEELWRIGHT, John, 163
WHITE, Anna, 213; Ebenezer, 107, 108;
    Penelope, 213; Samuel, 213;
    Susanna, 213
WHITING, Philander, 162
WILEY, Dorcas, 214
WILL, Harriet, 108; J. M., 108
WILLEY, Jane (Jennett), 54; Joseph,
    54; Margaret, 54
WILLIIAMS, Abigail, 213; Esther, 212;
    Mary, 105
WILSON, Jane, 52
WITCHER, Foxwell, 211
WITHAM, Joseph, 161
WITTAM, Peter, 212
WOOD, Daniel, 166; Joseph, 105;
    Thankful, 163
WOODBURY, Experience, 52; Frank, 215;
    Gladys E., 215; Grace M., 215;
    Hazel, 215; Helen Mae, 215;
    Joseph E., 215; Lillian Augusta,
    215; Ralph F., 215; Ruth M., 215;
    Samuel, 52, 105; Sarah, 105
WOODCOCK, Mary, 161
WORCESTER, Francis, 162; Samuel, 163
WORMWOOD, Ellen, 52
WORSLEY, Sarah, 166
WRIGHT, Aaron, 165, 166; Ann, 161;
    Joseph, 165; Justus, 166; William,
    161
WYATT, Mary, 54
WYMAN, Francis, 110; Love, 110;
    Lydia, 212; William, 110, 212

YORK, Joseph, 215; Patience, 110;
    Sarah, 215; Solomon, 212
YOUNG, Charles Franklin, 215; Daniel,
    215; Dorothy, 164; Franklin, 215;
    Matthew, 212; William, 212

LETTERS WRITTEN BY ISAIAH GRAVES FROM CALIFORNIA (continued from page 194)

San Francisco, Feb. 15, 1854
Dear Father, ... I thank you for your courteous letter in regard to keeping my business to myself. I never have informed anyone of my affairs. All the stories you may hear at home about me came from people that know nothing of my affairs. i have been here some time and have not been doing a great deal, and have invested some $1800 in potatoes, and as I have not been silent in regard to my affairs Lynn people here think I must have made a big pile of money. I feel very sorry that there are any stories of any kind about me at home, for I shall feel ashamed to come home now and be laughed at. ... Give my love to Aunt Mary, Grandfather and Grandmother and my respect to all my friends. It is very hard for me to tell when I shall return home. My health is very good.

Monteyuma Hill, Cal., July 12, 1954
Dear Father, ... I have been keeping a store here in the mountains since May last, as it is a new place I have not done much, the diggens are new and they are not fairly opened yet. It takes a great deal of labor to prospect the hills that contain gold...

San Francisco, Oct. 15, 1854
Dear Father, ... For the past year I have been losing money very fast, everything appears to go wrong that I take hold of. Last fall I speculated in potatoes until I sunk some $2000. I left for the mines in February last leaving some $2500 in the hands of H.A. Breed. I came down to San Francisco last week and found he had failed, leaving me without any security worth anything, and I can see no prospect of getting anything from him. I was very much to blame for trusting him after being warned by you, but he promised me faithfully that whatever might happen I should not lose anything by him. When I came down here last week I called on him and he would give me no satisfaction, he told me he had nothing, but if ever got able he would pay me. He had assigned over all his property and as there was nothing to get hold of I shall have to pocket the loss and make the most of it. I think he has some property in Lynn, I wish you would try and find out something about his affairs at home, and if there is anything to get hold of I will send his note home to you. He has his wife and the Col. here with him. I think he has covered up a good deal of property through them. I have some security on some land at Sacramento by which I may realize 25 cents on the dollar, that is all I can expect to get. ... I did expect to have been at home before this but I have had such bad luck that I can hardly say when I shall come. I want to hear from you very much...

Orleans Flat, Cal., Sept. 10, 1955
Dear Father, ... I am very sorry I disappointed you so much in not coming home this season. I can assure you that the disappointment has been greater to me than it could have been to you, for I am as anxious to return home again, and to see my friends as they can be to see me. You think my feelings must have changed since i left home, I feel grieved to think that you could have mistaken me so much, forgotten home and friends, no, I never could as long as my heart beats and memory lasts, when I forget you I shall cease to live.

* * * * * * * * * * * * * * * *

(Isaiah Graves finally returned home to Lynn, Mass. in 1856, seven years after leaving his native city. See page 191)

Compiled by Marilyn R. Fitzpatrick

Edited by Madelyn C. Liberti

ABANATHA
    Elizabeth, 144
ABBEY
    Joseph, 144
ABBOT
    ___, Dea., 119
    Samuel, 52
ABBOTT, 69
    ___, Dr., 187
    Arthur, 144
    Elizabeth (Gary), 24
    J.M., 196
    William, 24
ABORN, 69
    Carrie Helen (Nichols), 37
    Ebenezer, 102
    John Cushman, 37
    Margaret (Moulton), 102
ACEY
    Hannah (Green), 156
    John, 156
ADAMS
    Abigail, 5
    Abigail Smith, 5
    Elizabeth (Geary), 32
    Hannah, 5
    John, 65
    John Emery, Col, 99
    Jonathan, 32
    Relief, 75
    Samuel, 34
    Sara (Moody), 99
    Sarah Allen Plumer, 94
    William, 144
ADERAFT
    Wm. H., 198
AIREY
    Hazel Elizabeth, 8
AKERMAN
    Joseph Lord, 144
ALDEN
    John, 157
    Sarah, 164
ALDRICH
    Albert J., 109
    Elizabeth Amelia (Rivers), 109
ALEXANDER
    Charles L., 214
    Margaret, 204
    Margaret J. (Seeley), 214

ALFORD
    ___ (Gedney), 68
    Benjamin, 68
ALGER
    Horatio, 181
ALLE
    Sarah, 166
ALLEN, 99
    Andrew, 117
    Charity, 211
    Charles, 117
    E. E., 120
    E. W., 118, 120
    Effy, 211
    Ethan, 92, 211
    George, 117
    Hannah, 37
    Hannah (Gordon), 92
    Harriet N., 151
    Isaac, 151
    Jane, 42
    Joanna, 164
    John, 78
    John Gordon, 92
    Louvia Jennet (Frye), 92
    Mary (Fairbanks), 24
    Mary Egery, 92
    Nancy M. (Crane), 92
    Rachel, 49
    Rebecca (Green), 211
    Robert, 117
    Sarah, 54, 214
    Sarah Ann (Blaisdell), 151
    Susanna, 205
    Thomas, 164
    Walter, 117
    William, 117
    William Sylvester, 92
    William, Jr., 92
    William, Lt., 211
    Zilpha (Gilbert), 92
ALLEY/ALLY/ALLEE, 99
    Anna, 133
    Anna (Tarbox), 136
    Caleb B., 133
    Catherine, 133
    Charles Otis, 152
    Daniel, 133
    Dorcas (Wiley), 214
    Elizabeth Chase (Huse), 152
    George Warren, 136

Hannah, 133
Hugh, 144
John, 133
John B., 133
Jonathan, 133
Joseph, 152
Joseph, Jr., 136
Josiah Otis, 152
Lotta, 152
Lucy Backman (Knowles), 152
Mary, 214
Mary (Alley), 214
Mary Ann, 136
Mary Ann Coleman, 143
Mary Ann Coleman Orne, 142
Mary B., 133
Mercy (Buffum), 133
Micajah, 214
Nancy G. (___), 152
Nathan, 214
Peace B., 133
Rebecca (Haskell), 142
Samuel, 142
Sarah, 133
ALLIS
    Frederick S., Jr., 138
ALLYN See ALLEN
AMES
    Nathan, 119
    Oakes, 186
AMMIDON
    M., 196
AMORAGE
    George, 184
ANDERSON
    C. F., 198
    Clara, 165
    Isaac, 165
    Jonathan, 165
    Marion, 90
    Mary (___), 165
    William, 165
ANDREWS See also ANDROS
    Amos, 144
    C., 197
    J. E., 198
    John, 144
    Rebecca (Cole), 55, 109
    Robert, 144
    Thomas, 55, 109

ANDROS/ANDROSS
Margaret, 54
Mark, 144
ANNABLE
John, 144
ANTHONY
John, 52
Susanna (Potter), 52
ANTHROM
Thomas, 11
APLETON
Samuel, 121
APPLE JOHN, 73
APPLETON
B., 119-120
Samuel, 138, 144
Samuel, Jr., 138
Samuel, Maj., 138
ARCHAMBEAU
Catherine, 211
Catherine (Torique), 211-212
Joseph, 211
ARCHIBALD
Mary (Hendestead), 205
ARMITAGE
Joseph, 121
ARMSTRONG
Elsie, 151
Isaac, 151
Nellie (___), 151
ARNOLD
Christian (Peake), 162
Dorcas, 54, 162
Sarah (Smith), 162
Stephen, 162
William, 162
ASH
Sarah, 108
ASTOR
John Jacob, 59
ATKINSON
Harriet C., 36
Sarah, 78
ATTWELL, 192
Amos, 193
Amos M., 191
Eugene, 193
Eugene B., 191
ATTWILL See also ATWILL
Annie Louise, 37
Benjamin E., 133
Harriet Elizabeth, 37
Isaac Meade, 37

ATWILL
Alfred, 133
Betsy F., 133
Edwin, 133
Gustavus, 133
Jacob W., 133
John D., 133
Joseph, 133
Martha, 133
Martha (Ingalls), 133
Mary, 133
Nelson R., 133
Richard J., 133
William A., 133
ATWOOD
____, Mrs., 119
AUSTIN
Ann, 3, 5
Elizabeth, 125
Jane (Canney), 125
Mary, 126
Matthew, 125
AVERELL
Charles, 144
AVERILL
David, Jr., 42
Mary M. (Lee), 42
Sarah, 207
Susan, 41
AYERS
John, 144
Olive, 127
AYRES See AYERS

BABB
Isaac, 128
Lucinder (Leighton), 128
Margaret Hannah, 127
BABCOCK
Henry, 110
Sarah (Fisk), 110
BABSON
Abigail, 93
Eleanor (Hill), 129
Eunice, 129
Isabella (___), 129
James, 129
John J., 17
Martha, 21, 82
Mary (Dolliver), 129
Richard, 129
BACHELLER
Mary (Geary), 32
Nathaniel, 32

BACHELOR
Samuel, 119
BACHILER
Ann (Bates), 52
Christian (Weare), 52
Helen (___), 52
Hester (Mercer), 109
Mary Magdelane (Beedle), 52
Nathaniel, 109
Stephen, Rev., 52, 109
BACON
Elizabeth, 161
BAILEY
___, Dea., 162
Amos, 144
Benjamin Webster, 162
Betsy, 38
Dudley, 162
E., 196
Elizabeth (Williams), 153
George M., 93
Iddo, 153
James Iddo, 153
Jessie Helen (Sprague), 93
Margaret Ann (Hurley), 93
Margaret Joy, 92
Mary, 39
Mary (___), 154
Norman Sprague, 92
Talitha, 153
William, 120
BAKER, 103
___, Mr., 121
Abigail, 49
Abigail (Sallows), 49
Bethiah, 49
Cornelius, 49
Deborah (Morgan), 49
Edward, 131
Elizabeth, 131-132
Hannah, 49
Hannah (Woodbury), 49
Jabez, 49
John, 49, 121, 144
Jonathan, 49
Mary, 75, 105
Mary (Trask), 49
Nelson M., 131
Priscilla, 49
Rachel (Allen), 49
Robert, 49
Samuel, 49
Sarah, 125

BALCH
Benjamin, 144
Cornelius, 144
Daniel, 119
David 3rd, 144
Mary (Trask), 49
Samuel Jr., 49
BALDWIN, 99
___, Mrs., 119
D. S., 196
John, 198
BALLATT
S., 25
BALTIMORE
Lord, 4
BANCKES
Richard, 24
BANCROFT
Elizabeth (Geary), 30
Timothy, 30
BANKS, 171
Charles, 26
Edward, 23
BARBER
Mary/Polly, 107
William, 144
BARKER
Charlotte (Nutting), 143
Charlotte (___), 142
George, 142
Geroge F., 143
Mabelle C., 142-143
Robert, 144
BARNES
Jemima, 92
R., 198
Susan, 92
BARRETT
Hannah (Merrill), 165
James, 101
Lemuel, 165
BARRINGTON
Laurence W. L., Mrs., 3
BARROWS
Sidney Biddle, 59
BARTHOLOMEW
___, Mr., 120
BARTLETT
David, 164
Dorothy (Young), 164
F., 196
Joseph, 53
Mary (Currier), 53
Melinda, 77

Richard, 164
Tirzah, 52
BARTON
John, 157
Rebecca, 35
Ruth, 93
BASSETT
Joseph, 71
BATCHELDER See BACHILER
BATCHELOR See BACHILER
BATES
Ann, 52
Clement H., 170
Isabel, 35
John, 170
Sarah, 35
BATT
Thomas, 144
BATTEL
A. J., 196
BATTER
Edward, 68
BAXTER
Jennie, 94
R., 198
BAYLEY
C. W., 197
BEAL
Celia, 38
E. C., 120
Elisha, 39
Lydia (Tower), 39
BEALL
Ann Maria (Stricker), 95
Mary, 95
Ninian, 95
BEAN, 171
BEARD
Timothy Field, 59, 66
BEAUDOIN
Domithilde, 204
BEAUVAIS
A. B., 200
BECKFORD
Benjamin, 144
BEEDLE
Mary Magdelane, 52
BEERS
Caroline, 203
Sarah, 42
BELCHER
Abigail, 29
Celia (Beal), 38
Elijah, 107

Elijah Jr., 39
Emma Whitford (Putnam), 38
Lucy (Newcomb), 39
Lydia (Lord), 38
Mary (Pierce), 107
Pearl Frances, 38
William, 38
William Francis, 38
BELL
Isaac, 52
Nancy, 52
Phoebe, 151
Sophia (Gunterman), 52
Zephenian, 52
BENCHLEY, 116
BENNETT
David, Dr., 109
G., 196
Rebecca (Spencer), 109
BENSON
Mary Sumner, 6
BENTON
J. A., Rev., 183
BENWAR
C., 197
BERRY
Elizabeth, 126
Susah, 39
BERTRAND
Felicite, 80
Julyia, 80
BIEHN, 171
BILES
Jonathan, 13
Margaret (Corey), 13
Mary, 35
BILL
Benjamin, 36
Tabitha (Nichols), 36
BIRD
Ann, 92
Sarah, 170
BIRDSALL, 170
BIRNEY
Lawrence, 85
BISHOP
Ann (Douglas), 24
Ann (Kenney), 110
Bridget, 15
Elizabeth, 205
Elizabeth (Grandy), 205
John, 110
Levi, 205
Lydia, 110

Paul, 118
Thomas, 24
BLACK, 171
Daniel, 144
BLACKBURN
J., 200
BLAISDELL
Sarah Ann, 151
BLAKE
Almira, 214
Anna, 214
Deborah (Dalton), 109
Eunice, 214
Ezra, 214
Hannah, 214
Jasper, 109
John, 214
Jonathan, 214
William, 214
Zacharia, 214
BLANCHARD
Lavina, 135
BLANCPAIN, 171
BLANEY
John, 144
BLASHFIELD
Henry, 105
Mary (Morgan), 105
Mercy, 105
BLASS
F. E., 196
BLOOD
C., 196
BOARDMAN
B. G., 120
Dan, 144
Thomas, 120, 144
William, 119-120
BODEN
Mary, 39
BODGE
Hannah, 127
BOGART
Clara (Anderson), 165
BOHAN
P., 199
BOLAND
Ann, 87
BOLDUC
Antoine, 203
Arthur Joseph, Sr., 203
Constance Lea, 203
Lea (Cantin), 203
Lucille (Cote), 203

Mabel Constance (Rogan), 203
Marcel, 203
Marie (Tremblay), 203
Raoul, 203
BOLT
Henry, 119
BOLTON
Thomas, 71
BOND
W., 199
BONNEY
O., 196
BOODEN
Abashaba, 42
BOOLS
Joseph, 144
BOREMAN
Mary, 129
BOSWORTH
Helen P., 72
BOURMAN See BOARDMAN
BOURNE
Elizabeth (Holmes), 163
Thomas, 163
BOUTWELL
Ruth, 33
BOVEE
Elizabeth, 54, 162
BOWELS see BOOLS
BOWEN
Elizabeth, 87
John, 198
Patrick, 87
BOWLEY
Betsey, 203
BOWMAN
Alan P., 195
BOWREMAN
Thomas, 144
BOYLAN See also BOYLAND
Catherine, 151
BOYLAND
Catherine (Burns), 152
Mary (Clancy), 152
Michael, 152
Patrick, 152
BOYNTON
Asa, 79-80
Asa, Sr., 79
Betsey (Wheeler), 80
Carrie, 80
Charles C., 80
Cynthia, 80
Eliza J. (Cadot), 80

Felicite (Bertrand), 80
Helen (Pell), 79
Henry, 80
James, 80
Jane Ann, 80
John, 79
John L., 80
Joseph Capt., 79
Joseph E., 80
Julyia (Bertrand), 80
Lucy, 80
Lydia, 80
Margaret (Feurt), 80
Mary, 80
Mary (Edmunds), 79-80
Mary (Stewart), 79
Nancy (Feurt), 80
Nathaniel, 79
Orin, 80
Peter, 80
Peter Feurt, 80
Rhoda (Sumner), 80
Richard, Sgt., 79
Sarah (Dressler), 79
Sarah (Swan), 79
Urania (Bush), 80
William, 80
William L., 80
BRACKETT
Love, 212
Lydia, 212
Lydia (Marston), 212
Samuel, 212
BRADBURY
Hannah, 119
Jane, 130
Mary (Perkins), 130
Sarah, 130
Sarah (Pike), 130
Thomas, Capt., 130
Wymond, 130
BRADFORD
Deborah, 50
William, 16
Wm., 196
BRADSTREET
___, Dr., 119
Ann, 16, 138
Anne, 5
Simon, 138, 144
BRAGG
Edward, 144
Sally (Shores), 53
William, 53

BRAINERD
    Laurence, 24, 26
BRAINES
    Thomas, 24
BRAMAN
    Amasa, 106
    Amasa, Dr., 106
    Mary Polly (Brigham), 106
BRANT
    Ida C., 93
BRAY
    Abigail, 95, 129
    Dorothy/Dolly R., 94
    Eleanor (Dodge), 129
    Mary (Collins), 129
    Mary (Emerson), 212
    Mary (Wilson), 129-130
    Sarah, 130
    Thomas, 129-130, 212
    Thomas, Dr., 129
BREED, 85
    A. B., 86
    Allen, 55
    Elizabeth, 55
    H. A., 222
    Keezia, 134
    Mary, 211
    Warren Mudge, 179
BREEN
    Caroline (McGlaughlin), 93
    Helen, 87, 137, 178
    Helen Gallagher, 85
    James, 93
BRENT
    Margaret, 4-5
BREWER
    Elizabeth, 130
    Nellie, 54
    Ophelia, 151
    Peter, 130
BREWRE
    James, 71
BREWSTER
    William, 16, 59, 61, 209
BRIANT
    James, 191
BRIDE
    R., 197
BRIDGES
    ___, Capt., 121
    F. M., 196
    Sarah, 161
BRIGGS
    E. A., 196

S. A., 196
BRIGHAM
    Mary Polly, 106
    Mehitabel (Grout), 106
    Moses, 106
    Phoebe, 95
BRIMHALL, 198
BRITE
    Mary, 11, 13
BROCKLEBANK
    Samuel, 144
BROOKIN/BROOKING
    Mary (Walford), 109
    William, 109
BROOKS
    Geraldine, 6
    Mehitable, 163
BROOM
    Persis (Chapman), 73
    William, 73
BROWN, 69
    Abigail, 161
    Alice M., 192
    Betsey, 53
    Clarence Donald, 151
    Clarence Revere, 151
    Dorothy, 76
    E. Ebenezer, 212
    Ebenezer, 109
    Edward, 144
    Elizabeth, 40, 79
    Gail L., 151
    George Washington, 151
    H., 197
    Hannah (True), 109
    Henry, 76
    J., 196
    J. D., 196
    Jeremiah, 144
    Joan L. (Gardner), 151
    John, 71, 144
    Jonothan, 212
    Joseph, 212
    Josiah, 162
    Katharine, 29
    Loraine M. (Westfall), 151
    Mariam, 52
    Martha, 130
    Martha (Martin), 75
    Mary, 165
    Mary E., 137
    Mehitable, 92, 127
    Nathan, 144
    Phoebe (Bell), 151

Polly, 162
Ruth, 212
Ruth (___), 212
Samuel, 120, 212
Sarah, 212
Sarah (Martin), 76
Seth Ingersoll, 71
Sobriety (Moulton), 109
Thomas, 75, 109
Thomas Jr., 212
Thomas Sr., 212
W. H., 197
BROWN/BROWNE
    Chad Rev, 117
    Edward, 117
    James, 117
    John, 117
    Thomas, 117
BROWNE
    Sarah, 162
BROWNING
    Daniel, 109
    Malachi, 109
    Mary (Collier), 109
    Susannah, 109
BRUCE
    Chs., 196
    Samuel, 69
    W., 196
BRUER See BREWER
BRUNSON
    J., 197
BRYNER
    John, 199
BUBIER
    ___, Mayor, 191
BUCKNAM
    Anna, 33
    Wilmot F., 26
    Wilton F., 23
BUFFINGTON
    James, 144
BUFFUM
    Mercy, 133
BUGBEE
    Sarah (Canney), 122
BULKELEY
    Frances, 42
    Peter, 42
    Peter, Rev., 42
    Rebecca (Wheeler), 42
BULLOCK
    Elizabeth, 90
    Henry, 90

John, 90-91
Mary, 90-91
Mary (Maverick), 90
BURBANK
E. L., 196
Elijah, 106
Elizabeth (Gibbs), 106
BURDITT
Elizabeth, 35-36
BURKE, 171
Edward D., 20
BURNAP
Ann/Agnes (Miller), 162
Robert, 162
Sarah (Browne), 162
BURNHAM
Daniel, 120
Eunice, 75
John, 144
Noah, 144
Robert, 144
Soloman, 144
William, 144
BURNS
Ann (Conley), 152
Catherine, 152
Thomas, 152
BURR
Esther Edwards, 5
BURRELL
Anna, 163
BURRILL
Alden, 131-132
Elizabeth (Baker), 131-132
Elizabeth (Baker), 132
Esther Foss, 162
Hannah (___), 162
Josiah, 162
Shubel/Shubael, 131-132
BURROUGHS, 164
George, Rev., 15
Hannah (Van Valkenburg), 54
John, 54
Sarah (Johnson), 164
BURT
J. P., 196
Rebecca, 41
W. A., 198
BURTON
Abigail (Moulton), 102
John, 102
Margaret (French), 213
Simon, 213

BUSH
C., 197
Urania, 80
BUSHEY
Angelette, 53
BUSSELL, 25
BUTCHER
Elizabeth, 129
BUTLER
Daniel, 212
John, 212
Margaret (___), 212
Ruth (___), 212
William, 144
BUTTS
Mary, 162
BUXTON
Anthony, 11, 144
BYAM
Mary, 81-82
BYLES
Anna, 129
Elizabeth (Patch), 129
Jonathan, 129
Priscilla (Morgan), 129
William, 129
BYROM
Sarah Elizabeth (Sanders), 108
W., 108

CADOT
Claudius, 80
Eliza J., 80
CADWALADER
John, Gen., 172-173
Lambert Col., 173
Maria, 173
Sarah, 172-173
Tom, Maj. Gen., 173
CADY
Honora, 109
CALDWELL
Aaron, 144
Abigail (Bray), 129
John, 129
Lydia (Lull), 129
Sarah, 129
Sarah (Dillingham), 129
Sarah (Foster), 129
William, 129
CALHOUN
R., 199
Samuel, 199
Wm. B., 199

CALVERT
Leonard, Gov., 4
CALWELL
Dan, 138
CALY
Sarah, 129
CAMERON
Isabella, 50
Sarah, 50
CAMP
Elisha Dr., 77
Keziah (Durkee), 77
CAMPBELL
Elizabeth (Murray), 4
Nicholas, 71
Thomas, 4
CANIE See CANNEY
CANNE See CANNEY
CANNEY
Aaron, 127
Abigail (Tibbetts), 127
Almira. E. (Frazier), 127
Anne, 126
Betsey (Foss), 127
Betsy Ann (Tirrell), 127
Charles, 127
Charles E., 127
Cynthia A. (Huntoon), 128
Daniel, 126
Deborah, 126
Deborah (Nutter), 127
Deborah (Stokes), 126
Elizabeth, 124, 207
Elizabeth (Berry), 126
Elizabeth (Cator), 127-128
Elizabeth (Woodhouse), 127
Elizabeth C. (Kimball), 127
Emma (Edes), 127
Francis S., 127
George F., 127
Grace (Hartford), 125
Grace H. (Frost), 128
Hannah, 125
Hannah (Bodge), 127
Hannah (Sawyer), 126
Hannah C. (Hanson), 127
Hanora Helen (Haskell), 122
Henry, 207
Hulda (Stanyan), 126
Ichabod, 126
Isaac, 126-128
Jacob, 127
James, 126
James M., 122

Jane, 124-125
Jane (___), 125
John, 124, 126-127
John L., 122
John W., 128
Joseph, 125
Lydia, 125
Lydia O. (Sherburne), 122-123
Lyman, 128
Margaret E. (Caswell), 127
Margaret Hannah (Babb), 127
Martha, 125
Mary, 125
Mary (Clements), 125
Mary (Dam), 125
Mary (Loome), 124
Mary (Tuttle), 126
Mary (___), 125
Moses, 123, 126-127
Nancy T. (Demeritt), 127
Nicholas, 124
Olive (Ayers), 127
Olive S., 128
Phebe, 125
Rebecca (Otis), 126
Richard, 125-126
Robert S., 207
Robert Sayward, 122
Samuel, 125, 127
Sarah, 122, 125-127
Sarah (Daniels), 126-127
Sarah (Hackett) Rankin, 125
Sarah (Hanson), 126
Sarah (Nelson), 126
Sarah (Taylor), 125-126
Sarah (___), 127
Sarah J. (Jenness), 126
Susan Frances (Sargent), 127
Susanna, 126-127
Susanna (Perkins), 127
Susanna (Stanyan), 126
Thomas, 122-126
CANNY See CANNEY
CANTIN
Augustin, 203
Domithilde (Beaudoin), 204
Elizabeth Adeline (Leclerc), 203
Joseph, 203
Lea, 203
CAPRON
Sarah, 41
CAREW
S., 196

CARGILL
Daniel, 54, 162
Dorcas (Arnold), 54, 162
Electa (Rockwell), 162
Elizabeth (Bovee), 54, 162
James, 54, 162
Preston, 162
CARPENTER, 171
G. A., 199
Keziah, 95
Priscilla, 161
CARR
Ann, 164
E. I., 53
George, 53, 164
CARRIER
Martha, 15
CARTER
Charity, 53
Edward, 164
Elizabeth, 164
J. M., 199
Jane, 164-165
Lucretia, 164
Mary, 164
Mary (___), 164
Michael, 164
Phebe, 109
Sarah, 164
Thomas, 164
CARVER
Roger, 24
CASPAR
Elizabeth, 153
CASSADY
James, 198
CASTLEBERG, 198
CASWELL, 103
Margaret E., 127
CATOR
Elizabeth, 127-128
John, 127
Mary (Gorver), 127
CATTER
N., 119
CAVANAGH, 102
CAVIS
J. M., 196
CENNEY See CANNEY
CHADBOURNE, 99
CHADDUCK
John, 121
CHADWELL
Elizabeth, 136

Harris, 35-36
Lydia, 35-37
Ruth, 35-36
CHAFEE
F. A., 199
CHAFFE
Hannah, 77
CHAMBERLAIN
Betsey (Grant), 206
Eliza, 205
Experience (___), 109
J. P., 199
Jacob, 109
John, 161
Rebecca (___), 109
Rodolphus, 205
Sarah (Bridges), 161
William, 109
CHAMBERLIN
Elizabeth, 55
CHAMPION
Deborah, 5
CHANDLER
W. C., 86
CHAPLIN
Duncan, III, 95
CHAPMAN
Albion, 144
Amos, 144
Benjamin, 144
David, 144
Dudley, 144
Duncan, 144
Ebenezer, 144
Edward, 72, 144
Elizabeth, 72
Elizabeth (Simons), 72
Ephraim, 144
Horace, 144
Howard V., 144
Ichabod, 144
Joan, 129
John, 72, 144
Josiah, 144
Leeman, 144
Lucy (Cooley), 72
Martha (Perley), 72
Mary (___), 72
Michael, 144
Nathaniel, 72, 144
Persis, 73
Ralph, 144
Samuel, 144
Symon, 144

Washington, 144
William, 144
CHAPPLEMAN
Michael, 144
CHARDER
Mary, 211
CHASE
Judith, 55
R. C., 197
Thomas, 71
CHEEVER
Sarah, 95
CHENEY
Martha, 164
Mary, 162
CHIARELLO
Marion (Ryker), 40
CHICKERING
John, 119
CHIELDS
G., 198
CHOATE
Abraham, 153
Mary/Polly W., 152
Sarah, 204
Sarah (Potter), 153
CHRISTOPHER
Collins Jackson, 204
Joseiah, 204
Margaret (Alexander), 204
Orinda, 204
Orinda (Stevens), 204
CHUBBUCK
Martha, 163
CHURCH
Ambrose, 91
E. S., 196
H., 198
Joshua, 101
Keziah (Goss), 101
L., 196
CHURCHILL
Benjamin, 163
Hannah (Pontus), 163
John, 163
Thankful (Wood), 163
CHUTE
James, 144
CLAFLIN/CLAFLEN
Adelaide, 94
Ann Tyler (Thacher), 94
Eliza Fertig (Scott), 94
Hannah (Richardson), 95
Harvey, 94

Harvey Thacher, 94
Keziah (Carpenter), 95
Noah, 2d, 95
Noah 3rd, 95
CLAGGETT
Lettice (Mitchell), 105
Rebecca, 105
Sara (Morrill), 105
William Rev., 105
Wyseman, 105
CLANCY
Mary, 152
CLAPP
Gosham, 199
CLARK
Abigail, 105
Abraham, 126
Albert Center, 93
Anna (___), 126
Benjamin, 71
Catherine, 204
Elizabeth Wood (Marr), 93
Emily, 37
Enock, 127
Gorham, 94
Hannah (Kingsbury), 204
Ichabod, 165
Jane, 109
Laura Brown (Douglass), 93
Lewis, 204
Lucee, 76
Martha, 24
Mary, 126
Moses, 119
P., 199
Redigon, 212
Sarah, 207
Sarah Allen Plumer (Adams), 94
Susanna (Canney), 127
W. J., 197
William Biship, 93
CLARKE
Daniel, 144
Joseph, 37
Sarah Ann, 37
CLARY
George M., 80
Urania (Bush), 80
CLAY
Molly, 40
Rachel (Pennell), 107
Richard, 107
CLAYTON
Charles D., 162

Laura B., 162
Mary, 162
Mary (___), 162
Mary H., 162
CLEAVES
Anna, 92
Benjamin, 13
Ebenezer, 13
Eleanor, 13
Hannah, 13
John, 13
Margaret (Corey), 13
Martha, 13
Martha (Corey), 13
Rebeckar (Conant), 13
Robert, 13
William, 13, 102
CLEMENT
Allen B., 151
Charlotte (___), 151
Elsie (Armstrong), 151
Harriet N. (Allen), 151
Louise M., 151
Phillip G., 151
Phillip Henry Bartlett, 151
Samuel, 119
Sarah, 130
CLEMENTS
Counsellor Job, 125
Margaret (Dummer), 125
Mary, 125
CLINTON
Lawrence, 144
CLOTHIER
Samuel, 120
CLOUGH
Abia (Tomson), 130
Caleb, 130
Elbridge G., 106
Elizabeth, 130
Elizabeth B. (Tucker), 106
Florence M., 106
George W., 106
Henry, 106
Henry C., 106
Isaac H., 106
James Jr., 106
James S., 106
Jane, 166
Jane (___), 130
John, 130
John T., 106
Lydia, 106
Mercy (Page), 130

Sarah, 130
Sarah E., 106
Susan J., 106
Susanna (Palmer), 106
Susanne P., 106
Thomas, 106
COATES
John, 144
COBURN
A. W., 197
G. D., 197
Stephen, 144
COCHRAN
John, 157
COCKERILL
Hannah, 129
CODDINGTON
John Insley, 169
COE
Ebenezer, Lt., 95
Elizabeth, 95
Eunice (Jaggers/Jagger), 95
COFFLEY
Agney, 166
COGSWELL
James, 59
COIT
Abigail, 129
John, 129
Mary (Ganners), 129
Mary (Stevens), 129
COKER
Mary (Moody), 52
Robert, 52
COLBY
F., 196
John, 119
Sarah, 108
Sarah (Ash), 108
COLDOM
Elizabeth, 10
COLE
Job, 74
Moses, 119
Rebecca, 55, 109, 164
COLLIER
Jane (Clark), 109
Mary, 109
William, 109
COLLINGWOOD
G., 197
COLLINS
Francis, 129
George, 198

Hannah (Cockerill), 129
Mary, 129
Mary P., 81
COLMAN
Thos., 199
COLSON
Adam, 71
M. A., 200
W. P., 197
CONANT
Rebeckar, 13
CONLEY
Ann, 152
Mary, 137-138, 152
CONNER
Anna (Evans), 213
Benjamin, 213
Jemima (___), 213
Joseph, 213
Susanna, 162
Thankful Ingalls Weeks (Locks),
213
CONNIFF
Alice Elizabeth, 151
Anne (Quinn), 151
John, 151-152
Peter, 152
Sarah (Shaughnessy), 152
CONNORS
Ann, 108
Mary Ellen, 108
COOK
Frances (___), 109
Hannah, 54
Humphrey, 120
James, 105
Lewis D., 169
Mary (Williams), 105
Richard, 109
Thomas, 120
Z., 120
COOKE
Henry, 144
John, 11
Rachell (Varney), 121
Thomas, 120-121
COOLEY, 99
Lucy, 72
COOLIDGE
Jonathan, 118
S., 71
COOMBS
Martha (Walker), 165
Sylvanus, 165

COOPER
Ann, 161
John, 161
Mary, 5
Priscilla (Carpenter), 161
COPELAND, 69
COREE see COREY
COREY/CORY
Deliverance, 13
Elizabeth, 13, 102
Giles, 11-15, 102
Margaret, 13
Margaret (___), 11, 13
Martha, 12-13
Martha (___), 11, 13
Mary, 13
Mary (Brite), 11, 13
Martha, 15
CORRY/CORY See COREY
CORWIN
Jonathan, 12
CORY See COREY
COSTIGAN
Olive (Hurd), 42
Thankful W., 41
William, 42
COTE
Lucille, 203
COTTON, 116, 211
Lydia Minerva (Frost), 211
COURTNEY
Thomas, 8
COVINGTON
L., 197
COWAN
J. H., 197
COWLES
J. P., Rev., 141
COX, 85
Benjamin, Jr., 181
J., 198
Jane (Carter), 164
Philip, 164
COY
Elizabeth, 76
CRAM
Rachel, 38
CRANE
John, 71, 92
Nancy M., 92
Silas, 144
Susan (Poland), 92
CRATHORNE
Jonathan, 3

Mary (___), 3
CREEL
    Elizabeth, 52
CRISPIN
    Wm., 199
CROCKER
    A. S., 199
CROCKETT
    Abraham, 164
    Davy, 124
    Eleanor (Urin), 164
CROMWELL
    Oliver, 174
    Thomas, 174
CROSBY
    Deliverance (Corey), 13, 102
    E. M., 199
    Henry, 13, 102
CROSS
    Mary, 110
    Robert, 144
CROSSE
    Mary Fisher, 5
CROSSETT
    Isa, 106
CROWLEY
    Thomas, 125
CROWNINSHIED, 172
CUE
    Robert, 144
CULLING
    C. C., 198
CUMING
    Anne, 4
    Betsy, 4
CUMMINGS
    Mary, 55, 110
CUNNINGHAM
    James, 184
    Rebecca A., 108
CURRAN
    Mary, 203
CURRIER
    Abigail (Toppan), 53
    Ann (Poor), 164
    Diamond, 164
    Eleanor (Urin), 164
    Elizabeth (Todd), 53
    Esther (Henderson), 164
    J. J., 53
    John, 164
    John, Capt., 53
    Joseph, 53
    Joshua, 164

Judith (Pressey), 53
Mary, 53
Mary (Poor), 53
William, 53
CURTAIN
    J., 197
CURTIS
    Hannah, 24
    John, 162
    Mary (___), 162
    Sarah, 162, 166
    Stoddard, 144
    William, 144
CURWIN See also CORWIN
    ___, Mr., 11
CUSHING
    A., 197
CUSHMAN
    C. C., 198
    G. H., 197
CUTTER
    William Richard, 25-26
CUTTING
    C., 198
    D., 198
    John, Capt., 166
    Mary, 163
    Mary (___), 166

DAESSY
    M., 198
DAGGETT
    Joseph, 145
DAGLE
    J., 197
DALAND
    Phillip, 145
DALEY
    F., 196
    J., 198
    Lucy, 71
    T., 196
DALLIN See DARLING
DALTON
    Deborah, 109
    H. N., 199
    Philemon, 163
DAM
    Elizabeth (Pomfret), 125
    John, Dea., 125
    Mary, 125
DAME
    Mary, 127

DAMON
    Elizabeth, 29-30, 32-33
    Lucy Ann (Emerson), 30
    Mary, 32
    Samuel, 145
    Thomas, 30
DAMPATCHER
    J., 196
DANE
    Abiah (Harris), 211
    Abigail (___), 211
    Daniel Harris, 211
    Hannah, 21, 83
    John, 145
    Lemuel, 211
    Mary Dean, 141
    Mary E. (Hamer), 211
    Nancy, 211
DANFORTH
    Persis, 32
DANIELS
    Charity (___), 126
    Jacob, 126
    Sarah, 126-127
DANVIS
    Robt., 198
DARBY
    Hannah (Geary), 31-32
DARLING, 53
    Ann Elizabeth, 142
    Bessie May, 142-143
    Christopher, 145
    Edward Christopher, 142-143
    Edward Lee, 142-143
    Emeline Lee, 142
    Emma M. (Fewkes), 143
    Emma Matilda (Fewkes), 142
    Francis Turner, 142
    Lois Maria, 142
    Louise Mariah, 142
    Mabelle C. (Barker), 142-143
    Margaret Ellen, 142
    Mary Ann (Keezer), 110
    Mary Ann Coleman (Alley), 143
    Mary Ann Coleman Orne (Alley),
        142
    Michael C., 142
    Michael Christopher, 143
    Sally (Lee), 142-143
    William, 110
DARRAGH
    Lydia (___), 4
    Lydia Barrington, 5

DOANE
    Gilbert H., Dr., 170
DODD
    Elizabeth, 214
DODGE
    Barnabas, 145
    Barnabus, Capt., 8
    Edith (___), 129
    Edward, 129
    Eleanor, 129
    Elizabeth, 108
    Ezekial, 145
    George, 145
    Isaac, 145
    John, 129, 145
    Jonathan, Jr., 145
    Joshua, 145
    Mary (Haskell), 129
    Mary (___), 129
    Mary Ann, 215
    Peter, 145
    Pickering, 140
    Richard, 129, 145
    Thomas, 119
DOGGETT See DAGGETT
DOLE
    D. N., 119
    E., 119
    S., 119
DOLIBER
    Donald, 177
    Samuel, 71
DOLLIVAN
    William, 84
DOLLIVER See also DAYLBER
    Mary, 129
    Mary (Elwell), 129
    Samuel, 129
DOOR
    Betsy, 39
DORE
    James, Jr., 165
    Lydia (___), 165
DORMAN
    John Frederick, 174
DORR
    B. Dalton, 163
DOUGHTY
    James, 212
    Mary (Robinson), 212
DOUGLAS
    Ann, 24
DOUGLASS
    John, 93-94

    Laura Brown, 93
    Margaret (Pushee), 94
    Nancy (Norwood), 94
DOVOVAN
    Julia, 93
DOW
    Henry, 145
    Wm., 198
DOWLING
    James, 199
DOWNER
    Mary, 110
DOWNES
    Mary Ann, 39
    Massey, 54
DOWNEY
    Honora (Cady), 109
    Patrick, 109
    Thomas J., 109
DOYEL
    P. H., 198
DRESSER
    B., 198
DRESSLER
    Sarah, 79
DREW
    Betsey (Rose), 106
    Charles, 106
    Malvina, 128
DRISCOLL
    ___, Mr., 86
DUBESTER
    Henry J., 116
DUCHOW
    J. C., 196
    W., 196
DUDLEY
    Elizabeth (___), 163
    Samuel, 163
    Thomas, 138, 145
    Thomas, Gov., 16, 163
DUMMER
    Margaret, 125
DUN
    T., 196
DUNHAM
    Abial, Capt., 95
    Mahetabel (Knapp), 95
    Salona, 95
DUNKS
    Amelia, 106
DUNN
    P., 197
DURANT, 185

DUREY
    Ann, 138
DURHAM
    Caroline (Sanders), 108
    William N., 108
DURKEE
    Abigail (Durkee), 75
    Alba, 77
    Alonzo Martin, 77
    Annah, 77
    Arba, 77
    Benjamin, 75-77
    Benjamin, Capt., 75
    Catherine (McRae), 77
    Chloe, 76
    David Martin, 76
    Ebenezer, 76
    Eliphalet, 75
    Eliphalet, Jr., 76
    Eliphalet, Sr., 76
    Elizabeth, 74-76
    Elizabeth (Lord/Ford), 50
    Elizabeth (Martin), 75-76
    Erastus, 77
    Hannah (Chaffe), 77
    Henry, 75
    Jane, 74-76
    Jerusha, 74
    Jerusha, 75-76
    Keziah, 77
    Keziah (Martin), 75, 77
    Lora, 77
    Lora (Martin), 75-77
    Lorenzo Martin, 77
    Lucy (Warner), 77
    Mary, 77
    Mary (Baker), 75
    Mary Almira, 77
    Melinda (___), 77
    Mercy, 74-75
    Miranda (Spencer), 76
    Nathaniel, 75, 77
    Rebecca (Gould), 74
    Relief (Adams), 75
    Rhoda (Mott), 77
    Samuel, 77
    Sarah, 74-76
    Thomas, 50
    Thomas, 75
    Wiliam, 50
    William, Jr., 74-75
DUSTIN
    Hannah, 5
    Lydia, 15

DWINELL See DWONILL
DWONILL, 145
DYER
    Elizabeth (Nichols), 36
    Jane (Carter), 165
    Joseph, 36
    Michael, 165

EASTY/ESTY
    Mary, 15
EAMES
    Maria, 215
    Nancy H., 215
EARLE
    Alice Morse, 6
EASTMAN
    Calvin, 113
    Mary (Smith), 113
EATON
    Benjamin, 130
    Betsey, 31
    Elizabeth (Geary), 31
    James, 31
    John, 130
    Joseph, 130
    Lilley, 29
    Lydia (Pierce), 31
    Martha (Rowlandson), 130
    Mary (French), 130
    Sarah, 130
    Sarah (Morrill), 130
    Thomas, 31
    Thomas, Capt., 31
EAYRES
    Joseph, 71
EDES
    Emma, 127
EDGAR
    Henry, 84
    Sarah (___), 84
EDMUNDS
    Joseph, 79
    Mary, 79-80
    William, 121
EDWARD
    Joseph, 120
EDWARDS
    Dan'l, 198
    David, 162
    Lucretia, 105
    Mary (Sweet), 162
    Miriam, 165-166
    Rice, 145
    Sarah Pierpont, 5

EGERY
    Mary, 92
EICHEL
    Elizabeth (Weagle), 204
    Johann George, 204
ELBRIDGE
    Elizabeth, 25
ELDRED
    Catherine, 107
ELDRIDGE
    Anna/Amy (Tourtelotte), 213
    Joseph, 213
ELIOT
    John, Rev., 24
ELLINGWOOD
    Martha (Robson/Rowlandson), 214
    Ralph, 214
ELLIOTT
    Ambrose, 204
    Anna, 105
    Anna (___), 105
    Mary Elizabeth, 204
    Sarah (Choate), 204
    William, 105
ELLIS
    A.L., Mrs., 50
    Betsey, 108
    F., 196
ELLISON
    Addie (Philbrick), 92
    Barney, 92
    Delos, 92
    Jemima (Barnes), 92
    John, 92
    Mary (Tamplins), 92
    Mary Egery (Allen), 92
    Oscar Delos, 92
    Ruth Emily, 92
    Sarah Ann (Nash), 92
ELLMES
    Hannah L., 38
ELLSWORTH
    Jeremiah, 145
ELMER
    John, 164
    Rosamond (Ginnvarie), 164
ELMS
    J. O., 198
ELWELL
    Joan (___), 129
    Mary, 129
    Robert, 129
    Sarah, 161

ELY
    Enoch, Capt., 77
    Keziah (Durkee), 77
EMERSON
    ___, Mrs., 120
    Betsey (Brown), 53
    Lucy Ann, 30
    Mary, 212
    William, 53
EMERTON
    Susan Ann, 191
EMERY
    Deborah, 212
EMMERSON
    Thomas, 145
EMMISON
    ___, Dr., 171
EMMONS
    Eunice, 54
    Huldah (Shackley), 214
    John, Jr., 214
ENDECOTT
    Thomas, 145
EPES
    Daniel, 145
ERVIN
    W., 197
ERVING
    Wm., 198
ESAW
    Peter, 199
ESTERBROOK
    J. E., 197
ESTES
    Caleb, 110
    Lydia (Bishop), 110
EVANS
    ___, Gov., 88
    Anna, 213
    Anna (Weaver), 213
    David, 213
EVELETH
    Sylvester, 145
EVERITT
    Harold, 47

FADDEN
    Carrie Belle, 203
    James, 203
    Lovina (Wood), 203
    Mehitable (Dean), 203
    Nathaniel, 203
FAGAN
    Mary Ann, 109

FORDEN
M., 198
P., 198
FOSS
Betsey, 127
FOSTER
Ann, 15
Betsy, 54
Christina Elizabeth, 93
Eben, 206
Elizabeth, 214
Elizabeth (Rogers), 163
Ezra, 191
G., 200
George, 191
Gladys E. (Woodbury), 215
Jacob, 129
Judith (Wygnol), 129
Martha (Kinsman), 129
Moses, 163
Reginald, 145
Renald, 129
Samuel H., 119
Sarah, 129
Susan, 205
Susannah (Kennedy), 206
FOWLER
Deborah, 54
Joseph, 120
Philip, 145
FRANCIS
Ebenezer, 140
William, 118
FRANKLIN
Benjamin, 4, 61
Deborah Read, 5
FRAZIER
Almira E., 127
John, 198
FREEMAN
Dorcus (Hicks), 163
Edmund, 163
Rebecca, 163
Rebecca (Prence), 163
FRENCH
Abigail (___), 213
Beman, 163
Humphrey, 213
John, 130
Lucretia (Edwards), 105
Margaret, 213
Margaret (Gilmore), 163
Mary, 130
Mary (Noyes), 130

Parker Hardin, 105
Rebecca (Claggett), 105
Sarah (Morrill), 213
Stephen, 213
Thomas, 145
FRIIS
___, Mr., 186
Leo J., 184, 189
FRIZZELL
Annie (Thompson), 39
John, 39
Sarah Mussinger, 38
FROST
Grace H., 128
Lydia Breed (Hill), 211
Lydia Minerva, 211
Marcells, 128
Mary Breed, 211
Susan, 36
Susan Melissa (Tuttle), 128
William, 211
William, Capt., 211
FROTHINGHAM
___, Mr., 36
Maria (Nichols), 35
Nath'l, 71
FRYE
Chauncey, 92
John, Jr., 92
Louvia Jennet, 92
Mary Ann (Heywood), 92
Mehitable (Brown), 92
FULLENWIDER
Barbara, 40
FULLER
Edward, 169-170
J. A., 199
Jas., Jr., 199
John, 145, 163
L., 196
M. J., 197
Mary (___), 163
Thomas, 12
W. H., 199
FULLERTON
John, 165
Ruth (Sampson), 165

GAFLEY
T., 198
GAGNON
Felicite, 203
GAINES
John, 145

GALE
C. A., 196
GALLAGHER
Alice, 87
Ann (Boland), 87
Bill, 87
Catherine, 152
Elizabeth (Bowen), 87
Ella, 87
Francis, 87
Francis L., 87
Maria (Murray), 86
Marie, 87
Patrick, 86-87
Ted, 87
William, 86-87
GALLIJAN
T., 196
GAMMALL
T., 71
GANNERS
Mary, 129
GARDINER
C., 197
GARDNER
Abbie Ann (Lee), 94
Bethia, 22
Charles, 38-39
Clarence E., 151
Eugene Walter, 151
Frederick, 151
Hannah, 22
Hannah (Whiting), 38
Hannah Whiton, 38
Joan L., 151
Louise M. (Clement), 151
Milton D., 151
Ophelia (Brewer), 151
Sarah (Wiggins), 151
Silence (Sprague), 39
Thomas, 145
Thomas, Jr., 22
Wilson Herrick, 94
GAREY See GERRY
GARLAND
Ellen (Wormwood), 52
Josiah, 52
Mariam (Brown), 52
Mariam (Moore), 52
Thomas, 52
GARNER
P. G., 198
GARRET See GERRET

Susannah (Williams), 31-32
Tabitha (Skinner), 25
Thomas, 23-25, 27-34
Thomas Capt., 25
Thomas Jr., 29
Thomas Russell, 88
Typhena/Triphenia, 27-28
William, 23-24, 27-28, 30-33
William, Dea., 24
Wm., 88
GERRY See GEARY
GETCHELL
E., 197
GIBBS
C., 196
Elizabeth, 106
GIDDINGS
Sarah, 108
GIFFORD
J. R., 197
Phoebe (Reynolds), 40
Rhody (Tully), 41
Samuel, 40
Sarah Jane, 40
Thomas, 41
GILBERT
Mary, 25
Zilpha, 92
GILES
Eleazer, 11
Patience, 212
GILLINGS See GIDDINGS
GILMAN
Arthur, 118
Bela, 106
Catherine (Wheelock), 106
Charles E., 106
Henry H., 106
J., 119
Lewis E., 106
Mary Ellen, 106
Nathaniel, 106
W., 119
GILMORE
Alex, 36
David, 163
Ida Frances (Lakeman), 36
John, 163
Margaret, 163
Mary (Stewart), 163
Mitchell, 163
GIMSON See JAMESON
GINNVARIE
Rosamond, 164

GIPSON See also JIPSON
Gertrude (Gerry), 41
Madaline Dorothy, 41
Ralph Emerson, 41
GLADSTONE
___, Mr., 188
GLATIENBERG
Anna Mary, 204
GLEASON
Geo., 199
GLIDDEN
Edward, 145
John, 145
Rachel Ann, 39
William, 145
GLOVER
A. B., 197
B. S., 196
Hannah, 25
GODFREY
J. F., 199
GODING
Amasa, 41
Dorcas W. (Goss), 41
E., 196
Elizabeth (Parker), 42
Eunice Estelle, 41
Hannah (Howes), 41
Jonas, 42
Llewellyn, 41
GODSOE
James E., 110
Rhoda E. (Keazer), 110
GOELET
Hannah, 88
GOLDSMITH
Beatrice, 95
Beatrice (Marsh), 152
GOLDSTONE
Mary, 190
Sarah, 42
GOOCH
Elizabeth Peck, 153
Lydia, 207
GOOD/GOODE
Sara, 79
Sarah, 15
GOODALE
Elizabeth (___), 11
Jacob, 11
John, 145
Louisa, 30
Robert, 145
Ruth, 30-32

Zachariah, 11
GOODHUE
Anna, 214
William, 145
GOODNOW
S., 199
GOODRIDGE
David, 75
Elizabeth (Martin), 75
Joanna, 108
GOODWIN, 48
Ann Elizabeth (Darling), 142
Francis Turner (Darling), 142
Jimmy, 99
John M., 142
GOOKIN
G. D., 197
GOOLD
Abigail, 29
Abigail (Belcher), 29
John, 29
GORDON
Esther (Snow), 92
Hannah, 92
John, 92
Mary Ladd, 163
GORE
Sammuel, 71
GORHAM
Amelia (Dunks), 106
Roger, 95
Seth, 106
GORTON
John, 67
Samuel, 67
Thomas, 67
GORVER
Mary, 127
GOSLING
Marion, 88
GOSS
Dorcas W., 41
Elihu, 101
Elizabeth (Witham), 42
Ephraim, 101-102
Keziah (Geary), 101-102
Richard, 145
Thomas, 42
GOTT
Ambros, 93
Charity (Carter), 53
Clara Marie, 93
Eunice (Emmons), 54
John, 93

Margaret (Andross), 54
Peter, 54
Ruth (Barton), 93
Samuel, 54
Sarah Ann (Herrick), 93
Stephen, 54
GOULD
___ (Geary), 29
Abigail, 29
Dorcas, 33
Henry, 109
Henry, Jr., 55
Jacob, 26
Phebe, 207
Rebecca, 74
Rebecca (Cole), 55, 109
Ruth (Wyman), 31
Thomas, 29, 31
GOURDEAU
Genevieve, 204
GRADNER
Katherine F. (O'Donnell), 151
GRAFFAM
Caleb, 39, 107
Charity (Mayberry), 39, 107
Enoch, 39, 107
Harry Bion, 39
Ida Belle (Grant), 39
Jeanette Dora (Lombard), 39
Jesse Lewis, 39
Leander Lewis, 39
Lillian A. (Pierce), 38
Lottie Judson (Sawyer), 39
Mary (Swett), 107
Mary B. (Swett), 39
Merle Grant, 39
GRAFTON, 103
GRANDY
Elizabeth, 205
GRANGER
Charles, 131-132
Elizabeth, 131-132
Elizabeth (Baker), 131-132
Peter, 131-132
GRANT
Annah (Durkee), 77
Betsey, 206
Betsy (Green), 40 107
Edward C., 77
Emma J., 41
Francis, 145
Ida Belle, 39
James, 40, 107
Joseph W., 39

Lydia, 107
Mary (Boden), 39
Mary (Devlin), 41
Moses, 71
Moses, II, 39
Rachel Ann (Glidden), 39
Thomas, 41, 145
Ulysses S., Pres., 186
W. H., 200
GRAVES
Alice M. (Brown), 192
Anna (Ireson), 191
Edwin Johnson, 192
Hannah (Kendall), 95
Isaiah, 191-192, 222
Isial, 179
Julia Abbie (Nichols), 192
Mark, 130
Mary, 130
Mary Annie/Annie M., 192
Nancy Lord, 191
Philip, 191
Reuben, 95
Sally, 95
Samuel, 191
Samuel Albert, 192
Susan Ann, 191-192
Susan Ann (Emerton), 191
GRAY
H. C., 197
Matilda C. (___), 187
GREAVES
John, 145
GREELY
Stephen, 119
GREEN, 103
Abigail (Geary), 33
Betsy, 40, 107
Charity (Tucker), 211
David, 33
Elizabeth (Roads), 211
Elizabeth (___), 109
Elizabeth Wood, 94
Frances ___), 109
Hannah, 74, 155-156
Henry Judge, 156
John, 33
Jonas, 33
Keziah (Geary), 33
Mary, 106
Mary (___), 110
Nathaniel, 71
Peter, 211
Rebecca, 211

Richard, 110
Ruth, 33
Samuel H., 211
Thomas, 109-110
Thomas, Gov., 4
Wm., 198
GREENE
David L., 157
David L., Dr., 15
GREENLEAF
___, Mrs., 119
Eben, 119
Elizabeth, 25, 34
Enoch, 25
Joshua, 119-120
Rebecca (Russell), 25
GREENOUGH
John, 119
GREENWAY
John, 129
Mary, 129
Mary (___), 129
GREENWOOD
Val, 116
GRENUILL
Thomas, 24
GRIFFEN
Ebenezer, 76
Elizabeth (Martin), 76
GRIFFIN
Hannah, 206
Humphrey, 145
John Little, 145
Tamazine, 94
GRINDLE
Joanna (Hutchins), 40
John, 40
Rebecca, 39
GRINER, 199
GROUT
Mehitabel, 106
GROVER
Elizabeth (___), 162
Stephen, 162
Thomas, 162
GROVES
___, Wid., 212
Anna (Elliott), 105
Patience (___), 110
Peter, 105
William, 110, 212
GROWLEY
Johanna, 93

GUINES
Rebecca, 174
William, 174
GUNDERSON
Bernice B., 50, 74-75, 155
GUNN
C. M., 108
GUNTERMAN
Sophia, 52

HACKETT
Sarah, 125
HADLEY
Jane (Martin), 156
HADLOCK
Abigail (Martin), 156
John, 156
HAFEN
Ann W., 89
HAFFIELD
Richard, 145
HAINES
Eleanor, 212
Joshua, 165
Lucy (Moulton), 165
Richard, 174-175
HALE
Elizabeth, 107
John, 145
R. Wallace, 95
Thomas, 119
HALEY
T., 196
HALL
Amos B., 134
Augustus H., 134
Edward R., 134
G.K., 60
George E., 134
Huldah (Hanson), 134
Mary A., 134
Mary Ann, 134
Paul, 134
Phinelia El, 134
Richard, 163
HALLAHAN
T. H., 198
HALLOCK
R. L., 197
HALSEY
Ann, 42
HAMBLIN
T., 197

HAMER
Charity (Allen), 211
Eleanor (Lyon), 211
Josiah, 211
Josiah/Jessie, 211
Mary E./Ellen, 211
Thomas, Capt., 211
HAMILTON
Ann(geline), 204
Anna (Kavanagh), 204
Daniel, 204
David, 205
Elizabeth Schuyler, 5
Mary (Gavel), 205
HAMLIN
Molly (Clay), 40
Samuel, 40
Temperance, 107
Temperance Lewis, 39
HAMMOND
Elizabeth (Wells), 95
George, 95
Henry, 95
Mary (Beall), 95
Nancy, 94
HANCHETT
Eliza Ann, 107-108
HANCOCK
Judith (Winthrop), 68
Richard, 68
HANDERSON See also HENDERSON
Elizabeth (Hopp), 153
Ira, 153
HANOUSEK
Augusta L., 93
Joseph, 93
Sophia (Kinzel), 93
HANSON
Clarissa (___), 127
Hannah C., 127
Huldah, 134
Lydia (Canney), 125
Mary (Austin), 126
Samuel, 127
Sarah, 126
Stephen, 126
Tobias, 125
HARDING
Abigail (Littlefield), 206
Israel, 207
Lydia, 206
Lydia (Gooch), 207
Stephen, 206

HARDY
Abigail, 154
HARKIN
Barnet, 20
HARLAKENDON
Mabel, 174
HARLOW
J., 196
HARMON
Ruth, 165
HARRADEN
Benjamin, 10
Deborah (Norwood), 10
Edward, 10, 130
Elizabeth, 130
Hannah (York), 130
Mary, 10, 18, 20
Sarah (Haskell), 10
Sarah (___), 10, 130
Susanna, 21
HARRIMAN, 198
HARRINGTON
Augustus, 180
C. F., 196
Elisha, 162
J., 196
Susanna (Conner), 162
HARRIS
Abiah, 211
Edward, 145
Elizabeth, 161
Elizabeth (Nicholson), 211
Ephraim, 145
J., 200
Job, 145
John, 145
Mary/Polly, 215
Peter, 145
Ralph, 145
Samuel, 211
Thomas, 145
HARRISON
Hannah, 34
HARROD
, Mrs., 119-120
HART, 211
Isaac, 145
Jonathan, 207
Lydia, 206
Lydia (Neale), 207
M., 119
Nancy, 5-6
Sarah, 41

HARTFORD
    Grace, 125
    William, 125
HARVARD
    John, 16
HARVEY
    David, 55
    Judith (Chase), 55
    Phillis E., 8
    Phyllis, 10
HASKELL
    Hanora Helen, 122
    Jonathan, 130
    Joseph, 130
    Joseph, Dea., 130
    Lucy, 95
    Mark, 145
    Martha, 213
    Mary, 129-130
    Mary (Graves), 130
    Mary (Sawyer), 130
    Mary (Tybott), 129-130
    Mary (___), 165
    Rebecca, 142
    Sarah, 10
    Sarah (Davis), 130
    Thomas, 165
    William, 129-130, 145
HASKINS
    G. H., 197
HASTINGS
    Cora Minnie, 203
    John (M), 203
HATHAWAY
    E., 196
HATHORNE
    John, 12
    Sara, 52
HAWKES, 69
HAWKINS
    Alan H., 41
    Charles, 161
    Emily, 37
    Emma J. (Grant), 41
    Eunice Estelle (Goding), 41
    Fannie (___), 161
    Hayward Ludlow, 41
    Herschel James, 41
    James, 41
    James Ludlow, 41
    John Michael, 42
    Madaline Dorothy (Gipson), 41
    Nancy (Todd), 42
    Rebecca (Burt), 41

William, 161
HAWORTH
    H., 196
HAY
    Dorcas (Gould), 33
    Isabella, 154
    John, 174
    Patrick, 27
    Peter, 33
    Rebecca, 174
    Susanna/Susannah, 21, 31, 33
    William, 174
HAYDEN
    Phebe, 55
HAYES
    ___, Mrs., 187
    P., Pres., 187
HAYNES
    ___, Gov., 175
    John, Gov., 174
    John, Rev., 174-175
    Mabel (Harlakendon), 175
HAYWARD, 69
HEALEY
    J. C., 198
    Mark, 85
HEARD
    Albert F., 140
    Albert Farley, 142
    Alfred F., 141
    Amos, 142
    Augustine, 138, 140-142
    Augustine, Capt., 139-140
    Augustine, Jr., 140
    Augustine, Sr., 140
    Charles, 140
    Daniel, 141-142
    Daniel S., 140
    Elizabeth, 142
    Elizabeth (Knowlton), 141
    Elizabeth Ann (Farley), 142
    Elizabeth Ann (Story), 140, 142
    George, 142
    George F., 141
    George W., Dr., 140
    George Washington, 142
    Hannah Staniford, 142
    John, 139-142
    John, Jr., 140, 145
    Katherine, 207
    Luke, 145
    Margaret, 142
    Mary, 140-142
    Mary (Stevens), 142

Mary Dean (Dane), 141
    Nathan, 141
    Nathaniel, 142
    Samuel, 141
    Sarah, 142
    Sarah (Staniford), 142
    Sarah/Sally (Staniford), 140
    Susanna (Spiller), 142
HEATH
    Rachel, 76
HEATHERED, 103
HECK
    Barbara (___), 3
    Barbara Ruckle, 6
HECKENDORN, 195
HECKER, 154
HEIRMAN
    P., 198
HENDE
    Elizabeth, 75-76
HENDERSON See also HANDERSON
    Ada Mary (Fisher), 153
    Esther, 164
    Evangeline Fay (Wright), 153
    Hugh Goudy, 153
    Ira, 153
    James, 153
    John, 145
    Lloyd Fisher, 153
    Melinda, 54
    Robert, 95
    Robert Fisher, 153
    Sarah (Allen), 54
    Sarah Maria (Traver), 153
    Talitha (Bailey), 153
    William, 54
HENDESTEAD
    Mary, 205
HENESY
    D., 198
HENFIELD
    John, 199
HENNEFELD
    Paul, S/Sgt., 50
HENRY
    Joseph, 198
    Thomas, 198
HENRY VIII
    King, 174
HEPKER
    Gail, 95
    Gail L. (Brown), 151
HERBERT
    Harriet, 37

HERLIHY
    Richard, 180
HERON
    John, 199
HERRICK
    Abigail (Babson), 93
    Abigail Lufkin, 94
    Andrew, 109
    Betsey (___), 165
    Dorothy/Dolly R. (Bray), 94
    Ebenzer, 165
    Emmeline T., 93
    Jonathan, 84
    Kimball, 93
    Mary, 165
    Mary (___), 165
    Nathaniel, 109
    Samuel, 109
    Sarah Ann, 93
    Theophilus, 94
HERSEY
    Betsey (Bowley), 203
    Caroline M. (Thompson), 203
    Carrie Belle (Fadden), 203
    Charles Sumner Sr., 203
    Constance Lea (Bolduc), 203
    Harriet Adeline, 203
    Stephen, Jr., 203
    Stephen, Sr., 203
HERTZ
    Jana, 95
HERVEY
    Joseph, 119
HESNEY
    R., 197
HEWES
    Anna (Wellman), 190
    Anna M. (Lathrop), 188
    Charles, 187
    David, 181-184, 186, 188-189
    George R. T., 71
    Hannah (Johnson), 190
    Hannah (Norden), 190
    Hannah (___), 190
    Joel, 181, 190
    Joel, Col., 190
    John, 190
    Joshua, 181, 190
    Joshua, Lt., 189
    Lucy, 190
    Mary (Goldstone), 190
    Matilda C. (___), 187
    Ruthe, 187, 190
    Ruthe (Tapley), 181, 190

    Samuel, 190
HEWES-ELWELL
    Rebecca, 93
HEWETT
    Diana B. (Spring), 166
    Ephraim Gay, 166
HEYWOOD
    Mary (Egery), 92
    Mary Ann, 92
    William, 92
HICKEY
    Pat, 198
HICKS
    Dorcus, 163
    Samuel, 163
HIGGINS, 197
HILD
    Anna Katherine (Weber), 154
    Augustus, 154
    Katherine Wilhelmina, 153
HILDEBRAND
    M., 200
HILDRETH, 99
    Mary, 54, 162
HILL
    Abigail (Baker), 49
    Deborah, 166
    Eleanor, 129
    Hulda, 126
    Isabel (___), 9
    John, 33, 49
    John Jr., 33
    Joseph, 211
    Lydia Breed, 211
    Mary (Breed), 211
    Ruth (Boutwell), 33
    Susannah (Hay), 31, 33
    Thomas, 186
HILLERETH
    Herman Dr., 180
HILLIARD
    Elizabeth, 161
HILLIER See also TILL/TILLE
    Deborah, 55
    Hugh, 55
    Rose (___), 55
HILLIS
    Jane, 40
HILLMAN
    Louise, 16
    Paul A., 16
HILLS, 99, 103
    Obadiah, 145

HILTON
    Edward, 124
    Mary, 110
HISCOCK
    Creighton, 145
    David, 145
    Henry, 145
HOAG
    J., 196
HOAR
    Lydia, 175
HOBBS
    Hannah (Canney), 125
    Henry, 125
    Jonathan, 145
    Josiah H., 145
HOBSON, 59
HODGDON
    Caleb, 54
    Joel D., 53
    Salome (Fellows), 53
    Sarah (Roberts), 54
HODGES
    G. Z., 197
HODGKINS
    Hannah (Saville), 83
    Timothy, 83
    William, 145
HODGMAN
    Abigail (Geary), 29
    Benjamin, 29
    David, 29
    Elizabeth, 29
    John, 29
    Jonathan, 29
    Josiah, 29
    Thomas, 29
    Timothy, 29
HOGAN
    P., 197
HOLBROOK, 197
    Alice, 55
    F. W., 197
    H., 197
    M. D., 197
HOLDEN
    Dana, 35
    Eli, 35
    Ezra, 35
    Hannah, 35
    John, 32
    Keziah, 31, 33
    Marian, 35
    Mary (Damon), 32

Phebe, 30, 32, 35
Phebe (Nichols), 35
HOLLAND
Andrew, 199
HOLLINGSWORTH
Anne, 6
HOLLIS
A. J., 199
HOLMES
E. R., 197
Elizabeth, 163
Margaret (Patterson), 95
S. R., 197
Sally (Graves), 95
Sarah Maria, 94
Thomas, 95
Thomas, 95
W. C., 199
HOLT
John, 24
Loammi, 215
Mary/Polly (Harris), 215
Nicholas, 99
Sarah (Gary), 24
Sarah Elizabeth, 164
William, 164
William H., Jr., 214
HOLTZE
C., 200
HOMANS
Peter, 145
HOMER
J., 197
HONEY
Calvin, 197
HOOD
Abner, 134
Benjamin, 134
Content, 134
Ebenezer, 134
Keezia (Breed), 134
Richard, 134
Theodate, 134
HOOKER
Elizabeth (Hilliard), 161
Henry, 161
HOOPER
Annie Margaret, 152
Joseph, 118
HOOTEN
John, 71
HOPKINS
Stephen, 16

HOPP
Elizabeth, 153
HORGAN
J., 198
HORNE
Jane (Clough), 166
John, 166
HOSMER
Josiah, 197
HOTCHKISS
Henry, 211
Lois, 211
Lydia, 211
HOUGH
Benjamin K., 81
HOUGHTON
S. B., 198
HOUSE See HOWES
HOVEY
Arria, 81
Daniel, 145
Harriotte Johnson, 81-82
James, 81
HOW See HOWE
HOWARD
Algerman S., 145
Grace, 75-76
J. A., 199
John, 74-76
Mary (Martin), 75
S., 71
HOWE/HOW
Abraham, 145
Alfred, 145
Calvin, 145
Edward C., 71
Elizabeth, 15, 79
Leonard, 145
Nathaniel, 145
HOWES
Adeline (Speed), 41
George W., 41
Hannah, 41
HOWLAND
L. L., 197
HOWLETT
Mary, 206
Samuel, 145, 207
Sarah (Clark), 207
Thomas, 145
HOYT
Chase, 94
David W., 155
Hannah, 10

Tamazine, 93
Tamazine (Griffin), 94
HUBBARD
Betsy, 95
Betsy (Hubbard), 95
Elisha Dea., 95
Elizabeth, 77-78
Elizabeth Peck (Gooch), 153
John, Capt., 153
Lucy, 152-153
Mercy, 95
Mercy (Hubbard), 95
Peter, 95
Phoebe (Brigham), 95
Samuel Brigham, 94
Samuel Woodward, 95
Sarah Jane, 94
Sarah Maria (Holmes), 94
Tuttle, 153
HUCKINS
Rose (____), 110
Thomas, 110
HUGGINS see HUCKINS
HUGHES
J., 199
HUME
Eleanor, 213
Eleanor (____), 213
John, 213
HUMPFREY
Joseph, 68
HUMPHREY
Effingham, Jr., 195
John, Sir, 68
Z., 14
HUNN, 103
HUNNEWELL
Ric'd, Jr., 71
HUNT
C. A., 200
E. B., 200
Rosewell P., 79-80
Samuel, 79
HUNTOON
Cynthia A., 128
George W., 128
Malvina (Drew), 128
HURD
Olive, 42
HURDLEY
Wm, 71
HURLBURT
Sarah, 205

HURLEY
    Augusta L. (Hanousek), 93
    Jeremiah, 93
    Johanna (Growley), 93
    John, 93
    Julia (Dovovan), 93
    Margaret Ann, 93
    Timothy, 93
HUSE
    Elizabeth, 153
    Elizabeth Chase, 152
HUSSEY
    Andrew, 199
    Anna (___), 165
    J.W., 199
    James, 165
    Susannah, 126
HUSTED
    Angell, 107
    Rebecca (Sherwood), 107
    Samuel, 107
    Sarah (Knapp), 107
HUTCHINS
    Joanna, 40
HUTCHINSON
    Anne (___), 3
    Anne (___), 4
    Anne Marbury, 6
    Edward, 163
    Mary, 163
    Richard, 145
HUTTON
    Richard, 28
HYDE
    Samuel, 55
    Samuel, Rev., 55

INCHES
    Margaret (Shippee), 54
    Melinda (Henderson), 54
    Rachel (Lambert), 54
    Thomas, 54
    Thomas, Dr., 54
INDIAN
    John, 78
INGALLS
    Edmund, 145
    Hannah, 131-132
    Martha, 133
    Samuel, 145
INGOLLSON
    Daniel, 71
INMAN
    Elizabeth (Murray), 4

    Ralph, 4
IRESON
    Anna, 191
IVES
    David P., 71
    Isaac, 211
    John, 211
    Lois, 211
    Lois (Hotchkiss), 211
    Lydia (Hotchkiss), 211

JACKMAN
    Joseph, 118-119
JACKSON, 69
    Abigail (Tupper), 213
    Abraham, 119
    Donald Dale, 178
    Joseph William, 213
JACOBS
    George, 15
JACOBUS
    Donald Lines, 156, 171, 174
JAGGER/JAGGERS
    Eunice, 95
JAMESON
    Hester (Martin), 156
JANVRIN
    Elizabeth (Ladd), 152
    Elizabeth Chase (Huse), 152
    Joanna (Thurla/Thurlow), 152
    Joseph Adams, Jr., 152
    Joseph Adams, Sr., 152
JAYNES
    Alva, 80
    Cynthia (Boynton), 80
JEFTS
    Henry, Jr., 29
    Mary (Geary), 29
    Mary (Pierce), 101
    Peter, 101
JENKIN
    John, 119
JENNESS
    Sarah J., 127
JENNETT
    Jane, 54
JENNINGS, 171
JEWELL
    Sarah, 3
JEWETT
    Ebenezer, 145
    Ezehiell, 145
    Hannah, 119
    Joseph, 145

JEWIT
    Abraham, 145
JIPSON See also GIPSON
    Abashaba (Booden), 42
    Edith Ellen (Davis), 41
    James, 41
    Jane (Neal), 41
    Wellington, 41
    William, 42
JOHNNY APPLESEED, 73
JOHNS
    T. W., 198
JOHNSON, 85
    ___, Mrs., 119-120
    Cornelia Ann, 205
    Daniel, 200
    David, 206
    E. C., 198
    Edward, 94
    Eleazer, 120
    Eliza Ann, 136
    Elizabeth (Chadwell), 136
    Elizabeth (Nichols), 35
    Hannah, 190
    Hannah (Newman), 106
    Irene Sanders, 157
    Isabell (MacDonald), 94
    James, 94
    Jane (Roduck), 206
    Jeremiah, 106
    Joseph, 205
    Joseph C., 200
    Luther, 35
    Lydia, 136
    N., 199
    Richard, 136
    Rufus, 136
    Sarah, 164
    Susan (Foster), 205
    Susan (Gay), 93
    Susan (MacDonald), 94
    Timothy, 136
JOLIET, 8
JONES
    ___, Capt., 16
    Anne, 55
    D. W., 119
    J. W., 198
    John, 42
    Mary, 155
    Nathan, 145
    Phebe, 109
    Sarah (Farwell), 42

JOPPLIN
Robert, 145
JORDAN
A. K., 200
Francis, 52
Jane (Wilson), 52
Mary, 52
Mary McFadden, 165
JOSLIN
John F., 40
Lucy L., 40
Ludy (Fisk), 40
Nathan F., 40
Sarah Jane (Gifford), 40
JOSLYN
Roger D., 113, 116
JOWETT
William, 145
JOY
Sarah, 213

KALLOCH, 99
KANNEY See CANNEY
KATTAN
G. W., 197
KAVANAGH
Anna, 204
Sarah (Hurlburt), 205
Simon, 205
KEAZER
Clarissa D., 110
Rhoda E., 110
Susan, 110
KEBEE
Elisha, 11
KEEFE
Bridget (___), 204
John, 204
KEENE
Alonzo, 198
KEEZER
Clara H., 110
Mary Ann, 110
Nancy, 41
KEITH
Emma Clark (Wales), 204
George Chester, 204
H., 197
J. W., 198
Louisa Clark, 204
Martin, 204
Mary Elizabeth (Elliott), 204
W., 200

KELLEY
Joseph J, Jr., 6
M., 197
KELLOGG
Abigail (Miller), 106
Joseph, 106
KELLY
J., 198
O., 196
P., 198
KELSEY, 99
KEMP
Almira (Sinnett), 205
Cora Olive (Stone), 205
Cornelia Ann (Johnson), 205
Hannah (Snow), 206
John, 205
Lillian Violet, 205
Timothy, 206
William Henry, 205
KENDALL
Ephraim, 145
Hannah, 95
KENDRICK
Alonzo, 179
KENNEDY
Susannah, 206
KENNERSON
David, 71
KENNEY, 198
Ann, 110
Hannah, 214
KENNEY See CANNEY
KENT
Hannah (___), 166
John, 145
Richard, 166
KENTON
Mary (Rapp), 204
KERIGAN
M., 198
KERN
T., 199
KEZEIR
Elizar, 91
KIDDER
J. T., 198
KIERNAN
Ellen, 151
KIGHT, 198
KILBURN
Lucy, 54
KILLAM
Austin, 145

Daniel, 28
Triphena (Geare), 28
KIMBALL, 211
Abigail (Perkins), 212
Benjamin, 145
Elizabeth C., 127
James, 119
John, 145
John, Sgt., 52
Mary (Jordan), 52
Mary Breed (Frost), 211
Moses, 118
Nelson, 164
Richard, 120, 145
Samuel, 212
Sarah Elizabeth (Holt), 164
Thomas Albert, 212
KING
G. W., 199
Lavinia Marie, 205
Sarah Elizabeth, 54
KINGSBURY
Hannah, 204
KINGSLEY
S. B., 198
KINNEL
John, 199
KINSMAN
John, 145
Martha, 129
Mary (Boreman), 129
Robert, 129, 145
William, 145
KINZEL
Sophia, 93
KIRBY
George, 174
KITCHEN, 10
KITFIELD
Asa E., 180
KLEIN
Alden J., 8
Frederic, 9
Hazel Elizabeth (Airey), 8
Shirley, 10
Shirley Elizabeth, 8, 10
KLUTTS
J. C., 198
KNAPP
Abigail (Westcott), 107
Mahetabel, 95
Moses, 107
Sarah, 107

KNEELAND
    Edward, 145
KNIGHT
    A. Y., 197
    Agnes (Coffley), 166
    Darius, 76
    Elizabeth (Durkee), 76
    Richard, 166
    Sarah (___), 4
    Sarah Kemble, 6
KNOULTON
    John Tertius, 145
KNOWLES
    Elizabeth (Bacon), 161
    Lucy Backman, 152
    Nathaniel, 161
    Samuel, 161
    Sarah (Elwell), 161
KNOWLTON
    Dan, 138
    Elizabeth, 75, 141
    Ezekiel, 213
    John, 84, 119, 145
    Joseph, 145
    Lois, 205
    Mary (___), 84
    Richard, 146
    Sarah (Leach), 213
    William, 146
KOEHLER
    Sarah, 95
    Sarah Rose (Murray), 151
KOEN
    Mary Elizabeth, 201
KORY See COREY

LA SALLE, 8
LADD
    Daniel, Capt., 152
    Elizabeth, 152
    Elizabeth (Huse), 153
LaGRO see GROVES
LaGROVES
    Nicholas, 110
LAKEMAN
    Charles, 36
    Ida Frances, 36
    Mary Frances (Nichols), 36
    William, 146
LAMB
    A., 197
LAMBERT
    Daniel, 146
    Deborah (Fowler), 54

    Jesse, 54
    Rachel, 54
LAMBIRD
    P. M., 198
LAMPSON
    Robin, 189
LAMSON
    William, 146
LANCASTER
    Davis, 162
    Sarah (Curtis), 162
LAND
    J., 200
LANE
    Daniel, 105
    Elias, 105
    Giddings, 105
    Hannah, 215
    James, 105
    John, 146
    Judith, 105
    Lydia, 105
    Mary, 105
    Mary (___), 105
    Peter, 105
LANG
    Sarah (Sherburne), 165
    William, 165
LANGTON See also LAUGHTON
    Joseph, 121
    Rachell (Varney), 121
LARCUM, 103
LARKIN, 103
    John, 161
    Leah (___), 161
    Thomas, 161
LARRABEE
    Charles L., 135
    Ellen R., 135
    Lydia (Mitchell), 107
    Nancy, 40
    Sarah L., 135
    William, 107
LATHROP
    Anna M., 188
    John, Rev., 188
LATIMER
    J. B., 197
LAUGHTON See also LANGTON
    Joseph, 121
LAUNDER
    Thomas, 24
LAW
    Henry, 69

LAWRENCE, 69
    Nathaniel, Dea., 29
LEACH
    Abigail, 39
    Amos, 75
    Betsy (Door), 39
    George, 39
    John, 40
    Mercy (Martin), 75
    Polly (Simpson), 40
    Sarah, 213
LEATHERLAND
    William, 146
LEAVENS
    Esther (Williams), 212
    Frances, 212
    John, 212
LeBARON
    Elizabeth (Washburn), 211
    James, 211
LeBRETON
    Peter, 120
LeCLERC
    Elizabeth Adeline, 203
    Pierre, 204
LEDGERWOOD
    Jane (Hillis), 40
    Nancy, 40
    Samuel, 40
LEE
    Abbie Ann, 94
    Abigail Lufkin (Herrick), 94
    Ann Mother, 3, 6
    Elizabeth, 84
    Jacob, 94
    John, 146
    Joseph, 71
    Mary M., 42
    Nathaniel, 84
    Sally, 142-143
LEFFINGWELL
    Sarah, 29
LeGRO See GROVES
LEIGHTON
    Clarissa D. (Keazer), 110
    Joseph J., 110
    Lucinder, 128
LEMMON
    Elizabeth (___), 25
    Joseph, Dr., 25
LeNOIR, 171
LENOX
    James, 59

LEONARD
    Dolly Ann (Rich), 205
    Elfrida (Wheelock), 205
    Florence Rich, 205
    Gilbert, 205-205
    H. N., 199
    Joseph Warren, 205
    Norah, 152
    O. B., 169-170
    Polly (Gerry), 206
LEPINGWELL
    Sarah, 29
LESHER
    Catherine, 40
    Catherine (___), 41
    Nicholsen, 41
LeSHURE
    W. C., 198
LEWES
    Mercy, 14
LEWIS
    Alonzo, 191
    C., 198
    Mercy, 77-78
LIBBY, 48, 99
LIDDEASON
    Job, 175
LINCOLN
    ___, Pres., 185
    Amos, 71
    B., 199
    Frances (Leavens), 212
    Joseph, 212
    Susan, 212
LINDBERG
    Marcia Wiswall, 23, 131, 137, 181
LINDER, 99
LINDSAY
    Thos., 200
LINKON
    Jerush, 75
    Mercy, 75
LITCH
    Caleb, 154
    Mercy, 153
    Mercy (Dean), 154
LITTLE
    D., 119
    Edward, 119
    Jane, 40
    Moses, 105
LITTLEFIELD
    Abigail, 206
    Benjamin, 206

Hannah (Proctor), 206
James, 207
Katherine (Heard), 207
Olive, 205
LITTLEHALE
    Richard, 84
    Sally Byles, 81
    Sarah (___), 84
LIVINGSTON
    ___, Gov., 6
    Susan, 6
LOCKE
    Benjamin, 80
    Cynthia (Boynton), 80
    James, 119
    John, 127
    Mary (Dame), 127
    Sampson B., 127
    Sarah (Canney), 127
LOCKER
    Abigail, 215
LOCKS
    Thankful Ingalls Weeks, 213
LOCKWOOD
    Stephen C., 141
LOKER, 103
LOMBARD
    Bethiah (Smith), 40
    James, 40
    Jeanette Dora, 39
    Lydia (Grant), 107
    Richard, 39, 107
    Solomon, Jr., 107
    Temperance (Hamlin), 107
    Temperance Lewis (Hamlin), 39
LONG
    W. H., 197
LOOME
    Mary, 124
LOOMIS
    Mary (Canney), 125
    Nathaniel, 125
LORD
    Benjamin, 119
    Elizabeth, 50
    Hannah Whiton (Gardner), 38
    Jeremiah, 39, 107
    John, 39
    Lucietta Gertrude, 38
    Lydia, 38
    Lydia (Rideout), 39, 107
    Mary, 106
    Peter Ross, 38
    Polly (Ross), 39

Robert, 146
Samuel, 146
Sarah Ann (Philbrick), 38
Sarah Mussinger (Frizzell), 38
Thomas, 119
William Henry, 38
William Hugg, 38
LORING
    J. M., 200
    Matthew, 71
LOTT
    Sarah (___), 52
LOUNGER
    John B., 198
LOVEJOY
    Abigail (Tarr), 203
    Charles, 135
    Cora Minnie (Hastings), 203
    Denise, 95
    Edgar Eugene, 203
    Elbridge, 135
    Ellen Maria (Deane), 203
    Harriet, 135
    harriet Adeline (Hersey), 203
    Harriett Amelia, 153
    harry Cleveland, 203
    Jerry, 95
    Jerry Hersey, 203
    Jerry Hersey, Sr., 203
    John, 135
    John Eugene, 203
    Lavina (Blanchard), 135
    Mary (Ober), 153
    Nathan, 203
    Susanna (Rideout), 154
    William, 153
    William Nevins, 154
LOVELL
    Sarah, 24
LOVERING
    Esther, 214
LOVET
    Annis (Swetland), 206
    Hannah, 206
    John, 207
    Simon, 206
LOW
    Anna, 95
    David, Jr., 146
    John, 146
    Thomas, 146
    Thorndick, 146
LOWE
    Aaron Jr., 146

LUCAS
    Eliza, 4
    George, Lt. Col., 4
LUDDEN
    Anna Mae, 41
    Hannah (Woodbury), 42
    John Brown, 42
    John Emerson, 41
    Susan (Averill), 41
LUDINGTON
    Sybil, 6
    William, 101
LUFKIN
    Mary Sophia, 94
    Nancy, 215
    Sophia Walker (Rust), 94
    William, Jr., 94
LULL
    E., 196
    Lydia, 129
    Lydia (Smith), 129
    Thomas, 129
LUMMUS
    Jonathan, 146
LUNDGREN
    Elizabeth (Dodd), 214
    Hellen E., 214
    Nils Peter, 214
LUNT
    Hannah (Cook), 54
    Johnson, 54
    Massey (Downes), 54
    Samuel, 54
    Samuel Allen, 108
    Sarah (Giddings/Gillings), 108
LURVEY
    Elizabeth (Potter), 8-9
    Moses, 8-9
    Peter, 8, 10
LUSCOMB
    William, 146
LUSHER
    Catherine, 40
    Catherine (Lesher), 40
    Peter, 40
LYDON
    John, 203
    Mary (Curran), 203
    Winifred, 203
LYNDE
    N., 197
LYON
    Eleanor, 211
    Mary, 137

MacBEAN, 171
MacDONALD
    Isabell, 94
    Susan, 94
MacMAHON
    Elizabeth, 55
    Mary (McDermott), 55
    Michael, 55
MADISON
    Dolly Payne, 6
    James, 34
MAGOUN
    Faith, 131, 133
MAKEPIECE
    Abigail, 215
MANN
    G. H., 197
    H. S., 197
MANNING
    Margaret (Heard), 142
    Nicholas, 157
    Richard, 146
    Thomas, 142
MANSFIELD, 70-71
    Abigail Somes (Davis), 94
    Adelaide (Claflin), 94
    Alfred, 94
    Andrew, 68-69
    Daniel, Dea., 71
    Deborah, 135
    E. Gerry, 68
    Elizabeth, 135
    George Rogers, 94
    James, 94
    James S., 94
    John, Col., 95
    Lydia, 54
    Rebecca, 54
    Sarah (Cheever), 95
    Sarah Jane (Hubbard), 94
    Susan (Murphy), 94
MANSUR
    Samuel, 119
MANUEL
    Mary, 25
MARBLE
    Carrie, 37
    Eva Stanton, 37
    Frank Herbert, 37
    Harriet Maria (Flagg), 37
    James, 37
    Lena Marcelia, 37
    Maria, 37

MARCHANT
    Abigail O., 81
MARDEN
    Barbara Brown, 10
MARQUAND
    Joseph, 119
MARQUETTE, 8
MARR
    Chester, 94
    Elizabeth Wood, 93
    Elizabeth Wood (Green), 94
MARSH
    ___, Mr., 35
    Beatrice, 152
    Charles W., 153
    Charles Wallace, 152
    Elizabeth (Parratt), 163
    George Warren, 152
    Isaac, II, 153
    Isaac, III, 152
    John, 75
    Lotta (Alley), 152
    Lucy (Hubbard), 152
    Mary, 130
    Mary Louise (Rice), 152
    Mary/Polly W. (Choate), 152
    Old Lady, 153
    Onesiphorus, 163
    Sarah (Martin), 75
    Sarah (Nichols), 35
    Warren, 152
MARSHALL, 34
    Edmund, 146
    Moses F., 164
MARSON
    Elizabeth (Harris), 161
    Samuel, 161
MARSTON, 99
    Lydia, 212
MARTIN, 71
    Aaron, 76
    Amasa, 76
    Anna, 75
    Anna (Slate), 76
    Benjamin, 76
    Carrie Curtis (Smith), 40
    Catherine (Lusher), 40
    Charlotte, 75
    David, 40, 75-76
    Dinah (Utley), 76
    Dorothy (Brown), 76
    Ebenezer, 74, 76
    Ebenezer, Jr., 41
    Elizabeth, 75-76

Elizabeth (Coy), 76
Elizabeth (Durkee), 74-75
Elizabeth (Ford), 75-76
Elizabeth (Hende), 75-76
Elizabeth (Knowlton), 75
Elizabeth (Thomson), 75
Eunice (Burnham), 75
Eunice (Flint), 76
George, 74, 146, 155-157
George II, 76
George Jr., 74
George Sr., 74
George, 3rd, 74-76
Gidwon, 76
Goody, 78
Grace, 76
Grace (Howard), 75-76
Hannah, 74
Hannah (Green), 74
Hannah (___), 155
Harriet Jane, 40
Jane (Durkee), 74-76
Jerush (Linkon), 75
Jerusha, 76
Jerusha (Durkee), 74-76
John, 156
John Jr., 75
John Peter, 40
John S., 74-76
Jonathan, 76
Joseph, 75-76
Joshua, 75
Keziah, 75, 77
Lora, 75-77
Lucee, 76
Lucee (Clark), 76
Lucy, 76
Manassah, 75
Martha, 75
Mary, 75, 213
Mary (Baker), 75
Mary (Millard), 76
Mercy, 75-76
Mercy (Durkee), 74-75
Mercy (Linkon), 75
Naomi (Upton), 76
Nathaniel Ford, 75
Rachel (Heath), 76
Rebecca, 76
Richard, 156-157
Sabra (Sharp), 76
Samuel, 75
Samuel, Sr., 75
Sarah, 75-76

Sarah (Capron), 41
Sarah (Durkee), 74-76
Sarah (Martin) Marsh, 75
Sarah (Simmons), 76
Sarah (Storey), 75
Susan (Plumb), 76
Susanna, 15
Susanna (North), 74, 77-78, 155-157
Teressa (Denison), 40
Theodore Mills, 40
William, 76, 156
Zerviah (Dayley), 76
MARTINE
George, 157
MASON, 109
Anna, 92
Anna (Cleaves), 92
Ebenezer, 92
Helen (___), 52
John Capt., 124
John L., 54
Sally (Tarbell), 55
MASSEY
S., 198
MASURY
Margaret, 190
MATCHET
Susan, 214
MATHER
Cotton, 12
Samuel, 4
MATHEWS, 103
MATHISON
F., 197
MATTHEWS
John, 212
MAVERICK
Mary, 90-91
Moses, 90-91
MAXIM
Martha (Chubbuck), 163
Nathan, 163
MAY
Ann (Parker), 29
Benjamin, 29
Hannah, 29
James, 29
John, 29
John, Jr., 29
Mary, 29
Rebecca, 29
Sarah, 29
Sarah (Geary), 29
Thomas, 29

MAYBERRY
Charity, 39, 107
MAYHEW
Mary (McFadden Jordan), 165
Nathaniel, 165
Thomas, 146
MAYNARD
J., 198
McBRIDE
David, 154
Joseph, 153
Mary Ann (Saunders), 153
Sarah Margaret, 153
Susanna (Reed), 154
McCALGIN
M., 200
McCALL
Archibald, 172
Elizabeth (___), 172
McCARTHY
D. O., 196
McCAULEY
Mary Ludwig Hayes, 6
McCLELLAN
Ruth M. (Woodbury), 215
McCLOUD
Margaret, 206
McCLURE
Mary, 163
McCOOL
J., 197
McCRACKEN
George E., Dr., 15
McDERMOTT
Anne, 203
Mary, 55
McDONALD
George, 199
J., 199
McDONELD
B., 196
H. H., 196
McDONOUGH
T., 199
McDOWNEY
___, Mr., 86
McELHENY
R. D., 199
McFEE
Elinor (Van Pelt), 165
John, 165
McGERR
M., 199

McGLAUGHLIN
    Caroline, 93
    Hannah (Mundee), 93
    Samuel, 93
McINTOSH
    Peter, 71
    Walter, 34, 50
    Walter H., 118
McLEAN
    Isabelle, 50
McLEISH, 116
McMAHON, 199
McNAMARA
    Anna (Murray), 86
McNAUGHTON
    J., 200
McNUTT, 211
    (Archambeau), 211
McPHERSON
    Alexander, 50
    Isabella (Cameron), 50
    Mary Isabelle, 50
McQUESTEN
    Margaret (Nahor), 105
    William, 105
McRAE
    Catherine, 77
MEACHAM
    Jeremiah, 11
MEDCALF
    Joseph, 120
MELVILLE
    Thomas, 71
MENZIE
    James, 68
MERCER
    Hester, 109
MERRETT
    Mary (Sandin), 161
    Nicholas, 161
MERRIAM
    Anne (Jones), 55
    Elizabeth ( ), 55
    Joseph, 42
    Sarah, 42
    Sarah (Goldstone), 42
    William Jr., 55
MERRILL
    Daniel, 130
    Elias, 130
    Elizabeth (Clough), 130
    Hannah, 165
    Hannah (Rogers), 55
    Joseph, 55

    Mary (Pillsbury), 55
    Mary (___), 130
    Moses, 130
    Nathaniel, 130
    Rhoda, 130
    Rhoda (True), 130
    Richard, 55
    Sarah (Clough), 130
    Susanna (___), 130
MERRITT
    M. B., 197
MERRYMAN
    Hannah Bailey, 206
MERWIN
    David, 77
    Elijah Botton, 212
    Mary (Durkee), 77
    Susan (Lincoln), 212
MESERVE
    Clement, 52
    Sarah (Decker), 52
METCALFE
    Joseph, 146
MIDBURY
    P., 199
MILBERRY
    Lillian Estelle, 204
    Rosamond D. (Morris), 204
    William Henry, 204
MILLARD
    G., 196
    Mary, 76
MILLER
    Abigail, 106
    Ada B. (Tripp), 55
    Frederick, 55
    John, 166
    Lucinda, 166
    Mary (___), 166
    W. A., 196
MILLETT See also MYLET
    Abigail (Coit), 129
    Anna (Byles), 129
    David, 129
    Elthea Prince, 128
    Eunice (Babson), 129
    John, 129
    Mary (Greenway), 129
    Moses, 128-129
    Rhoda (Prince), 128
    Sarah (Caldwell), 129
    Thomas, Ens., 129
    Thomas, Lt., 129

MILLS
    Albert, 200
    Barbara, 204
    Sally, 204
MILTON
    Hannah (Parsons), 53
    John, 53
MINNEGERODE
    Meade, 6
MITCHELL
    ___, Dr., 105
    Grayson Dr., 22
    J., 196
    J. E., 196
    Lettice, 105
    Lydia, 107
MOLE
    ___, Mrs., 11
MOLLINEUX
    William, 71
MONNETTE
    Orra Eugene, 169
MONROE, 69
    Hannah, 32
MOODY
    Catherine (___), 52
    Chas., 199
    David, 119
    Dorcas, 166
    Hannah, 177
    Mary, 52
    Moses, 119
    Sara, 99
MOORE
    ___, Mr., 120
    Caleb, 11
    Joseph, 164
    Mariam, 52
    P. C., 199
    Sarah (Johnson), 164
    Thomas, 71
MOORING
    Jane, 41
MORALL
    Jacob, 77-78
MOREHOUSE
    G. W., 197
    W. P., 196
MOREY
    Roger, 12
MORGAN
    Anna (Ober), 129
    Deborah, 49
    Elizabeth, 32

Elizabeth (Dixey), 129
Margaret (Norman), 129
Mary, 105
Paul, 20
Priscilla, 129
Robert, 129
Samuel, 129
MORGRAGE See Mudridge
MORGRIDGE See Mudgridge
MORIARTY
George Andrew, Jr., 172
MORISON
W. A., 199
MORRILL
Abraham, 130
Abraham, Sgt., 213
Judith, 109
Sara, 105
Sarah, 130, 213
Sarah (Bradbury), 130
Sarah (Clement), 130
Sarah (Joy), 213
MORRIS
Barbara (Mills), 204
D., 198
John K., 204
Rosamond D. Morris, 204
MORROW, 12
MORSE, 103
Helen Mae (Woodbury), 215
MORTIMER
George G., 50
Harry H., 50
Henry/Harry, 50
Isabelle (McLean), 50
John A., 50
Mary Isabelle (McPherson), 50
Minnie M., 50
William, 50
MORTON
Ann (Cooper), 161
Archibald, 204
Elizabeth, 204
Ephraim, 161
George, 161
MOTT
Adam, 52
Elizabeth (Creel), 52
John, 52
Rhoda, 77
Sarah (___), 52
MOULTON
___, Mrs., 119
Abigail, 102

B. F., 196
Clarence, 69
Elizabeth, 102
Elizabeth (Corey), 13, 102
James, 146
John, 13, 102
Lucy, 165
Margaret, 102
Miriam, 102
Sobriety, 109
MOUNTFORD
Joseph, 71
MUDGE
Ann A., 132
Elizabeth (Baker), 131-132
Enoch, 132
Ezra, 132
Hannah, 132
Hannah (Ingalls), 131-132
Hepsy, 132
John, 132
Joseph, 132
Lydia, 131-132
Mary, 132
Nathan, 131-132
Shubel, 132
Simon, 132
MUDGRIDGE, 213
MULLETT
Abigail (Russell), 211
Thomas, 211
MULVANY
E., 199
MUNDEE
Hannah, 93
MUNGER
Mary Ann (Dodge), 215
Reuben S., 215
MUNROE
H. S., 198
MURCH
Deborah (Emery), 212
Samuel, 212
MURPHEY
John, 198
S., 196
MURPHY
Ann (Connors), 108
Anna (Low), 95
James F., 108
Lawrence, 108
Margaret (Murray), 85
Susan, 94
William, 95

MURRAY
Alice Elizabeth (Conniff), 151
Anna, 86
Anne, 85-86
Bridget, 85
Catherine (Boylan), 151
Elizabeth, 4, 6
Elizabeth (___), 152
James, 85
John, 85
John Francis, 151
John P., 151
Margaret, 85
Maria, 85-86
Mary (Conley), 152
Mary E. (Riley), 86
Patrick, 151
Sarah Rose, 151
Timothy, 152
William, 85-87
MUSSEY
___, Dr., 80
Mary (Boynton), 80
MYLET See also MILLETT
Henry, 129
Joan (Chapman), 129

NAHOR
James, 105
Margaret, 105
NASH
Ann (Bird), 92
Anna (Mason), 92
Francis, 108
Jonathan, 92
Joseph, 108
Lemuel, 92
Sarah Ann, 92
Susannah (Shaw), 108
NASON
Benjamin, 125
Georgiana, 38
Richard, 125
Sarah (Baker), 125
Sarah (Worsley), 166
Thomas, 166
NEAGLES
Sarah, 38
NEAL
Betsey (Patterson), 42
Jane, 41
Johnson, 42
NEALE
Jeremiah, 91

Lydia, 207
NEELAND
    Philip, 146
NEKOROWSKI
    Gail Goodwin, 17
NELLEDGE
    ___, Mrs., 119
NELSON
    Glade Ian, 15
    Joseph, 146
    Sarah, 126
NEWCOMB
    Lucy, 39
NEWHALL, 85
    Abigail (Locker), 215
    Abigail (Makepiece), 215
    Allen, 36
    Elisha, 33
    Ellies, 134
    Hannah, 134
    Hanson, 36
    Jacob, 215
    Jacob Landlord, 215
    Joana (Farington), 134
    Joanna, 134
    Joseph, 68-69, 71
    Josiah, 70, 134
    Locker, 215
    Lydia, 134
    Mary, 36-37
    Micajah, 134
    Micha, 36
    Nathaniel, 134
    Noah, 69
    Otis, 134
    Paul, 134
    Rebekah/Rebecca (Geary), 33
    Rufus, 47
    Sarah, 134
    Sarah (___), 215
    Susanna, 134
    Thomas B., 85-86
    William F., 134
NEWMAN
    Benjamin, 106
    Hannah, 106
    Hannah (Orn/Orne), 106
    Nathaniel, 119
    Thomas, 146
NEWMARCH
    John, 146
NEWTON, 102
    Elizabeth, 138

NICHOLS
    Abigail, 35
    Alexander, 54
    Andrew, 36
    Anna, 35
    Annie Louise (Attwill), 37
    Caleb, 35
    Caroline (Smith), 37
    Carrie Helen, 37
    Charles, 36
    Charles Augustus, 37
    David, 35
    Dorcas (Smith), 36
    Ebenezer, 35-36
    Edward, 35-36
    Elizabeth, 35-36
    Elizabeth (Burditt), 35-36
    Emily, 37
    Emily (Clark), 37
    Emily (Hawkins), 37
    Ester, 35
    Ester R., 36
    Esther (Sargent), 36
    Fanny, 35
    Frank Herbert, 37
    Franklin, 36
    Fred Hammond, 37
    Frederick, 37
    George, 37
    George Herbert, 37
    Gilbert, 36
    Hannah, 35-36
    Hannah (Allen), 37
    Hannah (Nichols), 36
    Hannah (Whittemore), 35
    Harriet (Herbert), 37
    Harriet C. (Atkinson), 36
    Harriet Elizabeth, 37
    Harris, 37
    Isabel (Bates), 35
    James, 35-37
    Jemima, 35
    John, 35-37
    John Edwin, 36
    John Harris, 37
    Joseph, 37
    Joshua, 35
    Josiah, 35
    Julia Abbie, 192
    Lemuel, 36
    Lois, 206
    Louise Mudge, 37
    Lydia (Chadwell), 35-37
    Lydia Caroline, 36

    Margaret (Willey), 54
    Maria, 35
    Marian, 35
    Mary, 35
    Mary (Biles), 35
    Mary (Felt), 35
    Mary (George), 108
    Mary (Newhall), 36-37
    Mary Frances, 36
    Melville Shepard, 37
    Mildred Aimee, 37
    Miriam Cecelia, 37
    Nancy, 36
    Nancy (Wait), 36
    Nathan, 35-37
    Nathan Augustus, 36
    Nathan Herbert, 37
    Nathaniel, 35
    Phebe, 35
    Phebe (Oaks), 35-36
    Polly (Watts), 35
    Rebecca (Barton), 35
    Richard, 35
    Richard Johnson, 37
    Ruth, 32
    Samuel, 35
    Sarah, 35-36
    Sarah (Bates), 35
    Sarah A. (Williams), 36
    Sarah Lizzie, 37
    Susan, 35
    Susan (Frost), 36
    Susan (Truman), 35
    Tabathy, 35
    Tabitha, 36
    Tabitha (Floyd), 35
    Thomas, 36, 108
    Thomas Attwill, 37
    Thomas Oaks, 35, 36
    Thomas Parker, 37
    Timothy Johnson, 37
    William, 35-36, 146
    William Henry, 37
    William Stephen Wait, 36
NICHOLSON
    Elizabeth, 211
NICKERSON, 99
NORDEN
    Hannah, 190
NORMAN
    Margaret, 129
NORTH
    Richard, 74, 155
    Susanna, 74, 77, 155-157

253

G. W. H., 200
George Whitefield, 215
Giles, 13
Hannah, 130
Isaac, 205
J. H., 197
John, 13-14, 215
Jonathan, 71
Joseph, 13
Lucy (Gerret), 215
Margaret, 13
Martha, 13
Mary, 14-15
Mary (Corey), 13
Mary Ann, 205
Mercy, 13
Nancy (Lufkin), 215
Nathan, 205
Sophia D. (Tappan), 215

PARRATT
Elizabeth, 163
PARRY
Henry, 172
Sarah (Cadwalader), 172
William, 9
PARSONS
Angie, 215
Bridget (___), 121
C. A., 196
Hannah, 53
PARTRIDGE
Ann (___), 126
William, 126
PATCH
Elizabeth, 129
Elizabeth (Owley), 129
Hannah (Woodbury), 129
James, 129
John, 146
Nehemiah, 146
Nicholas, 129
Richard, 146
Robert, 146
William, 146
PATTER
T., 197
PATTERSON
Betsey, 42
Margaret, 95
PAYNE
William, 146
PAYSON
Jose/Joseph, 71
PAYSON-FOLGER, 99

PEABODY
John, 119
PEACH
Barnard, 78
PEAK
___, Rev., 119
PEAKE
Christian, 162
PEARCE See PIERCE
PEARSON
Jeremiah, 106
Mary (Green), 106
Obadiah, 119
Theodore, 120
PEARY
Elizabeth (Canney), 207
Smith, 207
PEASLEE
Robert, 22
PECK
Samuel, 71
W. H., 200
PEDERICK
John, 146
PEIRCE See also PIERCE
John R., 38
Sarah (Waite), 38
PELEGGIFLORA, 197
PELL
Helen, 79
PENGRY
Moses, 146
PENNELL
Rachel, 107
PEPIN
Teresa Celeste, 212
PERKINS
___, Mr., 119
Abigail, 212
Abigail (Williams), 213
Ann (___), 212
Anne, 213
Anne (Canney), 126
Catherine (Towne), 206
Christina Elizabeth (Foster), 93
Eleanor Foster, 93
Eliphalet, 206
Elishua, 206
Emmeline T. (Herrick), 93
Gilbert, 94
Hannah, 206
Horace Walter, 93
John, 212-213
Joseph, 126, 146

Levi Gilbert, 94
Luke, 212
Mary, 130, 206
Mary (Perkins), 206
Mary (Wildes), 206
Mary Marie Antonette (Worden), 94
Mary Sophia (Lufkin), 94
Phebe (Gould), 207
Sarah (___), 212
Susanna, 127
Thomas, 206-207
True, 146
Walter Francis, 93
PERKYNS
William, 146
PERLEY
Lois, 108
Martha, 72
Sidney, 26, 90
PERRIN
Otis Jr., 199
PERRY See also PEARY
Curtis E., 200
Ezra, 163
John Hill, 207
Rebecca (Freeman), 163
PERVIERE
Abigail, 107
PETERSON
H., 199
PEVIERE
Abigail, 39
PHELPS
Henery, 12
John, 12
PHILBRICK
Abigail (Perviere), 107
Abigail (Peviere), 39
Addie, 92
James, 39, 107
Sarah Ann, 38
Susan (Barnes), 92
Thomas, 146
William H., 92
PHILBROOK
Jonathan, 146
PHILLIPS
Caleb, 24
Elizabeth, 94
F. M., 197
F. W., 197
Hannah (Gary), 24
James D., 14
Kezia, 55

PHIPPEN
    David, 146
PHIPPS
    John, 199
PHIPS
    Mary (Spencer), 109
    William, Sir, 109
PICKARD
    John, 146
    Samuel, 146
PICKENS
    A., 196
PICKERING
    Alice (Flint), 55
    Elizabeth (___), 55
    John, 55
PICKET
    Margaret, 33
PIERCE, 103 See also PEIRCE
    Adelaide Augusta (Wheelwright), 38
    Bertram Henry, 38
    Daniel, 176
    George, 176
    John, 176
    John Warren, 38
    John Warren, Jr., 38
    Lillian Ardelle, 38
    Lucietta Gertrude (Lord), 38
    M., 197
    Mary, 101, 107
    Nicholas, 119
    Pearl Frances (Belcher), 38
    Richard, 176
    Robert, 176
    Thomas, 176
    William, 107, 176
    Winnifred, 50
    Wm., 71
PIKE
    Elias, 120
    Enoch, 119
    Israel, 130
    Joseph D., 118
    Lois (Perley), 108
    Richard, 120
    Sarah, 130
    Thomas, 108
PILLSBURY
    Daniel, 166
    Job, 166
    Katherine (Gavett), 166
    Mary, 55
    Sarah (Alle), 166
PINCKNEY, 34

PINCKNEY See PINKNEY
PINKNEY
    ___, Col., 5
    ___, Judge, 5
    Eliza (Lucas), 5
    Eliza Lucas, 6
PITCHER
    Molly, 5, 6
PITMAN
    H. Minot, 175
PITTS
    A., 196
    Lendall, 71
PLUMB
    Susan, 76
PLUMMER
    David, Dr., 177
    Enoch, 119
    Enoch, Jr., 119
    Hannah (Moody), 177
    Samuel, 177
POLAND
    Susan, 92
POLLARD
    ___, Capt., 72
POMFRET
    Elizabeth, 125
PONTUS
    Hannah, 163
POOL
    Caleb, 146
    Esther, 81
    John, 146
POOLE
    Elizabeth, 6
POOR
    Amos, 164
    G. P., 197
    H. G., 197
    Martha (Cheney), 164
    Mary, 53, 164
POORE
    Mary, 213
POPE
    R. P. S., 198
PORTER
    Dudley, 118
    John, 146
    Thomas, 71
POTTER
    Anthony, 146
    Elizabeth, 8-9
    John, 146
    Sarah, 153

    Susanna, 52
POWER
    Pat, 198
POWERS
    James, 180
PRASASA
    F. A., 198
PRAT
    Abraham, 176
    Ephraim, 176
    John, 176
    Joseph, 176
    Joshua, 176
    Matthew, 176
    Micah, 176
    Phineas, 176
    Richard, 176
    Samuel, 176
    Thomas, 176
    William, 176
PRATT
    F. B., 196
    John, 166
    Martha (___), 166
    Mary Jr., 215
    Phineas, 166
    Richard, 166
PREBLE
    C. E., 196
PRENCE
    Mary (Collier), 109
    Rebecca, 163
    Thomas, Gov., 109
PRESCOTT
    Abigail (Brown), 161
    James B., 80
    Lydia (Boynton), 80
    Micah, 161
PRESSEY
    John, 79
    Judith, 53
PRESTON
    John, 24
    Sarah (Gary), 24
    Thomas, 11
PRICHARD
    Benjamin, 146
    Hugh, 119
    Thomas, 119
PRINCE
    ___, Mrs., 119
    Elizabeth (Harraden), 130
    Ezekiel, 120
    Honor (Tarr), 130

Isaac, 130
John, 71, 130
Jonathan, 130
Margaret (Skilling), 130
Mary (Haskell), 130
Rhoda, 128, 130
Rhoda (Merrill), 130
Sarah, 6
Thomas, 130
PRITCHARD
T., 120
PROCTOR
Edward, 71
Hannah, 206
John, 12, 15, 146
PRYAULX, 109
PUDEATOR
Ann, 15
PULSIFPHER
Benjamin, 146
PUNCH
Terrance, 91
PURKETT
Henry, 71
PUSHEE
David, 94
Jennie (Baxter), 94
Margaret, 94
PUTNAM
Ann, 14, 77-78
Ann (Carr), 164
Ann, Jr., 77
Eben, 181
Eben, 189
Emma Whitford, 38
Ephraim, 38
Georgiana (Nason), 38
John, 146
Phebe, 190
Rachel (Cram), 38
Thomas, 164
Thomas, Sgt., 77
William, 38
PUTNUM
Betsey, 70

QUARLES
William, 146
QUIMBY
A., 199
QUINN
Anne, 151
Catherine (Gallagher), 152
Mark, 152

Norah (O'Hare), 152
QUINTAN, 198

RADAMAKER
T., 180
RAILEY
T., 196
RAINER
J., 197
RAMSDELL
Abijah, 135
Daniel S., 135
Deborah (Mansfield), 135
Hudlah, 135
Mary, 135
Mary Annie/Annie M. (Graves), 192
Oliver, 135
Otis S., 192
Robert, 135
Sarah, 135
RAND
Edward, 120
RANDALL
J. H., 197
Lois (Knowlton), 205
Morris, 205
RANDOLPH See RANDALL
RANKIN
Joseph, 125
Sarah (Hackett), 125
RAPP
Mary, 204
RAYMOND
R. S., 196
RAYNER
Willm, 121
REA
Joshua, 11
RECARD
I. W., 197
REDD see REED
REED
Esther, 5
Esther Deberta, 6
Susanna, 154
Wilmot, 15
REEDER
Catherine, 154
REILLY
Henry Patrick, 108
Mary Ellen (Connors), 108
RENFIELD
L., 197

REVERE
Paul, 71
REYNOLDS
C., 198
Jacob, 41
Phoebe, 40
Sarah (Hart), 41
REYNOR
___, Rev., 124
RHOADES
Roland Jr., 95
RHOADS
Hannah, 56
RHODES
Hannah (Rhoads), 56
Hannah (Shillaber), 56
Henry, 55
John, 56
Samuel, 56
RICE, 198
Ann, 24
Annie Margaret (Hooper), 152
Benjamin, 71
Mary Louisa, 152
Peter Adam, 152
RICH
Angelette (Bushey), 53
Dolly (Davis), 205
Dolly Ann, 205
Margaret (McCloud), 206
Robert C., 53
Samuel, 205-206
RICHARD
Charles, 199
RICHARDS
___ (Gedney), 68
Hulday, 106
John, 68
Kenneth, 170
S. S., 196
RICHARDSON, 69, 199
Abigail, 31
Hannah, 95
Hannah (White), 95
J. A., 199
Katherine W., 179
Mary, 30
Ruth, 31-32
Sarah, 33
Vinton, 95
RICHMOND
J., 196
RICHTER
Kasper, 172

RIDEOUT
Abraham, 107
Lydia, 39, 107
Molly (Seavey), 107
Susanna, 154
RILEY
James, 86
Mary E., 86
RIMMEE
G., 197
RINDGE
Daniel, 146
RING
Andrew, 108
Batchelder, 108
Jarvis, 77
RINGGOLD
Samuel, Gen., 173
RIPLEY
Campbell, 146
RIPNER
E. A., 198
RIVERS
Elizabeth Amelia, 109
ROADS
Elizabeth, 211
ROBERTS
J. W., 197
Martha (Denin), 81
Sarah, 54
Sarah (Canney), 125
Thomas, Jr., 125
ROBINSON, 174
Abigail, 215
Abraham, 10
Howard, 118
John, 91
John, Rev., 10
Mary, 212
Mary (Harraden), 10
ROBOTHAM
Jane (Mooring), 41
Mary, 40
Robert, 41
ROBSON
Martha, 214
ROCKWELL
Electa, 162
Moses, 54
Rhoda (Spaulding), 54
RODGERS
John, 146
RODUCK
Jane, 206

ROGAN
Anne (McDermott), 203
Mabel Constance, 203
Robert, 203
Thomas F., 203
Winifred (Lydon), 203
ROGER
___, Mrs., 120
ROGERS
C., 198
Charles, 163
Effy (Allen), 211
Elizabeth, 163
Hannah, 55
Mary (Boynton), 80
Mary Ladd (Gordon), 163
Nathaniel, 146
Oscar, 95
Polly (Brown), 162
Robert, 211
Steven, 162
Thomas, 59, 80
William, 55
William E. P., 82
ROLLINS
Betsey, 106
Caroline, 106
Frances, 106
Hannah, 106
Hulday (Richards), 106
John, 146
Josiah, 106
Lucinda, 106
Lucy A., 106
Mary, 106
Samuel, 146
Sarah, 106
William A., 106
ROMAN
T., 196
ROPER
Joseph, 32
Ruth (Geary), 32
ROSE
Betsey, 106
Margaret S., 79
ROSEFELT
M., 197
ROSS
A. H., 196
Phebe (Geary), 31-32
Polly, 39
Timothy, 146

ROURKE
M., 199
ROW
John, Jr., 105
Mary (Baker), 105
ROWE
Allen, 181
Dorcas W., 41
ROWELL
___, Mr., 83
Mary (Saville), 83
ROWLANDSON
Martha, 130, 214
Mary (___), 5
Mary White, 6
RUBENKANP, 172
RUBINCAM
Milton, 169, 175
RUBINCHAMP, 171-172
RUSSELL, 69
Abigail, 211
Edward, 199
Elizabeth, 3
Elizabeth (Elbridge), 25
Geo., 199
John, 24
Kezia (Phillips), 55
R., 25
Rebecca, 25
Robert, 146
Samuel, 25
Sid, 47
Silas, 55
Thomas, 24
William, 71
RUST
Hazel (Woodbury), 215
Henry, 146
Sophia Walker, 94
RUTHERFORD
C., 196
F., 196
William, 146
RYKER
Barbara (Fullenwider), 40
Ed/Edward Leon, 40
Edward, 40
Harriet Jane (Martin), 40
Jane, 40
John, 40
Lucy L. (Joslin), 40
Marion, 40
Nancy (Ledgerwood), 40
Samuel, 40

SAFFORD
    John, 213
    Martha (Haskell), 213
SALLOWS
    Abigail, 49
SALMON
    Mary, 3
SALTER
    F., 200
SALTONSTALL, 138
    Robert, 68
SAMPSON
    B. C., 196
    Deborah, 5-6
    J. A., 197
    Ruth, 165
SANBORN
    John, 99
    Judith, 109
    William, 99
SANBORNE
    J. C., 200
SANBURN
    T. D., 197
SANDERS
    Betsey (Ellis), 108
    C. M. (Gunn), 108
    Caroline, 108
    Elizabeth (Dodge), 108
    Ellen J. (___), 108
    Fred Nathaniel, 108
    Henry, 108
    John, 108
    John L., 108
    Nathaniel, 10
    Permit Porter, 108
    Rebecca A. (Cunningham), 108
    Sarah Elizabeth, 108
    Thomas, 10
SANDIN
    Arthur, 161
    Mary, 161
SANFORD
    ___, Gov., 186
SARGENT
    C. H., 196-197
    Deborah (Hillier), 55
    Deborah (Tilly/Tillye/Hillier), 110
    Esther, 36
    John, 55, 110
    Maria (Eames), 215
    Mary (Viall), 55, 166
    Mehitable (Brown), 127
    Nathan, 55, 127, 166

Reuben T., 215
Samuel, 110
Susan Frances, 127
Tabitha (Nichols), 36
William, Rev., 55
Winslow, 36
SAUNDERS
    Joseph, 154
    Mary (Dine), 154
    Mary Ann, 153
SAVAGE
    James, 146
SAVELL See also SAVILLE
    Deborah, 161
SAVILLE See also SAVELL
    Abiah, 21
    Abigail O. (Marchant), 81
    Adeline Trask, 81
    Arria, 81
    Charles, 81
    David, 21
    Edgar, 81-82
    Elizabeth, 21
    Epes, 21
    Esther, 81, 84
    Esther (Pool), 81
    George, 17-18, 81-82
    George, Sir, 17
    Hannah, 21, 83
    Hannah (Dane), 21, 83
    Harriotte Johnson (Hovey), 81-82
    James, 21, 81
    Jesse, 17-18, 20-21, 82-83
    John, 20-21, 83
    Martha, 21
    Martha (Babson), 21, 82
    Martha (Denin), 81
    Mary, 20-21, 83
    Mary (Byam), 81-82
    Mary (Harraden), 18, 20
    Mary Dane, 21
    Mary P. (Collins), 81
    Nathaniel, 83-84
    Nathaniel Tucker, 81
    Oliver, 21
    Rhoda, 18
    Richard D., 17
    Richard Littlehale, 81-82, 84
    Sally B., 82
    Sally Byles (Littlehale), 81
    Sarah Byles, 82
    Susanna, 21
    Thomas, 17-21
    Thomas, Jr., 20

William, 17, 19, 21, 81-82, 84
William Oliver, 81
SAWYER
    Abigail (Leach), 39
    Benjamin, 109
    Charles Nathaniel, 39
    Charles William, 39
    Elizabeth (Brown), 40
    Flora (Deering), 39
    Hannah, 126
    Hannah (Parker), 130
    Hulda (Hill), 126
    James, 130
    Josiah, 39-40
    Lottie Judson, 39
    Mary, 130
    Moses, 126
    Nathaniel, 130
    Phebe (Carter), 109
    Phebe (Jones), 109
    Rebecca (Grindle), 39
    Sarah (Bray), 130
    Sarah (Geary), 31-32
SAYLES
    John, 175
SCALES
    James, 166
    Matthew, 166
    Sarah (Curtis), 166
    Sarah (___), 166
SCHAFF
    Philip, Dr., 187
SCHLESINGER
    Keith, 116
SCHOEFFLER
    William H., 43, 96
SCHWARTZ, 171
SCOTT
    Eliza Fertig, 94
    Elizabeth (Coe), 95
    James Scott, Dr., 94
    John, 120, 200
    Lettice (Denny), 95
    Margaret, 15
    Nancy (Hammond), 94
    Patrick, 95
    Richard, 120
    Thomas, 120, 146
    William, 95
SCRIBNER
    Carrie, 203
SCUYLER
    Cornelia Van Cortlan, 6

SEARLE/SEARLES
   Enos, 166
   Lucinda (Miller), 166
SEARS
   Mary (Hilton/Downer), 110
   Thomas, 110
SEAVEY
   Molly, 107
SEAWARD
   ___, Mrs., 119
SEELEY
   Margaret J., 214
SEERES See SEARS
SELLEA
   B. G., 198
SESSIONS
   Robert, 71
SEWARD
   William H., 186
SHACKLEY
   Huldah, 214
SHAFLIN
   Michael, 11
SHARP
   Sabra, 76
SHATSWELL
   John, 146
SHATTUCK, 103
SHAUGHNESSY
   Elizabeth (Welden), 152
   Francis, 152
   Sarah, 152
SHAW
   Benoni, 164
   Esther, 203
   J., 197
   John, 200
   Lydia (Waterman), 164
   Susannah, 108
SHEARS
   S., 199
SHEDD
   Joseph, 71
SHELDON, 48
   Sue, 78
SHEPARD
   Gerald Faulkner, 156
   Hannah, 108
   Hannah (Green), 156
   John, 156
   Samuel Swasey, 37
   Sarah Lizzie (Nichols), 37
SHEPPARD
   J. H., 196

SHERBOURNE
   A. S., 197
SHERBURNE
   Lydia O., 122-123
   Sarah, 165
SHERIDAN
   Elizabeth (MacMahon), 55
   Henry, 55
SHERMAN
   Betsy (Bailey), 38
   Mark J., 38
   Mary Nile, 38
   Ruth, 113
   Ruth Ann, 15
   Ruth Ann Wilder, 15
SHERWOOD
   Rebecca, 107
SHILLABER
   Hannah, 56
SHIPPEE
   Margaret, 54
SHORES
   Sally, 53
SIMMONS
   Sarah, 76
SIMONDS
   William, 146
SIMONS
   Elizabeth, 72
SIMPSON
   Eleanor (Hume), 213
   Isaac, 71
   Polly, 40
   Reuben, 213
SIMS
   Mary (Rapp), 204
SINKO
   Peggy Tuck, 116
SINNETT
   Almira, 205
   Hannah Bailey (Merryman), 206
   Stephen, 206
SKEHAN
   Arlene, 120
SKELTON
   Cynthia (Boynton), 80
   Samuel, 80
SKILLING, 130
SKINNER
   E. S., 196
   Tabitha, 25
SLATE
   Anna, 76

SLATER
   Peter, 71
   Peter, Capt., 71
SLEEPMANN
   H., 198
SLOPER
   Samuel, 71
SMALL
   John, 146
   Lydia, 190
   Thomas, 11
SMALLEY
   David, 170
   Ellen J. (___), 108
   Jonathan, 169-170
   Sarah (Bird), 170
SMITH
   Abigail, 105, 162
   Abigail (Clark), 105
   Alven Martyn, 155
   Amos, 105
   Anna (Goodhue), 214
   Anthony, 119
   Augustus Phineas, 107
   Benjamin, 93
   Bethiah, 40
   Caroline, 37
   Carrie Curtis, 40
   Catherine (Eldred), 107
   Charles G., 113
   Clara H. (Keezer), 110
   D. F., 196
   Daniel, 119
   Danny D., 128
   Dorcas, 36
   Edward, 162
   Eliza Ann (Hanchett), 107-108
   Elizabeth, 142
   Elizabeth (Foster), 214
   Elizabeth (Murray), 4
   Elizabeth (___), 214
   Esdras, 214
   Esther (lovering), 214
   Fred L., 128
   Frederick, 107
   George, 146
   Hannah, 105
   Hannah (Kenney), 214
   Hannah (Stone), 214
   Henry, 105
   Henry J., 110
   Henry, Jr., 105
   Isaiah W., 128
   J., 197

James, 4
Jane (Little), 40
Job, 214
Job, Jr., 214
John, 105, 146, 164
John F., 40
Joseph, 214
Lydia, 129
Marjory (Toothaker), 93
Mary, 113, 190
Mary (Robotham), 40
Mary (___), 165
Matthew W., 40
Meriah, 105
Phebe Toothaker, 93
Ralph, 99
Rhoda A. (Wills), 128
Richard, 146
Robert, 146
Ruth (Sherman), 113
Sarah, 105, 162
Sarah (Allen), 214
T. R., 198
Thomas, 146
Willima, 146
SNAIL
C. W., 198
SNOW
Esther, 92
Hannah, 206
SNYDER
J., 197
SOMERBY
Francis, 118
SOMES
Abigail, 94
Abigail (Bray), 95
Esther (Saville), 81, 84
George H., 82
George W., 81, 84
Samuel, Sr., Capt., 95
SOUTHER
A. F., 199
John, 146
SOUTHWICK
Betsy (Foster), 54
Lawrence, 146
Lucy (Kilburn), 54
Provided, 22
Sarah Elizabeth (King), 54
William, 54
SPALDING
Benjamin, 42
Elizabeth, 42

Josiah, 162
Olive (Farwell), 42
Sarah (Warren), 162
SPAULDING
Rhoda, 54
Sampson, 54
Temperance (Nott), 54
SPEAR
Thomas, 71
SPEED
Adeline, 41
SPENCER
Mary, 109
Miranda, 76
Rebecca, 109
Roger, 109
SPILLER
Amos L., 102
Edith (Winslow), 102
Eleanor V., 11, 113, 140, 169
Henry, 146
John, 102
Meredith, 102
Rebecca (Day), 102
Susanna, 142
SPINNEY, 69
Jacob, 200
SPRAGUE
A., 196
Charles Edwin, 93
Clara Marie (Gott), 93
David Edwin, 93
Elizabeth (Turner), 106
J., 199
James T., 93
Jessie Helen, 93
Micah, 106
Phebe Toothaker (Smith), 93
Rebecca (Hewes-Elwell), 93
Samuel, 71
Silence, 39
SPRING
Diana B., 166
Huldah (___), 166
William, 166
SPROAT
Earl, 79
SPURR
John, 71
ST. FRANCIS OF ASSISI, 73
STACY
Hugh, 146
STAINWOOD See also STANWOOD
Mary (___), 10

Philip, 10
STANDISH
Alexander, 164
Barbara (___), 164
Ebenezer, 164
Hannah (Sturtivant), 164
Myles, 164
Sarah (Alden), 164
Zerviah, 108
STANFORD
___, Gov., 188
Leland, 185-187
STANIFORD
John, 146
Sarah, 140, 142
Thomas, 146
STANLEY
Mary (Charder), 211
Sands, 211
STANWOOD See also STAINWOOD
J., 120
Joseph, 120
STANYAN
Ann (___), 126
Hulda, 126
James, 126
Susanna, 126
STAPLES
E. H., 196
STARBUCK
Mary Coffin, 6
STARR
James, 71
STEARNS
Isaac, 42
Raymond, 138
Sarah, 42
Sarah (Beers), 42
STEELE
J. S., 200
STEINFELTER, 196
STEPHEN
Delila, 153
Hannah (Sutton), 154
Thomas G., 154
STEPHENSON
Jean, Dr., 169
STETSON
C., 197
Hannah (Turner), 107
Isa (Crossett), 106
J. B., 197
Robert, 106
Robert, Jr., 106

STEVENS
    C. B., 198
    Cj, 91
    Ebenezer, 71
    Mary, 129, 142
    Orinda, 204
    Phillipa (___), 129
    Samuel P., 118
    William, 129
    William B., 26
STEWART
    John, 163
    Mary, 79, 163
    Mary (McClure), 163
STICKNEY
    ___, Mrs., 119
    William, 120
STODDART
    Alexander, 9
STODDER
    Hannah, 39
STOKES
    Deborah, 126
    Isaac, 126
STONE
    Abigail (Dixey), 206
    Benjamin F., 214
    Cora Olive, 205
    Dudley, 206
    Hannah, 214
    Hannah (Griffin), 206
    Hannah (Lovet), 206
    Hannah (Perkins), 206
    Hellen E. (Lundgren), 214
    Isaac, 120
    John, 95, 205-206
    John Littlefield, 205
    Jonathan, 206
    Lavinia Marie (King), 205
    Lydia (Hart), 206
    M. W., 200
    Nehemiah, 206
    Olive (Littlefield), 205
    William, 146
STOREY
    Sarah, 75
STORY
    Elizabeth Ann, 140, 142
    William, 140, 146
STOTT
    J., 197
STOWEL
    Anna (Martin), 75
    Ebenezer, 75

STRAIN
    Patrick, Rev., 85
STREETER
    Hannah, 29, 31
STRICKER
    Ann Maria, 95
STRICKLAND
    Allen, 105
    Sarah (Woodbury), 105
STURTIVANT
    Hannah, 164
SULLIVAN, 86
    Delina (___), 99
    Edmund, 99
SUMNER
    Edward C., Capt., 80
    Rhoda, 80
SUTTON
    Hannah, 154
    Richard, 146
SWAB
    Robert, 146
SWAIN
    Oliver, 181, 190
    Ruthe (Tapley), 190
SWAN
    James, 71
    Richard, 146
    Sarah, 79
SWASEY
    John, 146
SWEDENBORG
    Edmund, 72
SWEET
    John, 162
    Mary, 162
    Susanna (___), 162
SWEETSER
    B. G., 119
    Dana, 26
SWETLAND
    Annis, 206
SWETT
    Abigail (Smith), 162
    Elizabeth (Hale), 107
    Jabez, 146
    Jacob, 162
    Jacob, Jr., 162
    Joshua, 39
    Mary, 107
    Mary (Bailey), 39
    Mary (Butts), 162
    Mary B., 39
    Stephen, 107

SWIFT
    Betsey, 106
    Dean, 106
    Elnathan, 106
    Enoch, 106
    Hasadiah, 106
    Mary, 106
    Mary (Lord), 106
    Rebecca, 106
    Rufus, 106
    Sarah, 106
SYMONDS
    Catherine, 207
    James, 146
    Mark, 146
    Samuel, 121, 146
    Thomas, 146

TABER
    F., 198
TALBOTT
    Daniel, 154
    Elizabeth (Paris), 154
    Maria, 153
TAMPLINS
    Mary, 92
TAPLEY, 188
    Gilbert, 146, 190
    Gilbert, Jr., 190
    Gilbert, Lt., 190
    Harriet Sylvester, 189
    Joseph, 190
    Lydia (Small), 190
    Margaret (Masury), 190
    Mary (Smith), 190
    Phebe (Putnam), 190
    Ruthe, 181
    Ruthe, 190
    Tomasine/Tamsin (___), 190
TAPPAN
    ___, Mrs., 119
    Amos, 120
    B., 119
    Edward, 119
    Enoch, 119
    Enoch C., 120
    Joseph, 119
    Sophia D., 215
TARBELL
    Sally, 55
TARBOX
    Abigail, 85
    Anna, 136
    Edwin H., 179

John, 146
TARR, 116
   Abigail, 203
   Elizabeth (___), 130
   Honor, 130
   Richard, 130
TAYLER
   Catherine, 161
TAYLOR
   Anthony, 125
   C., 196
   Phillipi (___), 125
   Sarah, 125-126
   Susanna, 130
TEFFT
   Elenor, 41
TENNEY
   Perley, 119
TENNY
   John, 146
   Silas, 146
THACHER
   Ann Tyler, 94
   Noanna (Tyler), 95
   Peter, Dea., 95
   Salona (Dunham), 95
THAPPING/TAPPIN/TOPPIN/
   THAPPIN, 102
THAYER
   Alice (Holbrook), 55
   E. L., 197
   Jeremiah, 55
   Phebe (Hayden), 55
   Richard, 213
   Susanna (White), 213
   Uriah, 55
THOMAS
   E. S., 198
   J., 196
   L., 196
THOMPSON, 196
   Ann, 25, 34
   Annie, 39
   Caroline M., 203
   Charles, 34
   Esther (Shaw), 203
   Hannah (Harrison), 34
   Jacob, 203
   Lucy, 32
   Sarah, 25
THOMSON
   Elizabeth, 75
THORNDIKE
   Israel, 140

THORNGREN
   Richard, 71
   Richard, Mrs., 71
THURLA See THURLOW
THURLOW
   Joanna, 152
THURSTON
   Brown, 146
   Martha, 24
TIBBETTS
   ___, Capt., 126
   Abigail, 127
   Elizabeth (Austin), 125
   Henry, 125
   Jeremiah, 125
   Jeremy, 125
   Mary (Canney), 125
TILDEN
   Samuel J., Gov, 59
TILLYTILLE
   Deborah, 110
   H., 199
   Hugh, 110
   Rose (___), 110
TIRRELL
   Betsy Ann, 127
TITCOMB
   Ephraim, 119
   William, 120
TODD
   Abigail, 213
   Betsey, 213
   Elizabeth, 53
   Francis, 119
   G. L., 199
   Jane, 213
   Joseph, 146
   Mary (Martin), 213
   Nancy, 42
   Polly, 213
   Sally, 213
   Samuel, 213
   Samuel, Jr., 213
TOMSON
   Abia, 130
   Elizabeth (Brewer), 130
   John, 130
TOOTHAKER
   Marjory, 93
   Roger, 15
TOPPAN
   Abigail, 53
   Abraham, 130
   John, 53, 130

   Martha (Brown), 130
   Sarah, 130
   Susanna (Taylor), 130
TOPPER
   Thomas, 24
TORIQUE
   Catherine, 211-212
   Charles, 212
   Pasqual/Pierre, 211
   Teresa Celeste (Pepin), 212
TOURTELOTTE
   Anna/Amy, 213
TOWER
   Abraham, 71
   Lydia, 39
TOWN
   Catherine (Symonds), 207
   Jacob, 207
TOWNE
   Catherine, 206
   John, 146
TOWNER
   Stephen, 24
TOWNSEND
   Alonzo, 9
   D., 200
   Fanny Lurvey, 9
   Norman, 9
TOWSE
   Marion, 91
TRACY
   Nicholas, 119
TRAIN
   Hulday (Richards), 106
TRASK
   John, 213
   Mary, 49
   Penelope (White), 213
   William, 146
TRASKE
   John, 11
TRAVER
   Elizabeth (Caspar), 153
   Henry J., 153
   Sarah Maria, 153
TREADWELL
   Thomas, 146
TREDICK
   W. A., 199
TREMBLAY
   Felicite (Gagnon), 203
   Francois, 203
   Marie, 203

TRIPP
Ada B., 55
TRUE
Benjamin, 109
Hannah, 109
Henry, 130
Israel (Pike), 130
Jabez, 130
Jane (Bradbury), 130
Judith (Morrill), 109
Rhoda, 130
Sarah (Eaton), 130
Sarah (Toppan), 130
TRUMAN
Susan, 35
TUCK
J. W., 196
TUCKER
Benjamin, 71
Charity, 211
Elizabeth B., 106
John, 106
Lyman O., 7, 67, 71, 117
S. P., 196
T. J., 198
TUCKWELL
G., 198
TUESLEY
Elizabeth, 24
TUFTS
Mary (Pierce), 101
Peter, 101
TULLY
Rhody, 41
TUPPER
Abigail, 213
TURNER
Elizabeth, 106
Hannah, 107
Joanna (Goodridge), 108
Sarah (Colby), 108
William, 108
TUTHILL
Samuel, 175
TUTTLE
Anna (Burrell), 163
Henry, 180
James, 163
John, 146
John Ens., 126
Judith (Otis), 126
Mary, 126
Samuel, 175
Susan Melissa, 128

TWOMBLY
Elizabeth (___), 125
John, 125
Mary (Canney), 125
Ralph, 125
TYBOTT
Mary, 129-130
Walter, 129
TYLER
Noanna, 95

ULRICH
Laurel Thatcher, 50
UNDERWOOD
W. R., 196
UPHAM, 103
UPTON
Naomi, 76
URANN
Thomas, 71
URIN
Eleanor, 164
John, 164
Rebecca (Cole), 164
William, 146
UTLEY
Amos, 76
Dinah, 76
Grace (Martin), 76
Jerusha (Martin), 76
Joseph, 76

VAN PELT
Elinor, 165
VAN VALKENBURG
Francis, 54
Hannah, 54
Nellie (Brewer/Bruer), 54
VARNEY
Bridget (___), 121
Deborah (Canney), 126
Ebenezer, 126
Elizabeth (___), 126
Thomas, 126
William, 120-121
VEAZIE See also VEIZEI
Ann, 55
VEIZEI See also VEAZIE
Joseph, 55
VERNEY
Rachell, 121
VERY
Samuel, 11

VIALL
Mary, 55
Mary, 166
Nathaniel, 55, 166
Sarah (___), 166
VIBBER
Sarah, 14, 77
VICKERY
J., 200
Knott, 105
Martha (Dixey), 105
VIGER
Anne, 110
Joseph, 110
Mary (Cummings), 110
VINCEN/VINCENT
Rachel (Varney), 121
William, 121
VINING
Benjamin, 163
Mehitable (Broks), 163
VINTON, 103
Abigail, 29, 31, 33
Abigail (Richardson), 31
John, 31
VON KRONINSCHILDT
Johann Kaspar Richter, 172

WADE
Jonathan, 146
WAGNER
Anthony, Sir, 169
WAINWRIGHT
Francis, 146
WAIT
Marcus Swain, 205
Mary Ann (Parker), 205
Nancy, 36
Richard, 205
Susanna (Allen), 205
WAITE
Elizabeth (Bishop), 205
Florence Rich (Leonard), 205
Lillian Violet (Kemp), 205
Marcus Warren, 205
Nathaniel, 38
Richard, 205
Samuel, 146
Sarah, 38
Sarah (Neagles), 38
William, 95
William Henry, 205
WALCOT
Jonathan, Capt., 77

Mary, 77-78
WALCOTT
    Mary, 14
WALDRON
    ___ (Canney), 126
    Mary (Clark), 126
    Richard Kenney, 126
WALES
    Catherine (Clark), 204
    Emma Clark, 204
    Nathaniel, 204
    Nathaniel Jr., 204
    Sally (Mills), 204
WALFORD
    Mary, 109
    Thomas, 109
WALKER, 103
    Abigail (Geary), 30
    J. B., 196
    Martha, 165
    Obadiah, 30
    W. H., 197
WALL
    Caleb A., 71
WALTER
    Mary E., 131
WALTON
    Joshiah, 54
    Lydia (Mansfield), 54
    Rebecca (Mansfield), 54
    Timothy, 54
    William, 146
WARD
    Andrew, 7
    Benjamin, 7
    G. H., 199
    George, 7
    Hap, 71
    John, 7
    Jonathan, Col., 8
    Lawrence, 7
    Lizzie (Gerry), 88
    M., 197
    Marmaduke, 7
    Miles, 7
    Nathaniel, 7, 138
    Patrick, 200
    Samuel, 7
    Seth, 88
    Thomas, 7
    William, 7
WARDWELL
    Samuel, 15

WARMAN
    Frances, 24
WARNER
    ___, Capt., 120
    Frances, 24
    John, 146
    Lucy, 77
    William, 147
WARREN
    Abraham, 7
    Arthur, 7
    Ephraim, 7
    Jacob, 54, 162
    James, 7
    John, 7
    Mary, 105
    Mary (Hildreth), 54, 162
    Mercy Otis, 5-6
    Peter, 7
    Ralph, 7
    Richard, 7
    Sarah, 162
    Sarah (___), 54
    Sarah (___), 162
    Thomas, 7
    William, 7
WASHBURN
    Elizabeth, 211
    James, 161
    Mary (Woodcock), 161
    Sally (Flagg), 161
    Samuel, 161
WASHINGTON, 72
    George, 5
    Martha, 6
WATER
    John, 147
WATERMAN
    C., 198
    John, 164
    Lydia, 164
WATERS
    Henry F., 24, 26
    Thomas Franklin, 141
    Thomas Franklin, Rev., 138
WATHEN
    Ezekiell, 74
    Hannah (Martin), 74, 156
WATKIN
    William, 120
WATSON
    Elliot Burnham, 155
    G. W., 199

WATTS
    Polly, 35
WEAGLE
    Elizabeth, 204
WEARE
    Christian, 52
WEAVER
    Anna, 213
WEBB
    Timothy, 119
WEBBER
    Edward, 147
WEBER
    ___, (Hecker), 154
    Anna Katherine, 154
    Bertha Elizabeth, 153
    Henry, 154
    Henry Yost, 153
    Katherine Wilhelmina (Hild), 153
WEBSTER
    Noah, 174
WEED
    A., 196
WELBY
    Frances (Bulkeley), 42
    Olive, 42
    Richard, 42
WELDEN
    Elizabeth, 152
WELLINGTON
    E., 197
    J. K., 199
WELLMAN
    Anna, 190
WELLS
    Elizabeth, 95
    Jonathan, 105
    Thomas, 147
WENDELL
    Sarah, 25
WENTWORTH
    Elizabeth (Canney), 124
    William Elder, 124
WENTZEL/WENTZELL
    Anna Mary (Glatienberg), 204
    Conrad, 204
    Dorothy Louize, 204
    Edna Rosamond (Woods), 204
    Ethelbert Ellison, 204
    George Gilbert, 204
    James Frederick, 204
    Louisa Clark (Keith), 204
    Lucy Ann (Oickle), 204
    Orinda (Christopher), 204

Raymond Earle, 204
WESCOTT See also WESTCOTT
   Daniel, 165
   Joan (___), 107
   Maria, 165
   Mary (___), 165
WESSON See WESTON
WESTCOTT See also WESCOTT
   Abigail, 107
   Richard, 107
WESTFALL
   Joel, 151
   Loraine M., 151
   Mary (White), 151
WESTON
   Aaron, 53
   Jonathan, 53
   Jonathan, Jr., 53
   Mary/Molly (___), 53
WETMORE See WHITMORE
WHEATLEY
   Phillis, 5-6
WHEELER
   A., 119
   Ann (Halsey), 42
   Betsey, 80
   Elizabeth (Chamberlin), 55
   Elizabeth (Spalding), 42
   Ephraim, 42
   Frances (___), 55, 109
   Isaac, 55, 109
   John, 42
   Joseph, 42
   Josiah, 71
   Rebecca, 42
   Samuel, 120
   Sarah, 42
   Sarah (Beers), 42
   Sarah (Farwell), 42
   Sarah (Goldstone), 42
   Sarah (Merriam), 42
   Sarah (Stearns), 42
   Thomas, 42, 55
   Thomas, Sgt., 42
   Timothy, 42
WHEELOCK
   Abijah, 206
   Catherine, 106
   Elfrida, 205
   Lois (Nichols), 206
WHEELWRIGHT
   A., 120
   Adelaide Augusta, 38
   E., 120

Gershom, 38
   Hannah L. (Ellmes), 38
   John, 163
   Lewis L., 38
   Mary (Hutchinson), 163
   Mary Nile (Sherman), 38
WHIPPER
   J. P., 198
WHIPPLE
   Job, 175
   John, 121, 175
   John Elder, 139
   Lydia (Hoar), 175
   Matthew, 147
   Stephen, 147
WHITBREAD/WHITEBREAD, 171
WHITCOMB
   H., 197
WHITE
   A. C., 199
   Anna (___), 213
   C., 197
   Deborah, 154
   Ebenezer, 107-108
   Gilman, 119
   H. K., 196
   Hannah, 3d, 95
   Mary, 151
   Mary/Polly (Barber), 107
   Penelope, 213
   S., 197
   Samuel, 213
   Susanna, 213
   Thomas, 121, 147
WHITEHOUSE
   W., 199
WHITFORD
   Dorothy, 95
   Harry, Jr., 95
   Wm., 198
WHITING
   Geo. A., 198
   Hannah, 38
   Hannah (Stodder), 39
   Israel, 33
   L. C., 197
   Philander, 162
   Susannah (Geary), 33
   Sylvanus, 39
WHITMAN
   F. B., 197
WHITMORE
   T., 147

WHITREDGE
   Mary (Savell), 20-21
WHITTEMORE
   Charles, 36
   Eliza, 36
   Ester R. (Nichols), 36
   Esther, 36
   George, 36
   Hannah, 35
   Henry, 36
   John N., 36
   Joseph, 36
   Maria, 36
   Nathan, 36
   William, 36
WHITTIER, 188
   Jane Ann (Boynton), 80
   Thomas, 80
WHITTREDGE
   William, 21
WIGGANS
   ___, Capt., 124
WIGGINS
   Sarah, 151
WIGHT
   Abigail (___), 211
   Nathan, 211
WILCOMB
   D., 196
WILD/WILDES
   Ephraim, 206
   John, 207
   Mary, 206
   Mary (Howlett), 206
   Sarah, 15, 79, 207
   Sarah, 207
WILEY
   Dorcas, 214
   Edmond, Capt., 68
   Margaret (Winthrop), 68
WILKINSON
   Jemima, 6
WILL
   Harriett (___), 108
   J. M., 108
WILLARD
   Hannah Staniford (Heard), 142
   John, 15
   Lois (Geary), 31-32
   Sidney, Prof., 142
   Simon, 91
WILLCOMB
   Zeccheus, 147

WILLEY
Jane (Jennett), 54
Joseph, 54
Margaret, 54
WILLIAM
George, 80
Lucy (Boynton), 80
WILLIAMS
Abigail, 77-78, 213
Ann, 35
Betsey (___), 154
Betsy, 187
Dean, 187
Elizabeth, 153
Esther, 212
John, 154
Mary, 105
Richard, 174
Roger, 3
Sarah A., 36
Susannah, 31-32
WILLS
Elbridge, 128
Elthea Prince (Millet), 128
Rhoda A., 128
WILSON, 195
David, 50
Deborah (Bradford), 50
Dorothy, 50
Gowen, 50
James, 50
Jane, 52
Mary, 129-130
Putnam, 50
Sarah (Cameron), 50
WINDGARTERNER
G., 198
WING, 99
WINGATE
John, 126
Susannah (Canney), 126
WINN
Abigail, 31
Mary, 30
WINSLEY/WINSLO
___, Mr., 74
Mary (Jones), 155
Nathaniel, 155
WINSLO See WINSELY
WINTHROP
John, 5
Judith, 68
Margaret, 68
Margaret Tyndal, 6

Stephen, 68
WISE
John, 138
WITCHER
___ (Hill), 211
Foxwell, 211
WITHAM, 99
Catherine (Tayler), 161
Corinne B., 10
Corinne Wilmoth, 8
Daniel, 84
Elizabeth, 42
Henry, 10
Joseph, 161
Karl, 10
Mary, 84
WITT, 103
WITTAM
Peter, 212
Redigon (Clark), 212
WOOD, 103
Abner, 119
Bethia (Gates), 166
Daniel, 166
John, 120
Joseph, 105
Lovina, 203
Mercy (Blashfield), 105
Thankful, 163
WOODBERRY
Johannes, 147
Obadiah, 147
WOODBURY
Abigail, 129
Anna (Palsgrave), 129
Elizabeth (Patch), 129
Experience, 52
Frank, 215
G. W., 196
Gladys E., 215
Grace M., 215
Hannah, 42, 49, 129
Hazel, 215
Helen Mae, 215
John, 49
Joseph E., 215
Lillian Augusta, 215
Mary (Dennen), 215
Mary (Warren), 105
Nicholas, 129
Ralph F., 215
Ruth M., 215
Samuel, 52, 105
Sarah, 105

William, 129, 147
WOODCOCK
Mary, 161
WOODHOUSE
Elizabeth, 127
WOODIN
Bethia, 22
John, 22
John, Sr., 22
Mary, 22
WOODMAN
John, 122
Jonathan, 119
Sarah (Canney), 122
WOODS
Ann/Anngeline (Hamilton), 204
Edna Rosamond, 204
Edward Melven, 204
Elizabeth (Morton), 204
John, 204
Lillian Estelle (Milberry), 204
Mary (Rapp), 204
Robert Wentworth, 204
WORCESTER
Elizabeth (Parratt), 163
Francis, 162
Mary (Cheney), 162
Samuel, 163
WORDEN
Mary Marie Antonette, 94
WORMWOOD
Ellen, 52
WORSLEY
Sarah, 166
WORTHEN
Ezekiell, 74
Hannah (Martin), 74
WRIGHT
Aaron, 165-166
Amy Bertha (Davidson), 153
C. S., 198
Catherine (Reeder), 154
Dan, Jr., 154
Delila (Stephen), 153
Dorcas (Moody), 166
Evangeline Fay, 153
George Harvey, 153
Harvey, 153
Joseph, 165
Justus, 166
Miriam (Edwards), 165-166
N. H., 119
Priscilla (Carpenter), 161
Ruth (Harmon), 165

Sarah Margaret (McBridge), 153
Walter Clarence, 153
William, 161
WYATT
Mary, 54
WYETH
Joshua, 71
WYGNOL
Judith, 129
WYMAN
Abigail (Winn), 31
Elizabeth, 29-33
Francis, 110
Love (___), 110
Lydia, 212
Lydia (Brackett), 212
Mary (Cross), 110
Mary (Richardson), 30
Mary (Winn), 30
Nathaniel, 30-31
Phebe, 29, 31

Ruth, 31
Sarah (Brown), 212
Thomas Bellows, 26, 28
William, 110, 212

YELL
John, 147
YORK
Abigail (Robinson), 215
Hannah, 130
Hannah (York), 10
Hannah (___), 130
Joseph, 215
Patience, 110
Patience (Giles), 212
Samuel, 10, 130
Sarah, 215
Solomon, 212
YOUNG
Charles Frank, 215
Charles Franklin, 215

D. Thomas, 71
Daniel, 215
Dorothy, 164
Eleanor (Haines), 212
Franklin, 215
Hannah (Lane), 215
Jeremiah, 119
Lillian Augusta (Woodbury), 215
Matthew, 212
N. S., 200
Nancy H. (Eames), 215
Sarah (York), 215
William, 215
YOUNGLOVE
Samuel, 147

ZENNINGS
John, 171
ZENNINI, 171
ZIMMERMAN, 171

BEANTOWN BONANZA

Boston -
Dropoff spot for colonial immigrants,
Pioneer Podunk town
Of hardscrabble rustics
Who subsisted by fishing, farming,
Grazing cows on Boston common.
In early days religious decree
Spawned patently pertinent blue laws,
Oppressive then, ridiculous today,
Spurned and expunged in recent times.
Boston survived morbidity of witch-hunts,
A spate of Mother Goose rhymes,
Gave birth to Ben Franklin and later
Cradled a president or two,
Set a pace in printing and education,
Became a universe of learning.

Boston disliked taxes with its tea,
(Gave a grand teaparty to prove it),
Would not be stamped to economic death,
Had obsession against oppression.
It spewed out many patriots
Who might have been traitors
Except that one George Washington,
Through much military ledgerdermain
And inherent Yankee perseverance
Managed to quash the British tyranny,
Forcing evacuation of the Redcoats
Then quartered in Bostontown,
The nation's birthplace of liberty.

Boston, always a sprightly community,
A first in so many phases
Of knowhow, courage and culture,
Became hub of big wheel demographics,
Produced many VIPs of lasting fame;
Winthrop, Revere, Adams, Kennedy.
A center of commerse and shipping,
First of corn and worldly wherewithals,
And more latterly adding scientifics,
Ingenious electronic and atomic contrivance,
A busy seaport to this very day.

Boston -
Was a pumpkinseed of initial planting
With scads of historical and vital records,
Easy pickings for scavenger genealogists
Who love her archives and history.
Bassinet of an infant nation,
The morrow's monument to yesterday,
Boston from the very beginning
Was more than just codfish and beans.

                    - Sid Russell

INCIDENCE OF APPLE

Sir Isaac Newton,
I continually confuse you
With Izaac Walton, but I know
That he was the "compleat" fisherman,
While you did intellectual casting,
Fishing around, beneath an apple tree,
To hook the fact of the falling apple
And thusly angle your way,
Into our books of knowledge.

Sir Isaac Newton,
I have eaten your fig bars
With somewhat cathartic result,
But honestly, I simply cannot
Masticate or swallow that story
About the first big apple action,
Since Adam and Eve's most
Notable previous involvement
At Eden with pome and Pythian,
Where the apple was not the fallen.

Indeed; had the apple hit your head,
You would have fulminated
New cussword invective, rather
Than formulating a new law of science.
Still your fruited fish story
Has brought to humanity's attention,
The gravity of an earthy situation,
So much so I can stand and criticize
Without the need of even holding on.

I am attracted to your theory,
Yet as I, too, ruminate upon
The rudimentary, I still am unimpressed
By the fable of the fallen fruit -
Either you should have remained
In the baker business making cookies,
(Apple strudel also sold very well)
Or found a new recipe for story telling.
Enough now, of scribble about you,
Sir Isaac, I have better things to do,
Like going fishing. Who knows? I may find
A law of piscatorial determination;
Why I am fallen and hooked on fishing.

WHITHER AWAY AND WHY?

The Bible proscribes ancestor worship
And the genealogist does not engage in such,
But peers into bygone eras, uncovers history
Of his progenitors whom he gets to know,
And sometimes to love and admire,
But never with the adoration accorded God.
We wonder about those people of dimlit past;
The vague beginnings of mankind
(Which the good book defines by allegory)
And the backward progression
Of each ancestry, which at some point
Necessitated a million or more forebears
Numerically non-extant. What of that past?

What of the present?
Why the continuing redundancy of people
And what the purpose or mission of man?
Is he here merely to form the human links
In a chain of continuity, stretching from
We know not where to a nebulous future?
Are we as some would like to believe,
Bits of a jigsaw puzzle that assembled
Will present the most beautiful mosaic?
Are we shuffling or cloning our mortal genes
To make all human id and ego homogenous?
Will the ultimate man be better?

Are we insignificant animal abstraction,
Static impossibles that survived
As pitiable creatures of happenstance?
What of the mind and spirit, are they
Unripe fruit awaiting eventual maturity?
Can we be weeds or flowers in a garden
Universe or instruments of euphonious music?
Are people as pearls upon a silken cord,
Diamonds being polished for a proper setting,
Or mere maggots in a planetary cheese?
Perhaps we are pebbles in an ocean of froth,
Grains of sand on the shore of a cosmic sea
Washed by each tide closer to infinity.

It really boggles the mind,
Yet we shall continue from behind
The mystic curtain that enshrouds our view,
To seek the broad panorama through
A tiny peephole of our fathers' faith,
To probe the past and its ancestral people
Until our dying day or dusk, until
We know or have no need to know.

                    Sid Russell

ANCESTOR IN QUESTION

Great, great, great grandfather Silas,
That's an awful lot of greats, but were
You great in any other sense beyond kinship,
A great husband, lover, father or farmer?

I know that you had Kezia highly pregnant
A long time before being wed, or was
Gestation period in those days only five months?
A few years later you moved kit and caboodle
Away up country to a God-forsaken wilderness
For reasons I cannot truly ascertain.
Were you warned out of town for any reason,
Did you skip out on a lot of debts,
Did you have other local girls in a family way?
That is not what the golden rule meant by:
"To love thy neighbor."

Whatever,
Up there in the antedeluvian boondocks,
I'll bet that Kezia worked twice as hard,
While you went fishing for horned pout
In that reedy pond of yours. But then you
Skeddaddled into the army for three years,
Soldiering in the revolution while Kezia
And eleven-year-old Seth ran the farmstead.
I preseme that you had a grand time making
Hanky-panky with all of those camp-followers,
Spending your army pay continentals
On every fat strumpet that took your eye.

Anyway, after more years, after Kezia died
And you had that enormous army pension,
(A princely eight dollars a month) you probably
Became one lonesome tomcat who caterwauled
At every warm-blooded widow in the county.
If this were the case, perhaps you were
Exceptionally great at something after all.

I am only guessing, making a case by innuendo.
You were honorably discharged from the service,
You did build a house that still stands.
People figured you to be one of the good guys
And spoke well of you in the town history,
But human nature being what it is,
And myself an inherently, shenanigan-wise,
Suspicious chip-off-the-old-block,
I can't help wondering.

                    Sid Russell

Heritage Books by Essex Society of Genealogists, Inc.:

Essex County Deeds, Abstracts of Volumes 1–4 (1639–1678)
Copy Books, Essex County, Massachusetts

Essex County Deeds, Abstracts of Volume 5 (1678–1681)
Copy Books, Essex County, Massachusetts

Essex County Deeds, Abstracts of Volume 6 (1681–1684)
Copy Books, Essex County, Massachusetts

CD: The Essex Genealogist, Volumes 1 and 2 (1981–1982)

The Essex Genealogist, Volume 1 (1981)

The Essex Genealogist, Volume 2 (1982)

The Essex Genealogist, Volume 3 (1983)

The Essex Genealogist, Volume 4 (1984)

The Essex Genealogist, Volume 5 (1985)

The Essex Genealogist, Volume 6 (1986)

The Essex Genealogist, Volume 7 (1987)

The Essex Genealogist, Volume 8 (1988)

The Essex Genealogist, Volume 9 (1989)

The Essex Genealogist, Volume 10 (1990)

The Essex Genealogist, Volume 11 (1991)

The Essex Genealogist, Volume 12 (1992)

The Essex Genealogist, Volume 13 (1993)

The Essex Genealogist, Volume 14 (1994)

The Essex Genealogist, Volume 15 (1995)

The Essex Genealogist, Volume 16 (1996)

The Essex Genealogist, Volume 17 (1997)

The Essex Genealogist, Volume 18 (1998)

The Essex Genealogist, Volume 19 (1999)

The Essex Genealogist, Volume 20 (2000)

The Essex Genealogist, Volume 21 (2001)

The Essex Genealogist, Volume 22 (2002)

The Essex Genealogist, Volume 23 (2003)

The Essex Genealogist, Volume 24 (2004)

The Essex Genealogist, Volume 25 (2005)

The Essex Genealogist, Volume 26 (2006)

The Essex Genealogist, Volume 27 (2007)

The Essex Genealogist, Index to Volumes 1–15 (1981–1995)

The Essex Genealogist, Index to Volumes 16–20 (1996–2000)

The Essex Genealogist, Index to Volumes 21–25 (2001–2005)

www.ingramcontent.com/pod-product-compliance
Lightning Source LLC
Chambersburg PA
CBHW080416270326
41929CB00018B/3043